POLITICAL IDEOLOGIES
Left Center Right

SIXTH EDITION

Charles Funderburk
Robert G. Thobaben
December Green

PEARSON
Custom
Publishing

Cover Art: *One from Many*, Robin MacDonald-Foley.

Copyright © 2006, 2000 by Pearson Custom Publishing
Copyright © 1997 by Longman Publishers USA
All rights reserved.

Permission in writing must be obtained from the publisher before any part of this work may be reproduced or transmitted in any form or by any means, electronic or mechanical, including photocopying and recording, or by any information storage or retrieval system.

All trademarks, service marks, registered trademarks, and registered service marks are the property of their respective owners and are used herein for identification purposes only.

Printed in the United States of America

10 9 8 7

ISBN 0-536-21629-0

2006480028

AG

Please visit our web site at *www.pearsoncustom.com*

PEARSON CUSTOM PUBLISHING
75 Arlington Street, Suite 300, Boston, MA 02116
A Pearson Education Company

Contents

Chapter 1

Ideology

Beliefs so compelling that multitudes fight and die for them; ideas so powerful that leaders can use them to transform societies; principles that bring order out of chaos and make reality readily comprehensible—these are some of the themes and issues of ideological analysis.

All ideologies share common qualities, including a theoretical and historical foundation, a conception of human nature, and a view as to the causes of, and solutions to, social, economic, and political problems. In modern usage, ideology is particularly concerned with political beliefs, values, ideals, and moral justifications pertaining to the form and role of government and the nature of a state's economic system. Of particular importance in the modern era is the role of ideologies as political belief systems that can be used to mobilize people for action. Ideologies do this by providing a framework within which individuals can organize political reality, by motivating people to join political parties and mass movements, and by providing justifications that assist leaders in mobilizing their followers.

IDEOLOGY: LEFT, CENTER, AND RIGHT

The focus of this text is modern ideology. We will not, of course, ignore the historical and philosophical antecedents of ideology, but our emphasis is on the development of ideologies in the twentieth century. Our analysis includes major ideologies of the political left, center, and right.

The Left

The origins of the terms *left wing* and *right wing* can be traced to the habit of the more liberal and radical political parties in nineteenth-century European parliaments of sitting to the left of the presiding officer's chair; nobility, monarchists, and more conservative parties were seated to the right. Needless to say, today these terms have a great diversity of meanings.

The term the political *left* is used to describe ideologies that exhibit the following qualities:

1. A hostility to *private property,* especially private ownership of large concentrations of capital, and a preference for state ownership of the means of economic production as the best method to eliminate excesses and exploitation resulting from private ownership and control of the means of production.
2. An emphasis on *social class* as a key concept, explaining political conflict and justifying redistribution of property.
3. *Equalitarianism* in the economic sense of elimination of extremes of wealth and poverty.
4. A belief in the *welfare state* as necessary to promote equalitarianism.
5. A belief in significant and rapid *social and political change* as necessary to implement this program.

Communism, socialism, and social democracy are the ideologies of the left, which will be examined in detail in later chapters. Differentiating them is partly a matter of economics and partly a matter of politics. *Socialism* refers to government ownership of the means of economic production, distribution, transportation, and communication, and basic welfare services. As a practical matter, socialist parties have often been content to socialize some of the major means of production including heavy industry, transportation, and communications while leaving small business in private hands. A socialist state provides extensive welfare and public services to its citizens, including medical care, education, and unemployment compensation. *Social democracy* emphasizes creation of an extensive welfare state and a network of social programs to reduce poverty and provide citizens with a wide-ranging network of social services. Social democrats are less interested in socialization of economic assets. *Communist* states may collectivize nearly all of the economy including agriculture. Some variations of communism (e.g., in China) permit businesses and farms to function along market economy lines within the communist framework of state ownership of the means of production.

A second and more basic difference between communism and socialism is political. Once in power, communist ideology does not acknowledge the legitimacy of opposition political parties. Although communist states describe themselves as "people's democracies," they are in fact one-party governments. Only the Communist party is permitted and policy alternatives may be debated only within the party according to the principle of "democratic centralism." Of the many variations of communist ideology, only Eurocommunism recognizes the right of loyal opposition outside of the Communist party and is therefore compatible with parliamentary democracy.

Socialist ideology provides an economic framework compatible with several different forms of political organization. Socialism is not inherently one party or authoritarian in its politics. The socialist belief in state ownership of the means of economic production and state welfare may be implemented within the framework of parliamentary democracy and constitutional government. Consequently, Democratic Socialist parties participate in parliamentary politics throughout Europe, Australia, Scandinavia, Canada, and parts of Asia and Latin America. When Democratic Socialist parties have gained control of governments, they have instituted sweeping economic and social changes on occasion and modest reforms at other times. They have not attempted to eliminate the political opposition or to disrupt the processes of parliamentary constitutional government.

In summary, communist ideology is based on the thought of Marx and Lenin. It seeks the elimination of large holdings of private capital and the socialization of the means of economic production. To attain political power, communists espoused Lenin's doctrine of revolution and/or Mao's doctrine of guerrilla warfare. After attaining control of the state, communists outlawed and eliminated other political parties. Socialism, while opposed to some features of capitalism, is not necessarily Marxist. Socialist goals of state ownership of major means of production, distribution, and welfare can be, and frequently are, attained within the framework of parliamentary democracy and constitutional government.

The Center

The political *center* consists of the major political ideologies between the left and the right. These include *liberalism* and *conservatism,* which have in common two distinguishing features: (1) compatibility with the capitalist economic system and (2) a commitment to constitutional government. Both ideologies accept the desirability, or perhaps inevitability, of private ownership and control of the means of economic production and distribution. Consequently, in their modern

3

manifestations they defend the free-enterprise system but acknowledge the need for some measure of government regulation.

Ideologies of the center have a long tradition of constitutional government, emphasizing property rights, civil liberties, citizen participation, and proper procedures as basic to good government. In their modern variations, both liberalism and conservatism advocate religious freedom, or at least toleration, and permit workers to bargain with employers within the capitalist framework. Liberalism in particular rests on principles based on the natural rights of individuals and limited government based on consent. Conservatives place greater emphasis on social stability, continuity, tradition, and authority. Both emphasize orderly procedures and compromise within the political process.

The Right

Ideologies of the *right* share with conservatism an emphasis on custom, tradition, and authority. Citizen obligation is defined in terms of obedience to authority. Individualism is sacrificed for the sake of an ordered society. A premise of fascism is that individuals can find identity and meaning only by surrendering their individuality to the state and the society it represents.

The term *fascist* originally referred to the movement led by Benito Mussolini that came to power in Italy in 1922. In modern usage, fascism has assumed a broader meaning and is now used loosely to describe, in addition to Italian fascism, right wing authoritarian movements such as the Falangists in Spain and the totalitarian ideology of Nazi Germany. Consequently, our analysis of ideologies of the right focuses on fascism in this broader sense and includes the Nazis as well as some contemporary manifestations of right wing authoritarianism.

What distinguishes fascism and other right wing ideologies from conservatism is their appeal to *extremism* and their admiration of the *authoritarian state*. *Extremism* is the rejection of the orderly processes of constitutional government and individual rights and the intolerance of alternative points of view. Extremists are predisposed to resort to violence to attain their ends. Extremism is one characteristic of the anti-democratic right. In addition, fascists advocate a highly centralized, powerful state with authoritarian leadership. The state and the party that controls it become the vehicles through which the fascist program is implemented, opposition eliminated, constitutional government dismantled, and dissident cultures and races suppressed. Extremists, right wing authoritarians, and fascists have in common their hostility to democratic and constitutional government, socialism, individualism, liberalism, tolerance, and freedom of thought. They emphasize nationalism, jingoism, and irrationalism, are predis-

4

posed toward violence, and in the case of fascists, glorify violence. Fascists also admire strong and heroic leadership, a highly centralized and powerful state, and place the collective wisdom of society, culture, and race above that of the individual.

POLITICAL IDEOLOGIES: LEFT, CENTER AND RIGHT

Left			Center		Right		
Totalitarian/Authoritarian/Democratic					Democratic/Authoritarian/Totalitarian		
Communism	Socialism	Liberalism	Conservatism		Authoritarianism		Fascism
1 2	3	4 5	6 7 8		9 10	11	12

Key: 1 = Soviet Union under Stalin; 2 = China today;
       3 = Tanzania; 4 = Sweden under Social Democrats;
       5 = United States under Roosevelt; 6 = United States under Clinton;
       7 = United States under Eisenhower; 8 = United States under W. Bush;
       9 = Indonesia; 10 = Iran;
       11 = Italy under Mussolini; 12 = Germany under Hitler.

Figure 1.1 The political spectrum.

NATIONALISM

Nationalism is a doctrine that advocates the supremacy of the nation-state as the appropriate means of political organization worldwide. Originating in the late eighteenth century, this doctrine came to prominence in nineteenth-century Europe and has emerged as the prevailing conception of political orga-nization in the modern world. Nationalism asserts that humanity naturally divides itself into nations; that various characteristics including language, race, culture, and religion define nationalities and set them apart; and that national self-government is the only legitimate kind of government.[1]

In different contexts, various characteristics may be emphasized as constitut-ing the essence of a nation. It may be appropriate to speak of black nationalists, Islamic fundamentalists, or Serb nationalists, depending on whether racial, reli-gious, or cultural heritage defines the nationality. Nationalist movements are emphatic in the belief that the individual finds freedom and meaning only within the context of national identity, and that nations must constitute sover-eign states. The overriding demand of nationalist movements is for national self-determination.

5

Nationalism itself may be viewed as an ideology, or at least as a movement. Nationalism also functions as a tool for political leadership by generating a strong emotional bond between the nation-state and its citizens. Because of the power of nationalist sentiments, nationalism and the international system of nation-states define the basic context in which ideological debate and action take place.

Nationalist Movements

We have defined nationalism as the doctrine that asserts the right of a nationality to form a state, that is, to become self-governing by exercising political authority within a territory. As a movement, the focus of nationalism is that a nation be constituted as a sovereign state. Nationalist movements are attempts to uphold national identity by means of political action.

As an ideology of national self-determination, nationalist sentiment provides the basis of struggles for national independence by motivating increasing numbers of ethnic groups, religious sects, and cultural and racial groupings to agitate for political autonomy. Heightened nationalist sentiments encourage ethnic, cultural, and religious groupings to seek greater autonomy, or perhaps separation and independence. Militant nationalists, or separatists, often employ disruptive and violent tactics, leading to confrontations with the central authority of the state. Separatist movements are active around the globe, aggressively demanding, in the name of national self-determination, greater autonomy and political independence.

Nationalism and the State

Nationalism may function as a centralizing and unifying force when nationalist feelings are *generalized* to the state. In multi-ethnic states, national unity requires that nationalism transcend particular cultural and ethnic group identities. If feelings of patriotism and loyalty to country coexist with, or supersede, ethnic, cultural, and religious identity, then nationalism comes to reflect the ideology of attachment to the *nation-state* and its interests. It is in this sense of nationalism—as unifying ideology and source of identity with the nation-state—that nationalist sentiments are especially useful to political leaders. Those who control the governmental apparatus of the modern nation-state may benefit not only from the power of the state but from the loyalty and patriotism of its citizens as well. The merger of political control vested in the state and the emotional bonds of nationalism provides a powerful basis for mass mobilization and compliance.

Nationalism and Politics

The importance of nationalism in modern politics defines the context in which ideologies function. The case of Marxism is illustrative. Theoretically an anti-nationalist ideology emphasizing class solidarity across national boundaries, Marxist-Leninist thought was gradually modified by its practitioners to be more compatible with nationalism. Noteworthy in this respect were the policies of Joseph Stalin in the Soviet Union and Josip Broz Tito in Yugoslavia. Stalin's policy of "socialism in one country" relied on patriotism and force to promote Soviet economic development and national independence. Tito's concept of "national communism" proclaimed that communist nations could remain independent of foreign domination while developing their own paths to communism. Lately, the Chinese have been experimenting with a market economy within a communist framework. The development of these variations of national communism illustrates both the flexibility of ideology and the necessity of adapting ideas to the national context.

IDEOLOGY AND AUTHORITY

To complete our discussion of the left-right political spectrum, let us consider the relationship between ideology and the structure of political authority. Political systems may be classified in a variety of ways. One of the most basic distinctions between nation-states concerns the scope of governmental authority and limitations placed on it and the relationship between citizen and state. On this basis, political systems may be placed in one of three broad categories: constitutional democracy, authoritarian state, or totalitarian state. The relationship between ideology and political authority is illustrated in Figure 1.1.

Constitutional Democracies

The term *democracy* originally referred to rule by the people and a system of government in which citizens participated directly in making government policy. The evolution of the nation-state as the dominant form of political organization has effectively eliminated the possibility of direct citizen participation in national decision making. Consequently, democracy has been redefined as a system of representative government and competitive elections. For example, R. M. MacIver, in *The Web of Government*, states that:

Democracy is not a way of governing, whether by majority or otherwise, but primarily a way of determining who shall govern and, broadly, to what ends. . . . The people, let us repeat, do not and cannot govern: they control the government.[2]

Specific criteria are implicit in the conception of representative democracy, including the following.

Free Elections All citizens are entitled to vote by secret ballot in regularly held elections. Competing parties are free to offer candidates in opposition to government officeholders. Both government and opposition parties honor the election results.

Representatives The elected body of representatives has real legislative authority, including the power to enact taxes and budgets and to debate and deliberate government policy.[3]

Constitutional Government In addition, the modern conception of democracy requires that political power be exercised within a framework of *constitutional government*. This requires structures and processes of orderly government that authorize and limit the use of political power. Specifically, government officials are required to exercise power under the rule of law by following a set of procedures that define and limit governmental authority. Constitutional government provides for the protection of *civil liberties,* especially freedom of speech, association, religion, and due process of law.

The redefinition of *democracy* as the equivalent of constitutional government based on representative institutions, free elections, and party competition has become the prevailing viewpoint in contemporary Western political thought. We acknowledge that this conception has ideological assumptions and constitutes one of several competing definitions of democracy. It has the advantage, however, of widespread currency and clarity.

This conception of constitutional democracy is rejected by those on the political right as irrelevant and in conflict with human nature. Many leftists would denigrate it as "bourgeois democracy," contending that the trappings of representative government perpetuate rule by the capitalist class. In the leftist view, democracy is not only a process but an *outcome.* By eliminating large holdings of private property, and the inequality and exploitation resulting from the unequal distribution of wealth, the interests of the majority are not simply debated but are reflected in government policy. Many of those on the political left accept the principles of constitutional democracy. Democratic socialists

8

believe that the goals of a just society and a more equal distribution of wealth can be attained within a system of constitutional government, and they are content to work within the rules of representative democracy for peaceful change.

Authoritarian States

In an *authoritarian political system,* state power is not subject to constitutional limitations. Claims to governmental authority may rest on divine right, ancestral lineage, personal charisma, religious position, one-party dominance, force, or some combination of these. Emphasis is on obedience and acquiescence of the populace rather than on accountability of rulers to the public. Frequently, the right of those in power to rule is defended simply by the fact that they are in power. State power is used to control political activity and suppress opposition. Constitutional limitations on state power and protections for civil liberties are nonexistent, circumvented, or ignored.[4] The political right, as defined here, is clearly predisposed to authoritarianism, as are some variations of leftist ideologies. Suppression of dissent, elimination of opposition, control of the press, restriction of civil liberties, and establishment of one-party government are characteristic of ideologies that reject constitutional government.

Totalitarian States

Throughout history the majority of governments have been authoritarian. Twentieth-century trends, especially modern technology with its capability for mass mobilization, have permitted authoritarianism to evolve to a new level, creating governments with the potential for total control of society. In *The Politics of Mass Society,* William Kornhauser advanced the thesis that modern societies are in danger of developing in a particular direction. The erosion of tradition and the weakening of family and social ties tend to produce "mass man"—the anonymous, highly mobile individual without traditional social ties, memberships, and connections. Millions of such individuals constitute an amorphous mass directly accessible to government manipulation by means of modern communications technology. By actively seeking to replace traditional social groups (family, church, and private associations) with state-sponsored structures, government might gain direct and total control over the individual and society. Total penetration of society by the state permits the government to control economic, social, and cultural life.[5] Therefore, *totalitarianism* is a product not only of ideology but also of technology and social change.

Totalitarian states go beyond authoritarianism in both scope and intent. The scope of political control is sweeping, as is the elaborate enforcement network that relies on the secret police and systematic state terrorism. The two most infamous examples—the Soviet Union under Stalin and Germany under Hitler—resulted in the extermination of millions of people.

The intent of totalitarianism is not simply to promote obedience and acquiescence but also to require commitment. The objective is to reconstruct the individual and society in accord with an ideological vision. The certainty that derives from absolute truth brooks no compromise and justifies ruthless pursuit of ideological goals. An ideology that rejects the limitations of constitutional government in combination with a disciplined, centralized party and modern technology permits a degree of mass mobilization inconceivable prior to the twentieth century.

CONCLUSION

The various themes and ideas introduced here are developed and elaborated in subsequent chapters. This chapter provides the basis for further discussion of the major ideologies of the political left, center, and right in terms of their historical antecedents, core values, goals, leadership, and organization of political power for the state and society.

NOTES

1. Elie Kedourie, *Nationalism* (New York: Praeger, 1960), pp. 9–63.

2. R. M. MacIver, *The Web of Government* (New York, 1947), p. 198. Cited in Henry B. Mayo, *An Introduction to Democratic Theory* (New York: Oxford University Press, 1960), p. 59.

3. Alan Bullock and Oliver Stallybrass (eds.), *The Harper Dictionary of Modern Thought* (New York: Harper & Row, 1977), p. 161.

4. Leslie Lipson, *The Great Issues of Politics*, 4th ed. (Englewood Cliffs, N.J.: Prentice-Hall, 1970), pp. 215–225.

5. William Kornhauser, *The Politics of Mass Society* (New York: Free Press, 1959), pp. 21–128.

Chapter 2

Marxism and Communism

KARL MARX

SOCIAL CHANGE: FROM FEUDALISM TO CAPITALISM

The history of modern social change begins with the transition of society from *feudalism* to *capitalism*. This change was profound in that it transformed all conditions of life in the Middle Ages—small, self-sufficient agricultural communities dominated by the lord's castle; physical isolation of the people living on the European continent; rigid feudal relationships between vassal and lord, apprentice and master; lack of a central government; and primitive agricultural methods that produced goods for consumption or barter. The one unifying element in feudal society, the only ideological force that linked all of the complex relations together, was the Catholic church.[1]

One single factor more than any other undermined feudalism, the revival of commerce. Ironically, the Crusades unwittingly renewed contacts between East and West and generated a renewed interest in intellectual pursuits. New cities were established at the crossroads of commercial exchange, and merchants, bankers, and entrepreneurs became the mediators of a new spirit that shattered the bonds of medieval tradition. Cultural change found its reflection in the *Renaissance*, economic change manifested itself in capitalism, and religious change erupted in the Reformation. Change became the rule of life in all things—ideas, institutions, and individuals.[2]

An exact date for these changes cannot be established, but they were definitely underway during the 1400s. Over the next three or four hundred years, a new class, the bourgeoisie, asserted its demand for political and economic power. The old class, the landed aristocracy, struggled in vain against the new owners of the dominant means of production. This economic revolution was followed by an even more staggering phenomenon, the Industrial Revolution, which functioned to further solidify and strengthen the dominance of the emerging class of political and economic leaders.

The results of this primitive capitalism were absolutely fundamental in all social relationships. In economic life, skilled craftspeople lost their security and way of life. Where they formerly owned their own tools, worked within the protection of their guilds, and lived in a rural agricultural society, they now found themselves working with tools owned by the bourgeoisie, living an economic life at the mercy of the owner with no union or guild to protect them in an urban-industrial setting. In addition, because of the division of labor implicit in the new capitalism, the craftspeople found themselves performing simplistic tasks that were psychologically and physiologically destructive. These workers had no political rights to jobs, could not organize into unions to protect themselves, suffered under horrible working conditions for subsistence wages, and begged for work as periodic unemployment occurred.[3]

Protest was inevitable and it came from many sources, both utopian and scientific—the old landowning class, humanitarians, some students of economics such as Robert Owen, and socialists.[4]

KARL MARX: THE MAN AND HIS TIMES

At the time of Marx's birth in 1818 the Napoleonic occupation had only recently ended and the German princes were in the process of reestablishing control over previously lost territories. Their goal was to regain their principalities and organize them on the basis of feudal relationships. They totally rejected, of course, the three ideological doctrines that Napoleon had introduced, in theory if not in practice, to the German community—liberty, equality, and fraternity—and opted instead for a return to traditional authoritarian kingdoms and the ruinous economic policies of mercantilism that discouraged trade and enterprise. Many intellectuals fled the country, but one group was particularly sensitive to the reactionary policies of the German princes—the Jewish community. The Napoleonic period had reduced some social, economic, and political barriers for Jews, but now the barriers were being rapidly reconstructed. Jews were being pushed out of trades and professions they had only recently occupied and forced back into the ghettos. Many of them were reluctant to reenter the isolated, estranged world of the ghetto. This was the case of Herschel Levi, Karl Marx's father. Levi changed his name to Herschel Marx, acquired new friends, and became a Lutheran in 1817, one year before the birth of his famous son.[5]

Karl Heinrich Marx was born on May 15, 1818, in Trier, Germany, which is located on the Mosell River in an area of the German Rhineland known for its fine wine. Marx's father was a lawyer, and his home in Trier reflected the middle-class values of this group. Although his father had converted to Christianity, Marx's mother remained a Jew all her life. In fact, the Marxes were known as the rabbis of Trier with seven rabbis in the genealogy leading to Karl Marx. Marx's Jewish heritage, though rejected as significant by Russian communists and generally ignored by scholars as a crucial intellectual influence, probably was a powerful factor in his development.

During the years 1818–1843, Marx was intellectually influenced by his father, schoolteachers, and future father-in-law, Ludwig Von Westphalen. The earliest available writings of Marx include only his *Arbitur*, a German gymnasium (high school) examination, letters written to his parents while at Bonn University, and poetry he sent to his sweetheart, Jenny Von Westphalen. In the academic year 1835–1836, Marx studied at Bonn University, but in the fall of 1836, his father ordered him to transfer to the University of Berlin, believing that his son had spent too much time drinking, dueling, and writing poetry at Bonn. In Berlin, Marx became deeply involved with the Young Hegelians, lived a Bohemian lifestyle, and immersed himself in the study of philosophy. Here he experienced what must be considered an intellectual revolution—he embraced Hegelian dialectics as his epistemological tool. (In philosophy, *ontology* asks the question, "What constitutes ultimate reality?" whereas *epistemology* asks the question, "How can I come to know this reality?") Marx adopted Hegel's scheme of dialectical, vis-à-vis Aristotelian, logic as the rational key to understanding humanity, the world, and change.

Marx completed his Ph.D. at Jena in 1841 but was considered too radical to assume an academic post. Thus, he took a job in Cologne in 1842 as a journalist. Although the articles he wrote then would be considered liberal by today's standards, as his interests moved to the area of political economy his articles were viewed as too strident and the paper for which he wrote, *Rheinishe Zeitung*, was closed by the authorities in 1843.

Marx moved to Paris in 1843 following his marriage. There he read Feuerbach's essay, "The Essence of Christianity," and embraced matter, as opposed to mind, as his ontology. He was now philosophically set; that is, he had formed the philosophical basis for his emerging social theory. Life in Paris was a busy time for Marx. There he wrote "On the Jewish Question," an essay on religious alienation, and "The Economic and Philosophical Manuscripts of 1844" (also published as "The Paris Manuscripts" in 1930), a monumental anthropological

13

contribution that sought to explain the nature, causes, and dimensions of alienation and human estrangement. Here, too, Marx met Friedrich Engels, a man who was to be his lifelong friend and collaborator.[6]

Marx was forced to leave Paris by the authorities in 1844 and moved to Brussels, Belgium, where he lived for four years. This was a period of tremendous political and intellectual activity. Marx organized the Communist Correspondence Committee and made contact with revolutionaries in London and Paris. In Brussels he wrote, among other works, "Theses on Feuerbach," a critique of Feuerbach's understanding of humankind and materialism; *The German Ideology*, the first clear expression of historical materialism and his theory of social change and development; and a short statement of principles commissioned by the League of Communists, *The Communist Manifesto*.[7] This short document describes the history of humankind as class history, prophesies the victory of the proletariat (propertyless wage-laborers) over the bourgeoisie, describes the relations of communists with the proletarian class, criticizes other types of socialism as ineffective, and calls on communists to adopt the correct tactics to succeed in their revolutionary struggle. It closes with a clarion call for proletarian unity.[8]

No sooner was *The Communist Manifesto* published than the 1848 revolutions broke out. Europe was ablaze—Paris, Berlin, Milan, Brussels, and other cities were in flames. Marx went back to Paris briefly but soon returned to Cologne where he reopened the paper he formerly worked on, renaming it the *Neue Rheinishe Zeitung*. But the revolutions were quickly suppressed by the political authorities and Marx was arrested. He was tried, convicted, and ordered to leave the country. He did so, but not before committing a last act of defiance—he printed the last copy of the *Neue Rheinishe Zeitung* in red ink and then left immediately for Paris. Marx lived in Paris for only a few months and then moved to London, where his intended three-month stay lasted some 30 years (1849–1883).[9]

In London, Marx resumed his political activity (organizing, writing journalism, attending meetings with European radicals, and working with German refugees) and intellectual work. From 1852 to 1862, he contributed over 350 articles to the *New York Daily Tribune*, wrote a penetrating analysis of the class struggle in France in an essay entitled "The 18th Brumaire of Louie Bonaparte," produced an 800-page text entitled *The Grundrisse* (1857) that some scholars contend is the "prism" of all his work (published in 1953), and wrote his analysis of capitalism entitled *Das Kapital* (1867). A major political task that Marx was involved in from 1864 to 1872 was the organization of the First Internationale. His "Address to the Working Class" became the international guiding policy and constitution of the Internationale. He was the undisputed leader of this international organization of working people and at one time almost succeeded in controlling labor in Europe through the association of unions he led from London. Marx's wife died in 1881, and Marx was buried beside her in Highgate Cemetery in London when he died on March 14, 1883.

UNDERSTANDING MARX'S THOUGHT

Marx's thought runs the gamut of intellectual endeavor. Few philosophers in human history are more comprehensive and thorough in their inquiry, collection of data, analysis, and explanation. For convenience, we have organized Marx's ideas into five parts. The first two sections concern intellectual influences on Marx and his philosophical principles. The last three sections concern the essence of Marx's thinking as revealed in his writing on anthropology, sociology, and economics. It is in these areas that Marx's significance as a philosopher and social scientist is determined.

Intellectual Influences on Marx

The influences of German, French, and English philosophers on Marx, as well as his own Jewish heritage, are important to an understanding of his writing. Marx wrote profusely, detached the parts he thought were most valid, and combined them into a comprehensive theory. His thought is thus a combination of German idealism and romanticism, French rationalism, English liberalism, and Jewish universalism.

Kant, Hegel, and Feuerbach were the major German thinkers that most influenced Marx. From Kant, Marx learned of the limits of scientific method and formal logic, thus making way for his employment of dialectical logic in social analysis. Next, Marx owes a tremendous intellectual debt to Hegel, from whom he adopted his epistemology (dialectics) and the notion of alienation. For Marx, like Hegel, dialectical logic replaced Aristotelian logic, which he saw as a superior tool in social analysis. Hegel also influenced Marx's ideas on change as a rule of life (in people, society, and institutions) and on the concept of progress. Finally, Ludwig Feuerbach, an often neglected historical figure, provided Marx with the intellectual reasons for turning from Hegelian idealism to materialism. For Feuerbach, God was nothing but an ideal of the perfection all people yearn for, so that God was simply human beings worshipping themselves.

Marx was impressed by the French utopian socialists of the eighteenth and nineteenth centuries (Babeuf, St. Simon, Fourier, and Proudhon). These men argued for the abolition of private property, the crucial role of the intellectuals in the revolution, communal living relations, and atheism. These and other French radicals influenced Marx's sociology as it was later developed.

Marx was very familiar with the work of the English theorists, Adam Smith and David Ricardo. In fact, the genesis of Marx's economics, the labor theory of value, is drawn directly from Smith's book, *The Wealth of Nations*. In addition, Smith's commentary on monopoly, the division of labor, the role of government in protecting property, and the parasites of society (lawyers, professors, clergy) later found new expression in Marx's writing.[10]

Most Marxists, particularly Lenin, were not pleased by the presence of the biblical heritage in Marx and spoke of the "three sources" of Marxism as German philosophy, English economics, and French socialism. Although the Jewish tradition was then conveniently ignored, it is now viewed as an equally important fourth source for several reasons.[11] First, to Marx and to the Jew, the law is revealed over time, and in each epoch humanity perceives a partial, though fuller, understanding of the law.[12] Second, the division of time into three parts characterizes Marx's and Jewish thought. The Jewish Garden of Eden, the Fall, and the Redemption parallel Marx's primitive communism, the epoch of property, and the era of socialism/communism.[13] Finally, the family, with its organizing principle of love, is the salient feature of Judaism as it is in communism. Therefore, love is the essential category for Marx and for Jews.[14]

Marx's Philosophy (Dialectical Materialism)

Philosophy is an inquiry into fundamental principles. At the core of philosophy is ontology and epistemology.

Ontology asks the question, "What constitutes ultimate reality—matter (materialism) or mind (idealism)?" As idealists, Plato and Hegel conceived of an ultimate reality that transcends matter and is a product of mind. For Plato, it was a universal justice that existed above the particular justice of humanity. For Hegel, it was the concept of the absolute idea that makes him also a universalist.

Marx and Machiavelli rejected this position and instead embraced matter as the only ultimate reality. They rejected the idea of supreme values existing as extra-historical categories (such as justice, liberty, property, natural law) and any analysis of such topics. How, they questioned, can one analyze what does not exist? For Marx, matter in motion, developing by contradictions, is the fundamental reality.

Epistemology asks the question, "How can I come to know the nature of reality?" Two types of logic traditionally answer this question: Aristotelian logic and dialectical logic. *Aristotelian logic* (formal logic), with its powerful rules of identity, non-contradiction, and excluded middle, supplies us with one answer. However, some contend that these laws implicitly state the nature of ultimate reality as a static condition and then use this suppressed ontological premise as the basis for correct thinking.[15] They argue that relativity theory and quantum theory, the two basic theoretical positions in modern physics, see matter as being and not being at the same time. Matter may be either a particle or a wave depending on one's perspective, and this matter is in continuous motion—dancing and vibrating in rhythmic patterns. All seemingly inert things are then only bundles of dynamic energy.[16] These concepts of physics suggest that the laws of formal logic be employed as "models" rather than "laws" and that other perspectives may also be useful.

Dialectics is "an angle of vision," a perspective through which we can observe human beings, society, and change. A dialectical vision sees all matter in motion and development based on internal contradictions. The notion of contradictions suggests to us that reality is composed of the coexistence of incompatible forces. The master/slave relationship is instructive here. Each is defined by the other—each idea is a contradiction of the other. We cannot talk about each one individually, for each is necessary to the definition of the other.[17] Advocates of dialectical logic (such as Marx) claim that continuous change is the rule of life and that we must not mistake slow change for no change.

Aesthetics, Ethics, and Religion   *Aesthetics*, the principles determining the beautiful in nature, arts, and taste, were important to Marx. He viewed all forms of art (music, painting, writing, dancing, and so forth) as creative labor in that artists are trying to say something in their work. Marx contended that these artistic statements have both ideological (reinforcing the status quo) and revolutionary (challenging the status quo) dimensions. Art can, at least in part, transcend mere ideology and point the way to a new day or new human being. The concept of "pure art," art for art's sake, he rejected as a cliché used by some people to control others.

Ethics involves distinctions between right and wrong, moral duty and obligation, moral principles and the relation of means and ends. We contend here that, contrary to most analyses, Marx was a moral philosopher. He certainly made a moral judgment in his theory of human history and development. He saw the evolution of communism as the end of the exploitation and alienation of human beings, a cause worth living and dying for.

Marx's position on *religion* may be summarized as follows: Religious distress is at the same time the expression of real distress and the protest against real

17

distress. Religion is the sigh of the oppressed creature, the heart of a heartless world, just as it is the spirit of a spiritless situation. It is the opium of the people.[18]

Marx's analysis points out five positive features of religion, and only then does he characterize it as opium, a painkiller and sedative. Marx was not a theist, he was an atheist; but it is also appropriate to note he was not an antitheist as was his disciple Lenin.

Marx's Anthropology

The discovery and publication of "The Paris Manuscripts" required "a radical reinterpretation" of Marx's work by scholars and shifted their focus from economic study to philosophy.[19] Marx was now seen not as a mere economist but as a philosopher and sociologist for whom the central category of analysis is humankind. And the human individual is the "missing link" between base/superstructure relations, the central focus and responsible agent of change.

Three concepts that Marx employed help to clarify these ideas—the notions of praxis, the human individual, and alienation.

Marx's conception of *praxis* refers to an activity specific to human beings. We frequently talk about theory and practice, but practice is not praxis. For example, when the Bowerbird builds a complex nest, practice occurs. Although isolated for six generations, when provided with the appropriate building materials, the bird constructs the nest that it is genetically encoded to build.[20] This is practice. Praxis is the interaction between thought and action—each impregnated with the other. Praxis occurs when human beings construct a building first in the mind and then practically on a site. Animals produce of necessity. Human beings can, and do, employ ideas of beauty and justice in architecture.

Ironically, much of the conventional wisdom in the West and the perspective of orthodox communists on Marx's ideas relating to the *human individual* bear a striking resemblance. According to the common views of these uncommon "allies," the group is the central measure of value, whereas the individual is unimportant and a mere pawn of great historical forces that alone account for all historical change. However, humanist Marxists charge that nothing could be more incorrect. And they justify their position with selected testimony from Marx's writing.[21]

a. "The first premise of all human history is, of course, the existence of living human individuals." (*The German Ideology*)

  b. "The Materialist Doctrine that men are products of circumstances and upbringing and that, therefore, changed men are products of other circumstances and changed upbringing, forgets that it is men that change circumstances and that the educator himself needs educating." (*Theses on Feuerbach, no. 3*)

  c. "The moral entity, the grammatical being known as society, has been invested with attributes which have no real existence except in the imagination of those who turn a word into a thing." (*The Poverty of Philosophy*)

These quotations are among many others that suggest that the humanist perspective warrants serious consideration.

Alienation refers to the separation, isolation, and reification of individual and social life. In addition, it suggests loss of control over one's life and manipulation by others.

Marx discusses economic alienation in great detail. Here he notes that in the *act of producing*, workers deny themselves, mortify their bodies, and ruin their minds; they are appendages to a machine. In relation to the *product* they produce, they are further alienated in that it belongs to another, they may not even recognize it, and when they do they often cannot purchase it. They also have no control over what becomes of the product. Alienation from the capitalist is complete, but workers are also estranged from their *fellow workers* and in competition and conflict with them for jobs. Social class alienation refers to links that bind and isolate human beings into distinct groups. *Class consciousness* is awareness (or unawareness) of one's place in society.

Political alienation refers to the relationship of individuals to society through the institution known as the state. The state exercises control over individuals through government (parliament, courts, police, and so on). In most countries of the world today, this relationship is authoritarian; that is, the many are ruled by the few over whom they have little or no control. Finally, *religious alienation* occurs in a person's inner life. Marx viewed religious leaders who claimed to speak in God's name as reinforcers of society's superstructure by teaching submission to authoritarian regimes.[22]

Historical Materialism (Marx's Sociology)

Historical Materialism is Marx's theory of social change and development and is considered by Marxists to be his most important scientific contribution. It is an extension of the principles of dialectical materialism to the study of social life.

19

The first exposition of the theory, considered central to Marx's thought, appeared in *The German Ideology*. To Marx, human society is not a set pattern of changeless socioeconomic and political institutions. On the contrary, it changes in important quantitative and qualitative dimensions through time and place. Each social system is more progressive than its predecessors, each the outcome of the forerunner. The general theory purports to explain the basic causes of social change, how and why human history has developed, and what the future holds.

Marx's theory of historical materialism is presented here through the framework of four distinct epochs of human history—primitive communism, property, socialism, and communism—and is followed by Marx's ideas on social change and human development. (See Figure 2.1.)

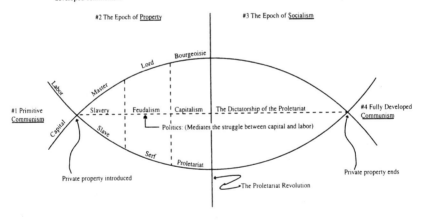

Marx's Premises
1. Change is the rule of life. Everything is in transition– human beings, the state, ideas
2. The change is progressive. Society is moving from lower to higher stages of social organization.
3. The engine (The locomotive) of change is technological development.
4. Four distinct epochs of human history are conceived by Marx– Primitive Communism the epoch of property (with three sub-stages as shown), the epoch of socialism, and fully developed communism

Figure 2.1 Marx's evolutionary and developmental theory of social change

Primitive Communism *Primitive communism* is a communism of scarcity. Humanity's alienation and struggle are against nature and the natural forces that impinge on life. All people in all societies must interact with their environment and wring from it the food, clothing, shelter, and fuel without which life cannot be sustained. To cope with this fundamental reality, primitive human beings did two things—they developed tools and instruments to interact more effectively with their environment, and they established social relationships (institutions, organizations, and so on) to apply those tools in the most efficient manner. In primitive communism, although personal possessions existed, the right to natural resources was held in common, and there were no hereditary rulers. Leadership was assigned to those individuals who demonstrated intelligence and skill in solving group problems. Politics, as we know it, did not exist, and resolution of the tensions that arose as to how to best cope with nature were resolved by the mechanism of collective decision-making.

With the development of new tools (technology) and the construction of new social relationships to apply them to the environment, a time arrives when an agricultural surplus exists—that is, a surplus that cannot be consumed in a few days or weeks. This surplus impels human history, for it portends a "change-of-state" that will subsequently introduce a new epoch in human history. When the decision is made to pass control of the surplus to a particular group within the community (be they the oldest, the wisest, the best fighters, or whatever), the basis for class society is established and the move from the epoch of primitive communism to the epoch of property is made.

Property   The *epoch of property*, in Marx's discussion, involves three specific stages that he characterizes as the periods of slavery, feudalism, and capitalism. In the epoch of primitive communism, the human's basic alienation was against nature, but here the estrangement is founded in a struggle against other human beings. This is the beginning of not only class, class consciousness, and class conflict but also of politics with its attendant institutions of parliaments, police, and kings—all designed to aid in the state's role of reinforcing the status quo and mediating conflict between the classes. In each of the three periods of property—slavery, feudalism, and capitalism—it is the control of the productive forces that determines one's class position. Marx sees two major classes in each period. In the slave system, it is master versus slave; in the feudal period, it is lord against serf; and in the capitalist system, it is the bourgeoisie in conflict with the proletariat. One class exploits and the other is exploited. Minor classes (farmers, technicians, intellectuals, petit bourgeoisie) also exist, and Marx discusses the nature and role of these groups in his inquiry of capitalist society. But in his analysis these groups are prone to switch allegiance as they interpret their own interest, while the basic class struggle in society is carried on by the two major classes.

In focusing on the capitalist system. Marx's analysis begins with a discussion of the *economic base*. Here he introduces two important concepts to explain his theory—the mode of production and the relations of production. The mode of *production* concerns what is produced (cocoa beans or F-16 airplanes), how it is produced (Is cloth the product of a hand loom or of the assembly line?), and how it is exchanged (barter or money-financed). It is, in short, a measure of the level of technological development of a society. The concept of *relations of production* refers to the property questions, that is, who owns, controls, or exercises authority over the mode. In Marx's theory, the dynamic of social change is *fundamentally* located in this economic base. For every stage of development of the mode of production there is a corresponding (a most rational) relations of production. Given the continual development and application of science and knowledge to technology, the mode eventually comes into conflict with the existing relations of production. This conflict must be resolved because, argues Marx, there is simply a better way to do things.

The *class struggle* is the social reflection of this tension between the mode and relations of production, and Marx states that "the history of all hitherto existing society is the history of the class struggle."[23] Class, of course, designates a group of people with a common relationship to the mode of production in the society. Those who control are invariably reluctant to voluntarily give up that control and the privileges—material and psychological—associated with it. Marx tells the story of the efforts of the guilds to retain control even though the new factories were in production. To the capitalist class, these guilds were barriers to development.

The *superstructure* that Marx talks of is always associated with a particular set of relations of production. Here he refers to the institutions of law, politics, religion, aesthetics, philosophy, and so on that are created by the property-owning class to reinforce their position in society. The superstructure is established on top of the economic base, "the real foundation," and constitutes the ideological forms and illusions in which human beings become conscious of the tension and conflict in the economic base. There are two interpretations of the base/superstructure relationship, which are diagramed in Figure 2.2. In model 1, the base determines everything. The nature of the superstructure and human consciousness act *only* as reinforcing agents. In model 2 of the figure, the base is seen as the most important single factor, *but* the superstructure and human beings can and do affect the *rate* and *direction* of social change and development. Here human beings are *not* pawns of external historical forces but crucial agents in the process of social transformation and progress.

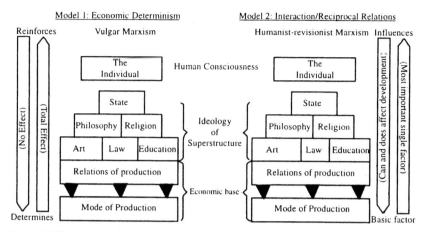

Figure 2.2 The base/superstructure relationship

Revolution and social change occur in history as social groups become more polarized and impoverished and when there exists a Communist party prepared to lead the exploited class to victory. The revolution may be either violent or peaceful, but Marx says that in most cases it will involve open conflict. However, both Marx and Engels insisted that if there are democratic institutions strong enough to implement the will of the majority, then force and violence are not absolutely necessary. For example, Marx believed that the transition to socialism would occur non-violently in Britain, the Netherlands, and the United States.

Socialism   The guiding motto of the *epoch of socialism* is "from each according to his ability— to each according to his work."[24] Socialism is a transition period that occurs after the epoch of property has ended and before the establishment of communism. Marx labeled this era the *Dictatorship of the Proletariat*. This revolutionary epoch is brought about by a crisis in capitalism and is preceded by a system that reflects centralization and concentration of capital, extreme division of labor (robotizing of labor), falling rates of profits, and an ever increasing organic dimension to capital. Marx described the nature of socialism as follows: the mode of production is socialized, the re-education and socialization of people with bourgeois ideas occurs via the school system and the mass media, and the proletariat establishes itself in political power.

Communism The motto of the epoch of communism is "from each according to his ability, to each according to his need."[25] It is a communism of abundance rather than scarcity. It is a classless society as the institution of private ownership of productive forces has ended. The state has withered away, and all coercion to shape behavior has disappeared. Communism sees the individual as a species being. Real community exists, and it is an association founded on love, not power. The government of persons is replaced by the administration of things, and work time gets shorter as human beings no longer need to devote themselves to meaningless effort. Men and women are no longer bound by traditional roles, instead, they become accomplished in many activities. It is the transition of humanity from profane to redeemed life.

Marx saw a future that promises the earthly redemption of the entire human race. His vision is an extremely powerful, motivating, and mobilizing force when coupled with his sociological and anthropological study, which purports to describe empirically the nature, causes, and solution to all human problems. But his claim of scientific explanation and prediction in the theory of historical materialism is still clouded by the conflict over its correct interpretation and by its application in practice. Marxism is a powerful ideology, this cannot be denied. It is something less as a philosophy—that is, as a clear, coherent, and rational explanation of the human condition.

Marx's Economic Thought

The economic corollary to Marx's analysis of the origin, development, and demise of capitalism as a social system (historical materialism), which was first outlined in *The German Ideology* (1845–1846), did not become widely known until 1867 with the publication of *Das Kapital*. Our discussion of the work is organized into two categories of analysis—Marx's (1) economic theory and (2) critique of the contradictions of capitalism.

Economic Theory The *labor theory of value* is the first of two concepts that Marx employed as foundation stones for his economic theory. The labor theory of value has its origin in John Locke's notion that labor congealed in resources is the only justification behind claiming them as one's own property.[26] Adam Smith and Ricardo went on to make the labor theory of value the basis of their classical economics.[27] Drawing on the work of these theorists, Marx distinguished use value from exchange value. The *use value* of something is simply its utility or its usefulness (e.g., water or air). Use value is independent of the quantity of labor congealed in it and becomes a reality through consumption. *Exchange value* is concerned with labor and with the proportions in which values in use exchange for one another. The exchange value of something is what one can receive by trading it for something else; value exists only when there is a division of labor that makes exchange necessary. Analytically, a *commodity* is a combination of use (quality) and exchange (quantity) values. The former defines its specific use value; the latter is a measure of the socially necessary human labor that a commodity possesses. The value of any commodity is the amount of labor required for its production. Thus, according to Marx, for something to have value not only must it have use value, but it must also be a product of labor. Commodities produced in capitalist society must have both of these characteristics.

Marx's *theory of surplus value* was praised by Engels in his eulogy to Marx.[28] *Surplus value* is the value produced by the labor power of workers above that required for their subsistence. It can be increased by prolonging the working day or by increasing the workers' productivity. Surplus value is appropriated by the capitalist in the form of profit. *Accumulation* is employing surplus value as capital and converting it into more capital. In the idiom of the day, the theory of surplus value argues that rewards due to workers as a result of labor power expended is stolen from them by the capitalists. That is, laborers work partly for themselves and partly for someone else, just as the serf toiled and paid ground rent in the form of labor and grain to the local duke. Marx insisted that the secret of the social order is precisely how the dominant powers extract the surplus from the direct producers. In the capitalist system, labor itself is a commodity—the worker's labor power is necessary to both production of the commodity and to the worker's own survival. Marx's thesis is that human beings create wealth, not money, and that our failure to recognize this function creates inhuman rather than human institutions.

The Contradictions of Capitalism Marx viewed capitalism and all other forms of social organization as transitory and as having a tendency toward self-destruction. He believed that the very success of capitalist development would cause its collapse as a social system. Marx expressed this idea in *Kapital* and called it the "contradictions of capitalism"—the fundamental flaws in the system that destroy it internally.

Unlimited production versus limited consumption Capitalism's tremendous capacity to produce and expand, together with its vigorous effort to save on labor time, is a crucial contradiction of the system because the latter tendency functions to limit consumption. As buyers (customers), workers are crucial to the market system. But as sellers of their labor power (a commodity), workers compete with capitalists, who continually struggle to hold down workers' wages. Contrary to previous economic systems, in which the crisis was scarcity, in the capitalist system it is glut. Demand, to be effective, implies money in the hands of workers which in turn implies jobs. But overproduction results in the following sequence of events: high inventories, slumping sales, the loss of jobs by workers, lower demand, more layoffs, and still lower demand (a problem that Keynesian economics sought to solve by stabilizing demand). Workers want to purchase, but they cannot because they do not possess the economic means to do so. Therefore, capitalist efficiency in production creates longer and deeper periods of depression and prosperity.[29]

Competition versus monopoly The mechanism of capitalism that provides its internal dynamic is competition. In theory, a number of economic actors in competition for the dollars of buyers produce the best possible product because they are threatened by the activity of others in the field. The inefficient fail, the "fittest" survive, and the buyer benefits. The system functions inexorably from competition toward monopoly as small individual capitalists are destroyed in the economic warfare with their larger competitors. Marxists today characterize our economic system as monopoly capitalism.

More constant capital versus less variable capital Marx contended that the distinction between constant and variable capital is crucial because it contains "the whole secret of surplus-value formulation."[30] *Constant capital* refers to machinery and tools; variable capital describes human labor. As competition increases, the individual capitalist tries to gain an advantage over competitors by replacing workers (human labor), investing more money in high technology and machinery, and even by robotizing industry. Although this reduces the opportunity for profit derived directly from labor, the increased productivity of the remaining workers, whose labor is now applied to a higher level of technology, generates a total profit that is larger. The problem is that the new higher profit is only a temporary phenomenon and will soon be eliminated as competing capitalists revolutionize their own tools and machinery and match that of the initial innovator. What is left is a lower price for the entire industry. The best example today might be the much lower cost of computers and CD/DVD recorders.

All this results in what Marx described as a failing rate of profit. The application of more science and technology to industry coupled with less use of workers necessarily brings with it less profits over the long run. Thus, capitalists, in the struggle to survive and grow, are their own worst enemy; their struggle for efficiency causes their ultimate destruction.

Capitalist means versus socialist ends Marx argued that, by organizing labor as a social process, the bourgeoisie create the proletariat. Consider Adam Smith's example of the small factory owner who makes pins. The capitalist divides the labor process into four steps (draw the steel, put a head on it, sharpen the point, package the pins) and increases production from 100 pins a day to 1,000. But the social problem is that a pin maker (the feudal role) has become a mere worker. By vastly improving technology and productivity, as in Smith's example of producing pins, socialism is actually created. The capitalists, by turning workers into wage earners, by bringing people together to produce a product collectively, and by bringing workers into intimate and frequent contact with each other, actually create the class that will be their undoing.

Class and class consciousness are the unforeseen consequences of capitalist production. Paradoxically, it is the capitalist that unwittingly creates the labor movement and finally the revolutionary proletariat—the very group that will ultimately replace the bourgeoisie as the authority over productive forces.

Concentration of wealth and control versus private ownership *The Communist Manifesto* holds that competition leads to monopoly and a greater concentration of wealth and control by the few over the many. Capitalism, by this process, is the principal destroyer of private ownership. The big owners (conglomerates, multinationals) destroy or buy out the small owners through mergers. Capitalism is not changeless as theory would have us believe. Rather, it is a dynamically changing system where, ironically, the very principles on which it is constructed—profit, private ownership, a market economy, and competition—are being eroded and corroded by the institutions it has created.

CONCLUSIONS

Marx's greatest achievements are three. First, he pointed out the monumental role that economics plays in our lives. He wrote more than sixty volumes associated with this topic and sought to demonstrate empirically the inner connections among our social, intellectual, and political institutions with the economic

27

basis of society. Since Marx's death over 100 years ago, the evidence that supports his assertions about these close relationships is accepted by virtually all professional economists and political scientists.

Second, Marx's evolutionary and developmental theory of social change, and the group tensions that produce such change, rank him as a sociologist with such giants of other fields as Darwin (biology), Teilhard de Chardin (religion), Whitehead (philosophy), and Einstein (physics). Each contributed to a new perspective on the world, a world in motion and change rather than one of staticity.

Third, Marx synthesized the random thoughts of scholars in philosophy, sociology, economics, and religion into a unified body of thought that affects virtually every aspect of our lives—theoretical and practical.

Marx's greatest weakness was in the area of politics. He was blind to many of the mysteries of power (the dictatorship of the proletariat, the nature and role of the Communist party, and the abuse of power by bureaucrats and experts). He deserves credit for his achievements, but his failures must also be acknowledged. It is a strange paradox that the man who saw the intimate connection between politics and economics neglected the very lesson he struggled so hard to teach others. Economics is important, but the primacy of political power and politics is neglected at great peril.

The two fundamental roles of the physician, diagnosis and prescription, if applied to Karl Marx, constitute a useful metaphor for an analysis and evaluation of his work. As a diagnostician, Marx offers us some brilliant insights into the nature of human beings, society, social problems, and the human condition. But in his prescription, in the remedy he suggests for humanity, he failed. Unfortunately for Marx, both dimensions are of equal import to a social philosopher, and it seems likely that history, in evaluating his total contribution, will find him wanting. Marx helped create an undemocratic world that was unable to compete with its democratic opponent.

COMMUNISM

Following Marx's death in 1883, the political parties in Europe dedicated to his principles were confronted with four major problems. First was the issue of nationalism. Socialists and Marxists feared that workers caught in the fervor of their own nation's war efforts would abandon international socialism to pursue national interests and ideology. The rapid collapse of the First Internationale in the flames of the Franco-Prussian War of 1870 was still fresh in their minds as new political conflicts over empire and national boundaries emerged—conflicts that ultimately led to World War I in 1914.

Second, the movement toward parliamentary democracy and away from absolutism in Europe had gained such momentum that many socialist parties abandoned illegal tactics in favor of legal processes. This was especially threatening to the parties that embraced Marxism, for they taught that the duty of the communist parties of Europe was to seize political power. To these Marxists, an effective socialist party simply could not be democratic. Socialists that embraced such "bourgeois democratic" institutions were not seen as true revolutionaries.

Third, the rise of labor unions in Europe was viewed by many in the social democratic parties of Europe (the original parties of Marx) as a betrayal of socialism. They argued that the labor union movement sought accommodation with capitalism, while Marxists wanted the system destroyed. To many Marxists, the union movement presupposed the existence of private ownership of productive forces and asked only for a "larger share of the pie" of profit.

Finally, there was a serious problem associated with the correct interpretation of Marx's work. This disagreement concerned the degree of violence necessary to establish socialism and the role of the worker in the revolutionary process. Ideologically, the answers to these questions ran from right to left. Edward Bernstein, a member of the German Social-Democratic party, argued on the "right" that Marx must be revised and updated to reflect the realities of the twentieth century. He contended that with the establishment of democratic institutions and labor unions to mediate the struggle between workers and capitalists, there was no longer a need for the violence that Marx foresaw. Workers could achieve their political and economic goals through peaceful parliamentary politics and union action. For Bernstein, then, the role of the worker in violent revolution was irrelevant. In the "center" of the political spectrum, Karl Kautsky, also a member of the German Social-Democratic party, argued that violence may or may not be necessary. According to him, political conditions determine rational action for Marxists, and if genuine democratic processes prevail, then violence may not be needed. Kautsky also argued that where violence was necessary workers would spontaneously arise to seize power and establish a new social system. To him, no intellectual saviors were needed. Finally, the "left" position supported by Lenin argued that parliamentary democracy was a sham and that violence was absolutely necessary to establish and maintain a socialist state. In addition, Lenin stated that the workers naturally tended toward a trade union mentality and thus must be led by an elite group of professional revolutionaries (the "vanguard of the proletariat") in the Communist party if they were ever to establish an authentic socialist system.[31] The practical resolution of these theoretical issues came in the communist revolutions of the twentieth century, and it is to these that we now turn.

This analysis of communism is divided into three parts: (1) Russian communism, because it was the oldest example (74 years) and because the former Soviet Union was one of the two superpowers in the world; (2) Chinese communism, in both its Maoist and post-Maoist expressions; and (3) the last bulwarks of communism.

RUSSIAN COMMUNISM

The Soviet Union was the largest country in the world (8.6 million square miles), about two and one-half times the size of the United States. It was situated one-third in Europe and two-thirds in Asia, and it contained every type of climate except subtropical. The Soviet Union was technically a federation membered by 15 republics, the largest being the Russian Soviet Federated Socialist Republic (SFSR). Its total population was approximately 280 million (the U.S. population is about 285 million), with the Russian SFSR having 140 million people, or 50 percent of the total population.

Prior to the Mongol invasion of 1240, the center of Russian civilization was Kiev, the capital of the first Russian state established in the ninth century by Scandinavian chieftains. After the Mongols overran the country, they moved the center to Moscow to facilitate political control and collection of taxes. This change naturally gave preeminence to the Moscow prince. This Mongol-Tartar rule lasted over 200 years and ended when Ivan the Great drove out the invaders. Thus began a 500-year period of Tsarist rule that lasted until 1917. In total, 700 years of absolute autocracy characterized Russian politics (1240–1917). The Tsar was believed to be ordained by God to rule, and the counterpart of this absolute autocracy at the local level was the practice of patriarchalism. In the patriarchal system the village was dominated by a council of elders and the family by its patriarch. Unquestioned obedience was demanded by the rulers and in turn given by the ruled.[32]

The Renaissance and Reformation had little impact on Tsarist Russia, and the practice of Byzantine Christianity always functioned to reinforce Tsarist rule. Western ideas and the beginning of modernization began in Russia in the nineteenth century, but it was not until 1861 that the feudal system of lord and serf was legally ended with the emancipation decree of Alexander II. The weakening of Tsarist rule began with the Napoleonic Wars when the Russian intelligentsia (politically active intellectuals) was exposed to Western ideas of liberty. This resulted in the abortive December 1825 revolt by a group calling themselves the Decembrists. Minor reforms and freedom for the serfs in 1861 were followed by military defeat in 1905 in the war with Japan and the disaster of World War I, which brought the Bolsheviks to power on November 7, 1917, and ended Tsarist rule.

Lenin

Vladimir Ilyich Ulyanow (Lenin) was born in 1870 in Simbirsk, Russia, to middle class parents. Lenin's father was a teacher and later a school administrator, and Lenin led a good life in a solid family setting. His brother, Alexander, with whom Lenin had a good relationship, was a bright student, whereas Lenin, who was also very intelligent, was more athletic and extroverted. In March 1887, Alexander participated in an attempt to assassinate Tsar Alexander III. The attempt failed, and he was caught, tried, and hanged. This was a crushing blow to Lenin; it alienated him from political authorities and strengthened his will to overthrow the regime. Lenin was the top graduate in his high school class and entered Kazan University in the fall of 1887. He was suspended for participation in a student protest, but subsequently was readmitted and received his law degree in 1891.[33]

Lenin studied Marx's thought and became a disciple of George Plekhanov, the "father" of Russian Marxism. In 1893 he moved to St. Petersburg to do political work, and it is there that he met Krupskaya, his future wife. While in St. Petersburg, Lenin organized a Marxist group and was subsequently arrested and exiled to Siberia for three years. Krupskaya followed him there and they were married in 1898. In 1900 he was released, left the country, and lived in exile (primarily in Switzerland) until 1917 except for the period 1905–1907. During this two year period, Lenin returned to Russia for the time of turmoil prompted by "Bloody Sunday" on January 22, 1905, in St. Petersburg. In this incident, Father Gapon led thousands of peasants and workers to the Tsar's palace to plead for his help. He was, after all, viewed as "their little father." But instead of help they received bullets.[34] This further speeded the drift toward revolution. In 1903, at the Russian Social-Democratic Workers Party's Second Congress, Lenin won a decisive vote on the nature of the party. He was concerned that the party be a highly centralized and organized group, while the opposition fought for a more democratic and broader based party. Lenin's group won and called themselves the *Bolsheviks* (majority) while the losing group, headed by Yulii O.

Martov, became known as the *Mensheviks* (minority). In 1917, with Russia involved in a disastrous conflict with Germany (World War I), Lenin who had been living in exile in Switzerland, crossed enemy territory in a sealed train to the Finland Station in Russia. This trip was made possible by the permission of the German high command who sought to further enfeeble the collapsing Tsarist regime by permitting the passage of one of its principal agitators—Lenin. This strategy worked, and on November 17, 1917, the Bolsheviks seized power and ended Tsarist rule in Russia. In the spring of 1918, Lenin signed the disastrous Treaty of Brest-Litovsk with Germany, giving up about 25 percent of Russian land and population. However, from Lenin's point of view it did create the conditions for him to solidify his political position and begin building socialism in Russia. After a period of "war communism" from 1918 to 1921, during which Lenin was wounded in an assassination attempt, he initiated the New Economic Policy, a program designed as a "holding operation" for the new social system. In May 1922 Lenin had a stroke and less than a year later, in March 1923, he suffered a second major stroke. These blows to his health ended his political leadership. On January 21, 1924, he died at age 54.[35]

Lenin's charismatic personality, candor, hyperactivism, and especially his genuine audacity in politics best characterize him personally. Intellectually, Lenin absolutized violence as the only road to socialism, but his capacity for analysis and polemical discourse (50 volumes) is truly remarkable. Politically, Lenin's concern with efficiency produced a centralized party that evolved into a new bureaucratized ruling elite. But his style of politics and his capacity for organization and leadership mark him as one of the giants of twentieth-century revolutionary politics.

Leninism

Marx predicted that the proletarian revolution would occur in the most advanced industrialized capitalist countries. But the revolution that Lenin directed occurred in a backward country compared to the other industrialized states of Western Europe. Russia was fundamentally still an agricultural society. Thus, the task for Lenin was to reconcile the economic facts of life in Russia and the ideas of Karl Marx as expressed in his fundamental theory of historical materialism. Lenin accomplished this task by analyzing his ideas in three major areas—the theory of the Communist party; the nature of the state and the seizure and consolidation of power; and the strategy and tactics of party politics.

Theory of the Communist Party "What Is to Be Done," Lenin's most important essay on the theory of the party, was published in March 1902 and designed to persuade the membership of the Russian Social-Democratic party at the Second Congress of 1903 that his conception of the party was the correct one to follow. The essay forms the basis of the Bolshevik-Menshevik split.

Lenin expressed his ideas on two major topics—the nature of the "triple struggle" that faced the party and the necessity of a disciplined revolutionary party to lead that struggle. Lenin's "triple struggle" involved theoretical, economic, and political dimensions. His theory is simple and clear: *maintain theoretical purity*.

The second dimension of party struggle is economic. Here Lenin's thesis is that the party is not interested in reforming but in changing the existing economic system and relations of production. This is the crux of the difference between the party and the Bernstein group that is doing mere "trade union" work.

Lenin's order regarding politics was to do "good political work," which included agitation, propaganda, and education. "It is not enough to explain to the workers that they are politically oppressed. . . . *Agitation* (exacerbating or creating problems) must be conducted with regard to every concrete example of this oppression."[36] Propaganda, the political exposure of all dimensions of Russian autocracy, is also a key political activity.

The second major part of "What Is to Be Done" outlines Lenin's conception of the Communist party. The party is to be the vanguard of the revolutionary forces, united and organized in a manner that surpasses the best military units.

The characteristics that Lenin applies to the party in a famous quotation is "small," "experienced," "secret," "professional," "solid organization," "united," "vanguard," "limited membership." Here he separates himself from Marx who visualized a mass movement that would spontaneously seize power. Lenin contends that while the masses may embody spontaneity, the party alone embodies consciousness. Only the party has the knowledge, insight, and selfless dedication to organize and lead the revolt.

"The State and Revolution" "The State and Revolution" outlines Lenin's thought on the nature of the state and the seizure and consolidation of state power. It is considered one of the most important works of Marxism and was written during the summer of 1917, on the eve of the October Revolution.

The essay describes the state as the produce of irreconcilable class tensions. The chief instruments of state power employed by the rulers to maintain the system are the police and the army. Force and the coercive power of the bayonet and prison are the means the state employs to control behavior.

The Strategy and Tactics of Party Politics   These topics are best expressed by Lenin in "Imperialism. The Highest Stage of Capitalism." Written in 1916, the essay attempts to prove that Marx's predictions were being realized, and it supplies Marxists with a powerful theory of international relations.

In "Imperialism: The Highest Stage of Capitalism," Lenin seeks to demonstrate that the evolution and development of the world's major economic actors has proceeded as Marx predicted and that capitalism has expanded into a mighty colonial empire, that is, that capitalism has transformed itself into imperialism. While the basic unit in Marx's perspective was the individual nation-state and entrepreneur capitalism, Lenin's analysis regards the entire world as an economic unit with monopoly capitalism as its principal economic system. Formerly, Lenin states, the conditions of revolution were analyzed from the point of view of individual countries. But in today's age of imperialism, the matter must be seen from the perspective of the world economy. Formerly, one analyzed the class consciousness of the national proletariat. Today, it is necessary to understand the consciousness of the international proletariat.

In one bold theoretical stroke Lenin explained the nature, causes, and consequences of international politics in the twentieth century. He "explained" the development and transformation of capitalism into imperialism (entrepreneur to monopoly capitalism); the causes of war between the imperial nations (their struggle for a share of the colonial world); the passivity of the working class in the developed nations (bribed with super profits); the struggle in the Third World to throw off the bonds of colonialism and neocolonialism (nationalist wars of liberation); the correspondence between the nationalist aspirations of Third World countries with the international communist movement; and the leadership of that movement by the Soviet Union.

Lenin's Russian messianic vision, his charismatic personality, his candor in relations with other people, and his real audacity in politics, coupled with his hyperactivism, mark him as one of the giants of twentieth-century revolutionary politics.

Stalin

Stalin (Iosif V. Dzhugashvili) was born on December 21, 1879, in the Gori, Tiflis region of Georgia. Although his father was a peasant, his mother was determined to prepare him for the Orthodox priesthood. He attended the Gori church school and later was admitted to the Tiflis theological seminary. He joined a revolutionary movement while a student at the seminary and was subsequently expelled for "devious political thinking." In 1901 Stalin joined the Tiflis Social-Democratic party and was sent to Batum to do party organizational work. There he instigated the Rothschild strike in February 1902, was arrested, and shortly thereafter began his first prison term in Siberia. In January 1904, Stalin escaped and returned to Batum.[37] By 1905 he was a dedicated Bolshevik, a man who put all of his faith in the party as the only mechanism that could save the proletariat. From a police report dated 1905, Stalin is described as about 5 feet 4 inches tall, average build, dark-brown hair, reddish-brown mustache and beard, smallpox marks on his face and a birthmark on his left ear.[38]

In the 1917 Revolution, Stalin played only a minor role compared to Lenin and Trotsky, but in 1922 he was named general secretary of the Central Committee Secretariat and shortly thereafter a member of the Politburo and Orgburo. It was his position on all three powerful bodies that disturbed Lenin and prompted him to talk of Stalin's "boundless power" and to express those misgivings in his "Testament."[39] With Lenin's death in 1924, Stalin became engaged in a vicious political struggle for power with Lev Kaminev, Grigory Zinoviev, and Leon Trotsky. Initially, he made a pact with Kaminev and Zinoviev to get rid of Trotsky. The plot worked, and in 1928 Trotsky was expelled from the party and subsequently sent into exile in Mexico where he was assassinated in 1940. Stalin then turned on his two conspirators who were first silenced and then executed along with many other Communist party, Soviet government, and Red Army officials in the purges called the Great Terror of the 1930s. Stalin was now the absolute ruler.

During World War II, Stalin continued his program of political repression even while his leadership enabled the Germans to enter the very suburbs of Moscow while inflicting terrible casualties on the Red Army and the civilian populace. The Soviet Union survived the struggle with Hitler's Germany and emerged as a major military power with an Eastern European empire. Stalin was now the undisputed leader of Russia and the World Communist Movement. In the last five years of his life, Stalin was consumed with expanding his personal role into what is now called the "cult of personality." He died on March 5, 1953, at the age of 73. Probably no person other than Hitler in the twentieth century is a match for Stalin in terms of personal vanity, ruthlessness, lust for power, and duplicity. He is surely "one of the greatest criminals in human history."[40]

Stalinism

Several characteristics of Stalin's rule combine to form what is today called Stalinism, the distorted Marxism operative in the Soviet Union during his 30 years in power (1924–1953).

- The nationalization of international communism: because of the "uneven and spasmodic" development of capitalism, a victorious revolution in one country is possible.
- Personal dictatorship: During his 30 years in power, Stalin transformed the party and government bureaucracy into personal instruments of power to serve his will.
- Totalitarianism and mass terror: everything was politicized in Stalin's Russia. There was no distinction between society and politics. The Great Terror of the 1930s solidified his personal powers.
- Coercive collectivization of the economy: the forced collectivization of agriculture and industry characterizes Stalin's economic policy.
- Empire and opportunity in foreign policy: this involved the subjugation of six eastern European countries, along with Stalin's opportunistic diplomacy—from his treaty with Hitler to his duplicity with Truman and Churchill.

Khrushchev, De-Stalinization, and the New Soviet Ruling Class

Nikita Khrushchev (1894–1971) became first secretary of the Communist party of the Soviet Union after Stalin's death in 1953. By 1956 Khrushchev had consolidated his position over his main rival Nikolai Bulganin and became the leader of the Soviet Union. In a six-hour speech, the most important given by a Soviet leader since World War II, delivered to the Twentieth Party Congress in Moscow in February 1956, Khrushchev shattered Stalin's reputation and outlined the ideological principles that were to guide Soviet foreign relations in the last half of the twentieth century.

After Khrushchev was relieved of power, Leonid I. Brezhnev assumed command. Some experts argue that Brezhnev became a spokesperson for a new class—the top 750,000 of the total party membership of 18 million. Serving as the "executive committee" of this new class were the interlocking members of the Central Committee's secretariat and politburo. Their main business was maximizing power (internally and externally) while improving the privileges of their hereditary members.

The Fall of Communism in the Soviet Union and Its Satellites in Eastern Europe

In March 1985 the election of 54-year-old Mikhail Gorbachev as secretary general of the Communist party signaled a generational change in the Soviet Union and its leadership. He presented himself to the Soviets and the world as a reformer of communism—communism with a "human face" reminiscent of 1968 and Czechoslovakia's "Prague Spring."

Externally, by late 1988 and throughout 1989, Gorbachev lost any semblance of effective control of the Central European satellites.

Internally, the legal monopoly of the Communist party, as set forth in Article 6 of the constitution, was formally abandoned by the Central Committee of the Communist party of the Soviet Union in February 1990.

The total collapse of the Soviet Union occurred in December 1991 when "eleven former republics of the Soviet Union formally constituted themselves today (December 21, 1991) as the Commonwealth of Independent States."[41]

CHINESE COMMUNISM

China comprises 3,691 million square miles of East Asia and is only slightly larger than the United States (which is 3,623 million square miles). However, China's population of 1.3 billion far exceeds the U.S. population of about 300 million and accounts for 23 percent of the 5.4 billion people living in the world today. One out of every 4.3 persons alive today is Chinese. The Chinese thus affect and are affected by virtually every event in world politics.[42]

Modern China (A.D. 1644–1949) is generally considered to begin with the Manchu, or Ch'ing dynasty in 1644. However, this foreign rule did little to change the fundamental culture of China, and the steady but gradual shift in power from the Manchus to the Chinese was clearly evident by 1865. The 20th century unification of China occurred in June 1928 under Chiang Kai-shek. The new nationalist regime, though fighting communist revolutionaries, was quickly recognized by most foreign governments as the legal authority in China. During this internal struggle for power, conflict between Japan and China began a conflict in which China was forced to give up Korea, Taiwan, and Manchuria. In July 1937, Japan invaded China. This war lasted until Japan was defeated in 1945. Then began, in deadly earnest, the bloody civil war between the Kuomingtang and the communists. The communists were eventually victorious over the

Kuomingtang, and Mao Zedong proclaimed the Chinese People's Republic in Beijing on October 1, 1949.

Communist China (1949–present) has existed for over fifty years, and in each decade dramatic changes have occurred.

The 1950s   The 1950s were a period of consolidation and experimentation. In 1950 the People's Republic of China (PRC) signed a friendship treaty with the Soviet Union and obtained in exchange economic and technical aid plus credit and trade agreements. In 1951 China occupied Tibet and "reintegrated" it as an "autonomous region" of the PRC. The first five-year plan for economic development was launched in 1953. During the 1950s all private enterprise was eliminated, and agriculture was gradually collectivized. Two dramatic experiments were attempted in this period—the "Hundred Flowers Movement" in 1956 and "the Great Leap Forward" in 1958. The former invited intellectuals to criticize the party, government, and the new system. This they did, and the PRC authorities quickly suppressed the program. The later innovation was a plan for rapid development in both agriculture and industry. But resistance to collectivization in agriculture and administrative breakdown in industry resulted in a short life for this program as well.

The 1960s   The 1960s were a period of self-reliance and self-purification (purge). The Sino-Soviet conflict in all its dimensions (military, diplomatic, economic, territorial, ideological) broke out in 1960, and the Treaty of Friendship collapsed when Soviet technicians left China with all their plans and hundreds of unfinished projects. China was now forced to solve its own internal problems. Externally, too, the PRC moved to achieve its goals through "self-reliance." In 1962 it invaded India to reclaim disputed territory given to that nation by the British in what was called the MacMahon Line. Also, in 1965, as the United States moved to escalate the level of fighting in Vietnam, China acted to provide significant material support and assistance for the Vietnamese. Then, in one of the most dramatic acts of self-purification and political purge the world has ever seen, the Great Proletarian Cultural Revolution (GPCR) was launched in 1966. This was a power struggle and purge of titanic proportions. Mao Zedong and Lin Biao, aided by the army and the Red Guard movement (young people in all walks of life), fought a life-and-death struggle with Liu Shao-qi and other high-level party members. Mao initiated the GPCR because he saw his revolution lost—lost to the bureaucracy of the Communist party, the very instrument that had brought him to power. For three years (1966–1969) a mighty struggle ensued. By 1969 Mao's coalition had prevailed, and more moderate, though still revolutionary, behavior prevailed in Chinese politics until Mao's death in 1976.

The 1970s The 1970s were a time of worldwide recognition and political transition. In October 1971 the General Assembly of the United Nations ousted the representatives of the Taiwan government and seated those of the PRC. China was also now one of the five permanent members of the Security Council. Then, in February 1972, President Richard Nixon visited China and met with Premier Zhou Enlai and Mao Zedong. The two countries opened offices in each other's capitals, and on December 15, 1978, the United States formally recognized the PRC as the legitimate government of China. In 1976 both Zhou Enlai and Mao Zedong died, and Mao's handpicked successor, Hua Guofeng, appeared to assume control of the PRC. But the transition was not destined to be smooth, as another power struggle emerged between the Gang of Four (one of whom was Mao's widow, Jiang Qing) and a group headed by Deng Xiaoping. This latter group prevailed; the Gang of Four was jailed, and Hua Guofeng was subsequently removed from power in 1979. The "pragmatists" on agriculture, industry, military professionalism, and foreign policy had replaced the Maoist ideologies.

The 1980s The 1980s were a period of sweeping reform in the economic system. Prior to this date, the Maoist view of development prevailed. This meant that China's policies were concerned not with modernization but with moving toward socialism. Self-reliance, large state and collective agricultural units, and heavy industrialization became the rule. When the reformers took over in late 1978 (December), important economic reforms were initiated and lasted throughout the 1980s. The goal of the reforms was to decentralize and liberalize the economy and to establish an "open door" policy to the outside world. Deng Xiaoping was determined to demonstrate that socialism could surpass capitalism. This socialism as development meant private ownership, stock ownership, free markets, a democratized management of economic units, material incentives, and even the introduction of stock markets into Shenzhen and Shanghai. Deng's policy was "whatever works"—indeed, the pragmatist reformers were in charge.[43]

In the Tiananmen incident of 1989 (April 15 to June 4), the Chinese government's repressive political crackdown turned foreign investors away. But China did *not* revert to an economic closed door policy. On the contrary, it continued and even worked to expand its new economic initiatives. Such remains the case today.

39

The 1990s In the early 1990s, "although Western countries continued to hold back, most of the countries of East Asia were once again fully engaged in business with the PRC."[44] Today the Shanghai stock market is in full operation, millionaires now exist in China, consumer standards are rising, and the *dakun*, the very wealthy, are shopping in posh boutiques buying Italian suits and French cosmetics. Private enterprise is flourishing in China in part because competition from state-owned companies is characterized by sloth and indifference.[45]

The alienating effects of urbanization are a problem in the 1990s, and it appears that Chinese socialism will become less important than China's development. The peasantry's per capita income has increased significantly; half of peasant income comes from sources outside the collective. Thousands of Chinese have had contact with the West through education abroad and through foreign investment and technology.

Perhaps the most significant event in the 90s for China was the establishment of Hong Kong as a special administrative region. On July 1, 1997, the seven million people who reside in Hong Kong were integrated into the PRC and the region reverted to Chinese administration. The Chief of State, President of China, Jiang Zemin, and a legislative council of sixty representatives, from seven political parties, began handling Hong Kong's political life. This bustling free market economy is highly dependent on international trade with imports of 208 billion and with China as its major export market and the United States as its second most important export point.

But the monopoly on political power is still complete. China's Four Basic Principles still prevail: the socialist road, the people's dictatorship, party leadership, and Marxist-Leninist-Mao Zedong thought are still being upheld. "Bourgeois liberalization," the "root cause" of the Tiananmen upheaval, is the target of daily government attacks. At the moment, the party leadership stands firmly in control of China's political institutions.

Mao Zedong—A Biographical Sketch

Mao Zedong was born in Hunan province on December 26, 1893. Mao's father was a successful peasant and his mother a devout Buddhist. It appears that the family generally enjoyed the basic necessities of life. As a boy Mao worked in his father's fields and attended a local school for a part of each day. Both Mao's father and teacher were apparently strict men, for he reported that he was beaten frequently. Mao loved reading and was anxious to continue his formal education. At the age of 16, he borrowed enough money from friends and relatives to attend the Tungshan schools in Siangsiang. After only one year at Tung-shan, he transferred to a secondary school in Changsha where he read his first newspaper, *The People's Strength*.[46]

When he was 18 years old, Mao joined the army and used most of his salary of $7 a month to buy newspapers. After a short tour of duty, he resigned from the army and returned to school where he spent six months reading on his own in the Hunan Provincial Library. Following this period of self-education, Mao spent almost five years at the First Normal School in Changshan (1912–1917). Here he was greatly influenced by Chen-ch'i who taught Mao the value of an ascetic lifestyle. When his mother died in 1918, Mao moved to Beijing. There he met Li Dazhao, who introduced him to Marxism. He read Lenin, Trotsky, and, of course, Marx and Engels, and by 1920 Mao was a dedicated communist. In Shanghai, in 1921, when the Chinese Communist party (CCP) was formed, Mao was present.[47] From 1924 to 1927 the communists collaborated with the Kuom-ingtang. It was during this period that Mao began his organization of the peas-ants in Hunan province. On April 12, 1927, Chiang Kai-shek attacked the communists in Shanghai, killing over 4,000 people. This began the period of armed struggle, and it is at this time that Mao and Zhu De began to build the Red Army.

In September 1930, Mao made a decision that was perhaps the most impor-tant in his life, for it split the CCP in two. The issue was who would be the driving force of the revolution—the peasant (Mao's position) or the industrial prole-tariat (the position of many CCP members and Moscow). Mao's view prevailed, and history has proven him correct.[48] Mao continued his organizational work among the peasants, and the army grew dramatically. But after a series of attacks by Chiang's forces, Mao began a retreat to a new base area on October 16, 1934—the Long March had begun. The March covered 6,000 miles, lasted over one year, and cost the communists 80,000 soldiers as Mao arrived in Yenan with only 20,000 troops. But they survived, and the new base camp was Mao's headquarters for the next 11 years (until 1945).[49] From 1936 to 1945, Mao and his Red Army, which had grown to almost a million soldiers at the time of Japan's surrender, fought the Japanese. In July 1946, the civil war between the Kuomingtang and communist forces was renewed and ended only when Mao proclaimed the establishment of the PRC on October 1, 1949.[50] In December 1949 Mao made the first of three trips to Moscow to sign the Sino-Soviet Treaty of Alliance. These were his only ventures outside of China proper.

Mao Zedong, "the great helmsman" as he was called, died on September 9, 1976, at the age of 82. With his death, the massive upheavals that had immersed the nation in chaos for ten years came to an end. Today, Mao lies in state in a mausoleum in Beijing's Tiananmen Square. He is still revered by the Chinese, but in the years since his death the new regime has sought to downgrade him from idol to human status. In China today he is still viewed as a great revolutionary leader, but a man who contributed to much of China's economic turmoil (the Great Leap Forward) and political chaos (the Great Proletarian Cultural Revolution).

Maoism

Mao's unique modification of Marxist-Leninist ideology may be usefully characterized within the framework of five doctrines: the revolutionary role of the Chinese peasant, guerrilla warfare, self-reliance, proletarianization (mind over matter or will versus history), and revolutionary nationalism.

The Revolutionary Role of the Chinese Peasant In "Report on an Investigation of the Peasant Movement in Hunan," written in March 1927, Mao Zedong discusses the revolutionary role of the peasants in China. He begins by dividing the peasants into three groups—rich, middle, and poor. The rich and middle-class peasants (10 and 20 percent, respectively) are not dependable, largely inactive, cautious, and vacillating in their attitude toward revolutionary activity. To Mao, it is the poor peasants, those 70 percent who are virtually destitute, who are the real agents of the revolution. "The poor peasants have always been the main force in the bitter fight in the countryside. . . . Leadership by the poor peasants is absolutely necessary. Without the poor peasants there would be no revolution. To deny their role is to deny the revolution."[51] It is the poor peasants who play the vanguard role in Mao's revolution and are the real heroes of the overthrow. For Mao, the mass of poor peasants are distinguished from rich and middle peasants by their relationship to land and labor. The rich and middle peasants own land and do not sell their labor for wages, while the vast majority of poor peasants own no land, rent the land they work on, and invariably are forced to sell their labor power to survive. This, says Mao, is the "principal criterion" distinguishing a rich and middle peasant from a poor peasant.[52]

Mao's entire strategy for overthrowing China's feudal relations has a rural orientation. The driving force of the revolution is the peasant; the agrarian revolution has its origin in the countryside; its basic structure is built on the peasant organizations; its immediate object of concern is to hit the landlords politically by executing, banishing, parading, locking up, and demonstrating against them;

42

and it is from the countryside that this revolutionary force will eventually sur-
round the cities and bring victory to this country of rural proletariat workers.

Guerrilla Warfare   The foundation of Mao's rural strategy lies in the truly
unique ideas expressed in *On Guerrilla Warfare*. This must rank as a work of the
first magnitude insofar as this type of warfare is concerned. For Mao Zedong,
"The seizure of power by armed force, the settlement of the issue by war, is the
central task and the highest form of revolution."[53] "Every Communist must
grasp the truth, 'Political power grows out of the barrel of a gun.'"[54] Although
the centerpiece of the text concerns the actual strategy and tactics of guerrilla
warfare, a number of other related doctrines are intimately related to success on
the battlefield, according to Mao. It is essential, of course, to rely on the peasants
in a people's war and to form them into a united front with students, intellectuals, workers, and even petty bourgeoisie. Mao believed, like Lenin, that these
alliances can be extremely useful, particularly because the Communist party
always is to play the leadership role in organization and planning. Mao also
gives great attention to what he calls the prominence of politics; that is, the fighting force must be built on a solid ideological base. Politics is the "commander"
and the "soul of everything"—it is the "lifeline" of the army. At one point Mao
comments that anyone can learn to shoot a rifle, but that one will only perform
that act if one is ideologically motivated to do so. Understanding *why* one fights
is infinitely more important to Mao than learning how to throw a hand grenade.

Mao describes the actual strategy and tactics of guerrilla warfare in his hand-
book for peasant revolutionaries in four clear, forthright theses. First, guerrilla
warriors must understand the *protracted* nature of the conflict. Guerrilla fighters
must be prepared to fight for 10, 15, or even 20 years. Psychologically, this pre-
pares Mao's fighters mentally to deal with a struggle that may last a generation
or more, and at the same time erodes the capacity and will of an enemy to carry
on the battle. Next, Mao talks about different types of warfare: terror, guerrilla
warfare, positional warfare, and mobile warfare (from the lowest to the highest
level of violence). Success on the battlefield can never come from guerrilla warfare alone. The fighting may move back and forth between the various types but
must ultimately reach the mobile stage if victory is to be achieved. He cautions
his troops to recognize the limitations of each form of warfare. Third, Mao
teaches tactics to his guerrilla fighters in a poem: "The enemy advances, we
retreat; the enemy camps, we harass; the enemy tires, we attack; the enemy
retreats, we pursue."[55] Note how Mao has built ideology into his tactics by the
concept of "enemy." It is important to remember that he is fielding an army of
peasants, civilians, who have had little or no formal education, let alone military

43

training. Finally, he comments on guerrilla war as a war of annihilation. The consequences of this type of battle involve, in theory, the total elimination of enemy units. This results in prisoners, captured weapons, a lowering of enemy morale, and an increase in guerrilla combat effectiveness. Mao again teaches this concept through a saying: "Pit one against ten, pit ten against one."[56] Briefly, this means that strategically the guerrilla fighters are weak as they are fighting a force ten times their size, while tactically it demands that the guerrilla fighters enter combat only when they substantially outnumber the enemy.[57]

Self-Reliance "On what basis should our policy rest? It should rest on our own strength, and that means regeneration through one's own efforts. . . . We stand for self-reliance."[58] The very act of liberation through guerrilla warfare is, to Mao, a supreme expression of self-reliance. Mao taught that only through the dedicated struggle of one's own people could the course of foreign intervention and domestic exploitation be ended. Guerrilla warfare was his formula for seizing power, and it demanded trial and error, spontaneity, and a willingness to rebel against all odds. For Mao, "a single spark will start a prairie fire"; that is, if just one person will rebel, the act will be seen by others and spread throughout the populace like a prairie fire. Everything must be done and can be done by the Chinese people. Mao instructs them to develop "savage bodies" through exercise so they can rid China of its tormentors. Those committed ideologically to the construction of a new society in China can accomplish this with determination and self-reliance. Nothing more is required. Plain living, hard struggle, reliance on one's own forces—these alone make everything possible for Mao.

Proletarianization "The Chinese national bourgeoisie retains a certain revolutionary quality . . . [unlike] the Russian bourgeoisie [which] was entirely lacking in revolutionary quality."[59] Thus, Mao declared the Chinese national bourgeoisie could become genuine members of the new socialist society through education. This process of transforming one's consciousness from a bourgeois to a proletarian mentality is called *proletarianization*. It is absolutely central to Mao's thought, as it stands in direct opposition to Marx's dictum that being, not consciousness, ultimately determines one's mentality. But for Mao, the human factor is always primary, and the human will can, under certain circumstances, transcend conditions. Mao clearly states that it is possible to build a proletarian mentality through education. He contended that because the Chinese people were "poor and blank"—"poor" in economic terms and "blank" in that they have never been exposed to the corrosive effects of materialism, consumerism, and individualism rampant in the Western world—they were peculiarly susceptible to proletarianization. To be "poor and blank" were perfect conditions for a revolutionary change of attitude.[60] Mao's struggle to ideologically remold the Chinese people reached its most extreme expression in the effort at thought control implicit in the millions of "little red books" published during the GPCR entitled *Quotations from Chairman Mao Tse-Tung*. Subjective forces can go beyond objective realities in Mao's thought. Thus, the role of ideology is crucial to Maoism.

Revolutionary Nationalism   Mao's revolutionary nationalism is passionately concerned with "the future of the motherland and the ideals of mankind."[61] Mao frequently expresses his love of China and its people, particularly the Hans, and he sought from an early age to end China's "century of humiliation" by foreigners. This same attitude and behavior pattern are reflected in his insistence that the Comintern cease its efforts to meddle in China's internal affairs and in China's 25-year dispute with the Soviet Union. When China entered the socialist camp in 1949, Moscow thought it had a new satellite. But Mao had no intention of turning China over to the Soviets. Maoism presents China as a model for Third World development, ridicules the United States and its nuclear weapons as "paper tigers," and argues that self-determination for China and the freedom of the Chinese people are dependent on the territorial integrity of China as a nation-state. If one looks at China's behavior in international politics today through the ideological prism of Marxism, one finds some difficulty in making sense of the world. If, however, one replaces Marxism with nationalism, then more order, consistency, and clarity prevail. Mao may be understood as a Marxist. He is equally understood as a nationalist, and his Chinese heritage will often prevail over his commitment to Western Marxism about which Mao had no first-hand information—only stereotypes. Mao's concern with China as a nation-state is also demonstrated in his struggle to unite Hong Kong and Taiwan with the mainland and for China to take its rightful seat as a permanent member of the United Nations Security Council. The United Nations and Hong Kong issues have been resolved. The Taiwan issue still remains.

Post-Mao Thought

With the death of Mao Zedong and Zhou Enlai in 1976, a two-year power struggle emerged in the CCP between the Gang of Four, headed by Mao's widow Jiang Qing, and the Pragmatists led by Den Xiaoping. Mao's illness and Zhou's death helped the Gang of Four in the struggle for power during the years 1974–1976. This "Red versus Expert" struggle involved all the major domestic and international issues facing China: In the *economy*, the Reds emphasized agriculture, whereas the Experts sought to reform China's enfeebled industrial base; in *foreign trade*, the Reds sought to modernize China through self-reliance, whereas the Experts eagerly worked to import foreign capital, skills, technology, and trade; in *education*, the Reds fought for ideological purity and dedicated students at the same time the Experts tried to reward the brightest students and those with specific skills in science and engineering; on the issue of the *military*, the Reds fought to preserve the militia and the idea of "people's war," whereas the Experts tried to modernize and professionalize the military by buying antiaircraft missiles from France, Harrier jets from Britain, and 707s from the United States; and in *ideology*, the Reds continued their struggle to have art and literature faithfully mirror ideology, whereas the Experts began to downgrade Mao from his idol status and encourage a degree of diversification in the cultural context of China's political economy. This struggle continued until December 1978 when the Pragmatist position prevailed and Deng Xiaoping and his followers assumed the leadership of China.

Since December 1978, China has been in the throes of great change. Witness the following developments now encouraged by the regime: the profit motive, private entrepreneurs, competitive markets, the dismantling of the commune system (Mao's proudest achievement), the establishment of individual family-run farms, advocacy of personal happiness, millions of self-employed people, skirts and dresses for women. Pierre Cardin invited to Beijing, foreign movies, dancing, a new college examination system, ideological innovation, 36,000 Chinese students studying abroad—one-half of them in the United States.[62]

Economic Changes   The heart of Deng Xiaoping's reforms lies in the economic changes he initiated. Even military preparedness does not get the same priority as China's "four modernizations" program, which involves agriculture, industry, science, and technology. Deng's rural reforms have raised living standards significantly; the CCP newspaper, *People's Daily*, printed an article that advocated the issuing of stock to concentrate capital and the payment of dividends from profits according to the number of shares one held; advertising of family-run restaurants and pedicabs is common; and increasingly, tools and equipment on the farm are privately rather than publicly owned.[63] China today advocates the concept of "one country, two systems." This is to be a new kind of communism with both socialist and capitalist institutions where planning and quotas are slowly giving some way to the market. All this is happening in a country that under the GPCR could not feed itself but now has surpluses of rice, cabbage, and fish—a nation where there has been a dramatic rise in the service sector of the economy.[64] Initially, China's economic reforms focused on the rural areas, but recently the reforms have shifted to the cities. The Chinese contend that, although Den Xiaoping played a key role in the economic reforms, this is not a "one-person show" and that the reforms are here to stay.

Politics For almost ten years, 1979 to 1989, three octogenarians ruled China—Deng Xiaoping, Hu Yaobang, and Zhao Ziyang. This trio controlled, respectively, the three main pillars of the Chinese political system: the military, the party, and the central government. But most specialists in Chinese politics believed that of the three, Den Xiaoping, with his military relationships, was the real ruler.

Deng, born in 1908, began his party work as an organizer. He studied in Paris and Moscow and then returned to China, joined Mao's guerrilla forces, and participated in the Long March. In the 1950s Deng was elected to the politburo, but was purged in the GPCR in 1966. He returned to power in 1974, was purged again in 1976, and returned to power a second time when the Gang of Four was arrested.[65]

In 1980 Hu Yaobang and Zhao Ziyang, two of Deng's supporters joined him as members of the Standing Committee of the politburo—the center of power in China. As general secretary of the party, Hu Yaobang controlled the daily life and direction of the party, while Zhao Ziyang headed the central government. Hu attempted to push political reforms that Deng thought unwise, and in 1987 he was forced to resign—ostensibly because of student demonstrations and his tolerance of "bourgeois liberalization." Hu died in April 1989, and it was his death that sparked the massive student demonstrations in Tiananmen Square that spring.

Zhao Ziyang then moved from his post as premier of the central government and replaced Hu Yaobang as party chief in November 1987 at the Thirteenth Party Congress, but his tenure was short-lived. He was ousted two years later as the party general secretary in June 1989. His crimes were his inability to handle the Tiananmen student demonstrations, his tolerance of "bourgeois liberalization," and the challenge he posed to Deng Xiaoping and the aged party leadership.[66]

The politically conservative leadership of the 50 million member Chinese Communist party prevailed over the most progressive elements in China's political elite. Zhao Ziyang was replaced as party chief by Jiang Zemin in June 1989, and Jiang subsequently was elected to be the nation's president in March of 1993. Jiang was certainly the personal choice of Deng Xiaoping—probably

47

because of his forthright actions designed to curb dissent and criticism during the Tiananmen crisis. (Deng died in February of 1997.)

Jiang Zemin was President from 1989 to 2003. He began the leadership transition to Hu Jintao in November of 2002 when he gave Hu the post of party chief. Hu then succeeded Jiang as President in March 2003. At this writing Hu is still in power. Hu is a careful not to antagonize his predecessor, Mr. Jiang, who still remains a powerful figure.

The Military   China's military problems were a continuing problem for Deng Xiaoping and continue to be so for the new regime. They have problems in the south with Vietnam, with whom they fought, and in the north with the Russians where about 25 percent of their army and air force personnel are stationed. The Russian troops are supported by significant offensive and defensive missiles, and the Chinese, although they have the manpower, do not have the weapons to match the Russian force. Internally, all effective challenges to power are now eliminated, and the army has been reorganized and streamlined from 4 to 3 million soldiers. Present efforts have been directed toward building a professional army rather than a militia, getting China's first nuclear submarines with nuclear weapons at sea, setting up new ICBM missiles (CSS-2 ballistic missiles and CSS-4 intercontinental missiles), and importing military equipment from Western powers to help build a modern army and air force.

Tiananmen Square, in June of 1989, was a major crisis for the military. The People's Liberation Army (PLA) and its relation to the Chinese people were damaged by the Tiananmen incident. The Goddess of Democracy statue was a challenge and the PLA leaders decided it must be crushed.

But the future for China is dazzling. China is now the world's largest producer of coal, steel and cement, the second largest consumer of energy and the third largest importer of oil.[67] China is the world's fastest growing large economy, the world's largest army (2.5 million men) and the fourth biggest defense budget. It is the powerful new force on the global scene.[68] China's modernization is pursued on a pragmatic path. Ideology is put aside when it comes to questions of economics. Today, Nationalism has replaced Communism as the ideological cement that holds China together—Mao is still a hero in China despite his failed policies. China is moving up in science and technology—challenging the United States.[69]

THE LAST BULWARKS OF COMMUNISM

With the total collapse of communism in the Soviet Union and Eastern Europe, the few communist regimes that remain (China, North Korea, Vietnam, Laos and Cuba) are all in trouble in terms of political legitimacy and/or economic effectiveness. Politically, the entrenched bureaucracy, corruption, and age of the party leadership all function to weaken the legitimacy of the regimes in the five "last bulwarks." Gone are the economic subsidies in oil and subsidized exports, gone are the military ties that linked these second- and third-rate military powers to the USSR superpower, gone are the technological advantages (particularly in weapons development) associated with close relations to a fraternal superpower, and gone is the ideological source of truth—the first communist state established by Lenin himself.

The shock to the morale of these "last bulwarks" is great and as such intensifies pressures for radical change. All had relied on the Soviets for everything from training and technical support to weaponry and intelligence. Student and ethnic unrest is a reality in these, the remaining bastions of communism. The old ideology and institutions must change but cannot.

What can we say about the future of communism in the "last bulwarks"? Much, obviously, depends on how the economies in these countries perform. Growth and modernization are extremely important. The regimes must become economically effective or they will collapse. A capacity for military repression may be a necessary condition of ruling; unfortunately for the leaders of the "last bulwarks," however, it is not a sufficient condition. Inefficiency, centralized control, and the decline in GNP and living standards must be resolved. In addition, the "vision" that sparked communist revolutions in the "last bulwarks" has been dimmed, if not extinguished. Even in Vietnam, now that the dream of a unified Vietnam has been realized, communist ideology has failed to mobilize the masses to strive for a new socialist reality. Ideological fatigue plagues the "last bulwarks," particularly the youth who see the changes occurring in the world through the worldwide communication network. The signals and messages from the world can no longer be blocked out—particularly so as joint ventures with non-socialist states are developed and the intrusive reality of the world wide web, the internet, spreads throughout the world.

Finally, all of the "last bulwarks" refuse to give up their control of political power. The consequences of the Soviet decision of February 1990 to formally abandon a power monopoly must be very unnerving to the entrenched party bureaucrats in China, North Korea, Vietnam, Laos, and Cuba. North Korea is particularly dangerous to United States security. There the communist regime

49

has launched long-range missiles over Japan, sold missiles to a number of middle-east states, shot at our soldiers in the buffer zone between North and South Korea, and massed a million man army within artillery range of 37,000 American troops on the DMZ.[70]

Free elections and competing political parties, the litmus paper test for democratic systems, remind one of Marx's metaphor in *The Communist Manifesto*, "A spectre is haunting Europe." The spectre that haunts the "last bulwarks" today is liberal democracy, and no "holy alliance to exorcise this spectre" can prevail because the great protector, the Soviet Union, no longer exists, rapid technological change demands reform, and aid from the West requires economic and political liberalization. Marx said that "The history of all hitherto existing society is the history of class struggles." The day of living "first class in a classless society" is coming to a close in the last bulwarks.

NOTES

1. J. Russell Major, *The Western World: Renaissance to the Present* (New York: J.B. Lippincott Co., 1966), pp. 122–127. Also, Michel Beaud, *A History of Capitalism 1500–1980*, translated by Tom Dickman and Anny Lefebuer (New York: Monthly Review Press, 1983), pp. 17–73; Robert L. Heilbroner, *The Making of Economic Society*, 4th ed. (Englewood Cliffs, NJ: Prentice-Hall, 1972), pp. 54–75.

2. Heilbroner, *Making of Economic Society*, pp. 78–98. Also, Robert L. Reynolds, *Europe Emerges: Transition Toward an Industrial World-Wide Society*, 600–1750 (Madison: University of Wisconsin Press, 1967), pp. 389–411; Malcolm E. Falkus, ed., *Readings in the History of Economic Growth* (London: Oxford University Press, 1968), see especially "Part Two: Economic Development in Western Europe," pp. 51–134.

3. Walter P. Hall, Robert G. Albion, and Jennie B. Pope, *A History of England and the Commonwealth* (Boston: Blaisdell, 1965), pp. 337–338.

4. Ibid., pp. 390–391, 428–438.

5. Isaiah Berlin, *Karl Marx: His Life and Environment* (New York: Oxford University Press, 1959), pp. 26–31.

6. Ibid., pp. 98–103. Also, David McLellan, *Karl Marx: His Life and Thought* (New York: Harper & Row, 1973), pp. 88–122.

7. Monty Johnstone, "Party," in *A Dictionary of Marxist Thought*, Tom Bottomore, ed. (Cambridge, MA: Harvard University Press, 1983), p. 360.

8. McLellan, *Karl Marx*, pp. 180–188.

9. Personal visit to Karl Marx's former home in Trier by Robert G. Thobaben in January 1981. The home is now a museum open to the public.

10. Adam Smith, *An Inquiry into the Nature and Causes of the Wealth of Nations* (New York: Random House [Modern Library], 1937), pp. 315, 718.

11. George Friedman, "Marxism, Judaism and the Death of God." Paper presented at the Conference on the Current State of Marxism, Ohio University, Athens, Ohio (November 10–13, 1977), pp. 9–10.

12. Ibid., pp. 10–19.

13. Ibid., pp. 19–29.

14. Ibid., pp. 30–32.

15. John Somerville, *The Philosophy of Marxism: An Exposition* (New York: Random House, 1967), pp. 42–44. (We are indebted to Somerville for his very clear treatment of ontology and epistemology.)

16. Fritjof Capra, "The Tao of Physics: Reflections on the Cosmic Dance," *Saturday Review* (December 10, 1977), pp. 21–28.

17. Robert L. Heilbroner, "The Dialectical Vision," *The New Republic* (March 1, 1980), p. 27.

18. Karl Marx, "Toward a Critique of Hegel's Philosophy of Right: Introduction," in *Karl Marx: Selected Writings*, edited by David McLellan (London: Oxford University Press, 1977), p. 64.

19. David Resnick, "Crude Communism and Revolution," *The American Political Science Review* (December 1976), p. 1136.

20. Robert G. Thobaben, Jr., lecture delivered at Wright State University for course entitled "Biopolitics" in October 1983.

21a. Adam Schaff, *Marxism and the Human Individual* (New York: McGraw-Hill, 1970), p. 51.

21b. Ibid., p. 72.

21c. Ibid., p. 78.

21d. *Karl Marx: Selected Writings in Sociology and Social Philosophy*, edited and translated by T.B. Bottomore and M. Rubel (New York: McGraw-Hill, 1964), p. 63.

21e. Ibid., p. 91.

22. Karl Marx, "Economic and Philosophical Manuscripts of 1844," (ed.), *Karl Marx: Selected Writings*, pp. 75–111.

23. Karl Marx, "The Communist Manifesto," in McLellan (ed.), *Karl Marx*, p. 222.

24. Karl Marx, "Critique of the Gotha Programme," in McLellan (ed.), *Karl Marx*, p. 568.

25. Ibid., p. 569.

26. George Sabine, *A History of Political Theory* (New York: Holt, Rinehart & Winston, 1961), p. 527.

27. Smith, *Wealth of Nations*, pp. 30, 64, 83.

28. *The Militant*, March 16, 1979, p. 30.

29. Michael Harrington, *Socialism* (New York: Bantam Books, 1970), pp. 119–120. (Our entire discussion in this part is informed by Harrington's analysis.)

30. Karl Marx, *Capital*, Vol. 1, "Constant and Variable Capital," in McLellan, pp. 470–474.

31. David E. Ingersoll, *Communism, Fascism, and Democracy* (Columbus, Ohio: Merrill, 1971), pp. 41–46. (A very thorough and lucid presentation of all the problems and answers discussed here.)

32. Bertram D. Wolfe, *Three Who Made a Revolution* (Boston: Beacon Press, 1948), pp. 11–23.

33. Ibid., pp. 60–90.

34. Robert C. Tucker, ed., *The Lenin Anthology* (New York: W.W. Norton, 1975), pp. xxxii–xxxvi.

35. Nina Tumarkin, *Lenin Lives: The Lenin Cult in Soviet Russia* (Cambridge, MA: Harvard University Press, 1983), pp. 112–131.

36. V.I. Lenin, "What is to be done," Vol. V, May, 1901–February 1902 (Moscow: Progress Publishers, 1964), p. 369.

37. Wolfe, *Three Who Made a Revolution*, pp. 399–436.

38. Roy A. Medvedev, "New Pages from the Political Biography of Stalin," *Stalinism: Essay in Historical Interpretation*, edited by Robert C. Tucker (New York: Norton, 1977), p. 201.

39. Ibid., pp. 201–203.

40. Ibid., p. 235.

41. Francis X. Clines, "11 Soviet States Form Commonwealth," *New York Times*, December 22, 1991, pp. 1 and 8.

53

42. *Facts on File*, Vol. I, 52, No. 2682, April 16, 1992.

43. Suzanne Ogden, *China's Unresolved Issues*, 2nd ed., (Englewood Cliffs, NJ: Prentice Hall, 1992), p. 333.

44. Ibid., p. 335.

45. Nicholas D. Kristof, "Entrepreneurs in China Attain the Age of Greed," *New York Times*, August 30, 1992, p. 3.

46. Anne Fremantle, *Mao Tse-Tung: An Anthology of His Writings* (New York: New American Library (Mentor Books), 1962), pp. vii–xii.

47. Mao Tse-Tung, *On Guerrilla Warfare*, translated by S.B. Griffith, USMC (Ret.) (New York: Praeger, 1961), pp. 12–13.

48. Ibid., p. 17.

49. Fremantle, *Mao Tse-Tung*, pp. xxxiii–xl.

50. Ibid., pp. xxxviii–xliv.

51. Mao Zedong, "Report on an Investigation of the Peasant Movement in Hunan," in *Selected Works of Mao Tse-Tung*, Vol. I (Peking: Foreign Languages Press, 1965), pp. 138–139.

52. Mao Zedong, "How to Differentiate the Classes in the Rural Areas," in *Selected Works of Mao Tse-Tung*, Vol. I (Peking: Foreign Languages Press, 1965), pp. 138–139.

53. Mao Zedong, "China's Characteristics and Revolutionary War," in *Selected Works of Mao Tse-Tung*, Vol. II (Peking: Foreign Languages Press, 1965), p. 219.

54. Ibid., p. 224.

55. Mao Zedong, "A Single Spark Can Start a Prairie Fire," in *Selected Works*, Vol. I, p. 124.

56. Ibid., p. 236.

57. Mao Tse-Tung, *On Guerrilla Warfare*, pp. 41–114

58. Mao Zedong, *Selected Works*, Vol. IV, p. 20 and Vol. III, p. 241.

59. Mao Zedong, *Selected Works*, Vol. II, 348.

60. Stuart R. Schram, *The Political Thought of Mao Tse-Tung* (New York: Praeger, 1970), pp. 350–352.

61. Mao Zedong, *Selected Works*, Vol. V, p. 405.

62. *New York Times*, December 10, 1978, by Fox Butterfield, pp. 42–144. Also see *Dayton Daily News* article by Jim Abrams of Associated Press, October 1, 1986, p. 2.

63a. *The Dayton Journal Herald*, October 2, 1984, p. 12.

63b. *New York Times* article by Cheng Chun, November 9, 1980.

63c. "Marx, Mao, and Markets," by Harry Harding, *The New Republic*, October 7, 1985, p. 38.

64. "Muddling after Mao," Merle Goldman, *The New Republic*, June 16, 1986, p. 39.

65. Byron S. J. Weng, "Economic Development and Democratization," *Asian Studies*, 36, 3 (July 1990): 8–10. See also Suzanne Ogden, *China's Unresolved Issues* (Englewood Cliffs, NJ: Prentice Hall, 1992), p. 335.

66. Ogden, *China's Unresolved Issues*, p. 337. See also the internet site for Political Leaders: 1945–2000, China.

67. Fareed Zakaria, "Does the Future Belong to China," *Newsweek*, May 9, 2005, p. 28.

68. Ibid., p. 29.

69. Ibid., p. 39.

70. Robert G. Thobaben, "Treat North Korea Like Enemy It Is," *Dayton Daily News*, December 1, 1998, p. 11-A.

SUGGESTED READINGS FOR KARL MARX

Berlin, Isaiah. *Karl Marx: His Life and Environment*. New York: Oxford University Press, 1959.

Harrington, Michael. *Socialism*. New York: Bantam Books, 1970.

Marx, Karl, and Friedrich Engels. *The Communist Manifesto*. Baltimore: Penguin Books, 1968.

McLellan, David. *Karl Marx: His Life and Thought*. New York: Harper & Row, 1973.

Ollman, Bertell. *Alienation: Marx's Conception of Man in Capitalist Society*. London: Cambridge University Press, 1971.

Somerville, John. *The Philosophy of Marxism: An Exposition*. New York: Random House, 1967.

SUGGESTED READINGS FOR COMMUNISM

Hicks, George (ed.), *The Broken Mirror*, Great Britain: Biddles Ltd., 1990.

Piediscalzi, Nicholas, and Robert Thobaben, *Three Worlds of Christian-Marxist Encounters*, Philadelphia: Fortress Press, 1985.

Schram, Stuart R., *The Political Thought of Mao Tse-Tung*, New York: Praeger, 1970.

Tucker, Robert C., *The Lenin Anthology*, New York: Norton, 1975. Especially, "What Is to Be Done" and "Imperialism: The Highest Stage of Capitalism."

Tumarkin, Nina, *Lenin Lives: The Lenin Cult in Soviet Russia*, Cambridge, Mass.: Harvard University Press, 1983.

Wolfe, Bertram D., *Three Who Made a Revolution*, New York: Norton, 1948.

Chapter 3

Democratic Socialism

L eftist objectives are pursued by a variety of means, including voting, mass activism, persuasion, education, and violence. The democratic left, as defined here, consists of those aspects of leftist ideology that are compatible with constitutional government and representative democracy. Marxist scholar Leszek Kolakowski was a leading advocate of a democratic and humanist socialism. Kolakowski describes the characteristics of the political left as including an emphasis on constructive change seeking abolition of social privilege, discrimination, and exploitation between classes and nations. The democratic left resists limitations on freedom of speech and expression, and strives to secularize social life and promote rational thought. For publishing these and other "revisionist ideas," Kolakowski was expelled from the Communist party in Poland.[1]

The call to resistance against authoritarian dogmatism is a major theme within the democratic left. The planning state, more than any other, requires checks on political power in the form of public opinion, a free press, civil liberties, and constitutional government. Stated more simply by poet and playwright Oscar Wilde: "It is clear, then, that no Authoritarian Socialism will do."[2]

Democratic socialists share with other leftists a *utopian vision* of an ideal society characterized by material abundance, social and economic equality, and considerable leisure time available for pursuit of higher human endeavors. Invariably, these utopian conditions are envisioned as resulting from the abolition or control of private property and inequality, and the diversion of profits from private owners to the public good. Historically, there has been a contrast between this socialist vision based on the restructuring of society and the *practical socialism* compatible with the realism and compromise required by representative government.

In summary, democratic socialism includes a commitment to constitutional government and representative democracy, redistribution of property or incomes to promote economic as well as political equality, and a utopian vision of a new social order in which modern technology is used to create the leisure time needed for individual intellectual and moral development.

THE DEVELOPMENT OF DEMOCRATIC SOCIALISM

Two fundamentally different approaches have characterized attempts to realize the socialist vision in a democratic context. We describe these as socialism from *below* and socialism from *above*.

Socialism from below consists of attempts to create the utopian society directly by establishing socialist communities and cooperatives at the local level. This approach has the advantage of not requiring the restructuring of society or the state. Within the existing society, like-minded individuals choose to involve themselves in communal and cooperative endeavors. Their objective is to implement socialism within their own community. This approach has the significant disadvantage of being dependent on voluntary participation. Not having the enforcement power of the state to command compliance and control resources, voluntary socialist communities have frequently failed or met with only limited success. Consequently, this approach is often described as utopian socialism.

Socialism from above strives to implement the socialist vision by means of political democracy. Through mass education and free discussion, the workers and their allies use political organization, activism, and bloc voting for the Socialist party to take control of the government. Once in command of the political structure, socialists use it to bring about fundamental social and economic change. Large industries may be nationalized (taken over by the government), and the wealth produced by society is distributed more equitably. A welfare state is established to marshal economic resources to eliminate poverty and promote human development. Because limits on state power and requirements for compromise are part of representative democracy, socialism in practice has frequently fallen short of the utopian vision.

Socialism from Below: The Utopians

For the average factory worker in nineteenth-century Europe, the Industrial Revolution had created a dreary world. To paraphrase Thomas Hobbes, life was nasty, brutish, and short. Day-to-day existence for factory workers consisted of long hours of routinized, deadening wage work in regimented conditions. Workers labored 16 hours a day for subsistence wages, frequently in dreadful and unsafe conditions. The wretchedness of factory labor was exceeded only by the squalor in which workers and their families lived. Rather than spending their days in school or idle play, children were frequently put to work in coal mines and textile mills. Seemingly, humans became enslaved by the machines they had created.

Visionaries and reformers known as *utopian socialists* envisioned a better world. Historically, their ideas were an intellectual protest against the excesses of emerging industrial capitalism. Their theories, and the experimental communities based on them, attempted to provide alternatives to the misery of industrial society and the violence of revolution. The utopians proposed to establish the ideal society based on new principles of human nature and social organization.

Foremost among the utopian socialists was Robert Owen, a British entrepreneur who made his fortune in textiles. After purchasing the textile mills in the Scottish village of New Lanark, Owen was able to conduct an experiment in social reorganization. Regarding human nature, Owen assumed, as did most utopians, that "mankind was no better than his environment and if environment was changed, a real paradise on earth might be achieved."[3] New Lanark was to be a demonstration project that would convince property owners and workers that, indeed, there was a better way.

The form of social organization advocated by Owen was a planned community of producers—essentially a producers' cooperative. These small communities (about 2,000 people or less) should be self-sustaining economic units. Factories, farms, and living areas were to be owned and run communally for the benefit of all the members.

Initially, New Lanark was owned by the partnership that purchased it, but it did serve to enable Owen to demonstrate the validity of his principles of planned communalism. Decent housing and working conditions were maintained, and schools and child care provided. Owen's reforms contributed to higher worker morale and productivity, and New Lanark returned a handsome profit. These relatively ideal conditions were maintained for 15 years until Owen sold his interest in the venture.[4]

In 1821 Owen wrote *Social System,* justifying communalism and critiquing private property. He was especially concerned about the unequal distribution of wealth and income. The objective of social organization should be the good of all, which, Owen insisted, could be attained only in a communal setting. Both labor and rewards should be distributed equally. In 1824 he ventured to America to establish a community based on these principles. After purchasing 30,000 acres in Indiana, Owen founded on July 4, 1826, the community of New Harmony. Despite the best of intentions, social organization broke down in New Harmony within three years and the venture collapsed. Assessing the failure of New Harmony and similar utopian communities, economist Robert Heilbroner states: "Dream worlds have a difficult time contending with the frictions of reality."[5] Owen and other utopian thinkers helped keep the socialist vision alive until the expansion of political democracy permitted a different approach.

Socialism from Above: The Democratic Socialists

The experimental villages and cooperatives of the utopians met with varying degrees of success or, more often, failure when confronted with the task of creating socialist communities within a political structure controlled by capitalists. In his comprehensive *History of Socialism,* Harry W. Ladler assesses the utopias as "isolated social experiments [based] on principles directly at variance with those of the outside world."[6] As the utopian communities floundered on the shoals of voluntarism, mass-based democratic socialism gained momentum because of the convergence of political and intellectual trends.

A political development of great significance for socialism was the growing *democratization* of politics. From the middle of the nineteenth century, mass participation in politics began to become a reality. The remainder of the century and the early twentieth century saw increasing numbers of people being permitted, and even encouraged, to participate in politics. The expansion of the franchise to include those other than the propertied classes, in combination with the development of organized political parties to mobilize voters, meant that mass-based democratic socialism was possible. The left, with sufficient popular support, could gain political power peacefully and institute social and economic change. The state need not be perpetually under the control of the capitalists. Stated differently, politics could be used to restructure economics, law, and property relations—all in all, a rather non-Marxist notion for the left to be contemplating.

A significant intellectual development accompanying political democratization was the rejection, or at least the *revision,* of key assumptions of Marxist thought by some leading Western European leftist thinkers. Two schools of thought are particularly important in the development of democratic socialist ideology. The Fabian socialists in England constituted less of a revision of Marxism than a straightforward democratic alternative. The revisionists of Germany, however, purported to provide an explicit reformulation directly challenging the revolutionary basis of Marxism.

Fabian Socialism

The Fabian Society was founded in England on January 4, 1888. The society was an outgrowth of meetings between small groups of students and intellectuals seeking to explore nonrevolutionary solutions to social and economic problems. The Fabians selected their name in honor of the Roman General Fabius Maximus, who achieved fame and military victories using a strategy of gradual attrition of the enemy. Adopting a philosophy of gradualism, the society counseled patience in its approach to politics. It attracted as members some of England's most notable men and women, including George Bernard Shaw, Sidney Webb, Beatrice Potter Webb, Ramsay MacDonald, Graham Wallas, and H. G. Wells. Shaw edited the Fabian Essays, which outlined the principles and program of the Fabian Society.

Webb, in the second essay, argued that in order to be successful in England, the transition to socialism must be democratic, gradual, and constitutional so as to be acceptable to the majority. Webb concluded that the extension of democracy to the economy could be attained peacefully by means of political organization, public education, and representative government:

[T]he inevitable outcome of Democracy is the control by the people themselves, not only of their own political organization, but, through that, also of the main instruments of wealth production; the gradual substitution of organized co-operation for the anarchy of the competitive struggle.[7]

With Webb having established that socialism is the extension of democracy to the economic sphere, an essay by William Clarke examined the economic basis of socialism. Clarke's analysis argued that the capitalist was no longer necessary to the industrial economy. Owners of capital had ceased to be a creative force in the economy, having become merely the recipients of profits, interest, and rent. No longer risk-taking entrepreneurs, they combined with their fellow capitalists to form monopolies and trusts to stifle competition. Not involved in the day-to-day activities of their firms, the owners hired salaried managers to

61

direct their businesses for them. This separation of ownership from management of capital was the basis of Clarke's conclusion that *managers* were necessary for the functioning of industrial society but *owners* were not. The capitalist could be replaced by hired managers, and the economy would be no worse off. Society would be considerably better off because the profits that would have gone to the capitalist could be used to address public needs.[8]

In summary, the Fabians proposed that socialists could, by democratic means, attain ownership by the state of the means of economic production and distribution. Major economic enterprises such as railroads, large industries, and resources (e.g., coal and iron mines) would be nationalized—that is, taken over by the government—with fair compensation to their owners. Industries and resources would be administered by professional managers, in the public interest.

Revisionism

Accompanying the development of Fabian socialism in England was a parallel movement in Germany. As the German Social Democratic party developed, it followed an orthodox Marxist party line. Shortly before the turn of the century, this orientation began to change as opposition to orthodox Marxism began to develop within the party.

A leading figure in the reinterpretation, or revision, of Marxism was Edward Bernstein. An activist in the Social Democratic party, Bernstein lived in exile from 1878 until 1900 in Switzerland, and later in England. While in England he became acquainted with the leaders of the Fabian Society, and some of his ideas reflect Fabian principles. Bernstein, for example, equated democracy with socialism and the elimination of gross inequalities. Democratic procedures are important, Bernstein agreed, but democracy involves more than constitutional government. Democracy also requires consideration of *social justice*. The goal of social democracy was "raising the worker from the social position of a proletarian to that of a citizen" and "the development and the securing of a free personality."[9]

Revisionists went beyond Fabian socialists by formulating an explicit critique of Marxism. Bernstein's analysis of developments in history and economics challenged some of Marx's assumptions and predictions. Bernstein's *Evolutionary Socialism*, published in 1899, precipitated a debate within the German Social Democratic party, and the party officially rejected his revision of Marxism. On his return to Germany, Bernstein assumed leadership of the revisionist movement until his death in 1932.

Bernstein's critique of Marxism consisted of six main points, which may be grouped into two broader categories as follows:

1. The *social and economic conditions* predicted by Marx as the cause of revolution in capitalist countries have not materialized. Marx's predictions of the disappearance of the middle class and the polarization of society into two antagonistic classes have not proven to be accurate.
2. *Representative democracy* has worked more effectively than Marx anticipated. Labor union activism and reform legislation have improved conditions and diminished the likelihood of revolution. Marx had underestimated the potential of representative government to improve social and economic conditions. Since the collapse of capitalism was not imminent, Bernstein reasoned that the proper course of action for socialists was to become active in the organized struggle for the political and economic rights of the working class.

With the Fabians and revisionists providing intellectual leadership and organized labor providing mass membership and financial assistance, democratic socialism became a force in parliamentary politics. Socialist intellectuals, trade unionists, social reformers, and the Independent Labour party came together around the turn of the century in England to produce a mass-based political party. In elections for Parliament in 1906, the Labour party astounded the Liberals and conservatives by running 50 candidates and electing 29.[10] These Labour victories ushered in a new era in socialist politics.

MODERN DEMOCRATIC SOCIALISM

British Socialist leader and member of Parliament J. Ramsay MacDonald wrote *The Socialist Movement* in 1911. MacDonald, who would later serve as prime minister on two occasions in minority Labour governments, described the essence of modern democratic socialism. To comprehend the nature of socialism it is necessary to consider what socialism is not. It is not, MacDonald stated, anarchism or communism, the abolition of private property, class war, or the negation of liberty.

Property

Having outlined socialist arguments against authoritarianism and in favor of democracy, let us now consider MacDonald's contention that democratic socialism does not seek the abolition of private property According to MacDonald, socialism strives to eliminate the evil consequences of private property and to promote the realization of its desirable possibilities. His analysis, in fact, assumes that individuality requires private property as a means of self-expression:

Man must control and own something, otherwise he does not control and own himself. . . . The ownership of things will always be a means of expressing personality, and this fact will not be forgotten in the evolution of Socialism . . . there is nothing in this concession contrary to Socialist theory.[11]

Beginning with this (seemingly) liberal premise, MacDonald arrives at a socialist conclusion: although ownership is basic to human nature, it is not in the interest of either society or most individuals for a handful of owners to control the major means of production and distribution for society. Concentration of huge amounts of property in the hands of a few owners has deprived society and most of its members of the benefits of property ownership. The unequal distribution of property means that only a few, "a very small class enjoy today the pleasure and the freedom which comes from private property."[12] Consequently, socialists advocate the public ownership of certain forms of property as a necessary condition to remedy the inequities in property ownership and the resulting exploitation and injustice characteristic of capitalism.

The Socialist Program

It was not until after the Great Depression of the 1930s that democratic socialists acquired the political power necessary to implement their program. Evan F. M. Durbin, an economist, a member of Parliament, and a junior minister in the postwar Labour government in Britain, wrote *The Politics of Democratic Socialism* (1940). This discussion of economic and social legislation summarized the political program advocated by democratic socialists. Durbin's four sets of legislative measures outlined below have been enacted into policy, in one form or another, by most European democratic socialist governments.

Full Employment   Because capitalism experiences recurring recessions in economic activity, these policies are necessary to maintain productivity and

employment during the transition to socialism. The programs consist of governmental actions that attempt to maintain and increase industrial activity.
Although these measures constitute a cornerstone of modern liberalism, liberals rely on this program to maintain capitalism and avoid the transition to
socialism.

Social Services   These measures consist of legislative and administrative
policies using governmental action to improve the condition of the poor.
Emphasis is on education, medical care, unemployment compensation and
retraining, and old age pensions. In addition, legislation is enacted to require
safe working conditions. Since these policies deal with the consequences of
inequality without disturbing the basic principle of the capitalist system (private
property), these measures are usually endorsed by modern liberals as well as
socialists.

Socialization   Socialization measures refer to "the acquisition by the State of
the power to decide the output, investment and employment policy of any economic undertaking."[13] The method often advocated by socialists is *nationalization,* meaning the compulsory purchase with fair compensation by the state of
the controlling property rights of economic enterprises. *Public enterprises* may
be established to deliver services that are not being provided by the private sector. Socialization measures transfer economic power to the state and are more
likely to be resisted by liberals and conservatives alike.

Egalitarian Measures   Taxation policies directed at reducing inequality by
redistributing income are an integral part of the socialist program. Like socialization measures, these policies generate little enthusiasm among liberals and
conservatives.

In 1951 the Socialist International met at Frankfurt, Germany. Among the
documents produced by the congress of this international meeting of socialists
was the Frankfurt Declaration, which constitutes a comprehensive statement of
the goals of modern democratic socialism. To summarize the main points of this
declaration:

1. Socialism does not require a rigidly uniform approach. Socialists are
   flexible about means but strive for the same goals—social justice, free
   dom, and world peace.
2. Socialism must be democratic and democracy can be realized only
   through socialism.

3. Socialism seeks the replacement of capitalism by a system based on a fair distribution of income and property.
4. Immediate aims of socialism are full employment, higher productivity, and social security.
5. Public ownership may include nationalization, creation of new public enterprises, or producers' and consumers' cooperatives.
6. Trade unions and cooperatives are necessary elements of democratic socialism.
7. Socialism seeks to abolish legal, political, and economic discrimination based on sex, regionalism, or racial and ethnic groupings.[14]

Democratic Socialism in Practice

Democratic socialist parties have held government power or have shared power in combination with other parties in most Western nations, including Great Britain, Austria, France, Italy, Germany, Norway, Sweden, Denmark, Spain, Canada, Australia, and New Zealand. Representative of democratic socialism as it is practiced today are Great Britain, France, and Sweden. As might be expected, a variety of policies similar to Durbin's four measures have been employed in pursuit of socialist goals.

Great Britain: Evolutionary Socialism

Given England's long tradition of social reform, British socialism following World War II may be viewed as a continuation of political and economic evolution rather than an abrupt change. Many social reforms already had been enacted by liberals, and much of the welfare state was already in place when socialists came to power in 1945. Consequently, the Labour government of Prime Minister Clement R. Attlee (1945–1951) concentrated primarily on socialization measures. Having a majority in the House of Commons for the first time, the Labour government nationalized the Bank of England, iron and steel companies, coal mines, civil aviation, railways, telephone and telegraph, electric and atomic energy, and some aspects of inland transportation. The criteria for nationalization were partly economic and partly political. Industries that constituted a monopoly, were inefficient, were suppliers of basic raw materials, or suffered from poor labor-management relations were viewed as candidates for nationalization.[15]

Social services were expanded in the areas of education, housing, and medical care. Especially popular was the national health service, which established a system of socialized medical care in competition with private health care. This program of alternative health care was financed primarily from taxation in combination with modest fees for particular services. British citizens were entitled to comprehensive medical care without additional charges. The vast majority of citizens chose to utilize the service, and most doctors affiliated with the pro gram. This national system of subsidized medical care proved sufficiently popular with the public that when the Conservatives returned to power under Winston Churchill in 1951, the national health service was left in place. The steel companies were denationalized (returned to private ownership).

When Labour returned to political power in 1964, Prime Minister Harold Wilson's government again expanded social programs, including increases in health-care benefits, old-age pensions, and tenants' rights. The Conservative government of Prime Minister Margaret Thatcher, on gaining power in 1979, enacted a policy of divestiture, meaning that some nationalized enterprises were sold back to the private sector. In the 1990s Labour selected Tony Blair as leader of the party. Blair's youthful appeal and advocacy of moderate policies contributed to his elevation as party leader and subsequent election as Prime Minister. The enduring competition between the Labour and Conservative parties has shown that significant economic changes may be enacted democratically through the political structure, that democratic socialists follow parliamentary rules and relinquish power when they lose elections, and that not all the gains of socialism are repealed when centrist parties oust the left from power.

France: Socialism with a Marxist Tinge   The French *Parti Socialiste* is the oldest existing mass-based party in France. Founded in 1905, the Socialist party has attempted to unite four diverse groupings: social reformers, Marxists, utopian socialists, and syndicalists (radical trade unionists). To promote solidarity with its more radical elements, the party has emphasized its Marxist heritage more than most democratic socialist parties by appealing to the working class with promises of radical economic change.[16]

From 1914 until 1957, French socialists occasionally shared power by participating in coalition governments. From 1958 until 1981, they were confined to opposition. In the 1970s they gained electoral strength, and in 1981 the Socialists gained control of the French presidency and Parliament. In addition, the French Communist party elected 44 deputies, prompting Socialist President Francois Mitterrand to include four Communist ministers in his cabinet in exchange for political support from their party. The Communist ministers received the relatively minor positions of transport, civil service, health, and professional training.[17]

Initially, the socialist program in France consisted of two main thrusts: nationalization and economic benefits. Nationalization, while satisfying demands of doctrinaire socialists, proved to be economically costly. Selected for nationalization were steel, electronics, chemicals, textiles, aeronautics, and 36 banks. Contrary to the assumptions of Socialist party leaders who believed that these industries would generate revenue for the government, many of the firms were at, or near, bankruptcy. In addition to inheriting these troubled businesses, the French government paid out an additional $10 billion in compensation to the owners.[18] These outlays combined with greater expenditures for expansion of social programs produced an economic crunch in 1983.

The Socialist package of economic benefits in France was directed at promoting redistribution, growth, and employment. The program included tax increases for corporations and higher income individuals, increases in the minimum wage, a shorter work week, five weeks of paid vacation, and an employment program with the goal of creating 50,000 public-sector jobs.

The 20 percent increase in social spending combined with nationalization costs and poor performance of the French economy led 18 months later to a shift to austerity policies. Faced with high unemployment and inflation, the Mitterrand administration imposed policies of wage restraint, higher taxes and fees, cuts in public-sector programs, and devaluation of the franc.[19] The economic conditions that led to socialism initially had worsened while the Socialists were in power, undermining the party's support. In the 1986 elections, the Socialists lost their parliamentary majority. In 1988, French voters reelected Socialist President Mitterrand but again denied the Socialists a majority in parliament. In the 1993 elections, the Socialists were defeated decisively.

Social Democracy: The Third Way   The Scandinavian countries of Norway, Denmark, and Sweden have for many years followed a path they describe as "the third way," meaning a system midway between socialism and capitalism. *Social Democracy* is an ideology that places greater emphasis on social services, welfare, and redistributive policies than on nationalization of the economy. Social Democrats are not doctrinaire socialists. They seek fairness, and they view the state as a means to achieve *social justice*. The socialization of the economy is not an integral part of the social democratic ideology. Social Democrats have created a system of regulated welfare capitalism. In the case of Sweden's economy, the government owns less than 5 percent of the country's industry, and cooperatives own about 4 percent. More than 90 percent is privately owned. There are in excess of half a million small businesses in Sweden, less than half of which are farms.[20] Large firms such as Volvo and Saab manufacture automotive, aeronautical, and marine products for world markets. In Sweden, state ownership is limited to the post office, telephone, railways, some of the bus lines, and natural resources. The government is a major shareholder in the airlines.

Social Democrats in Sweden have attempted to establish the middle way between capitalism and socialism. By this they mean the creation of an elaborate *welfare state* to protect Swedish citizens against the financial consequences of ill health, unemployment, and old age. In Sweden, social benefits are considerable, as are the taxes required to pay for them. The universal health-care program covers the costs of most hospitalization, doctor, and dental bills and some prescription drugs. Fees, when assessed, are modest. Education and child care programs are equally generous. Each family with children receives a small allowance for each child, as well as free school tuition, textbooks, dental care, and school lunches. College students receive a monthly allowance and are eligible for low-interest loans. Additional social programs provide vocational training and guidance, subsidized housing, old-age pensions, and extensive assistance to the disabled.

Needless to say, since extensive social services are provided at little or no cost, public demand for them is great. Long delays in obtaining hospitalization (except in emergencies) and public housing are commonplace. Overall, however, Swedes enjoy one of the highest standards of living in the world.[21]

Critics of social democracy insist that living standards ought not to be confused with quality of life. Conservatives have criticized social democracy as spiritually bankrupt, as well as excessively expensive and bureaucratic.[22] Social democracy requires an extensive welfare state, high levels of public services, and high taxes. The costs of supporting social democracy may be why some Scandinavian countries have begun to question it. In the fall of 1991 Carl Bildt, a conservative, became prime minister of Sweden. According to Bildt, "The time for the Nordic model has passed. It created societies that were too monopolized, too expensive and didn't give people the freedom they wanted; societies that lacked flexibility and dynamism."[23]

Socialism in the United States

The United States is the least socialized of major nations. A survey published recently by the International Monetary Fund reported that more than 95 percent of the American economy is run by private enterprise. Unusual among industrial nations, the telephone and telegraph, television, radio, energy, and transportation industries are mostly in private hands. In many other nations most, or all, of these are run by the government. The United States Postal

Service, ports, waterways, and airports are the chief publicly owned enterprises in the United States.[24] The large degree of private ownership and control of the economy is a testament to the ideological triumph of liberal capitalism in America. There was a time not too long ago, however, when socialism was politically relevant in the United States.

The socialist movement in America began to gain momentum with the arrival, between 1830 and 1850, of significant numbers of immigrants from Germany. Included among the waves of immigrants were an assortment of revolutionaries, anarchists, and trade union activists. In 1877 the Socialist Labor party was founded, with the stated objective of promoting the emancipation of industrial labor. Daniel DeLeon joined the party in 1890 and was a force in American socialism during the next 25 years. He was an outspoken advocate for moving beyond trade union objectives of improving wages and working conditions to strive for fundamental change in the property system.

For the most part, American socialism was divided and ineffective until Eugene V. Debs emerged as leader of the movement. Debs was active in the Social Democracy party, which evolved in 1901 into the Socialist party of America. In 1912 the Socialist party had 118,000 dues-paying members and had elected over 1,000 candidates to public office in the United States, including 56 mayors and one member of Congress. Debs ran for president as the party's candidate four times. In 1912 Debs received nearly 900,000 votes for president, and in 1920, while in prison for antiwar activities, he received 920,000 votes.[25]

After Debs died in 1926, Norman Thomas assumed leadership of the party. In 1932 Thomas got 885,000 votes for president, but socialist support throughout the United States declined rapidly thereafter. The popularity of New Deal liberalism, as well as internal divisions in the socialist movement, contributed to the decline of support for socialist candidates.

Another difficulty faced by the socialists was their inability to win the support of the majority of American workers. The prevailing ideology of American labor has been liberalism, not socialism. Labor has been more interested, and more effective, in organizing for specific short-term economic gains (higher wages and benefits) than for comprehensive political action. This was particularly true of the craft unions but also proved to be the case for the industrial unions, which in many countries are more likely to support socialists.[26] The emphasis on self-interest and personal gain, so fundamental to liberalism, pervades American labor as it does the society as a whole. It has been difficult for a more long-term communal or cooperative outlook to take hold.

Last, and certainly not least, governments in America have been energetic about repressing and discrediting socialist ideas. The antiwar stance of the party in World War I resulted in socialist leaders being imprisoned and harassed. According to historian Harry W. Laidler:

The socialist press was, for the most part, suppressed, and numerous socialists were arrested. Eugene V. Debs was sentenced to the Federal penitentiary for an antiwar speech he delivered in Canton, Ohio. Leading members of the national executive committee were likewise convicted, although the United States Supreme Court later set their convictions aside.[27]

The left wing of the socialist movement split off to form the Communist party of America in 1919. This distinction has often been lost, however, as liberals and conservatives alike have denounced the democratic left as "reds," "pinkos," and fellow travelers. The one-sided triumph of liberal capitalism in America has meant that one of the world's significant democratic ideologies is widely misunderstood, mistrusted, and discredited.

CONCLUSION

The expansion of political democracy has provided leftists with an alternative to revolutionary socialism. The democratic left has attempted to implement socialist ideas within the framework of constitutional and representative government. Participation in the process of representative government involves power sharing and necessitates ideological flexibility and political compromise. Consequently, democratic socialists have relinquished the Marxist rhetoric and utopian zeal of the revolutionary left.

The goal of the revolutionary left is to socialize capital and thereby eliminate poverty and exploitation. The primary goal of democratic socialism might better be described as the elimination of poverty and exploitation by various means, including the socialization of some private capital. Many democratic socialists advocate a system of competition between public and private capital that retains most economic enterprise in private hands. The goal of modern democratic socialism is not to eliminate private property but rather to eliminate or control the undesirable consequences of private property.

NOTES

1. Leszek Kolakowski, "The Concept of the Left," in Irving Howe (ed.), *Essential Works of Socialism* (New York: Bantam Books, 1971), pp. 682–691.

2. Oscar Wilde, "The Soul of Man Under Socialism," in Irving Howe (ed.), *Essential Works of Socialism* (New York: Bantam Books, 1971), p. 416.

3. Robert L. Heilbroner, *The Worldly Philosophers: The Lives, Times, and Ideas of the Great Economic Thinkers,* 6th ed. (New York: Simon & Schuster, 1986), p. 111.

4. Ibid., pp. 107–113.

5. Ibid., p. 124.

6. Harry W. Laidler, *History of Socialism* (New York: Crowell, 1968), p. 107.

7. Sidney Webb, "Essay number 2," in G. Bernard Shaw (ed.), *Fabian Essays in Socialism* (Gloucester, Mass.: Peter Smith, 1967), p. 52.

8. William Clarke, "Essay number 3," in G. Bernard Shaw (ed.), *Fabian Essays in Socialism,* pp. 109–130.

9. Edward Bernstein, *Evolutionary Socialism* (New York: Schocken, 1970), pp. 148–149.

10. Laidler, *History of Socialism,* pp. 316–318.

11. J. Ramsay MacDonald, *The Socialist Movement* (New York: Henry Holt & Co., 1911), p. 129.

12. Ibid., p. 127.

13. E. F. M. Durbin, *The Politics of Democratic Socialism: An Essay in Social Policy* (New York: Augustus M. Kelley, 1965), p. 294.

14. Laidler, *History of Socialism,* pp. 863–864.

15. Emile B. Ader, *Socialism* (Woodbury, N.Y.: Barron's, 1966), pp. 120–123.

16. William Safran, *The French Polity,* 2nd ed. (New York: Longman, 1985), pp. 120–123.

17. D. S. Bell and Byron Criddle, *The French Socialist Party* (Oxford: Clarendon Press, 1984), p. 114.

18. Safran, *The French Polity,* pp. 257–258.

19. Ibid., pp. 257–261.

20. Fredric Fleisher, *The New Sweden* (New York: David McKay, 1967), p. 100. Also, Kurt Samuelsson, *From Great Power to Welfare State: 300 Years of Swedish Social Development* (London: George Allen & Unwin Ltd.), 1968, p. 276.

21. Ibid., p. 196.

22. Erik V. Kuehnelt-Leddihn, "Paradise Lost," *National Review,* December 9, 1988, p. 24.

23. William E. Schmidt, "In a Post-Cold War Era, Scandinavia Rethinks Itself," *New York Times,* February 23, 1992, Section 5, p. 3.

24. Carl Hartman, "U.S. Economy Holds Position as World's Least Socialized," *Dayton Daily News,* October 28, 1984, p. 2E.

25. Laidler, *History of Socialism,* pp. 577–590.

26. John D. Stephens, *The Transition from Capitalism to Socialism* (Chicago: University of Illinois Press, 1986), pp. 149–153.

27. Laidler, *History of Socialism,* p. 590.

SUGGESTED READINGS

Ader, Emile B., *Socialism,* Woodbury, N.Y.: Barron's, 1966.

Durbin, E. F. M., *The Politics of Democratic Socialism: An Essay in Social Policy,* New York: Augustus M. Kelley, 1965.

Howe, Irving, ed., *Essential Works of Socialism,* New York: Bantam Books, 1971.

Laidler, Harry W., *History of Socialism,* New York: Crowell, 1968.

Shaw, G. Bernard, ed., *Fabian Essays in Socialism,* Gloucester, Mass.: Peter Smith, 1967.

74

Chapter 4

Liberalism

L iberalism is the oldest of the modern political ideologies, having its roots in the seventeenth century. The rise of science in the seventeenth century followed by the Enlightenment produced among the educated and informed segments of society an outlook of openness to new ideas, a faith in human reason, a belief that science would lead to progress, and a skepticism toward tradition and authority. Prevailing conceptions of the state, property, the individual, and society were transformed. The development of liberalism was a reflection of, and a contributing factor to, these changes.

THE LIBERAL TRADITION

The values embodied in the classical liberal tradition include private property, constitutional government, and individual liberty. Underlying these values is a faith in the capacity of human reason and a belief in progress.

The Liberal View of Reality

Ideologies begin with first principles. These are suppositions that cannot be proven and so are simply assumed to be true. For Marxists, a key assumption is that material conditions shape ideology, the state, law, and human nature. Liberals attribute a much greater impact to human nature, ideology, and politics as determinants of social, economic, and political institutions.

Liberals believe that human nature is universal and immutable, and that human nature and the natural laws on which it rests are accessible to human understanding. Once human nature is understood, it is possible to design institutions that are compatible with human nature. Liberals regard this as clearly preferable to the alternative of forcing humans to fit into social systems that are not compatible with human nature. Fundamentally, liberals believe that *human nature requires liberty*, and that successful social and political institutions must be based on this principle.

The Individual and Society

One of the earliest systematic statements of the principles of liberalism is found in the writings of John Locke (1632–1704), an English philosopher and political theorist. His *Two Treatises of Civil Government* (1690) constitute one of the leading justifications for limited government.[1] Arguing against the theory of divine right as the basis of civil authority, Locke defended constitutional government within the framework of natural rights, private property, individual liberty, and religious toleration.

Natural Rights   Locke's conception of the individual rests on the assumptions of natural rights and human rationality. Locke assumed that individuals are naturally free and equal in the sense that everyone is entitled to natural rights. The individual's basic natural right is the right to property—meaning life, liberty, and property (i.e., estate and material goods). In addition to these rights, every individual has the obligation to obey the law of nature—that is, to respect the natural rights of others. Thus, individuals have natural rights and obligations prior to or in the absence of government. Such rights are not conferred by society or government; they are the *inherent rights* of free individuals.

These assumptions, together with Locke's belief in human rationality, led him to conclude that the "state of nature" was not particularly harsh or unpleasant. By this Locke meant that human beings in the absence of society and government—in their natural state—were capable of viable existence as reasonable beings apart from society. This image of asocial individualism as constituting the natural condition of humankind is a distinctive and controversial assumption of liberal thought.

Each of these assumptions has implications for Locke's conception of the relationship between the individual and civil society. Locke argued that since individuals are naturally free they can be bound only by their own consent, freely given. Rational individuals voluntarily depart the state of nature and

76

enter into civil society as a means of better protecting their property. Government is legitimate only when it rests on the consent of the governed. Individuals acquire the obligation of obedience by consenting to be governed.[2]

According to Locke, the laws of nature give individuals the right to acquire property—meaning material goods and land—by mixing their labor with it. This right of accumulation is limited only by the provision that the goods not spoil nor the land lay idle. Individuals are obligated to exercise this right in a manner that does not interfere with another's natural rights. With the introduction of money, the potential for accumulation becomes nearly unlimited because money may sit idle and earn interest.

Since Locke viewed government as being instituted primarily to protect the individual's natural rights, he regards government as having limited authority to regulate property (life, liberty, and estate). Individual rights limit community and governmental action regarding property.

The Social Contract   In the state of nature—meaning the absence of civil society—disputes concerning property will inevitably occur and likely be resolved in an unsatisfactory manner because individuals do not have government enforcement but only the law of nature as a guide. Rational individuals are capable of devising a better and more efficient way of protecting their property. They do so by means of the *social contract*. Rational calculation enables individuals to comprehend the desirability of government and the possibility of instituting civil society by means of a covenant. This same calculus enables individuals to see the necessity of limiting the role of government to that of safeguarding property, rather than attempting to promote the virtue of the citizenry.

In Locke's conception, the creation of government is a twofold process. By consenting explicitly or tacitly to join civil society, individuals enter into the social contract by which society is established. By relinquishing the absolute freedom of the state of nature, they are able to obtain the benefits of social order. Within society, a majority of *property holders* draft a second contract or covenant to establish a limited government. This political covenant, or constitution, is conditional. Government may properly exercise only the authority that citizens have consented to give to it. The governed may withdraw their consent to be governed, and if necessary they may defend their natural rights and freedoms by rebellion.

Locke's ideas, while well known in Europe, were especially influential in colonial America. Revolutionary leader Samuel Adams wrote in 1772:

Among the Natural Rights of the Colonists are those First: a Right to *Life;* Secondly to *Liberty;* thirdly to *Property* . . . All Men have a Right to remain in a State of Nature as long as they please . . . to leave the Society they belong to, and enter into another. . . . When Men enter into Society, it is by voluntary consent; and they have a right to demand and insist upon the performance of such conditions, And previous limitations as form an equitable *original compact.*[3]

The Declaration of Independence of the United States likewise demonstrates the influence of John Locke's ideas:

We hold these truths to be self-evident, that all men are created equal, that they are endowed by their Creator with certain unalienable Rights, that among these are Life, Liberty and the Pursuit of Happiness.—That to secure these rights, Governments are instituted among Men, deriving their just powers from the consent of the governed,—That whenever any Form of Government becomes destructive of these ends, it is the Right of the People to alter or to abolish it, and to institute new Government. . . .[4]

Liberalism refers generally to ideas and policies that increase human liberty and individual choice. Especially significant in liberal thought are questions of economic and political liberty.

Economic Liberty

In 1776, the year in which the Declaration of Independence was signed, Scottish political economist Adam Smith (1723–1790) published his *Inquiry into the Nature and Causes of the Wealth of Nations.* Because Smith's analysis suggested a new way of looking at political economy, it had a lasting impact on ideological thought in Western liberal societies. Smith argued for a laissez-faire approach to economics contending that increases in the production and distribution of goods could best be achieved not by imposing restrictions on the economy but rather by freeing it from government control.[5]

In the absence of extensive government intervention, how was the economy to be managed? The answer, Smith stated, was that an open, free, and competitive market was essentially self-regulating. The doctrine of *laissez-faire* (French for "let it be") advocated by Smith assumed that the market economy, if left to itself, has a natural tendency toward equilibrium. This is because a free market economy rests on the rational behavior of competitive individuals. Producers, investors, laborers, and consumers pursuing their self-interests converge in the marketplace to produce the most efficient decisions about wages, prices, production, and distribution. The profit motive and individual liberty combine to contribute to the general welfare by optimizing the efficient production and distribution of goods and services.[6]

To Locke's conception of natural rights and consent, Smith added yet another justification for economic liberty and limited government. The "public interest" was declared to result fortuitously from the process of competitive individuals freely seeking private gain within a system of limited government.

Political Liberty

Writing what is perhaps the best known essay in liberal thought, John Stuart Mill in *On Liberty* (1859) discusses the nature and limits of the power that society may legitimately exercise over the individual. In Mill's analysis, the most significant feature of human history has been the struggle between liberty and authority. Traditionally, those seeking to expand the scope of human liberty have sought to set limits to the power that rulers could exercise. These limitations defined the essence of "liberty." Mill suggested that the increasing popularity of democratic republics and demands for expanded voting rights created a new threat to liberty which Mill described as *social tyranny*.[7] Clearly in the age of popular government, limitations on the power of rulers are a necessary but not sufficient means to protect individual liberty. Equally important is protection for freedom of thought and expression of unpopular opinions:

Protection, therefore against the tyranny of the magistrate is not enough: there needs protection also against the tyranny of the prevailing opinion and feeling; against the tendency of society to impose, by other means than civil penalties, its own ideas and practices as rules of conduct on those who dissent from them. . . . There is a limit to the legitimate interference of collective opinion with individual independence: and to find that limit, and maintain it against encroachment, is as indispensable to a good condition of human affairs, as protection against political despotism.[8]

This threat to civil liberties results from the confusion of two issues that ought to remain separate, namely, what things society likes or dislikes and whether these should be *rules for individuals*. To clarify the boundary between prevailing opinion and individual liberty, Mill offers these guidelines:

- The only reason that people, individually or collectively, may legitimately interfere with another's liberty is self-protection; that is, to prevent harm to themselves or others. They may not interfere with an individual's liberty simply for his or her own good.

- Individuals may rightfully be compelled to participate in positive actions that concern the interests of others such as paying taxes, testifying in a court of law, supporting the common defense, and other measures to support the interest of society.
- There is a portion of a person's life and conduct that affects only that individual, or others with their voluntary consent. In this *private sphere* of human liberty, the individual should enjoy absolute freedom of thought, opinion, and expression on all subjects, as well as freedom of association for any purpose not involving harm to others. These liberties are essential in a free society.
- Freedom of *action* is necessarily limited by the principle that individual behavior not cause harm to others.[9]

Mill concludes by defending the proposition that society has no right to try to limit the individual's freedom of thought or expression of opinion even if those opinions are wrong. The justification for freedom of thought, expression, and action is not that people always choose "correctly" but that individuals should be free to choose.

MODERN LIBERAL THOUGHT

In his analysis entitled *Ten Philosophical Mistakes,* Mortimer J. Adler concludes that there is a fundamental error in the classical liberal conception of human nature and society. The source of this error is social contract theory. Adler contends that humans are by nature social animals, and that the origin of society and the state can be explained without recourse to social contract theory.[10] Adler's critique reveals a great deal about the transformation of liberal thought. In the modern era, liberalism has moved away from the view of human nature as selfish, competitive, and asocial. As social contract theory has receded in importance, a different ethical system has evolved to justify liberal values of individualism, liberty, and limited government. In the process, liberal conceptions of human nature, society, the state, and property have been altered.

The Individual and Society

As the image of the individual in liberal thought has shifted from that of selfish and competitive to cooperative and sociable, the ethical system underlying it has also changed. Liberty for the self-seeking, acquisitive individual was justified by a system of natural rights protected by a social contract. Modern liberals tend to justify freedom on the grounds of individual self-development. The focus remains on the individual. Ethically, liberty still rests on human nature and individual needs. It is the view of human nature that has changed.

Liberty Concern with the cultivation of human capacities has consequences for the meaning of liberty and other central ideas in modern liberal thought. Freedom from state authority and removal of barriers to individual freedom of thought and action is no longer a satisfactory definition of liberty. The full realization of individual potential requires an appropriate social setting. The *creation of social conditions* conducive to human development implies a program of social action. John Dewey, writing in *Liberalism and Social Action* (1935), argued that liberation of the capacities of individuals for free, self-initiated expression is an essential part of liberalism:

The majority who call themselves liberals today are committed to the principle that organized society must use its powers to establish the conditions under which the mass of individuals can possess actual as distinct from merely legal liberty. They define their liberalism in the concrete in terms of a program of measures moving toward this end.[11]

Dewey's distinction between legal (or formal) liberty and "actual" (or effective) liberty is embodied in modern liberal proposals for social programs that have the goal of establishing conditions compatible with, and supportive of, the development of individual intellectual, political, and moral capacities.

Equality In practice, liberal attempts to promote equality have involved two ideas, the first of which is *equality of opportunity*. Liberal policies in this area have been directed at removing barriers to equal access to resources and advancement by prohibiting discrimination based on race, gender, and national origin.

Second, modern liberals advocate *political equality* within the context of representative democracy. The defense of democracy is, again, on ethical grounds. Popular participation in public affairs is encouraged as a means of enhancing the civic, intellectual, and moral development of the citizenry. Individuals become more aware of, and are able to exercise some influence over, the issues affecting their lives. Liberal democracy is defended not because citizens always choose correctly but because they are permitted to choose. The *process* of civic education and participation is beneficial to the citizenry. Consequently, liberals advocate the extension of voting rights to all citizens by removal of restrictions based on race, gender, or property holdings.

Liberal Reform

As liberal thought evolved, the state assumed an important role in promoting individuality. The creation of conditions fostering positive liberty became the central objective of liberal proposals for social, economic, and political reforms. The genesis of modern liberal reforms can be traced to industrial England prior to World War I. During the period 1886–1914, the quality of life in industrial society became a leading issue on the liberal agenda. The social and economic conditions fostered by industrialization were regarded by liberals as fundamentally in conflict with human nature. The regimented drudgery of 14-hour work days in sweatshop conditions left workers little inclined to the "higher pursuits." In such an environment the free, conscious actions essential to individual intellectual and moral development were deemed impossible. If the new liberal view of human nature was correct, these conditions must be changed in order for citizens to have any hope of realizing their potentialities.

The New Liberals   The cadre of theorists and politicians instigating the reforms in England prior to World War I were referred to as *new liberals* because of their role in reformulating social policy. Prominent among them were L. T. Hobhouse and J. A. Hobson. A variety of reforms were proposed by the new liberals and enacted into law between 1905 and 1914. These reforms were aimed at improving social and economic conditions and were justified morally on the grounds of human improvement.

The outpouring of social legislation during this period included measures establishing compulsory public education, old-age pensions, and unemployment compensation. These *social policies* were justified in terms of their contribution to the community and individual well-being. Old-age pensions were a recognition of service to the community. A modern state, said Hobson, recognizes "its duty to secure its members against poverty in old age."[12] Unemployment programs reflected the acknowledgment of the individual's "right to work." If the industrial sector was unable to provide gainful employment for able-bodied workers, then state action was appropriate. Henceforth, unemployment was defined in modern liberal thought as primarily a social problem rather than a personal vice. Liberal *economic policies* included proposals for a progressive income tax and a stiff inheritance tax. These were justified by the liberals not simply by the need for government revenue but ethically as a means of redistributing income and offsetting unjust advantages of birth.[13] Reforms in the workplace included limitations on working hours and regulations to promote job safety.

Taming Socialism   The political and economic framework of the modern liberal state was in place in England by 1914. In economics, liberals have been critical of the inequalities inherent in capitalism but have advocated regulation and reform of the system of private ownership of property rather than its elimination. Modest efforts at income redistribution have been attempted through the tax and welfare systems. The welfare state assists the disadvantaged classes in society by providing a minimum of economic security, unemployment compensation, and old-age benefits. Civil liberties limit the intrusive power of the state and society over matters of personal choice. While the liberal reforms were significant for their time, they were relatively modest in comparison to proposals by the Fabian Socialists, the Labour party, and the more radical liberals. British liberalism flirted with socialism and ultimately tamed it by diluting reforms so as to leave the system of private property basically intact.

MODERN LIBERALISM IN THE UNITED STATES

Because the United States was a predominantly agrarian and individualistic society, modern liberalism evolved more slowly than in England. Between the end of the Civil War and the outbreak of World War I, American society was transformed. In 1870 the United States was a rural society with an agrarian economy. By 1920 a majority of Americans lived in urban areas and the economy had a strong industrial base. The forces of industrialization and urbanization produced fundamental changes in American society. The social ferment and activism beginning late in the nineteenth century contributed to the modernization of liberal ideology. As in England, the modern liberal state in America began to play an active role in social reform and regulation of the economy.

The Regulatory State: The Progressive Era

The emergence of the United States as an industrial and military power was not without its costs. The extensive changes in the American economy produced widespread dislocations among farmers and workers. This was especially the case among millions of immigrants who were imported as a source of cheap labor. Industrialization involved basic changes in the techniques and organization of production. The

83

transition from small-scale to large-scale enterprise resulted in a significant increase in the power of property owners in relation to laborers. In his history of liberalism, Harry K. Girvetz summarized the impact of industrialization:

[T]he result of this revolution has been to repose enormous powers in private hands so that, at the turn of the century, a great steel baron could control the economic destiny of thousands of his workers, own the houses they lived in, the stores they spent their wages in, the legislators who made their laws, the police who arrested them, and the courts that tried them.[14]

As economic power was centralized in the hands of the owners of capital, there were some developments strengthening the political position of the middle and working classes. One of these was the trend toward greater democratization of politics. The right to vote was extended to most able-bodied males including naturalized immigrants. Equally important was the growing concern with social and political reform. Squalid working and living conditions produced by rapid industrialization and urbanization generated social activism among the middle and working classes. Both of these developments—democratization and social activism—produced political pressure for government to become involved in efforts at social reform.

The Origins of Progressive Reform

The Progressive movement included Democrats, Republicans, liberals, and even some conservatives concerned about improving social, economic, and political conditions in America. A variety of reform-minded groups contributed ideas and proposals to the Progressive program. The beginning of liberal social activism is often dated from the publication in 1879 of *Progress and Poverty* by Henry George. Addressing the paradox of widespread poverty in the midst of great wealth, George argued that poverty is not inevitable, and is, in fact, contrary to natural law. Advancing a religious and ethical defense of social reform, George contended that social justice can be achieved without a revolution overthrowing capitalism. This was possible by means of social activism on behalf of the needy and disadvantaged. George's book became a best-seller and popularized an image of a more harmonious society based on cooperation.[15]

The call for social activism was answered by Christian reformers in the Social Gospel movement and its secular counterpart, the Settlement movement. Contending that social justice and Christianity were synonymous, the Social Gospel advocated Christian commitment to reform America. Settlement houses were established in the slums of America's cities in an attempt to help impoverished city dwellers. Both movements contributed to the moral zeal characteristic of the Progressive era. First-hand experience with slum conditions proved enlightening for middle-class reformers who soon began advocating better public facilities, schools, playgrounds, and government regulations pertaining to child labor, working conditions, factory inspections, and inheritance taxes.[16]

Political Reform   Progressive reforms in political institutions and practices were of two varieties—those aimed at eliminating political corruption and making government more efficient, and those intended to make politics more democratic. Conservatives were more supportive of the first type than the second. Progressives were concerned with the decline of standards in politics and business. Unregulated industrial expansion had produced crass materialism among the wealthy and corrupt political organizations supported by masses of immigrant workers. Progressive activism was directed at undermining corrupt political bosses by instituting a civil-service system to regulate government hiring and promotion. Civil service regulations were enacted at the federal level in 1883 (the Pendleton Act) and in many states and cities.

To increase political democracy, Progressives advocated adoption of the secret ballot, direct election of United States senators, direct primary elections permitting party voters to control nominations, and initiative, referendum, and recall. These latter provisions permitted voters to place issues on the ballot and to recall (or remove) unpopular elected officials. In addition, many Progressives supported suffrage for women. Corrupt campaign practices were outlawed and rational management techniques were applied to government budgets, purchasing, contracts, hiring, and firing.

Economic Regulation   Progressive economic reforms involved two areas of government regulation. The first focused on public health and safety; the second reflected concerns about concentrations of economic power. Policies in both areas were clearly influenced by liberal thought in that Progressives worked to preserve capitalism by reforming the economic system. Regulation of working conditions and housing was aimed at providing an environment less destructive to individuality. By regulating private power and protecting public safety, the Progressives attempted to make industrial capitalism more humane and compatible with liberal democracy.

The growth of concentrated economic power was a central concern to liberal thinkers. The structure of the modern corporation proved so efficient economi-

85

cally that it raised the very real possibility of the elimination of market competition. By means of corporate takeovers, mergers, trusts, and interlocking directorates dominance of the market by one, or a few, firms became economic reality. Use of government power to combat the trusts and monopolies became a central premise of Progressive politics. The Clayton Anti-Trust Act, passed in 1914, strengthened antitrust regulations by outlawing economic activities directed at eliminating competition. Legislation established an assortment of government agencies and commissions to regulate aspects of commerce and the economy. Noteworthy among them was the Federal Trade Commission (FTC), established to enjoin illicit activities in commerce, and the Federal Reserve Board (FRB), which placed the nation's private banking system under federal regulation.

In summary, the Progressive era marks the transition to modern liberalism in American ideology. Progressive thought de-emphasized materialism, competition, and acquisitiveness, focusing instead on improving prospects for individual development and social well-being. Progressives were generally optimistic, assuming that individuality could be nurtured by creating a suitable environment. They advocated vigorous government action to confront concentrated economic power, restore competition, regulate business for public health and safety, and attack corrupt practices in business and politics.

The Welfare State: The New Deal

The transition to modern liberalism during the Progressive era was incomplete. The basis for the regulatory state was established, but the welfare state was not yet an integral part of liberal ideology nor a national commitment. Much of the Progressive fervor was dissipated by World War I and the economic boom that followed. Then an economic catastrophe—the Great Depression—reshaped American ideological thinking for the next four decades.

The Great Depression   The Great Depression began in October 1929 when the stock market crashed, resulting in staggering losses for investors and businesses. This was followed by widespread financial panic and bank failures. Many of those not already wiped out by the stock market crash lost their life savings when the banks closed. Businesses failed, factories closed, and within two years one-fourth of the work force was unemployed. By 1933 national income had shrunk to less than half of what it had been four years earlier. Jobs, money, and credit were in very short supply. America was caught in a worldwide depression, and the self-regulating free-enterprise economy was paralyzed. The conservative public philosophy of unregulated industrial expansion was thoroughly discredited. The crucial issue was which philosophy would replace it. Serious doubts arose as to whether democratic government could cope with the economic crisis. Writing in *The Coming of the New Deal,* historian Arthur M. Schlesinger, Jr., describes the political atmosphere at the time of President Franklin Roosevelt's inauguration in 1933:

The machinery for sheltering and feeding the unemployed was breaking down everywhere under the growing burden. And a few hours before, in the early morning before the inauguration, every bank in America had locked its doors. It was now not just a matter of staving off hunger. It was a matter of seeing whether a representative democracy could conquer economic collapse. It was a matter of staving off violence, even (at least some so thought) revolution.[17]

Within a few years the ways in which Americans thought about government and the economy were fundamentally changed. Beginning in 1933, President Roosevelt and the Democrats in Congress produced a program of pragmatic social and economic legislation aimed at alleviating the economic chaos. This series of legislative enactments and presidential actions came to be known as the New Deal.

The New Deal   Initially, President Roosevelt's program was directed at stabilizing the banking system, making credit available to farmers and businesses, putting people back to work, and regulating the stock markets. Declaring a banking "holiday," Roosevelt called Congress to a special session to enact the Emergency Banking Act. Rather than nationalizing the banks, the bill provided government assistance to private banks to reopen. This, along with Roosevelt's reassuring speeches and confident demeanor, blunted the financial panic. "Capitalism," remarked New Dealer Raymond Moley, "was saved in eight days."[18]

Help for the unemployed and destitute was provided by public works projects and direct federal grants to the states for relief. Farm bills subsidized farm staples and made credit available to farmers to avoid foreclosures. Similar assistance was provided to homeowners to prevent foreclosures by passage of the Home Owners' Loan Act. Funds made available by this legislation eventually refinanced one of every five mortgaged dwellings in America's cities. Rural electrification was accelerated by creation of the Tennessee Valley Authority (TVA) and industrial mobilization was initiated with the National Industrial Recovery Act, a program of governmental-industrial cooperation. In order to reestablish balance in labor-management relations, legislation was enacted protecting the rights of labor to bargain collectively and establishing a minimum wage.[19]

87

Some policies, such as the Securities Exchange Act (1934), which sought to regulate the stock markets, were staunchly resisted by segments of the business community. Some business leaders contended, despite the crash, that regulation of the stock exchanges was unnecessary and would deter investment. James H. Rand, Jr., of Remington, Rand denounced the bill as pushing the nation "along the road from Democracy to Communism."[20] Roosevelt and the New Dealers prevailed in Congress, and legislation was enacted establishing the Securities and Exchange Commission to regulate stock exchanges.

Many New Deal programs were welcomed by the public, especially by citizens among the army of unemployed. The work relief and public works programs created employment for four million Americans. With Secretary of Interior Harold L. Ickes overseeing its activities, the Public Works Administration (PWA) spent $6 billion between 1933 and 1939. The PWA helped in construction of more than half of the nation's new educational buildings, courthouses, and city halls, and made major contributions to construction of hospitals, power plants, roads, bridges, and subways. Much of these funds were channeled through private contractors.[21]

The New Dealers' loss of confidence in the private economic market was reflected in a growing emphasis on planning for public development of resources. In that light, the Tennessee Valley Authority (TVA) was more than a public project for development of electric power, resources, and recreation. It was a thinly veiled warning to the power companies. According to New Dealer David Lilienthal, the TVA would stand as a reminder that, when power companies fail in their responsibility to the public interest, "the public, at any time, may assume the function of providing itself with this necessity of community life."[22]

The welfare state came of age in America in 1935 when Congress passed the Social Security Act. Schlesinger gave this assessment of America's old-age insurance program:

No government bureau ever directly touched the lives of so many millions of Americans—the old, the jobless, the sick, the needy, the blind, the mothers, the children—with so little confusion or complaint. ... With the Social Security Act, the constitutional dedication of federal power to the general welfare began a new phase of national history.[23]

Critics of the liberal welfare state, while not sharing Schlesinger's optimism, had to agree that the nation had entered a new era.

The Liberal Vision   By the end of World War II in 1945, the government had become a major investor in American society, having assumed responsibilities for social welfare and economic management. The liberal conception of government was written into law in the form of the Employment Act of 1946. This legislation embraced the liberal premise that full employment should be a goal of national policy, and that it is the "responsibility of the Federal government to use all practicable means . . . to promote maximum employment."[24] In short, the United States government is now responsible for promoting full employment and high levels of consumer demand, and for managing business cycles. In the cliché of the times: Big business and big labor require big government as a balancing force in the economy.

This was the crux of the postwar liberal vision: virtually unlimited progress and prosperity for all through government involvement in active partnership with business and labor to promote full employment, high levels of productivity, and economic stability. However, the enormous social benefits of the welfare state predicted by liberal theorists and planners did not materialize. Ambitious liberal plans for economic development included extensive programs of slum clearance, public housing, urban development, public transportation, conservation of resources, and an attack on industrial pollution. Social policies advocated by the liberals included equalizing pay for minorities and women, day-care centers, and comprehensive medical care and health insurance for all citizens.

The postwar liberal agenda was only partially attained. Historian Richard H. Pells has suggested a reason for this: the liberals were unable to devise and implement a political strategy capable of transforming America. Having been spared devastation by World War II, the United States enjoyed a period of postwar prosperity. This produced an impetus not toward social reform but conservatism.[25] In addition, a new competitor to the liberal social programs arose, one that would shortly consume nearly half of the federal budget. The decision to maintain a large peacetime military establishment was the fundamental decision made by the postwar liberals. The welfare state had to compete with the warfare state.

Cold War Liberalism

The postwar confrontation with communism proved to be a divisive issue among the liberals, separating them from the left and from one another. The struggle over defense policy reflected the existence of two distinct worldviews within liberal ideology. The *left-liberals* sought an alternative to the *cold war* (the ideological and political struggle between communism and the West). They emphasized the goals of peace, international cooperation, and anti-militarism in foreign policy, and social reform at home. Left-liberalism is perhaps best per-

89

sonified by Henry Wallace. After having served as vice president, Wallace was dumped from the Roosevelt team in 1944 and replaced by Harry S Truman. Since President Roosevelt died within a few months, this proved to be a fateful decision. Wallace formed the Progressive Citizens of America, an organization that included dissident liberals and communists.[26] Running for president in 1948 as the candidate of the Progressive party, Wallace finished fourth, receiving 2 percent of the popular vote and no electoral votes.

The victorious faction of mainstream or *cold war liberals* had a different view of international politics. They regarded the Soviet Union as a danger to world peace and a threat to American security interests. Perceiving Russia not as a socialist society but as a totalitarian state, they believed that liberalism should not include tolerance for Soviet aggression. Consequently, they decided to use the power of the United States to oppose Soviet policy. Being liberals, they favored modest social reforms at home. This combination of progressive social programs at home and tenacious anticommunism in foreign policy is best described as cold war liberalism. Initially a product of the Truman administration, cold war liberalism defined the policies of Presidents John F. Kennedy (1961–1963) and Lyndon B. Johnson (1963–1968) as well.

Containment   The cold war liberals implemented a foreign policy designed to contain the expansion of communism in general and the Soviet Union in particular. Before a joint session of Congress on March 12, 1947, President Truman set forth the basis of the *containment* policy. The *Truman Doctrine* stated that it was the policy of the United States "to support free peoples who are resisting attempted subjugation by armed minorities or outside, pressure."[27] The Truman Doctrine was implemented by massive economic aid to Europe (the Marshall Plan) and a system of military alliances for collective security. Initially, the strategy was successful. Europe was revived economically and militarily, establishing a barrier against further Soviet expansion in the West. Ultimately, containment proved to be a more viable policy for Europe than for Asia, especially as the emphasis shifted from economic to military assistance, and then to direct American intervention.

The liberal policy of containment was severely tested in Korea, where President Truman decided to respond militarily to communist aggression, and in Vietnam, where President Johnson did likewise. These two unpopular wars divided not only the liberals but the American public as well, challenging the feasibility of the containment policy.

The legacy of cold war liberalism is a defense policy involving large-scale peacetime arms buildups, military interventions, and wars in Korea and Viet-

nam. These policies were formulated and implemented during the administrations of three of America's most liberal presidents. Ironically, it fell to conservative Richard M Nixon to bring the containment policy under control. The *Nixon
Doctrine* stated that the policy of the United States is to intervene militarily
only when American strategic interests are threatened; in other conflicts with
communism the United States will provide military and economic aid, but local
forces must do the fighting.

Liberal Social Activism

Events of the 1960s renewed liberal efforts for extensive social reform. Liberal
activism was characterized by a strong concern for social problems including
civil rights, poverty, and the environment. By seeking to implement reforms
within established political and legal procedures, liberals faced the difficult task
of using the system's rules to change the system. Combining political clout,
social activism, and litigation, they were more successful than might reasonably
have been anticipated. The liberal program, as enacted, emphasized reform in
two areas: civil rights and social programs.

Civil Rights   The irony of this period of liberal reform was that a Southerner
presided over the most extensive changes in American civil rights policies in the
twentieth century. Assuming office on November 22, 1963, after the assassination of John Kennedy, President Lyndon Johnson used his personal persuasive
and political skills to salvage civil rights proposals bottled up in Congress. The
1964 Civil Rights Act integrated public accommodations nationwide and outlawed racial discrimination by private businesses that delivered services to the
public. The following year the Voting Rights Act was passed, permitting federal
authorities to oversee the voter registration process. This legislation resulted in
huge increases in black voter registration in the South. Exactly 100 years after
the Civil War, the liberals succeeded in finally transforming American civil
rights policies.

The Great Society   The culmination of postwar liberalism was the *Great
Society* legislation enacted during President Johnson's second term
(1965–1968). Clearly reflecting the liberal view that government programs and
money could improve the lot of the disadvantaged, the centerpiece of the Great
Society was the president's much publicized "war on poverty." Included in the
poverty programs were the Job Corps for training unemployed youth, Community Action Programs, legal aid for the poor, and Head Start to begin education

of preschool children. In 1966 these programs were expanded and supplemented by medical care for the aged, increased federal aid to education, increases in minimum wage and unemployment benefits, and model cities programs for urban development. Programs were devised to deal with black lung disease, the handicapped, nurses' training, mass transit, law enforcement, and hospital construction. There were food stamps and school lunch programs, rent subsidies, and housing for the elderly. Especially unpopular with conservatives were the Occupational Safety and Health Act and the Affirmative Action programs.

Critics of the liberal social programs questioned whether the government had either the capability or the duty to raise the standard of living of poor people, integrate the races, and revise long-standing social patterns. In particular, conservative critics pointed out that by shifting the emphasis of government action away from political equality and ending discrimination to social and economic equality, these programs made government responsible for problems it could not solve:

This inequality was impervious, unaffected by the economy's cycles, and irredeemable short of drastic action—the redistribution of income [and] large-scale integration of the races. . . . These solutions, the liberals found were beyond their reach.[28]

CONTEMPORARY LIBERALISM

By the end of the 1970s, American liberalism could be described, with only slight exaggeration, as an ideology advocating Affirmative Action, racial and gender preferences for hiring and promotion, homosexual rights, freedom of choice regarding abortion, expansion of welfare and social programs, and support of school busing but opposition to school prayer. Liberalism began to lose its base of support among the lower middle and working classes.[29]

The flurry of government social programs and regulations inspired a reaction not only among conservatives but within the liberal community as well. Some disenchanted liberals became conservatives. Others believed that liberalism was in need of a reassessment that would lead to new directions. The body of ideas and programs produced by this reassessment is known as *neoliberalism.*

During the 1980s, a group of prominent politicians endorsed a variety of "new liberal" ideas. Included among this group were Senators Bill Bradley (D-N.J.), Christopher Dodd, (D-Conn.), and Dale Bumpers (D-Ark.), and Albert Gore, Jr.

(D-Tenn.), and Governors Bruce Babbitt (Ariz.), and Bill Clinton (Ark.). These political leaders were joined by academics and journalists, such as Lester Thurow and Charles Peters, in calling for a redefinition of liberalism in a more moderate direction.[30] The fact that the presidential candidates of the Democratic party in 1992, 1996, and 2000 were chosen from among this group suggests a recognition that liberalism needed to adapt to changing circumstances, especially in social programs and economic policy.

Neoliberals believe that the Great Society approach to social problems is politically outdated and that liberalism cannot maintain political influence by relying primarily on the appeal of social programs for the disadvantaged. These programs worked well, providing necessary benefits, but no longer constitute the basis for majority support among the populace. Economic growth and prosperity have altered American class structure, increasing the size and influence of the middle class. Liberal policies supporting public education and equal opportunity have opened doors to advancement. Consequently the have-nots are no longer a majority whose needs have to be accommodated but a minority with declining political influence. Social programs must be maintained, but the welfare system should be reformed to emphasize incentives to work. Part of the new direction for liberalism includes a recognition that government cannot solve every social problem by legislation.

In summary, neoliberals emphasize economic growth, productivity, and free trade as the essence of the national interest. While not hostile to social programs for the disadvantaged, their economic proposals reflect the belief that spending for economic development will, in the long run, be more effective in alleviating poverty. The security of the nation requires a major effort to "invest in itself," meaning that national resources should be committed to human capital, education, and infrastructure.

NOTES

1. John Locke, *Two Treatises of Government* (New York: New American Library, 1965).

2. See, among others, John Plamenatz, *Man and Society,* Vol. 1 (New York: McGraw-Hill, 1963), pp. 220–241.

3. Samuel Adams, "The Rights of Colonists," in Kenneth M. Dolbeare (ed.), *American Political Thought,* rev. ed. (Chatham, N.J.: Chatham House, 1984), p. 38.

4. *The Declaration of independence of the Thirteen United States of America,* p. 1.

5. Fredrick M. Watkins, *The Age of Ideology-Political Thought, 1750 to the Present* (Englewood Cliffs, N.J.: Prentice-Hall, 1964), pp. 10–12.

6. Robert L. Heilbroner, *The Worldly Philosophers: The Lives, Times and Ideas of the Great Economic Thinkers,* 5th ed. (New York: Simon & Schuster, 1980), pp. 40–72.

7. John Stuart Mill, *Three Essays: On Liberty, Representative Government, The Subjugation of Women (*New York: Oxford University Press, 1975), pp. 1–9.

8. Ibid., p. 9.

9. Ibid., pp. 15–39.

10. Mortimer J. Adler, *Ten Philosophical Mistakes* (New York: Macmillan, 1985), p. 170.

11. John Dewey, *Liberalism and Social Action* (New York: Capricorn Books, 1963), p. 27.

12. Michael Freeden, *The New Liberalism: An Ideology of Social Reform* (Oxford: Clarendon Press, 1978), p. 241.

13. Ibid., pp. 194–244.

14. Harry K. Girvetz, *The Evolution of Liberalism* (New York: Collier Books, 1963), p. 251.

15. Stanley P. Caine, "The Origins of Progressivism," in Lewis L. Gould (ed.), *The Progressive Era* (Syracuse, N.Y.: Syracuse University Press, 1974), pp. 11–13.

16. Ibid., p. 14.

17. Arthur M. Schlesinger, Jr., *The Age of Roosevelt: The Coming of the New Deal* (Boston: Houghton Mifflin, 1959), p. 3.

18. William E. Leuchtenburg, *Franklin D. Roosevelt and the New Deal: 1932–1940* (New York: Harper & Row, 1963), p. 45.

19. Charles Funderburk, *Presidents and Politics: The Limits of Power* (Monterey, Calif.: Brooks/Cole, 1982), pp. 80–81.

20. Schlesinger, *The Coming of the New Deal*, p. 457.

21. Ibid., pp. 282–288.

22. Ibid., p. 331.

23. Ibid., p. 315.

24. Girvetz, *The Evolution of Liberalism*, p. 314.

25. Richard H. Pells, *The Liberal Mind in a Conservative Age: American Intellectuals in the 1940s and 1950s* (New York: Harper & Row, 1985), pp. 27–32.

26. Ibid., p. 69.

27. John Spanier, *American Foreign Policy Since World War II, 8th ed.* (New York: Holt, Rinehart & Winston, 1980), p. 26.

28. John Frederick Martin, *Civil Rights and the Crisis of Liberalism: The Democratic Party 1945–1976* (Boulder, Colo.: Westview Press, 1979), p. 191.

29. Alonzo L. Hamby, *Liberalism and Its Challengers: From FDR to Bush*, 2nd ed. (New York: Oxford University Press, 1992), Chapters 7 & 8.

95

30. Randall Rothenberg, *The Neoliberals: Creating the New American Politics* (New York: Simon & Schuster, 1984), p. 42.

SUGGESTED READINGS

Girvetz, Harry K. *The Evolution of Liberalism.* New York: Collier Books, 1963.

Hamby, Alonzo L. *Liberalism and Its Challengers: From FDR to Bush.* 2nd ed. New York: Oxford University Press, 1992.

Hofstadter, Richard. *The American Political Tradition.* New York: Random House (Vintage Books), 1954.

Leuchtenburg, William E. *Franklin D. Roosevelt and the New Deal: 1932–1940.* New York: Harper & Row, 1963.

Martin, John Frederick. *Civil Rights and the Crisis of Liberalism: The Democratic Party 1945–1976.* Boulder, Colo.: Westview Press, 1979.

Mill, John Stuart. *Three Essays: On Liberty, Representative Government, The Subjugation of Women.* New York: Oxford University Press, 1975.

Pells, Richard H. *The Liberal Mind in a Conservative Age: American Intellectuals in the 1940s and 1950s.* New York: Harper & Row, 1985.

Rothenberg, Randall. *The Neoliberals: Creating the New American Politics.* New York: Simon & Schuster, 1984.

Chapter 5

Conservatism

Conservatism is a state of mind as well as an ideology. As an ideology, *conservatism* shares with liberalism the attributes of the political center, including an acceptance of private property rights, constitutional government based on consent, a limited view of the potential of the state, and a rejection of political extremism. As a state of mind, conservatism differs more significantly from liberalism. Historically, liberalism has been oriented toward change and progress, whereas conservatism is skeptical about change and does not necessarily equate change with progress. Changes initiated and planned by the state might be described by a liberal as "reform" and by a conservative as "meddling," that is, meddling with the natural order of things. Conservatives view the social, economic, and political order in a society as natural, in that the society's culture and politics have developed over generations by a process of gradual evolution.

CLASSICAL CONSERVATISM

Perhaps the most basic differences between liberalism and conservatism involve the conception of society and the individual's place within society. Liberalism begins with a conception of individual and property rights and then constructs a theory of society to accommodate the individual's natural rights. Conservatism begins with a conception of society and fits into it individual and property rights. Classical Liberalism defines society as essentially a set of contractual relationships created by individuals for their own convenience; conservatism conceives of society as an entity greater than the sum of its individual parts. Liberals emphasize individual liberty; conservatives stress social order (or what they call "ordered liberty"). Liberals are oriented toward innovation; conservatives value tradition and stability.

The Nature of Society

A major principle of conservatism is that *society is not simply a set of contractual arrangements*. At the most basic level, what distinguishes conservatives from liberals is their differing conceptions of the nature of society. Consider the words of British political theorist Sir Edmund Burke: "People will not look forward to posterity, who never look back to their ancestors."[1] A leading politician and thinker of the late eighteenth century, Burke is generally regarded as the founder of conservatism. Burke's *Reflections on the Revolution in France* (1790) is among the first statements of conservative principles. An eloquent critique of the radicalism unleashed by the French Revolution, Burke's analysis of the nature of society forms the foundation of conservatism.

As in liberalism, conservative social theory incorporates the social contract and natural rights but prescribes to society a greater role in defining and interpreting their meaning. The social contract (a constitution) is not an instrument of mere utility. It is a sacred contract that "becomes a partnership not only between those who are living, but between those who are living, those who are dead, and those who are to be born."[2]

Organic Society   Classical conservatism views society as an organic entity characterized by unity, continuity, and stability. In other words, the organic conception of society is not an *analogy* but an accurate description of reality. Conservative social theory assumes that enduring societies possess attributes of living organisms including interdependence, unity, and continuity.

The *interdependent* nature of organic society means that each part of society—individuals, groups, classes, and institutions—has a functional relationship to the others. As with living organisms, there is potential for natural harmony within society whenever individuals, groups, and classes are working together in proper fashion. Natural harmony may be disturbed by social changes that are too rapid and too extensive.

The *unity* of society rests on a community of common interest. Societies that survive and flourish are those in which the collective interest of the whole community is placed above the particular interests of individuals, groups, and classes. A fundamental problem with liberalism, from the conservative's perspective, is that unity and the larger interest of the whole community seldom prevail over individual self-interest.

Social continuity is exemplified by conservatism's description of the community as comprising not only the living but also the dead and unborn. Continuity provides a basis for social stability. Society is not only a social contract but also a heritage. Traditions, customs, institutions, and laws represent the wisdom of past generations and constitute the best available guide for action. In Burke's words: "When ancient opinions and rules of life are taken away the loss cannot possibly be estimated. From that moment on we have no compass to govern us, nor can we know distinctly to what port we steer."[3]

Conservatives are not opposed to change, for they are well aware that change is inevitable. The conservative's goal is *conservation through change*. The direction and the pace of change may be influenced by enlightened conservative leadership. Change is necessary for growth and is part of the natural order of things—the natural development of the social organism. *Innovation* is another matter.

Radicalism involves extensive and rapid change and as such should be avoided. By disrupting social order and continuity, radical change poses a fundamental threat to the community. According to social critic Irving Babbitt, the result of radicalism is that

the State loses its historical continuity, its permanent self, as it were, that unites its present with its past and future. . . . The generations of men can no more link with one another than the flies of summer. They are disconnected into the dust and powder of individuality.[4]

The Individual

Burke and other classical conservatives emphatically agree with Aristotle's view of human beings as social animals. Burke's image of a ship adrift without compass or steering is an appropriate metaphor for describing the asocial individual—one who is drifting aimlessly without direction or hope. The existence of society and the state makes possible a meaningful existence for individuals. Only by participation in social life can the individual become a member of a community and realize the full potential of human existence.

The individual needs society not only because of the benefits it can provide. The need is more basic, being rooted in human nature. Professor Clinton Rossiter has succinctly captured the essence of the conservative view of human nature: "Man may not be perfected but he may be civilized."[5] Conservatives

99

contend that both reason and emotion play significant roles in governing human behavior. In order for humans to lead a civilized cooperative existence, their instincts and passions must be controlled and appetites curbed. Civilization requires the individual's participation within society, church, and state. Individuals may *learn* to be civilized if properly socialized and educated. Human nature requires the order and authority that only the state and society can provide. The individual derives considerable benefits from social existence. By means of participation in society, culture, religion, and work, the individual develops an identity as a contributing member of the community.

The State and Authority

In conservative thought, stability and authority are the keys to ordered liberty. Stability derives from social structure and the authority of institutions, especially church and state. Of all institutions the state is especially significant because of the scope of its authority and its monopoly on the legitimate use of force. The state maintains order, provides for the common defense, protects property rights, and establishes a system of justice.

Classical conservatism is not anti-statist. Although limited in power and potential, the conservative state functions positively as the *agent of society*. The state, like society, is an outgrowth of a lengthy evolutionary process and not the work of a single generation. The state plays a positive role in preserving tradition and order and in placing the interests of the community above those of individuals. The institutions and principles of constitutional government are among humanity's most noble and enduring creations. According to Burke, the state

ought not to be considered nothing better than a partnership agreement in a trade of pepper and coffee, calico and tobacco, or some other such low concern. . . . It is to be looked on with other reverence. . . . It is a partnership in all science; a partnership in all art; a partnership in every virtue, and in all perfection.[6]

Constitutional Government   Although the state functions positively as the agent of community interests and social order, it is, nevertheless, a limited government. The state is limited by the constitution, representation, human nature, society, and natural rights.

The nature of society constitutes a natural limit on the state. The family, church, and other social groups exist separately from the government but are an integral part of the community. They contribute to social order by educating and civilizing individuals, thereby assuring that the state does not monopolize these responsibilities.

Finally, government is limited by human rights that the community must protect and honor. These include life, liberty, and property. "Ordered liberty" includes freedom of expression and association and justice—the right to live under the rule of law.

Conservatives contend that people are not equal in many important respects. Individuals differ in talent, skill, motivation, intelligence, and potential. Inequalities are not to be lamented—they are simply part of the natural order. What nature has decreed, the state is unlikely to improve. Social classes, which reflect this natural hierarchy, make a positive contribution to social order. The state cannot and should not attempt to promote equality. Rather, the state should guarantee *equal rights*. According to Burke, "all men have equal rights but not to equal things," and citizens "have no right to what is not reasonable, and to what is not for their benefit."[7] All citizens are entitled to the advantages of civil society, including ordered liberty and the rights of individuals. As summarized by John Adams, one of America's more conservative presidents: "That men are born to equal rights is true. . . . But to teach that all men are born with equal powers and faculties to equal influence in society, to equal property and advantages through life is a gross fraud."[8]

Property

Like liberals, conservatives enthusiastically endorse private property as part of the natural state of affairs. There are numerous benefits that society and individuals derive from property ownership. Property is, in itself, a conservative agent, contributing to social stability by giving individuals a stake in society. Property ownership creates the "conservatism of possession." As described by Rossiter, this reflects the attitude of the citizen who has something substantial to defend against change. In addition, the possibility of acquiring property provides individuals with an incentive to work. This is significant because social progress is impossible without human industry. Most importantly, however, property is essential because of its contribution to ordered liberty. *Property makes freedom possible.* According to Rossiter, "Independence and privacy can never be enjoyed by one who must rely on other persons and agencies—especially the government—for food, shelter and material comforts."[9] Property gives the individual and society a measure of independence from the state. This makes freedom of choice a reality.

In summary, the core values of classical conservatism include social order, private property, and constitutional government. Individual liberty and rights, including property, exist within a social context in which the interests of the community are placed above individual self-interest.

MODERN CONSERVATISM

Modern conservatism is heir to both the conservative and liberal traditions. The classical conservative tradition remains alive in England's Conservative party and among the social conservatives in the United States. Modern conservatism also reflects the liberal tradition, especially in the economic policies of the free-enterprise conservatives in the United States.

Social Conservatism

Social conservatives have adapted the classical view of society to the modern context. They advocate individual liberty within a social context. Property is regarded not as an end in itself but as a means of conservative ends. The state is viewed in a relatively positive light amid concerns about the weakening of authority. Finally, social conservatives share reservations about the capacity of liberal democratic government to cope with the challenges of governing modern society.

Because social conservatives share a classical orientation, they insist that individual liberty be expressed within the limits of values established by society and that the collective interest be placed above self-interest. George F. Will is among the most visible and articulate of contemporary social conservatives. In Will's analysis, "society's institutions are concrete embodiments of social values which can claim precedence over the desire of the individual or even the collective will of the moment."[10] For Will, the central question facing society is, "What kind of people do we want our citizens to be?" The weakness of liberalism has led to a society in which values have sunk to the lowest common denominator. Instead of social order and virtue, liberalism has produced permissiveness and chaos. It is dangerous logic to teach people "that they need not govern their actions by calculations of public good."[11]

Many social conservatives, especially George Will, Russell Kirk, and Walter Lippmann, have been influenced by the British classical tradition. Other social conservatives reflect traditional values that are American in origin. The *Southern Agrarians* constitute a conservative intellectual movement that reached fruition shortly after World War II. Prominent among them in literature is Robert Penn Warren and, in social analysis, John Crowe Ransom and his student, Richard M. Weaver. In *The Southern Tradition at Bay*, Weaver articulated the Southern Agrarian theme of the superiority of southern traditional society over urban, industrial civilization. The feudal South, he argued, with its emphasis on tradition, civility, small property holders, religion, and stability, constituted the last nonmaterialist civilization in the Western world. The decline of Western liberal society was attributable to the abandonment of belief in transcendental values. Without the anchor of beliefs in immutable, eternal truths, society degenerated into relativistic amoralism.[12]

Traditional Values   Solutions for the ills of liberal society require enhancing the authority of social and political institutions in order to promote conservative values. Specifically, the state must use its authority for moral compulsion and, in addition, enact policies strengthening social institutions, particularly the family. Moral compulsion requires the state to make judgments and to enforce them with legal authority. "Proper conservatism holds that men and women are biological facts, but ladies and gentlemen fit for self-government are social artifacts, creations of law."[13]

The problem with modern liberal government is that for 50 years it has been moving in the wrong direction. Government has been expanding its distributive role (welfare and benefits) and contracting its involvement in cultivation of character and virtue. This, social conservatives assert, is the reverse of what government should be doing.

The civil rights laws of the 1960s integrating public accommodations and protecting voting rights were a demonstration of the government's power of moral compulsion. The irony, from Will's perspective, is that liberals seem incapable of similar moral choices in areas such as pornography and abortion. "So *Hustler* magazine must be protected or else *Ulysses* cannot be protected. That is, censorship of anything endangers everything because all standards are equally subjective."[14]

The social conservatives contend that liberalism has produced big government but not strong, effective government. This requires leadership willing to make difficult choices promoting an accommodation between the individual and society's interests based on conservative principles.

The objective of social policy should be to conserve and strengthen *institutions*, especially the family and private property. The family may be strengthened by promoting a welfare system that encourages families to stay together rather than splitting them apart. Tax incentives can contribute to social stability by encouraging more widespread ownership of property. In the area of education, tax credits or vouchers may be used to offset tuition payments to private schools. It is public business to improve the quality of citizens' education. This proposal would do so by increasing competitive pressure on public schools and by permitting less affluent families to exercise greater choice about educating their children. In general, policies that support and strengthen the family, schools, churches, private associations, and local governments are preferable.

To summarize, social conservatives keep the classical tradition alive in modern society. They seek a reasonable balance between individual liberty and social order. They look to institutions to provide a buffer between society and the state and to provide a social orientation for individuals. They advocate positive but limited use of the state to strengthen institutional life and nurture a citizenry capable of self-government.

Individualist Conservatism

In the United States there is an alternative tradition to the classical conception of conservatism. This version of conservatism is highly *individualistic* in conception and *anti-statist* in its orientation. In other words, it is a remnant of classical liberalism in America.

American conservatism, or at least conservative economics, was transformed into a variation of classical liberalism during the nineteenth century. The fundamentals of the liberal tradition are outlined in Chapter 4. The core values of liberalism include private property, competitive individualism, and constitutional government. These values were so widely embraced by American society that liberalism not only dominated the political mainstream, it came to be something of a national faith, being equated with "the American way of life."[15] Moreover, in the American version of liberalism, the emphasis is on promoting individual freedom by protecting property rights and limiting the power of government. The conservatism that emerged from the American political tradition consisted less of a modification of classical conservatism than an enthusiastic embrace of classical liberalism under a new label.

During the period 1865–1945, American conservatives appropriated liberal ideas as a means of limiting the authority of the state to regulate the economy. A new economic class, composed of industrialists and financiers, developed and eventually came to dominate the American economy. The desire of the business community was for economic expansion without interference by society or the state.

The economic, cultural, and political dominance of the business class was threatened by popular movements among the farmers (the Populists) and the middle and working classes (the Progressives) demanding government intervention to promote economic and political reforms. In response, the conservative business community embraced *laissez-faire* capitalism. The term "laissez-faire" is French and means "leave it alone," or "let it be." Advocates of laissez-faire economics favor unregulated capitalism and rapid economic expansion. Industrial and financial interests were able to defend against reforms using a strategy of classical liberal (laissez-faire) rhetoric. According to Rossiter, opportunistic conservatives appropriated classical liberal economics for their own purposes. Through their economic, political, and cultural influence they persuaded much of the nation that their narrow interpretation (laissez-faire or unregulated capitalism) was correct. In so doing, they abandoned key principles of conservatism.[16]

The classical conservative tradition was displaced in America by a new ideology ironically termed *laissez-faire conservatism*. The irony was twofold in that the new ideology was neither laissez-faire nor conservative. Classical liberal conceptions of individualism and property were redefined in the extreme, while the notion of liberal governmental intervention in the economy to aid commerce and industry was retained. As indicated earlier, ideologies are not necessarily logically consistent. The genius of laissez-faire conservatism was the use of liberal ideas to thwart social reform and economic regulation while encouraging state intervention on behalf of business interests. This uniquely American variety of conservatism rose to prominence between 1865 and 1885, to ascendancy between 1885 and 1920, and to dominance as "the American way" in the 1920s.

Social Darwinism   The vehicle for promoting laissez-faire conservatism was the concept of *Social Darwinism*. The popularization of this idea via journalistic, educational, and religious institutions profoundly affected politics and economics in the United States. Competitive individualism and materialistic acquisition of private wealth was elevated to the level of social dogma. Private property became sacred, wealth came to be a measure of virtue, and poverty was regarded as a form of justice.

A variety of writers, academics, politicians, industrialists, and ministers contributed to the impact of Social Darwinism. Herbert Spencer's anti-statist essays (e.g., "The Man Versus the State," published in 1884) laid the foundation, but the writing and lectures of William Graham Sumner were especially influential. Rising from humble origins, Sumner (1840–1910) became first an Episcopal minister and, subsequently, a professor of political and social science at Yale University.

Social Darwinism purported to apply some of the principles of Charles Darwin's *Origin of Species* to society, economics, and government. Briefly, Darwin's analysis suggested that biological evolution proceeded by means of a competitive struggle between species. Those that survived and flourished did so by successfully adapting to environmental conditions. Social Darwinism, by loosely applying similar ideas to society, provided a *pseudoscientific* basis for laissez-faire conservatism.

As defined by Social Darwinists, the public good is best served by permitting the competitive struggle between individuals to unfold naturally in a harsh or even brutal fashion. *Equality* is limited to the idea that all individuals are free to compete and achieve at the level their talents and drive permit. Individuals are equal in their rights to accumulate property, to be free from government interference, and in the lack of any right to government assistance. *Duty* is redefined to eliminate the notion of social responsibility, and *property* is elevated above all others rights, virtually immune from government regulation. Accumulation of great wealth is not only sanctioned but glorified as necessary for social progress. Poverty is regarded as the inevitable result of the inability of some individuals to compete successfully in the struggle for survival.[17] Ultimately, there are winners and losers. The outcome of the competitive struggle is reflected in the class structure of society. Therefore, extremes of wealth and poverty are natural. Millionaires are a product of natural selection, constituting a natural aristocracy elevated by superior talent to positions of leadership and power. Similarly, the poor and destitute are simply those who by definition are unfit and are receiving their due in accord with their talents and efforts.

The Role of Government   Because the competitive economic struggle is a natural part of social evolution, government interference in this struggle is regarded as unnatural and undesirable. The public interest (defined, essentially, as unregulated economic development) is best served by confining the role of the state to preserving order and guaranteeing property rights. Classical conservatism mandates an active role for the state as the agent of society that protects the interests of the community. Laissez-faire conservatism would seem to reduce the role of the state to that of an agency for enforcement of property rights and contracts.

Almost, but not quite. In an interesting twist of logic, laissez-faire conservatism permits the government to *aid* business but not to regulate it. The *doctrine of nonintervention* was developed to prohibit economic regulation but to *permit* government intervention in economic affairs to aid large property holders. Government assistance to business (in the form of tariffs, land grants, tax exemptions and incentives, subsidies to corporations, and anti-labor laws) is permissible and does not constitute government interference in the natural economic order.

The ideological achievement of laissez-faire conservatism is impressive in its scope and audacity. Economic regulation by the state is unacceptable because it interferes with the natural economic order. Regulation for public health, safety, and welfare (to prevent child labor, prohibit pollution, require compensation for workers injured on the job, enforce safety standards, regulate monopolies, or permit labor unions to organize) exceeds the legitimate bounds of the state's authority. Government assistance to owners of steel mills, factories, and railroad and oil magnates is the order of the day. It is not surprising that industrialists, developers, and financiers embraced this ideology with relish. The state was to function as an enforcement apparatus for the property-owning classes, provide aid to business enterprise, and virtually ignore the needs of the rest of society. The state, like the individual, was relieved of its social obligations.

Modern Individualist Conservatism

Stripped of some of its Social Darwinist flavor, individualist conservatism remains very influential in the United States. Among the leading spokespersons for individualist conservatism, Friedrich A. Hayek and Milton Friedman describe themselves as "liberals." Hayek is, in fact, the author of an essay entitled "Why I Am Not a Conservative."[18] Individualist conservatism represents a *revival* of classical liberalism. It involves not so much a desire to return to the past as it does the belief of its adherents that principles of liberalism were sound in the nineteenth century and are still applicable today. Economic liberalism and individualism are values *worth conserving.* The individualists share with other conservatives the belief in a limited role for government and the certainty that modern reform liberalism has gone off in the wrong direction.

Free-Enterprise Conservatives   The individualists consist of two groups— economic conservatives and extreme individualists, or libertarians. The first group, by far the more influential, are often referred to as *free-enterprise conservatives.* Well known among them are Friedrich A. Hayek, Milton Friedman, and George F. Gilder. They are distinguished from social conservatives in two ways. First, their concerns are primarily *economic.* Second, Hayek and Friedman, in particular, advocate a very *limited role* for government in the economy.

107

The task of revitalizing classical liberal economic thinking after World War II was assumed by European intellectual Friedrich Hayek. His writings helped to rejuvenate conservatism in America. Hayek was born in Vienna in 1899. He immigrated to England and became a professor at the London School of Economics in 1931. His writing was heavily influenced by the rise of totalitarianism in prewar Germany and the Soviet Union. Preservation of individual liberty is a major theme of his analyses. He wrote *The Road to Serfdom* (published in 1944) while still in England. When *The Constitution of Liberty* was published in 1960, he had been living in the United States for ten years.

The appeal of Hayek for conservatives rests on two ideas: liberty and collectivism. Hayek defines *liberty* as the absence of coercion by others. *Collectivism,* especially a monopoly of economic planning by the state, leads to totalitarianism. However, there is an alternative path—that of individualism and economic liberalism. Society, especially economic relationships, should be governed as much as possible by the principles of individual choice, while minimizing resort to coercion.[19]

Economist Milton Friedman likewise emphasizes free market economics, individualism, and limited government as the bases of a free society: "As liberals, we take freedom of the individual, or perhaps the family, as our ultimate goal."[20] In *Capitalism and Freedom*, Friedman explains why the power of government must be strictly limited in economic matters:

The fundamental threat to freedom is power to coerce, be it in the hands of a monarch, a dictator, an oligarchy, or a momentary majority. . . . By removing the organization of economic activity from the control of political authority, the market eliminates this source of coercive power. It enables economic strength to be a check to political power rather than a reinforcement.[21]

The Role of Government   Free-enterprise conservatives acknowledge the importance of effective government in modern society. They insist, especially in the economic sphere, that the responsibilities of government need to be clearly defined and limited. Friedman distinguishes between government as *rule maker* and as *provider* of goods and services. Production and distribution of goods and services are economic matters and should be the responsibility of the private sector.

Government's responsibilities are important but should be confined to the area of rule making and enforcement. As rule maker, government establishes a legal framework (liberal capitalism) and a monetary system. Government functions to enforce contracts, promote competition, and prohibit fraud. Government should not become directly involved in regulating production and distribution or impede competition. Government should not regulate wages and prices (e.g., by minimum wage laws and price or rent controls) nor hamper the flow of goods (by import quotas or tariffs) nor the production of goods (by farm subsidies and production controls). Government's role is analogous to that of a referee who enforces the established rules of the game in a neutral fashion.[22]

As part of its responsibilities, government provides for national defense, social order, education, and welfare for the destitute. However, government programs should be structured in ways that encourage participation by the private sector in meeting public needs. Private competition should be encouraged in areas that are now state monopolies (e.g., the post office). Competition between public and private schools can be encouraged through tax incentives. Even in national defense, competitive incentives are possible. Friedman was a long-time advocate of eliminating the draft and staffing the military on a volunteer basis by making pay and benefits more attractive, an idea that was eventually adopted.

Government must, of course, collect taxes to pay for its costs, but the tax rate should be kept low so as not to be a drag on the economy by discouraging capital formation. Generally, government should be involved in removing obstacles to free growth, not in erecting them. In clear cases of failure of the market, government regulation may be required. Pollution and hazardous wastes are examples of public interests justifying regulation. Market economies encourage pollution as a way to reduce costs. Imposition by regulation of increased costs (fines) and penalties is a necessary supplement to market economics.

Wealth and Poverty   Free-enterprise conservatives confront a problem that requires an explanation and, hopefully, a solution: the persistence of extensive poverty in wealthy capitalist societies. Decades of liberal capitalism have undeniably produced great wealth. If free market economics distributes goods and services efficiently, then why does not nearly everyone have enough to meet basic needs? George Gilder's analysis in *Wealth and Poverty* acknowledges the paradox of widespread poverty in the midst of great wealth and advances an explanation.[23] While inequality is inevitable in capitalist economies, extensive poverty is not. Poverty in American society results, Gilder insists, not from free market economics but from government policies that disrupt the market and hamstring free enterprise. Decades of liberal tax policy have been counterproductive because tax rates are too high and too progressive, impeding capital formation, generation of wealth, and economic expansion. An expanding economy is the only cure for poverty. Liberal politicians have attempted to use tax law to punish the wealthy and redistribute income. The proper role of tax policy is to encourage savings and investment to stimulate the supply side of the economy.

Liberal welfare policies are equally to blame for persisting poverty. Government attempts to directly assist the poor increase the tax burden and perpetuate the problem by fostering poor work habits and an attitude of dependency among welfare recipients. This self-perpetuating culture of welfare blocks the only proven method for escaping from poverty—hard work:

The ONLY dependable route from poverty is that in order to move up, the poor must not only work, they must work harder than the classes above them. Every previous generation of the lower class has made such efforts. But the current poor, white even more than black, are refusing to work hard. . . . The poor choose leisure not because of moral weakness, but because they are paid to do so.[24]

Libertarians The goal of libertarians is to maximize individual liberty in all areas of human endeavor. A free market economy is one of their numerous concerns. The libertarians' broader objective is to promote absolutely minimal constraint by society on individual freedom of thought and action. They regard customs, institutions and, sometimes, the family as unnecessarily constraining the individual's vision of the world. Because they seek to liberate human thought and action from social constraints, *libertarianism* is difficult to reconcile with traditional conservatism.

Novelist Ayn Rand was a prominent spokesperson for libertarianism. She immigrated to the United States from Russia between the world wars. Her experience in the Soviet Union naturally flavored her writing, which is extremely individualistic and anticollectivist. Among her better known novels are *The Fountainhead* (1943) and *Atlas Shrugged* (1957). Rand used the term *objectivism* to describe her version of libertarianism. Her philosophical tract *For the New Intellectual* (1963) and her novels are extreme statements of the libertarian position. Social Darwinist in flavor, they defend aggressiveness, selfishness, and individual achievement. She espoused strict laissez-faire economics and self-reliance. Philosophically, she was a rationalist, dismissing religion and custom as superstition and myth.[25]

Not all conservatives were willing to endorse Rand's extreme individualism. William F. Buckley, in a terse piece entitled " Ayn Rand, R.I.P.," stated:

Ayn Rand is dead. So, incidently, is the philosophy she sought to launch. . . . She was an eloquent and persuasive anti-statist, and if only she had left it at that—but no. She

110

had to declare that God did not exist, that altruism was despicable, that only self-interest is good and noble. She risked, in fact giving to capitalism that bad name that its enemies had done so well in giving it, and that is a pity.[26]

Anticommunism

Opposition to communism has been a characteristic of centrist ideologies since the Russian Revolution. As always, there are specific disagreements about strategy and tactics. Cold war liberalism, as discussed in Chapter 4, rested on a strategy of containment of communism using economic aid, military alliances, and nuclear deterrence. Conservatives generally advocated a more aggressive strategy for confronting communists and derided liberal policies as weak and ineffective, and occasionally, even as appeasement.

After the breakdown of Soviet-American relations following World War II, the perception of communism as a global menace came to dominate conservative thinking. In unifying around the issue, conservatives began to abandon their traditional isolationist ideas. Anticommunism made an indelible imprint on conservative ideology.

Big Government   The necessity of combating international communism and internal subversion had the effect of enabling many individualists to come to terms, of sorts, with big government. Although still favoring minimum regulation of business, conservatives could in good conscience argue for a larger defense establishment and expanded government authority to police subversive activities. Civil liberties might have to be curtailed to protect society against communist subversion. The anti-statism of the individualists was tempered by the overriding importance of anticommunism.

It was not an easy task to synthesize and unify the diverse strains of social, individualist, and anticommunist conservatism. A major forum for the consolidation of conservative ideology in postwar America was the journal *National Review*. The moving force behind *National Review* was William F. Buckley, who has been described as "the most important individual figure in the rise of conservatism and perhaps in postwar American political thought."[27] *National Review* gave some ideological coherence to the conservative movement by emphasizing the themes of (1) victory over communism; (2) anti-statism, meaning opposition to nondefense-related governmental growth; (3) a free market economy as the key to liberty and prosperity; (4) traditional conservative defense of the moral order; and (5) secular liberalism as the common enemy of all conservatives.[28]

CONTEMPORARY TRENDS IN AMERICAN CONSERVATISM

The New Right

The New Right is a mass movement with considerable popular support, especially among Christian conservatives. They command political attention by sheer weight of numbers as well as ideas.

Kevin P. Phillips coined the term *New Right* "to describe specifically the populist-conservative groups . . . emphasizing social issues, religious and cultural alienation, anti-elite rhetoric, lower-middle-class constituencies, populist fund raising and plebiscitary opinion-mobilization."[29] The New Right consists of two components. The *organizational and leadership* structure is comprised of secular political machinery aligned with fundamentalist Protestant religious organizations. The political arm raises funds by direct mail, publicizes political issues, and organizes political action committees to mobilize support for candidates.[30] These leaders work closely with conservative Christian organizations and their leadership, most notably television evangelists Jerry Falwell, Pat Robertson, and Jim Robison. Through personal influence and electronic evangelism, these ministers link the New Right to a significant popular following.

The *popular base* of the New Right consists of millions of evangelical Christians (commonly referred to as *fundamentalists* by the media) who share common concerns about social and moral issues. They are loosely allied with other conservatives, particularly lower-middle-class whites in the South and West, who share similar values. One analysis estimates this popular following at potentially 20 percent of the American population.[31]

Theo-conservatives   In analyzing Christian conservatism John Redekop identified several themes that have emerged as central to the New Right. The most important was that political and social conservatism has biblical sanction. According to evangelist Billy James Hargis, founder of the Christian Crusade, "Bible-believers" must necessarily be conservative in politics because "Christ is the heart of the Conservative cause." It follows that "if the conservative cause is of God and right, then people who fight it are fighting God."[32]

Other characteristics of Christian conservatism include, according to Redekop, intense anticommunism, opposition to modern social trends, emphasis on emotion over reason, the desire to simplify complexities, and support for limited government.[33] Seen in this context, the call by some speakers at the 1992 Republican convention for a religious and cultural "war" against liberalism is more easily comprehended.

The New Right Program
A brief perusal of the New Right political agenda suggests that Redekop was correct in describing Christian conservatism as opposed to several trends in modern society. The program, as outlined by Richard Viguerie, is opposed to big government, taxes, regulations, sex on television and in the movies, abortion, and forced busing to integrate public schools. The New Right advocates permitting state-sponsored prayers in public schools, constitutional amendments to outlaw abortion and school busing, vigorous prosecution of obscenity laws (including redefining pornography as "obscenity"), and laws requiring that creationism be taught in the science curriculum of public schools. In general, they favor legal techniques that will promote their religious beliefs and stifle the progression of secular liberalism.

The populist and reactive flavor of the New Right program is captured in Viguerie's description:

We are determined to achieve our goal of organizing the conservative middle-class majority in America. We are convinced that such a new American majority is an idea whose time is now. How will we do it? By appealing to:

- Hard-working citizens sick and tired of high taxes and ever-rising inflation.
- Small businessmen angry at excessive government regulations and federal red tape.
- Born-again Christians disturbed about sex on TV and in movies.
- Parents opposed to forced busing.
- Supporters of the right to life and against federal financing of abortion.
- Middle-class Americans tired of Big Government, Big Business, Big Labor and Big Education telling us what to do and what not to do.
- Pro-defense citizens alarmed by appeasement and weakness in U.S. foreign policy.
- Everyone who is unwilling to accept the liberal line that America has had her day in the sun, and that we must all tighten our belt and do with less.[34]

The New Right program demonstrates the paradox of anti-statist conservatives advocating policies requiring *big government* for implementation. Their goals of military superiority and state enforcement of morality presuppose an active, powerful, and intrusive government. Despite the anti-government rhetoric directed at the liberal establishment, this program assumes an expansion of state authority in several areas.

For these reasons the alliance between the New Right and individualist conservatives is uneasy at best. Consider this assessment by F. A. Hayek (from his essay "Why I Am Not a Conservative"): "Personally, I find the most objectionable feature of the conservative attitude is its propensity to reject well-substantiated new knowledge.... I can have little patience with those who oppose, for instance, the theory of evolution.... By refusing to face the facts, the conservative only weakens his own position."[35] Hayek's critique illustrates the gulf separating the individualists from their fellow conservatives. Whether the emerging unity of conservative ideology can be maintained, or whether the movement will be pulled apart by its centrifugal tendencies, are questions basic to the future of conservatism.

President Ronald Reagan   The program of the Reagan administration illustrates the interplay of conservative principles in American politics. In the area of *economics,* President Reagan enthusiastically embraced the principles of free-enterprise conservatism. This has been the principal theme of his rhetoric since the 1950s. Although initially a supporter of New Deal liberalism, Reagan gradually became more conservative. During this transition to conservatism, he refined his conception of government and economics in hundreds of speeches he gave as a public relations spokesperson for General Electric. By Reagan's account he gave as many as 14 speeches a day and spent two years on the road. Although the titles varied, including the likes of "Encroaching Control" and "Our Eroding Freedoms," the themes were always similar. Each speech was a rousing assault on big government, bureaucracy, wasteful government programs, and high taxes to illustrate the central premise that the ills of America all stem from a single source: "the belief that the government, particularly the federal government, has the answer to our ills and that the proper method of dealing with social problems is to transfer power from the private sector to the public sector."[36]

President Reagan's commitment to free-enterprise conservatism was apparent in the administration's program. In the president's first term of office, the administration was successful in obtaining congressional approval for a 25 percent cut in income taxes over three years. Deregulation of economic activity (begun in the Carter administration) was accelerated by review of existing regulations to propose elimination of those judged outdated and harmful to business activity. Income tax reforms enacted in 1986 simplified the tax code and reduced the top tax rate from 50 to 31 percent.

In *defense policy,* the Reagan administration's tough anti-Soviet rhetoric was accompanied by the largest peacetime military buildup in the nation's history. During the 1970s defense's share of the total federal budget had shrunk to 24 percent. The objective of the Reagan administration buildup was to increase defense spending and, in combination with cuts in non-defense spending, to produce a significant reordering of priorities in the budget.

The *social agenda* of the Reagan administration reflected the concerns of the social conservatives and the New Right. The rhetoric was strongly opposed to abortion, busing, pornography, and permissiveness. In terms of concrete legislative proposals, it is clear that the social agenda was not a high priority. The president expended his political resources promoting free-enterprise conservatism and protecting the defense buildup. The administration used the Justice Department in largely unsuccessful attempts to challenge Affirmative Action, restrict the right to abortion, discourage pornography, and restore prayer in public schools.

The Reagan presidency was the political manifestation of neoconservatism. Ideologically, the administration combined the free-enterprise economic program with elements of social and populist conservation. President Reagan is the prototype of the neoconservative politician—a disillusioned liberal who became an effective champion of the conservative cause.

President George W. Bush and the Neoconservatives

In *Reflections of a Neoconservative* Irvin Kristol notes with irony that it was "the socialist critic Michael Harrington who first applied the term 'neoconservative' to those who, like myself, had begun to move away from a liberalism that had lost its moral and political bearings."[37] The intellectual core of the neoconservative movement consisted of a cadre of social scientists and social critics who were at the forefront of criticism of liberal programs during the 1970s. In the area of economics, the neoconservatives gravitated to the position of free-enterprise conservatives, contending that liberal policies have caused government to assume responsibilities for problems that it cannot solve, and that government programs were so poorly designed and implemented that liberal "solutions" created new problems. Regarding the state and authority, neoconservatives lean more in the direction of social conservatism. They are not libertarian in the Ayn Rand anti-statist sense. Irving Kristol contends that liberalism, "which prescribes massive government intervention in the marketplace but an absolute laissez-faire attitude toward manners and morals, strikes neoconservatives as representing a bizarre inversion of priorities."[38] The foreign policy advocated by neoconservatives called for a tougher American posture in international affairs, a defense buildup and an emphasis on military preparedness.

The policies of the George W. Bush administration illustrate the interplay between the ideas of the free enterprise conservatives, the New Right, and the neoconservatives. In the area of social policy the administration promoted the ideas of the New Right and the theoconservatives. The economic policies of the Bush administration reflected the ideas of the Free Enterprise conservatives. In foreign policy and national security policy the President embraced the ideas of the neoconservatives.

Social and Economic Policy The emergence of the New Right as a political force has enabled political conservatives to mobilize public support by emphasizing a battery of social issues under the rubric of "family values." These issues include opposition to abortion (and often birth control as well), to stem cell research, and physician assisted suicide, opposition to homosexuality and same sex marriage, resistance to the teaching of evolution in the public school science curriculum, and opposition to erotica and pornography, to stem cell research, and to gun control. The New Right agenda includes support for the death penalty, prayer in public schools, the teaching of creationism and intelligent design as part of the science curriculum in public schools, and display of the Ten Commandments on public property. The Bush administration has embraced much of this agenda, advocating a greater role for the federal government in these social issues, including more federal involvement in the public schools and the use of public funds for faith based initiatives in delivery of social services.

Reflecting the ideas of economic conservatives, the Bush administration used executive authority and appointments to the Environmental Protection Agency, and the departments of Interior, Energy, and Justice, as well as legislative proposals to weaken environmental and clean air regulations, to push for deregulation of public lands to grant greater access to oil and timber companies, and to enact tax reductions for higher-income tax payers.

Foreign Policy: The New American Century It was in the area of foreign policy that President George W. Bush most reflected the ideas of neoconservative thinkers. One of the vehicles for promoting neoconservative ideas in the Bush administration has been the Project for the New American Century (PNAC). A conservative think tank established in 1997, PNAC is chaired by William Kristol and includes many prominent neoconservatives as members and associates. The PNAC Statement of Principles (June 3, 1997) is signed by a number of conservatives subsequently appointed to positions of authority in the W. Bush administration, including:

Dick Cheney	Vice President
Lewis Libby	Chief of Staff to the Vice President
Donald Rumsfeld	Secretary of Defense
Paul Wolfowitz	Assistant Secretary of Defense

Other signatories included Elliot Abrams, Gary Bauer, William J. Bennett and Jeb Bush.

The Project for the New American Century is a neoconservative organization with an assertive approach to foreign policy, including the belief that the United States should use its power to reshape international politics, particularly the Middle East. According to the PNAC Statement of Principles, "As the 20th century draws to a close, the United states stands as the world's preeminent power . . . Does the United States have the resolve to shape a new century favorable to American principles and interests?" In the PNAC Statement of Principles are several recommendations, including

- we need to increase defense spending significantly if we are to carry out our global responsibilities today and modernize our armed forces for the future
- we need to strengthen our ties to democratic allies and to challenge regimes hostile to our interest and values . . .[39]

An objective of The Project for the New American Century is to support policies they believe will shape the new century in a manner favorable to American principles and interests. The agenda of PNAC included, among other things, the removal of Saddam Hussein as President of Iraq. On January 26, 1998, PNAC sent a letter to President Bill Clinton calling for the removal of Saddam Hussein from power. Given the subsequent success of PNAC in gaining positions of power in the Bush administration, the roots of the American attack and occupation of Iraq were in place in well before the terrorist attacks on the World Trade Center in New York on September 11, 2001.[40]

117

The Bush Doctrine and Iraq   After the attacks on the World Trade Center in New York, the Bush administration stated that the policy of the United States government would be to retaliate against groups and states that harbor and support terrorists. The Bush Doctrine includes the policy of preemption, including launching attacks on terrorists *and* hostile states that the administration believes constitute a threat to the United States. In the neoconservative view, the attack on Afghanistan in 2001 was an application of the first principle of the Bush Doctrine, retaliation against terrorists, (in this case the Taliban); and the conquest and occupation of Iraq was an application of the second principle, preemptive attack.

CONCLUSION

Internal conflicts and contradictions are inherent in political ideologies. President Ronald Reagan's leadership provided coherence to American conservative ideology by emphasizing unifying themes of anticommunism, free enterprise economics and limited government. Tensions within American political conservatism have increased after the departure of President Reagan and the collapse of the Soviet Union. Particularly important is the growing influence within American conservatism of the so called *theo-conservatives*, or evangelical Christian conservatives. Former unifying themes of anticommunism, limited government and free enterprise economics have been displaced by emphasis on religious and moral themes, including infidelity, abortion, homosexuality, pornography and school prayer.

NOTES

1. Edmund Burke, *Reflections on the Revolution in France,* edited with an Introduction by Thomas H. D. Mahoney (New York: Liberal Arts Press, 1955), p. 38.

2. Ibid., p. 110.

3. Burke, *Reflections,* p. 89.

4. Irving Babbitt, "Burke and the Moral Imagination," in Russell Kirk (ed.), *The Portable Conservative Reader* (New York: Penguin Books, 1982), pp. 357–359.

5. Clinton Rossiter, *Conservatism in America: The Thankless Persuasion,* 2nd ed. (New York: Vantage, 1962), p. 27.

6. Burke, *Reflections,* p. 110.

7. Ibid., pp. 67, 71.

8. John Adams, "On Natural Aristocracy," in Kirk (ed.), *Portable Conservative,* p. 69.

9. Rossiter, *Conservatism in America,* p. 38.

10. George F. Will, *Statecraft as Soulcraft: What Government Does* (New York: Simon & Schuster, 1983), p. 77.

11. Ibid., p. 45.

12. For a discussion of the Southern Agrarians, see George H. Nash, *The Conservative Intellectual Movement in America: Since 1945* (New York: Basic Books, 1976), pp. 39–40.

13. Will, *Statecraft as Soulcraft,* pp. 90–91.

14. Ibid., p. 89.

15. Rossiter, *Conservatism in America,* pp. 67–96.

16. Ibid., pp. 128–162.

17. For a brief introduction to Sumner's political thought, see "What Social Classes Owe to Each Other" in Kenneth M. Dolbeare (ed.), *American Political Thought,* rev. ed. (Chatham, N.J.: Chatham House), pp. 340–356.

18. Friedrich A. Hayek, *The Constitution of Liberty* [Chicago: Henry Regnery Co. (Gateway edition), 1972], pp. 397–411.

19. Friedrich A. Hayek, *The Road to Serfdom* (Chicago: University of Chicago Press, 1956), pp. 35–42.

20. Milton Friedman, *Capitalism and Freedom* (Chicago: University of Chicago Press, 1962).

21. Ibid., p. 15.

22. Ibid., Chapter 2.

23. George Gilder, *Wealth and Poverty* (New York: Basic Books, 1981). This discussion is based on Gilder's analysis in chapters 1–10, pp. 3–114.

24. Ibid., p. 68.

25. See Ayn Rand, *For the New Intellectual: The Philosophy of Ayn Rand* [New York: New American Library, (Signet), 1969]. See also any of her novels.

26. William F. Buckley, Jr., *Right Reason* (Garden City, N.Y.: Doubleday, 1985), pp. 410–411.

27. Linda J. Medcalf and Kenneth M. Dolbeare, *Neopolitics: American Political Ideas in the 1980s* (New York: Random House, 1985), p. 132.

28. For a concise historical treatment of *National Review* and other conservative journals, see Nash, *Conservative Intellectual Movement,* Chapter 6, pp. 131–153.

29. Kevin P. Phillips, *Post-Conservative America: People, Politics and Ideology in a Time of Crisis* (New York: Random House, 1982), p. 47.

30. According to Richard A. Viguerie, *The New Right: We're Ready to Lead* (Falls Church, Va.: Viguerie Co., 1980), p. 14.

31. Phillips, *Post-Conservative America,* p. 199.

32. Hargis is cited in John Harold Redekop, *The American Far Right: A Case Study of Billy James Hargis and Christian Crusade* (Grand Rapids, Mich.: William B. Eerdmans Co., 1968), p. 43.

33. Ibid., pp. 183–184.

34. Viguerie, *The New Right*, pp. 15–16.

35. Hayek, *Constitution of Liberty*, pp. 404–405.

36. Cited in Lou Cannon, *Reagan* (New York: G. P. Putnam's Sons, 1982), p. 202.

37. Irvin Kristol, *Reflections of a Neoconservative* (New York, Basic Books, 1983), p. ix.

38. Ibid., p. 77.

39. *www.newamericancentury.org/statementofprinciples.htm.*

40. *www.newamericancentury.org/iraqclintonletter.htm*

SUGGESTED READINGS

Buchanan, Patrick J. *Where the Right Went Wrong.* New York: Thomas Dunne Books, 2004.

Burke, Edmund, *Reflections on the Revolution in France,* edited with an Introduction by Thomas H.D. Mahoney. New York: Liberal Arts Press, 1955.

Frank, Thomas. *What's the Matter with Kansas: How Conservatives Won the Heart of America.* New York: Henry Holt and Co., 2004.

Hayek, Friedrich A., *The Constitution of Liberty.* Chicago: Henry Regnery Co. (Gateway edition), 1972.

Ivins, Molly, and Dubose, Lou, *Shrub: The Short but Happy Political Life of George W. Bush.* New York: Random House, 2000.

Kirk, Russell, ed., *The Portable Conservative Reader.* New York: Penguin Books, 1982.

Nash, George H., *The Conservative Intellectual Movement in America: Since 1945.* New York: Basic Books, 1976.

Pemberton, William E., *Exit with Honor: The Life and Presidency of Ronald Reagan.* Armonk, New York: M. E. Sharpe, 1998.

Rossiter, Clinton, *Conservatism in America: The Thankless Persuasion.* 2nd ed. New York: Vantage, 1962.

Viguerie, Richard A., *The New Right: We're Ready to Lead.* Falls Church, Va.: Viguerie Co., 1980.

Will, George F., *Statecraft as Soulcraft: What Government Does.* New York: Simon & Schuster, 1983.

Chapter 6

Fascism and National Socialism

INTRODUCTION: ORIGIN, DEFINITION, AND RATIONALE

Fascism is a post-World War I phenomenon. It originated in Italy in 1922 and in Germany, where it was called national socialism, in 1933. Mussolini's fascist regime in Italy lasted 23 years (1922–1945), while Hitler and the Nazis (the national socialists) ruled Germany for 12 years (1933–1945). These two movements generated fanatical loyalty from millions of Italians and Germans and their tragic legacy, World War II and the Holocaust, has haunted us ever since. Although fascist movements emerged throughout Europe in many other states after World War I (e.g., in Austria, Britain, France, Belgium, Hungary, Denmark, Romania, Holland, and Spain), they were all "clumsy imitations" of Mussolini's and Hitler's regimes.[1] Therefore, our analysis focuses on the ideas and actions of these two principal forms of fascism.

Although there are differing opinions on whether fascism is a socioeconomic or a philosophical movement, there is general agreement on some of its objective characteristics. *Fascism* is a political system of the extreme right that exercises unlimited power by government over virtually all aspects of social, economic, political, and cultural life. It is both antidemocratic and anti-Marxist it openly denies liberal democracy's claim to political liberty, equality, and majority rule and communism's concepts of class struggle and collective ownership of all productive forces. Rather, fascism allocates all power to an elite group and retains private ownership of productive forces, while insisting that the economy function to serve the needs of the state and nation rather than the individual. It is a system that subscribes to the leader principle (*il Duce* and der *führer*), a one-party state, the use of secret police, propaganda, control of all media, and the ruthless suppression of any speech, press, association, or religion perceived by the rulers as a threat to the regime's exercise of power. Finally, it is militaristic and the most extreme form of overt nationalism in the twentieth century.

Why should we study and try to understand fascism? Did not the threat of fascism vanish with the defeat of Italy and Germany in World War II? On the contrary, the scourge of fascism, disguised by a host of other names, is present in the world today. It is therefore crucial to understand what fascism is and what life is like in this type of a totalitarian system. This knowledge is necessary in order to successfully combat fascist movements in our democratic societies today, to understand the world in which we live, and to recognize the social and psychological conditions that produced a secular faith system that captured the minds of millions. Therefore, the most effective way to cope with fascism is to understand the force and power of its ideas, to support rational thought and critical thinking rather than fanaticism, and to remember always that ends and means are equally important. Finally, it is sobering to recall that these two totalitarian systems—Italian fascism and German Naziism—thrived in civic cultures that embraced Christianity (Protestant and Catholic) and capitalism—even these two mighty ideological forces did not prevent the catastrophic move toward Teutonic cults and neomercantilism.

Philosophic "Roots" of Fascism

Unlike contemporary communism, which draws virtually all of its basic theory from the thought of Marx and Engels and its ideas on practice from revolutionaries like Lenin and Mao, fascism is a combination and blending of old prejudices and new myths twisted together to reinforce cultural fears, bigotry, and hatred. The fascists and Nazis drew on both major and minor philosophers from a number of countries to explain and justify their doctrines. Most were nineteenth-century philosophers, but the ideas of classical, medieval, and modern thinkers also were used to rationalize the new political philosophies. German, Italian, French, English, American, and Swedish philosophers unwittingly contributed ideas that lie at the root of fascist and National Socialist ideology. These ideas created a mentality in the people and civic culture of Italy and Germany that predisposed them to accept the totalitarian remedies suggested by Mussolini and Hitler—particularly when confronted with governments perceived as ineffective and illegitimate. We employ several concepts to explain the ideas and identify the theorists who contributed to the ideological development including irrationalism, the supreme value of the state, hero worship and elitism, war and international relations, racism and anti-Semitism, and geopolitics.

Irrationalism   German philosophers Arthur Schopenhauer and Martin Heidegger, along with French philosophers Henri Bergson and Georges Sorel, contended that life and nature are irrational, that life is too complex for reason, and that irrationality is therefore morally as well as intellectually affirmed. True knowledge cannot be derived by reason or by the scientific method; rather, only intuition, or instinct, can help us to understand the world. Intuition is a higher form of knowledge, and all great social movements are "pulled" by the power of a myth that cannot be analyzed. The philosopher Heidegger stated that truth is revealed only in revelation. The logical consequence of philosophies such as these is that what we call "reason" is built on postulates that are so unreasonable that genius, revelation, and intuition alone should guide our actions.

The State as Supreme Value   German philosopher Georg Hegel and Italian philosophers Giovanni Gentile and Alfredo Rocco are most noteworthy for their ideas on the concept of the state and the individual's relation to the state. For Hegel, the state is an end in itself; that is, it is the institution whereby God reveals his plan for worldly development. Gentile wrote of the supremacy and sanctity of the state, which he saw as the living embodiment of an ethical idea. Rocco, an extreme nationalist, argued that the Roman Empire was the high point of human civilization and that Italy is the spiritual heir to this legacy of Rome. He viewed the state as the central measure of value—the standard on which all things should be judged. Hegel argued that duty to the state rather than self-interest should motivate the actions of individuals. He believed that individual freedom can be realized only through the state, for only through society can people be delivered from enslavement. These ideas of Hegel, Gentile, and Rocco helped create conditions for society's acceptance of fascist thought in regards to the state.

Hero Worship and Elitism   German philosopher Friedrich Nietzsche, in *Thus Spake Zarathustra,* expressed his contempt for the common person and his adulation of the hero, what he called the *übermensch* or superman. German composer Richard Wagner also supported hero worship and German nationalism. Wagner's ideas were conveyed to the German people through a powerful medium—his music. Italian philosopher Vilfredo Pareto argued for a society

125

ruled by the elite, while Nietzsche saw the masses as a lower order, lacking creativity, blinded by originality, and fit only to follow the superiors in society. This hierarchical ranking of society extended also to the sexes, and Nietzsche, like Aristotle, expressed contempt for women in his writing. To Nietzsche, Wagner, and Pareto, only the hero and the elite immediately surrounding him should exercise power.

War and International Relations   Theorists Niccolò Machiavelli, Johann Fichte, Heinrich von Treitschke, Houston Chamberlain, and Sir Halford Mackinder advocated war and the use of violence to achieve state goals. British theorists Mackinder and Chamberlain espoused antiliberal doctrines and favored imperialism—the political and economic domination of one country by another. This doctrine was further developed by von Treitschke who held that war and violence are not only effective but also the best remedies available for any type of national illness. All of these theorists argued that the practice of cooperation and competition among states as a means to resolve differences is evidence of weakness. Conflict, war, and violence are politically more effective and psychologically therapeutic. Fichte and Machiavelli summarized the position well in arguing that "might makes right" in the relations among states. International law, treaties, and organizations should be supported so long as they serve national interests. When they do not, a prince, dictator, or king should ignore ethical considerations and concentrate on maximizing power, even if it involves war and violence.

Racism and Anti-Semitism   German composer Richard Wagner preached anti-Semitism as did his son-in-law H. S. Chamberlain. They viewed Aryans as a superior race and the Jewish people as inferior, and their diatribes against Jews exacerbated the racist myths in Germany that had existed since the time of Martin Luther.[2] Arthur de Gobineau, a nineteenth-century French noble, taught that the races should be arranged hierarchically. According to Gobineau, the white race was the most superior of all, the black race constituted the most inferior group, and the Mongoloids ranked somewhere in between. Gobineau claimed that only the Aryan race possessed the qualities of intellect and creativity necessary for leadership, and because Jews were a mixture of races, they were a corrupting influence.

Geopolitics   Rudolph Kjellén, a Swedish professor, argued that there was room for only one great power in Europe. He called his plan "geopolitik" and maintained that the growth and development of a state could be understood only in terms of its physical location, geography, relationship to other states, environment, and strategic position. Kjellén's ideas were adopted by Heinrich Haushofer and his Geopolitical Institute and formed the basis of Nazi thought in Hitler's Germany. Haushofer's thesis was that Germany formed the heartland that controlled the world island, which in turn controlled the world.[3]

Fascist and Nazi Similarities

Although most of the analysis that follows focuses on the major differences between the fascist movements in Italy and Germany in terms of their history, doctrine, and practice, it is useful to understand first the overall similarities of the two movements. The most succinct and useful description of the characteristics common to both movements is that of George H. Sabine in *A History of Political Theory*. Sabine notes that, although Italian fascism and German Nazism claimed to be socialist, they were actually nationalist—both made emotional appeals to people who were exhausted and demoralized by the war, inflation, and depression; both exalted idealism and elicited fanatical support from the people in all classes; both were anticommunist and antidemocratic; and both employed war as a unifying force to rally the nation behind their one-party totalitarian systems.[4]

ITALIAN FASCISM: 1922–1945

History: 1815–1915

The Risorgimento (1815–1870)   The three-stage struggle for freedom whereby Italy was transformed from a fragmented peninsula dominated by foreign powers to a united independent state is called the *Risorgimento* (or "resurgence"). The first stage (1815–1848) began when the Congress of Vienna redrew the map of Europe following Napoleon's defeat. After 14 years of dominance by Napoleon, Italy dreamed of independence, but when Prince Metternich, Austria's master diplomat, acquired the province of Lombardy and Venetia along with some satellite dukedoms, Italy was left divided and weakened. Conspiracies and rebellions against the Austrians followed, and some remarkable patriotic literature emerged. When the revolutions of 1848 broke out in Paris, Berlin, Vienna, and Milan, the Italians began a war to drive the Austrians from Italy. However, after six months the fighting ended and Austria prevailed.[5]

The second stage of the Risorgimento (1849–1861) was dominated by three revolutionaries—Count Camillo Cavour, Giuseppe Mazzini, and Giuseppe Garibaldi. Cavour was an aristocrat from Turin who acted as strategist and states person. Mazzini was a visionary and an intellectual whose writing and passionate speeches strongly contributed to the development of nationalism rather than regionalism. Garibaldi was a soldier, fighter, and romantic hero who led the troops in the fighting for unification. During this period, a revolt in Milan organized by Mazzini, a second war to secure independence in 1859 orchestrated by Cavour, and Garibaldi's astonishing military victories in Sicily and Naples resulted in the virtual unification of Italy by 1861. All that remained outside of Italian control was Rome, Venice, and the patriarchate of St. Peter.[6]

The third and final stage of the Risorgimento (1861–1870) opened with the unfortunate death of Cavour, a great loss for Italy. However, in 1866 Venice was given to Italy by Germany as a reward for its support in a war with Austria, and the Italians took Rome while the French were preoccupied in their conflict with Germany in 1870–1871. The Italians then seized the area controlled by the pope and in the Law of Guarantees left the church only three sites: the Vatican, a church (St. John Lateran), and the pope's summer residence, Castel Gandolfo. In 1870 Italy was finally united.[7]

The period 1870–1915 saw the death of the old leadership (Mazzini, Garibaldi, Pope Pius XI, and King Victor Emmanuel), Italy's involvement in the Triple Alliance (Germany, Italy, Austria) that lasted until World War I, and a ruinous race for armaments, colonies in Africa, and prestige. The conflicts in Ethiopia and Libya cost Italy a great deal of national treasure.

Italy and World War I: 1915–1918

When World War I began in 1914, Italy declared neutrality because it could do little else. The war in Libya had demonstrated weaknesses in the organization and equipment of Italy's armed forces, the Italian army was not prepared to fight an Alpine campaign, time was needed to gain popular support, and, most important, public opinion tended toward support for the Allied cause. In April 1915 Italy signed the secret Treaty of London with the Allies and in May withdrew from the Triple Alliance. Later that month, Italy declared war on Austria (war with Germany was declared over a year later, in August 1916). Initially, the fighting on the Austrian front went well, but when Russia collapsed in 1917 and the Austrians moved their troops to the Italian front the struggle intensified. Italy mobilized over 5 million men and lost almost 700,000 in the war. Still Italy fought well. At the battle of Piave, 29 Italian divisions held off 50 German and

Austrian divisions, and in the fall of 1918, Italy and its allies won a major victory in the battle of Vittorio Veneto.[8] In November 1918 the war ended after Italy and its allies had defeated Germany and Austria.

Fascism: 1922–1945

Following the end of World War I, Italy was faced with many domestic problems—demobilization, inflation, political instability, unemployment, strikes, and large budget deficits. In addition, the Paris Peace Conference resulted in huge territorial gains for England and France while Italy received little for its contribution to the Allied victory.

The disintegration of the parliamentary system was at hand in Italy in 1919, and reaction against it emerged in the form of fascist groups organized by Benito Mussolini in March of that year in Milan. The Fascist party program appealed to war veterans, landowners, the unemployed, industrialists, and nationalists who wanted to "crush the Reds." In 1920, as socialists increased their power in parliament, strikes and peasant land seizures shook Italy with the specter of radical social, economic, and political change. But Mussolini cemented his allegiance to the right by using his Blackshirts to break the power of the socialists and communists in Milan and Bologna, and thus won the overwhelming support of the middle class and the military. In 1921 the Fascist party won 35 seats in parliament, and in 1922, the fascists took control of many cities. They were supported by the neutrality and in some instances open support of the police and military. In October 1922, under the guise of stopping "the left," Mussolini orchestrated the famous March on Rome. When 60,000 Blackshirts began a march on the capital, King Victor Emmanuel III agreed to cooperate and invited Mussolini to form a new government—all with the acquiescence of the army and police.

During 1922–1926, Mussolini consolidated his power. He purged the bureaucracy, police, and military of all dissident elements; established a Fascist Grand Council that gave him exceptional power; eliminated political parties and labor unions not controlled by the fascists; subordinated the press, judiciary, and youth groups; abolished secret societies such as the Freemasons; and even controlled recreation through an association called Dopolavoro. The totalitarian state became a reality.

In foreign affairs Mussolini maintained a policy of peace for about 12 years. But in 1935 he attacked Ethiopia, in 1936 he sent Italian troops to Spain to help Franco in Spain's civil war, in 1939 Italian troops occupied Albania, and in June 1940 Mussolini joined Hitler when he attacked France—an opportunistic ven-

129

ture in that France had already been defeated. In 1942, when the Allies landed in North Africa, Mussolini began to lose support. After the invasion of Italy in 1943, Mussolini was driven from power by a vote of "no confidence" in the Grand Council. He was arrested, subsequently rescued by German paratroopers, and then set up in a "puppet" fascist state in northern Italy—all under German protection.

In April 1945, as Hitler's Third Reich collapsed, Mussolini was captured by partisan fighters near Lake Como and was executed along with his mistress. (Their bodies were strung up feet first in a gas station in Milan.) Thus ended 23 years of fascism in Italy.

Mussolini: A Biographical Sketch (1883–1945)

Benito Mussolini was born on July 29, 1883, in Predaggio, a small town in central Italy. His father was a blacksmith, a socialist, and an outspoken critic of the church. His mother was a devout Christian and an elementary schoolteacher. After completing his education in Italy, Mussolini went to Switzerland where he worked as a manual laborer. In 1904 he returned to Italy to fulfill his military service obligation and then became editor of a socialist newspaper.

At this time he was an advocate of violent revolution and a critic of nationalism as a capitalist ploy. In 1912 Mussolini was given the job of editor of *Avanti*, Milan's official voice of the socialist party of Italy. He was a successful editor until October 1914, when he took a pro-war stand. At that time he argued for Italian intervention in World War I in support of the Allied cause and for Italy's national honor—a complete reversal of his previous ideological position. In 1915, Mussolini was called to military duty and served one and a half years in the trenches. He was wounded and discharged in 1917.[9]

When Mussolini took power in Italy in 1922 he was 39 years old and loved to wear uniforms. He was a charismatic leader and began to use the name *il Duce* in 1921. He also was a vain man who shaved his head to look younger. He was married and had three children but kept a mistress, Clarissa, from 1934 to 1945.

Major Doctrines of Italian Fascism

The doctrines of communism have a single source—Karl Marx. Fascism, however, has no single prophet on which all agree. Although the origins of this extreme nationalist, idealist, anticommunist, and militarist ideology are diverse, its doctrines can be identified, analyzed, and explained. To accomplish this, the doctrines are separated into two groups that we call the "foundation stones" and the "building blocks" of Italian fascist thought. (The metaphors are employed to suggest that some doctrines of fascism are more important than others.)

The "Foundation Stones" of Fascism

The State As the Central Measure of Value   "The *foundation* of fascism is the conception of the state. Fascism conceives of the state as an absolute, in comparison with which all individuals or groups are relative, only to be conceived of in their relation to the State."[10] In fascist thought the state is seen as a living, breathing entity with an organic life of its own. It is only through the state that the human individual has any meaning. The individual is "transitory" while the state is concrete. The state alone has dignity and personality. It is the concrete manifestation of Italy's past, present, and future.[11]

Sovereignty (supreme law-making and law enforcement) is founded in the state, not in the individual as liberalism contends, and this sovereignty is unlimited, indivisible, and permanent. To fascists, the state demonstrates its will and consciousness through the exercise of its sovereignty. Fascist thought also reverses the relationship between state and nation. Most Western thought suggests that it is the nation (common language, religion, ethnicity, culture) that gives rise to the state (sovereignty, population, territory, government). Fascists maintain that the reverse is true—that the state creates the nation. That is, through the state a nation becomes conscious of itself; only the state can generate a collective will and identity. Simply, the state is the "end" and individuals are the "means" whereby this supreme value (the state) realizes itself in history.[12]

The Hero and the Will to Power   In "The Fascist Decalogue"—the ten commandments of an Italian soldier—two statements document the thesis of the critical role of the hero in history. Commandment eight states, "Mussolini is always right," and Commandment ten says, "One thing must be dear to you above all: the life of The Duce."[13] In Italian fascism, Benito Mussolini is the leader and the hero. Only Mussolini could express in words the collective thought of the Italian people. Only through Mussolini was the salvation of the Italian people possible, and only he could know the truth and make the truth a reality, for he alone had access to the inner voice that dictates the truth. Theorists of Italian fascism contend that Mussolini, through his speech and action, possessed the sincerity, courage, and faith of the hero that emerges so infrequently in history. And it is these exceptional individuals who change history.

The concept of the will to power suggests that the social, economic, and political environment can be changed by human will alone. Contrary to Marxism, which sees the tension between economic forces as the agent of change in human history, fascism contends that human will can transcend these conditions and transform the world. Social classes and new technology do not change the direction and velocity of human history, rather it is heroes such as Mussolini exercising their will to power who alone can eliminate the forces that enslave human beings and lead them to a new day of total redemption. Such a ruler needs absolute power and devotion from those he leads to accomplish the state's goals, and the freedom to pursue the "sacred duty."

Anti-intellectualism   Fascism is eminently anti-intellectual. Fascism does not separate "thought from action, of knowledge from life, of brain from heart, of theory from practice. . . . [of] all Utopian systems which are destined never to face the test of reality. . . . [Fascists scorn] the educated classes in Italy: the leterato—the man who plays with knowledge. . . . Fascism prefers not to waste time constructing abstract theories."[14]

Mussolini once said, "we think with our blood." Italian fascism expresses its distrust of reason and its embrace of anti-intellectualism in the writing of all its major theorists and activists. To these individuals, fascism is "above all, action and sentiment. . . . Were it otherwise, it could not keep up that immense driving force . . . to stir the soul of the people."[15] Mussolini argued that fascism was opposed to all materialistic abstractions and that fascists pursue not material pleasure but "spiritual existence." Through its employment of emotionalism, Italy's fascist leadership sought to give life meaning. By following the Duce without thought or analysis, Italians would find new purpose in their lives. Feeling and sentiment, not sterile logic and scientific method, are the true sources of information and all else is knowledge of an inferior order.

The "Building Blocks" of Fascism

Anti-communism and Anti-liberalism   Mussolini argued that fascism is "the complete opposite" of Marxism, that the materialist conception of history whereby historical change is driven by the clash of social classes is absurd, and that "holiness and heroism"—human action free of economic motivation—are the real engines of historical change.[16] Fascists maintain that the institutional bases of Western civilization—private property, religion, monogamy, and the state—are threatened by the doctrines of communism and that fascists are morally obligated to eliminate the threat of this new "Dark Age."

Fascism also bitterly attacks liberalism and the modern democratic state. The theory of liberalism that the state exists to serve the individual is rejected by fascism. Fascism denies majority rule, political equality, popular control of leaders, and political freedom. Instead, it argues passionately for the inequality of human beings and for government by an elite. Freedom, in fascist thought, is associated not with the individual but with the life of the state itself. The curtailment of personal freedom is therefore "a fundamental condition of the triumph of Fascism."[17]

Corporatism   Mussolini proclaimed that the corporate state was a dynamic new alternative to capitalism and communism. Corporatism linked employers and employees in huge bureaucratic institutions that then sent deputies to a corporative chamber in Rome to act as instruments of government control over the economy. The corporate state was based on 22 corporations, directing and coordinating the economy, and was a mechanism employed by Mussolini for the ruthless exploitation of labor. In theory, the corporation's task was to equitably settle problems that arose between management and labor. In practice, it functioned to seek the economic welfare of the state at the expense of the individual worker. The goal of corporatist doctrine was social and economic efficiency—the mobilization of economic forces in the service of the state. The institution of private property was never directly threatened, but capitalism and the free-enterprise system with its corollaries of individual freedom and self-interest was too divisive for Italian fascism, which constantly sought mechanisms to unify the diverse elements of society.

Nationalism and Imperialism   Mussolini and the Fascist party sought to reestablish the glory of Rome in twentieth-century Italy. Rome symbolized to the fascists a golden age for Italy, and they set out to reconstruct a new empire and strong Italian state. The struggles of Machiavelli and nineteenth-century revolutionaries Cavour, Garibaldi, and Mazzini to unify Italy had succeeded. It was time to expand and develop the "legacy of Rome" and bring its cultural vitality to others. Nationalism, self-determination, and freedom for the robust, energetic, and animated people of Italy was a reality, and the new empire was viewed as an extension of that vitality. Mussolini talked of the new empire as more than territory and economics—it was also "spiritual and moral." The fascists claimed that if Italians were to lead a meaningful life they would have to find salvation "through the renewed cult of the family, the church, the nation, and the state."[18]

133

Totalitarianism and Elitism   Fascism rejects government of "the multitude" in liberal democracies and advocates rule by those capable of rising above their own self-interests. In "The Philosophic Basis of Fascism" Giovanni Gentile states that fascist doctrine is totalitarian, meaning that nothing is outside the province of politics. To Gentile, the power of the state is absolute—it does not compromise, barter, or surrender any area of its discretion.[19]

This is precisely the point of totalitarian government—politics knows no bounds. Nothing is exempt. Everything becomes a public concern. In theory, and to a great extent in practice, fascist Italy attempted to operationalize the "totalitarian temptation" of Jean Francois Revel. All barriers to political encroachment were crushed in the areas of religion, education, press, sports, cinema, theatre, business, and family life. At the apex of this totalitarian regime was Mussolini—il Duce—the national hero and the fascist elite who controlled everything.

War and Violence   Fascism is anti-pacifist. It openly repudiates the doctrine of pacifism and rejects the possibility, probability, and utility of peace. War alone brings out the best in a person and a nation; it ennobles those involved in the conflict. According to Mussolini, combat, duty, and sacrifice are the hallmarks of fascism.[20] Mussolini and his fascists put this doctrine into practice in 1935, when they attacked and defeated Ethiopia, and in 1939, when they occupied Albania. War and conflict were also seen as means to fascist ends when Italy sent Italian troops to Spain in 1936 to aid Franco's forces and when Italy attacked France in 1940. Violence was also employed within Italy when circumstances warranted. For example, Mussolini had some of his most vocal opponents such as Giacomo Matteoti murdered and others such as Antonio Gramsci imprisoned. He also employed force, or the threat of force, to achieve political goals in Greece in 1923 and to control the city of Fiume in Yugoslavia in 1924.

Italian Fascism in Practice: Concluding Commentary

Although the preceding discussion of Italian fascism focuses on the significant political and economic practices of the regime, some clarification of church-state relations is necessary.

Christianity has existed in Italy since the first century AD. The church was forced to acquire and keep property in order to survive and fulfill its spiritual mission. This implied the need to own land, seminaries, and support systems to train the clergy. The needs of the church thus conflicted with those of the landowners and elite in Italy as they struggled for state support. This, in turn,

generated anti-clericalism. Mussolini and many of his followers were anticleri-
cal, but at the same time they embraced the Christian faith. The church had its
own supporting institutions—the Catholic Popular party, Catholic trade unions,
and the education system—that created barriers to Mussolini and the party in
their effort to control Italy. Therefore, in order to coexist, Mussolini and the Vatican entered into a convention, a treaty, and a concordat. The convention
resolved the Vatican's economic claims on the state, the treaty established
the sovereignty of the Vatican, and the concordat resolved the multitude of
church-state relations in Italy.[21] Problems arose, but the "two swords" of civil
and ecclesiastical power were assigned their respective jurisdictions. Essentially,
a religious boundary to Italian fascism existed during the years 1922–1945.

GERMAN NATIONAL SOCIALISM: 1933–1945

Germany: Land and People

Situated in Central Europe, Germany has no natural barriers except the Alps in
the south and thus has historically been an area of migration where intellectual
and political struggles frequently occur. At the end of World War II, Germany
was divided into two states—the Federal Republic of Germany (West Germany), which was about the size of Oregon (95,700 square miles) and had a population of 61 million; and the German Democratic Republic (East Germany),
which was about the size of Ohio (41,600 square miles) and had a population of
17 million. When Germany was reunited on October 3, 1990, the new state
totaled 137,300 square miles (Montana comprises 145,587 square miles), with a
total population of about 80 million people.

The German nation developed out of a number of tribes, and about 100 million people consider German their native language. The current GNP of Germany is the third largest in the world, reflecting the energy, efficiency, and
discipline of the people. Only the United States and Japan exceed Germany in
GNP.[22]

Who are the Germans? What values and beliefs motivate them? In *Germans*,
George Bailey characterizes them as people who worship nature ("the forest
people") and have a direct and mystical relationship with nature; as sensitive to
questions of rank and status with a class consciousness similar to other Euro-
peans; and as good and efficient at anything they attempt ("wenn schon, denn
schon"—if it is to be done at all, then do it properly). The German people love
Shakespeare, holidays, animals, and the theatre; they are fascinated by excessive

135

abstraction and the romanticism of gods and demons in literature; they are often prone to maintain formal (*sie*) rather than personal (*du*) relationships with friends they may have known for years; and finally, they are searchers who dream of the Holy Roman Empire in their quest for national identity.[23] Today it is not unusual to hear returning visitors to Germany comment on the efficiency of the bureaucracy, the importance of education to Germans, the pastoral landscape and charming small towns that dominate the countryside (40 percent of Germans live in villages of 20,000 inhabitants or less), the first-rate integrated transportation system, the unique accommodations for the traveler (Gasthaus or inn, and "Zimmer Frei" or rooms), and, of course, the world-famous Bier und Schnapps.

Why then did Germany, a nation that produced Luther, Bach, Kant, and Goethe, blindly follow Hitler; permit the horrors of Auschwitz, Sobibor, and Dachau; and participate in the Lebensborn program of racial breeding? History can give us some insights into these intriguing questions.

History

The First Reich

The origin and development of the German nation took place over many centuries. Although it began with Charlemagne in 800 AD, the term *Reich* was not used until 911. Otto I (936–973) was crowned emperor in AD 962 in Rome, and the First Reich—the Holy Roman Empire—reached its "golden age" under Frederick Barbarossa (1115-1190). But a problem that had plagued Germany for almost 2000 years remained—the division and territorial fragmentation of the nation caused by divisive internal forces (tribal distrust and differences in tradition, dialect, and culture, along with the unremitting struggle for control and power between tribal duchies). These factors re-emerged under Barbarossa's successors and were further exacerbated by the great religious schism, the Reformation, initiated by Martin Luther in 1517. Germany's entire social system was subsequently shaken by the Peasants' Revolt of 1525, the Catholic Counter-Reformation, and the Thirty Years' War (1618–1648). In this disastrous conflict, Germany was devastated and forced to make tremendous territorial concessions to its neighbors in the Treaty of Westphalia. All these actions bear witness to the depth of the change.[24] The crumbling First Reich finally collapsed under the onslaught of Napoleon's forces and was replaced by the "Deutsche Bund" (German Confederation) in 1815 after the Congress of Vienna, another blow to German unity.

The Second Reich   Otto von Bismarck (1815–1898), a count from a Prussian Junker family and prime minister of Prussia in 1862, sought to construct a "smaller German Reich" (one that did not include Austria) under Prussian leadership. He accomplished this goal by winning three wars: the German-Danish war in 1864 that forced Denmark to give up the dukedoms of Schleswig and Holstein; the 1866 seven-week war with Austria (the so-called German War) that forced Austria to give up its administrative role in Holstein; and the war with France (1870–1871), which required France to cede the territory of Alsace-Lorraine to Germany. With three great victories, German patriots in the southern principalities joined those of the north to form the German Empire (the Second Reich) with Wilhelm I of Prussia as emperor and Bismarck as Reich chancellor. Bismarck ruled until 1890, when he was dismissed by an ambitious and blustering Wilhelm II, a man with grandiose ideas of empire. These dreams resulted in the construction of a navy that threatened Great Britain, and the stage for war was set.

World War I and the Weimar Republic   In June 1914 the heir to the Austrian throne, Archduke Ferdinand, was assassinated. The incident triggered World War I, which began on August 1, 1914, between the Central Powers (Austria-Hungary and Germany) and the Allies (Russia, France, Britain, and Serbia). The Germans advanced rapidly and fought well but were defeated at the battle of the Marne, only 15 miles from Paris, in the autumn of 1914. With this defeat, the western front was stabilized and the fighting froze into trench warfare. With the great slaughter at the battle of Verdun and the bloody fighting on the River Somme in 1916, coupled with the United States's entry into the war in April 1917, the German will to fight weakened. The country had suffered economically and militarily, and on November 11, 1918, the war ended. In the Treaty of Versailles, Germany was forced to pay massive reparations, give up 12 percent of its national territory along with 6 million people, turn over much of its merchant fleet to the Allies, limit its armed forces, "demilitarize" the Rhine area, surrender all its colonies, and make massive coal deliveries to Allied powers for a decade.[25] Some historians contend that the "seeds" for World War II were sown in the Treaty of Versailles.

The *Weimar Republic* was established in January 1919 with power going to the Social Democrats. But it was a "republic without republicans," challenged by the extreme left (communists) and right (Nazis) and supported in only a half-hearted way by the major parliamentary political parties. Conspiracies and street violence were commonplace. In 1923 domestic instability reached its peak with disastrous inflation, attempts by communists to overthrow the government, and Hitler's abortive military putsch in Munich. After a short period of recovery during the years 1924–1929, depression and unemployment returned to Germany. The final blow was the American Wall Street crisis of October 1929, which shook the economic fabric of the nation to its core. The Nazi party, led by Adolf Hitler, had been growing throughout the 1920s, and, in the elections of 1930, the Nazis received over six million votes and were accorded 107 seats in the parliament. In the balloting of November 1932, the Nazis won 196 seats in the legislative elections and were the largest party in the Reichstag (the national legislature). On January 30, 1933, Hitler was appointed Reich chancellor by President Paul von Hindenburg.

Hitler and the Nazis: 1919–1945

Adolf Hitler was born on April 20, 1889, in Braunau-on-the-Inn, Austria, a small town located on the German-Austrian border. He was a mediocre student at the public school he attended in Linz and longed for a career as an artist or painter, a desire that was a source of serious conflict with his father, a retired customs official. After his parents' death, Hitler went to Vienna and for five years experienced "the most miserable time of my life."[26] There he painted small pictures of Vienna's landmarks and postcards, lived in abject poverty, and absorbed the virulent anti-Semitism that he later described in *Mein Kampf.*[27]

In the spring of 1912, at the age of 23, Hitler moved to Munich, the art center of Germany, and reported it as the "happiest and most satisfying time of my life."[28] On August 3, 1914, he directly petitioned King Ludwig III of Bavaria to serve in a Bavarian regiment. His request was granted and Hitler joined the German army where he served with distinction. He was wounded twice and twice decorated for bravery with the Iron Cross. Germany's defeat was a terrible blow to Hitler, one of shame and disgrace, and on his return to Munich in November 1918, he resolved to "become a politician." In September 1919, he was ordered to investigate a political group called the German Workers' party. He did this and a few days later accepted a membership card "with the number seven." Hitler proved to be a skilled orator, organizer, and propagandist and soon took over the leadership of the group. In 1920 the group's name was changed to the National Socialist German Workers' party, and the name "Nazi" emerged out of the German pronunciation of the first two words.

In 1923 Hitler, with the support of General Erich Ludendorff, attempted to seize control of the Munich government in a military putsch (military seizure of power). The attempt failed, and he was arrested, tried, convicted, and ordered to

Landsberg prison where he served one year of a five-year sentence. There he wrote *Mein Kampf* (My Struggle), which outlines Nazi ideology and politics. Although the years 1925–1929 brought economic recovery to Germany, they also saw a decline in the fortunes of the National Socialist party. But the world-wide trauma of 1929 revived the party, which won over 6 million votes in the 1930 elections. Two years and four months later, Hitler and the Nazis were in power.

How can we begin to explain and understand the power that Hitler was able to exercise over millions of Germans? Albert Speer, Hitler's close associate for 12 years, in *Spandau: The Secret Diaries,* saw Hitler as a master psychologist— able to perceive and act on the innermost hopes and fears of people—and a man with an "opaque personality." After more than a decade together, Speer wrote, "I could not say . . . whether he really liked me . . . I don't even know what he felt for Germany."[29] Others, too, saw Hitler as an absolute master of group psychology—a man who expressed in passionate language the deepest sentiments of the average German, who effectively used meaningful symbols (swastika, Teutonic knights, art) to transmit his ideas to the masses, who realized that enthusiastic political action and sacrifice demand emotional involvement, and who understood the need for a sustaining ideology.[30] To the German people, Hitler was a charismatic personality; he had extraordinary spiritual power and capability to elicit widespread popular support for the goals he sought.

Consolidation of Power   The Nazi consolidation of power occurred during the years 1933–1935. In February 1933 the Reichstag building was burned by a mentally retarded communist from Holland. This convinced many Germans that communist terrorism was a force to be feared. Thus, in the March elections, the Nazis further increased their deputies in the legislature and an Enabling Act was passed that gave the government complete power. In July 1933 the Nazi party was declared the only legal party in Germany. Then, in the summer of 1934, two events completed the totalitarianization of power. First, on June 30, 1934, Hitler and some of his closest associates in the Nazi party murdered Ernst Röhm and hundreds of other leaders of the *Sturmabteilung* (the SA, or Brown-shirts, who numbered about 2.5 million). For this treacherous act, Hitler received the support of the army (the Wehrmacht). Second, on August 2, 1934, Hindenburg died, and Hitler became chancellor and president of the Third Reich.

The party then nazified German culture by penetrating and dominating all types of groups (religious, art, media, education, sports, economic) except one— the Jewish community. German Jews were to be eliminated, and the legal basis

139

for their persecution was formalized in the Nuremberg Laws of September 1935, which deprived them of all rights. However, the massive, systematic persecution of Jews began in November 1938 with *Kristallnacht* (crystal night).

Foreign Policy   Nazi foreign policy between 1936 and 1939 is best characterized as daring, resolute, and bold. In just over three years, through diplomacy and military bluff, Hitler ordered his troops back into the Rhineland (1936), began his support of Franco in Spain's civil war (1936), completed the incorporation of Austria into the German Reich (the Anschluss of 1938), and occupied the Sudetenland in 1938, Czechoslovakia's westernmost territory, along with the balance of that state in early 1939. All of this occurred without the loss of a soldier to enemy gunfire. Hitler then demanded that Poland give up Danzig and create a route to Prussia. In August 1939, after the Poles refused, Germany and the Soviet Union signed a nonaggression pact and on September 1, 1939, Nazi troops crossed the Polish border.

World War II   World War II began with a series of lightning (*blitzkrieg*) attacks. By June 1940 Nazi forces had conquered Poland, Denmark, Norway, Belgium, the Netherlands, and France. In April 1941 Hitler attacked Yugoslavia and Greece and defeated both countries in less than a month. Then, in June 1941, Hitler attacked the Soviet Union, after which he decided to exterminate the Jewish population within the German sphere of power. It was the beginning of the "Final Solution,"[31] which resulted in the death of six million Jews.

By December 1941 Hitler's troops were in the outskirts of Moscow, the high point of his victorious campaigns. The Soviet's winter offensive and the entry of the United States into World War II occurred in that same month, and the next three years (1942–1944) brought a series of military defeats to Nazi Germany at the massive battle at Stalingrad (1942), the loss of North Africa (1943), the invasion and surrender of Italy (1943), and the Allied invasion of Western Europe (1944). In January 1945 Hitler went underground into the Reich chancellery bunker. By April 1945 Russian troops were moving into Berlin. Hitler held a series of farewell meetings with close associates and on April 28, 1945, he and Eva Braun, his mistress, were married. On April 30, 1945, Hitler and Braun committed suicide and their bodies were covered with gasoline and burned.[32] The Third Reich had collapsed, and the war that had cost 55 million lives ended on May 7, 1945.

Major Doctrines of German National Socialism (Naziism)

Although German national socialism (Naziism) and Italian fascism are similar in many ways, there are important differences in their theory and practice. In Italian fascism, the central measure of value was clearly the state; the exercise of political power involved some limits regarding corporate, church, and military elites; and little effort was made to implement a racial program. In Hitler's Germany, the reverse was true. In Naziism, the racial purity of the German nation was the supreme value, and a ten-year eugenics plan to eliminate undesirable people and breed desirable Aryans (the Lebensborn program of 1935–1945) lay at the very heart of Nazi thought and action. In addition, a great deal of tension, conflict, and struggle existed between the Christian church and the fascist state, and the exercise of ultimate political power was much more centralized and knew few, if any, limits. To aid readers' understanding, the doctrines of Naziism are divided into two groups—the ideological groundwork of Naziism and other pillars of Nazi doctrine.

The Ideological Groundwork of Naziism

On Race and Pure Blood   The national socialist doctrines of Aryan racial superiority, the centerpiece of Nazi ideology, are summed up by Hitler in the comment, "All that is not race in this world is trash."[33] In *Mein Kampf,* Hitler contends that the progress of humankind depends on racial struggle; that the emergence of the superior Aryan culture was made possible only when this group subdued inferior peoples and used them to implement their will; and that interracial mixing of blood enfeebles and eventually destroys the superior group. Hitler divided people into three groups—culture founders (Aryans), culture bearers (Asians), and culture destroyers (Jews and blacks). According to Hitler, anything that has value was created by the Aryan race, which possesses the "divine spark of genius," whereas Asians can only use that which is given them (technology, art, knowledge) and Jews and blacks act only as destroyers of Aryan culture.[34]

Hitler's ideas were further developed by Alfred Rosenberg, a Nazi theoretician, who argued that the Nordic race (and to Rosenberg Nordic *is* German) represents the "divine essence of man," that world history is a product of the "blue-eyed blond race" of Aryans—the world's only true "spiritual force"—and that "on the day when Nordic blood should completely dry up, Germany would fall to ruin."[35] Heinrich Himmler also contributed to the Nazi theory of race and blood. Himmler, head of the SS (*Schutzstaffel,* or headquarters guards) and German police, outlined his ideas on the racial myth in a memorandum. In it he attacked the Jews for international conspiracy and the Slavs for being subhuman, and he claimed the importance of maintaining the pure blood of the Nordic race through controlled breeding.

The logic of racism is painfully clear, and the political consequence of the German racial myth was staggering—the Lebensborn program, the Holocaust, and experimentation and euthanasia. The *Lebensborn program* was established in Germany in 1935 by Heinrich Himmler and continued until the end of the war. The program was designed to maintain and improve the inborn hereditary qualities of the German people through a program of breeding German women with the desired Nordic characteristics (eyes and hair color and other physical and mental qualities) to SS officers. Women were encouraged to "give a child to the führer," and women of all classes participated in the program. Fifteen Lebensborn homes were established, and through an ever-expanding program over 250,000 children were born. After a short stay in the Lebensborn home, the child was taken from the mother and adopted by a German family, and the mother returned to her previous occupation.[36]

The *Holocaust* refers to the six million Jewish victims of the "final solution" who were murdered in areas under German control during Nazi rule in Europe (approximately one-third of all Jews alive in the world at that time). The annihilation of Europe's Jews is intimately linked to the history of the SS. The Nazi party began its program of discrimination against Jews with the Nuremberg Laws of 1935; the SS then initiated the systematic persecution of Jews in 1938; and the "Final Solution," a plan to kill all Jews, was formulated at the Wannsee Conference in 1941. Restriction and emigration had only partially worked—genocide was the ultimate "solution." The exact date of the "Final Solution" has not been determined, but existing documentation using the concept is dated July 31, 1941 (letter from Hermann Göring to Reinhard Heydrich).[37] According to the Nazis, purification of German blood could be accomplished only by the extermination of Jews.

Experimentation and *euthanasia* were practiced on thousands of people in Germany who had mental or physical problems by physicians such as Dr. Joseph Mengele. Those who could serve in useful laboratory experiments were given the "opportunity" to forfeit their health and lives for the greater good. Those too old or ill to participate were simply killed by injection or gas.

The Volk   Hitler frequently spoke of the "folkish state" in *Mein Kampf* as a "living organism" whose highest purpose is the preservation of the German nation. Organism here implies the notion that Germany is a living, breathing entity with unique racial elements and that individual Germans will find meaning in their lives to the extent that they become one with the culture, creativity, beauty, and dignity of this jewel of the human race.[38] Ernst Huber, a theoretician of the Third Reich, further developed this important theme of German Naziism. Huber saw the people, the *Volk,* as determined by a number of characteristics—race, land, language, history, and consciousness—and the Reich as "people and state . . . conceived as an inseparable unity. . . . In the theory of the nationalistic (Völkish) Reich, people and state are conceived as an inseparable unity . . . the state does not form the people but the people mold the state out of itself. . . . The state is a function of the people."[39] In this doctrine, the "folkish state," or national community, is the supreme value and end, and individuals are only means, or instruments, by which the nation is glorified. The political corollary of this doctrine is an extreme nationalism that stands in opposition to international law and organization, equality of nations, and anything that separates and isolates Germans from each other. The German-American Bund of the 1930s is an excellent example of how this doctrine of blood and folk ties was employed to obtain external support for German policy. (Such groups existed in other countries as well.) Hitler called for "fanatical nationalism" in the struggle against democracy and communism, and believed that everything must be subordinated to the welfare of the "folkish state."

The Führer Principle and Elitism   The premise on which the führer principle and elitism rests is that since all value is derived from the Volk, and since individuals vary in the degree to which they mirror these Völkish qualities, then human equality is the greatest myth of all. Naziism denies as sheer nonsense the notion of fundamental, human equality and instead maintains that inequality and hierarchy prevail. The logic of this doctrine is that Germans (Aryan and Nordic types) are superior to non-Germans, men are superior to women, military men are higher than civilians, officers obviously stand higher and command enlisted men, and finally, an elite in the officer corps led by the führer, the absolute pinnacle of human perfection, must prevail over all. Naziism is, as noted, explicitly anti-feminist. In national socialist thought, women are second-class citizens and have no role in political decision-making.

In Naziism, the führer is seen as infallible, a man endowed with mystical insights. If there is disagreement between the leader and the elite, then the leader's will must prevail, for only he is capable of acting for the general rather than individual welfare. In *The Mind of Adolf Hitler,* Walter Langer contends that the great bulk of German people viewed Hitler as a superman, a man of tremendous will power, vision, and energy, almost a god himself.[40] To support the führer was the SS. Recruited particularly from the upper classes, they were attracted by Himmler's elitist propaganda, the uniforms, and the fact that it was a secret, elitist society. To emphasize the elitist nature of the group, Himmler used the death's head ring, a dagger given to all officers, and, in addition, for the top 12 SS officers, membership in the Round Table at Wewelsburg Castle.[41]

Perhaps Ernst Huber's summary of the führer principle will suffice. Hitler is portrayed as the sole bearer of the people's will, a man who unites in himself the sovereign power of Germany, the only person in the nation with the right to exercise absolute, unlimited authority—authority unhindered by any checks or limits.[42]

Other Pillars of Nazi Doctrine

Irrationalism   One of the most significant traits of German national socialism is its irrationalism. Naziism openly rejects reason and logic in human affairs and instead embraces feeling, passion, sentiment, and the irrational. Hitler and the Nazis brought answers to Germans, not questions, and these new solutions to old vexing problems prompted massive book-burning incidents at some of Germany's great universities. Students and faculty alike participated in this exercise in anti-intellectualism and irrationality. In *Mein Kampf,* Hitler expresses time and again his distrust, bitterness, and aversion to the so-called intelligentsia who look down with "infinite condescension" on those without degrees. In fact, he contends, these collectors of certificates (degrees) are "empty-headed." Intellectuals burden young minds with "ballast" they will never use and should be teaching not abstractions but "will and determination" and physical sport.[43] To Hitler and the Nazis, revelation and intuition in human affairs are better guides to truth than mere reason, and scientific analysis can never give us the insights into life that are possible with sentiment and feeling. Emotionalism is important in life. At one part in *Mein Kampf,* Hitler engages in a lengthy explanation of *why* a passionate speaker will have more effect and transmit more truth to people than any writer. What counts is the emotional interaction between speaker and audience and the fullness of life and authentic communication the experience encourages.[44] Some analysts claim that Germans do not sharply distinguish between *Glaube* (faith) and *Aberglaube* (superstition), that witches and demons still play a part in the German psyche, and that symbols like the swastika represent a deep desire to believe and be a part of something.[45] Perhaps all this can be summarized in the charge to the Germans by the Nazis to seek Hitler not through their heads but through their hearts.

Totalitarianism   *Totalitarianism* refers to the *scope* of power exercised by a political regime. Hitler and the Nazis organized the Third Reich on a totalitarian basis. Government power was absolute and unlimited. It was absolute in the sense that power was in the hands of only a few people (the führer and the Nazi elite)—a system of centralized leadership. It was unlimited in that no individual rights existed, only duty to the ruling group. The goal of the Nazi totalitarian organization of society was to control all aspects of life. No boundaries separated politics from any other activity. Everything in Nazi Germany was politicized and controlled (education, religion, the economy, sport, and so on). In a pluralist society, mediating groups stand between the individual and the ruling regime. In a monist system, these groups are pulverized, and any that do exist are penetrated and dominated by the regime. (See Figure 6.1.) Hitler's Germany may be the best example of a monist and totalitarian state. In Nazi Germany, it was impossible to legally organize a labor union or political party without Nazi party approval. The acts of any person in Germany perceived by the Nazis as weakening their control brought harsh punishment. And the Gestapo, SS (elite guards), SA (storm troopers), SD (secret police), and civilian police were constantly alert to arrest and punish those who violated or appeared to violate the total control of the regime.

War and Violence   War is an ideal and violence a necessary corollary of Nazi doctrine. Hitler made the following comments on war and violence in speeches he delivered:

> If men wish to live, then they are forced to kill others . . . the stronger has the right before God to enforce his will. . . . Only force rules. . . . Only through struggle have states and the world become great . . . there is no humanitarianism but only an eternal struggle . . . [man is] the most brutal and most resolute creature on earth. . . . In the power of the sword lies the vital strength of a nation. . . . One is either the hammer or the anvil.[46]

The political consequences of such ideas are psychological brainwashing, mass murder, enslavement of inferiors, and experimentation. To Hitler and the Nazis, war brings out the highest tensions in people. War makes authentic people out of mere mortals. Politics is, by definition, disagreement and conflict—a struggle

145

carried out by human beings who themselves are "the most brutal" of all living things on earth. Given the doctrine of racial superiority and the dogma of war and violence, conflict extermination centers, and labor camps were not an anomaly but a rule and accepted with regularity in Germany between 1933 and 1945. Only through war and violence could the Nazi regime transcend "bourgeois modernity" and return to a mythical past where Germans lived in harmony and racial purity with one another. Perhaps one example of this violence and brutality may prove the point. On May 27, 1942, Reinhard Heydrich, a top SS officer, was assassinated in Lidice, Czechoslovakia, by partisans. In retaliation, the Germans arrested 10,000 people, executed 1,300 of them (including all males of Lidice), and the village was burned to the ground.[47]

German Nationalism Versus Communism and Democracy

According to Hitler, Germans embrace two Gods, "A God in Heaven and a God on earth and that is our Fatherland. [We Germans embrace] fanatical nationalism. . . . We want all 60 million people to say *not* 'I am a democrat,' but 'I am a German.'"[48] Throughout *Mein Kampf,* Hitler states his hatred of democracy with its "ridiculous institution" of parliament, and communism with the "loathsome" doctrines of class struggle created by "the Jew Karl Marx." Everything that democracy stands for—political equality, freedom, and popular control of

GERMAN NATIONAL SOCIALISM 1933-1945

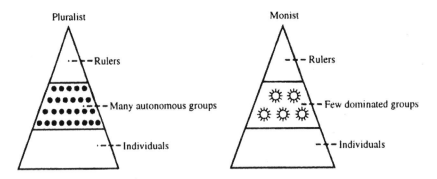

Figure 6.1 Pluralist versus monist societies.

government—was anathema to Hitler and the Nazis. These institutions are designed to maximize individual potential, while national socialist doctrine is the cult of the group. As such, they stand in direct opposition to each other.

Hermann Göring, commander of the German air force, saw Germany as a bastion against communism. War with the "red terror" was viewed as inevitable as national socialism and Marxism are poles apart. Marxism's doctrines of class struggle, internationalism, public ownership of property, and atheism, if put into practice, would destroy Germany as a nation-state.

These then constitute the major doctrines of Naziism. Their effect on public policy and behavior in Germany remains a legacy of treachery and savagery unmatched in human history. Many instances of such conduct exist, two of which are discussed here.

Naziism in Practice: Power and Persecution

"The Night of the Long Knives"   Consider these lyrics from a Nazi song: "Sharpen the long knives on the sidewalks, so that they may cut the clergymen's bodies better. . . . When the hour of retribution strikes we will be ready for mass murder."[49] During "The Night of the Long Knives" (June 30–July 2, 1934), hundreds were shot, tortured, and beaten to death. It was a slaughter that grew out of the rivalry and feuding between the political and military elements within the Nazi party. The target was Ernst Röhm and the SA. The conspirators included Heinrich Himmler and Reinhard Heydrich of the SS, Hermann Göring, head of the Gestapo, Joseph Goebbels (propaganda minister), Generals Blomberg and Reichenau of the German army, and Adolf Hitler, the führer and Nazi party chief. The motives of the plotters differed, but they agreed on one point—the power of the SA, a military force of two to three million soldiers (the numbers vary in different sources) must be brought under party control and the top leadership executed. The SA had been created in 1921 to protect speakers, keep order, and break up rival political gatherings. They were the "strutting bully-boys" of the New Order.

When Hitler took power in January 1933, Röhm, a close friend of Hitler and a former World War I soldier, hoped to take over the smaller German army. Thus, the German army officer corps feared Röhm and the SA, as they saw them as challengers for the army's historic role as the sole bearer of arms in Germany. Himmler, Heydrich, and Göring, though opposed to each other, hated the SA because their groups, the SS and Gestapo, were much smaller. Finally, Hitler feared Röhm and the SA as untrustworthy and potential challenges to his per-

147

sonal power. But more than that, Hitler knew he could not get the full support of the German army until the rival SA army was brought under control.

Himmler, Göring, Goebbels, Heydrich, and Blomberg finally convinced Hitler that Röhm planned a putsch. The excuse for the bloodletting was established. On the night of June 30, 1934, Hitler, Himmler, and other members of the SS and Gestapo began the orgy of murder. Röhm was killed on July 1, and the entire top leadership of the SA was imprisoned, tortured, or murdered. The number of people who died during this savage three-day period may never be determined for certain; but the documentation available today suggests that between 500 and 1,000 people were killed.

The results of the event changed the political and military organization of Germany: the power of the SA was broken, and, though never technically eliminated, the bulk of the membership was drafted into the armed forces, while many others were switched into the SS; the German army gave its full support to Hitler; and the SS turned out to be the big winner in the struggle in that subsequently the SA and Gestapo came under its control.[50]

The Holocaust   As noted earlier, the Holocaust refers to the extermination of Europe's Jews by Hitler and the Nazis in which six million Jews were killed. Nazi policy regarding Jews had initially been one of forced emigration, but by the summer of 1941 the intensification of hostility to Jews had increased, and annihilation replaced expulsion. To the existing concentration camps (Bergen-Belsen, Buchenwald, Dachau, and others), located throughout German-controlled territory, six major extermination camps were established at Auschwitz, Chelmno, Treblinka, Sobibor, Maidanek, and Belzec.

In May 1941 Himmler created four *Einsatzgruppen* (mobile killing units) to follow the German troops as they moved into the Soviet Union. Their task was to find and kill Russia's five million Jews. In Kiev, which was captured in September 1941, the Einsatzgruppen marched 35,000 Jews to Babi Yar, a ravine in the city, and killed them in two days. By their own records, the SS Einsatzgruppen personnel had killed one-half million Jews by December.[51] But this system was not efficient enough. The creation of the death factories such as Auschwitz made the mass killing possible. Poland's Jewish population of 3 million in 1939 was reduced to 30,000 by 1945. At these extermination centers, trains arrived bringing Jews from all parts of Europe. Many were dead when they arrived, but those who survived the trip were forced to strip naked, give up all valuables, have their hair shaved, and march past an officer for inspection. A few were selected to work or fill a needed trade, but most went directly to the gas chambers. Auschwitz reached the goal of Nazi efficiency with chambers that would hold 2,000 people. The doors of the chamber were closed and the gas, Zyklon B, turned on. Within 30 minutes everyone in the chamber was dead. From here the corpses were buried in pits or cremated. Two and a half million Jews were killed at Auschwitz alone.

The SS and German bureaucrats ran the camps with impersonal efficiency, for only this behavior could psychologically make mass murder possible. The death factories were considered a new social system—a "society of total domination." The Nazis commanded the Jews to lie down in mass graves to be shot, used their slave labor at the execution center to produce products and make it operate efficiently,[52] and even participated in ghastly medical experiments conducted by "physicians" such as Dr. Mengele at Auschwitz.

The question arises, *why* was there a lack of resistance? Although some isolated acts of resistance and massive resistance occurred at Sobibor and at the Warsaw Ghetto, "the overwhelming majority of Jews did not resist. They had been conditioned by their religious culture to submit and endure . . . in addition to the cultural conditioning . . . the organized Jewish community was a major factor in preventing effective resistance . . . the Germans utilized the existing leadership and organizations of the Jewish community to assist them"[53] with registration, records, resettlement selection, supplies, police, and so on. The 2,000-year strategy of "submit and endure" failed in World War II, and the concept of "never again" has become the operating principle of the state of Israel. This because Hitler and the Nazis revealed a potential for brutality and inhumanity unsuspected in human beings—genocide conducted by the state in the name of racial purity.

CONCLUSIONS

Is fascism still a threat in the modern democratic state? We contend that it is a danger today and a growing menace in the developed countries of Europe, the United States, and Japan because of a number of conditions—racism and nationalism, population growth and movement,[54] weakening of democratic habits, party and media focus on personality and image rather than issues, and protracted frustration over the inability of government to democratically resolve protracted domestic and international problems. Consider the following:

In France the National Front of Jean-Marie Le Pen is openly hostile to Arab and African immigrants. Le Pen and his party want them expelled from France, and the French metropolitan electorate in significant numbers support his proposals. Working on the hatred of Arab immigrants and the anger with the unemployment rate, Le Pen's movement is slowly growing, recruiting new members from many groups including small farmers, small shopkeepers, and monarchists. In the 1998 election in France, the National Front made gains that portend a role in coalitions. In fact, in three of the twenty-two regions, it is now a part of government. The Front favors blood-purity tests for family allowances.[55] The National Front clearly draws its strength from four of the five conditions noted above. Then in the fall of 2005, thousands of Arabs participated in hundreds of violent protests against French policy and practices that discriminate and alienate them from society. France has a social problem that can no longer be ignored.

In Germany, Neo-Nazi and other right-wing extremists have initiated scores of hate crimes. Two groups have even won seats in state parliaments—the German Peoples Union and the Republicans. Gangs of Neo-Nazi "skinheads" regularly provoke violence and threats against foreigners in Germany. The recruitment in extreme right-wing organizations is climbing steadily as Germans are left jobless and confused by problems associated with unification. The German People's Union won 13% of the legislative seats in Saxony-Anhalt with a call to expel "foreign bandits" and stressing "German jobs for Germans." Violence also is rising with 790 right-wing attacks recorded last year.[56] Recently, youths shouting Nazi slogans attacked a gay street festival in Berlin, and teenagers with shaved heads held protests with signs saying, "No Bordello in Dresden." This group calls themselves the German National Resistance, and their special targets are about five million immigrants in Germany today. Most of these immigrants came as laborers, and social welfare for them costs the government about $2 billion a year. In the area that formerly constituted the state of East Germany, unemployment runs as high as 45 percent in some areas, causing anger and frustration with government.

Neo-Nazi Kay Diesner and other Neo-Nazis are behaving like the Werewolves in the Third Reich according to chief prosecutor Guenter Moeller.[57] Black-shirted Neo-Nazis by the score were arrested by police in Germany on the 10th anniversary of the death of Rudolf Hess—a cult figure among Nazi youth in Germany and in Europe in August of 1997. Again, the conditions of racism, protracted economic problems, and population movements can be associated with right-wing extremism.

Elsewhere in Europe, new right-wing parties have also emerged in Britain, Belgium, and Holland. According to *The Independent* of London, British right-wing extremists are now forging close ties with Neo-Nazi groups in Germany— contacts some reports characterize as "intensive." The collapse of communism in the East has "unleashed forces of nationalism and ethnicity contained for the last 45 years by the exigencies of the Cold War." In Austria, the anti-immigrant party of Jorg Haider, The Freedom Party, has forged a coalition with the center-right Peoples's Party. The two parties will have a 104-seat controlling majority in the 183-member Parliament. Haider is a charismatic, right-winger who refers to concentration camps as "punishment" camps and praises veterans of the Waffen SS as "decent people of character." In Belgium, the Flemish separatist party, Vlaams Blok, pursues the same racist, anti-immigration agenda as the Austrian Freedom Party. In Norway the Progress Party, which fights immigrants and asylum seekers, has become the third largest party in the nation. In Switzerland, the voters made the anti-immigrant Swiss People's Party the second largest in that country.[58] The extreme right is alive and well in Europe today and growing in size daily.

In the United States, Neo-Nazi appeal is growing throughout the country. Three major types of hate groups are "operating in Ohio—white supremacists; so-called Christian conservatives such as the Covenant, The Sword and the Arm of the Lord, and the Identity churches; and patriot-survivalists groups." The intelligence Report published by the Southern Poverty Law Center of Montgomery, Alabama, lists Ohio as having twenty-four hate groups operating in the state—trailing only Alabama, Florida and California in the number of white-supremacist and watchdog groups.[59] In Alabama, white supremacists in Birmingham rallied in support of skinheads charged with killing a black man. These skinheads are youths who believe white culture is threatened by nonwhite immigrants, and as such they are viscerally anti-black and anti-Semitic. These groups thrive in many other places—the Patriots party in Florida; the Order, a splinter group of the Aryan Nation, in Idaho; the White Resistance in California; and the Aryan Nations and the Christian Identity Movement in Washington and Idaho. All openly support racist policy and exacerbate white-nonwhite tensions.[60] In 1983, a group of white supremacists with ties to the Neo-Nazi group Aryan Nation drew up a plan to bomb the same Oklahoma City federal building . . . (that) Timothy McVeigh, the prime suspect in the Oklahoma City blast, was later convicted of destroying. In the United States, especially in the event of another terrorist atrocity, fascism might well gain support. Remember: the recent scorn of traditional allies and of the United Nations; the claim of some that America is a "Christian nation;" the caricature of the "decadent liberal" without national loyalty, atheistic, and lodged in a position of cultural power in the academy, pro-choice, and pro-gay marriage. These demons survive "below the radar" in America.[61]

Japan has a history of racism, and a growing rightist minority is demanding that Japan assert its interests more aggressively. In the 1930s Japanese troops in a bloody sweep through China slaughtered over 200,000 civilians in what is known as the "Rape of Nanking." In addition, Korean women were forced to act as prostitutes (called comfort women) for Japanese soldiers during World War II. Unlike Germany, which has made an effort to "cleanse" itself of Naziism and accepted responsibility for the war, Japan has never accepted responsibility. Instead, the Japanese tend to see themselves as victims rather than the initiators of the war.[62] In addition, ultranationalist leaders in Japan argue that Japan was forced into war because it "had to rid Asia of white-skinned devils." The Yasukuni Shrine is Japan's national war memorial dedicated to those who died fighting for the Japanese Empire including the 1.7 million soldiers who died in the Pacific War and the 920 convicted of war crimes and executed. Some time ago, a group of 150 members of parliament and eight Cabinet members from both ruling and opposition visited the war shrine and signal the rising influence of right-wing and conservative forces in Japanese politics. And very recently, moviegoers thronged to see Pride, the Fateful Moment, about the life of Tojo—the wartime prime minister.[63] Today in Japan, the corporate culture is clothed in racism and sexism. To Americans, "Japanese businesses function in a blatantly racist and sexist manner."[64] An American who worked in Japan for 15 years in two different securities firms was told, "Don't hire blacks . . . ," and he was directed not to hire Jews.[65] This last admonition seems rather unwarranted since "there are only 150 Jewish families in Japan."[66] The latest wave of anti-Semitism hit Japan in the late 1980s. "Masaaki Nakayama, then Japan's Posts and Telecommunications minister [said], The Jews own all the 'seven sisters.' They control agriculture in America and the international precious metals market. Both George Bush and Michael Dukakis are related to Jews."[67]

In July of 1999, Japan's powerful Lower House passed a Bill to establish a task force to review the post war Constitution—the idea being to strike out the no-war provision. This seems ominous in light of the fact that Japan has emerged as the country that has the second largest military expenditure in the world, led only by the United States.[68]

The heart of the problem in Japan is its homogeneous and insular society—a patriarchal society clothed in the garments of Confucianism. By and large, the Japanese simply believe that a multiracial society is inferior to one with racial and blood purity. Given a racist and ultranationalist perspective, relatively young democratic institutions, a background of virtual worship of the emperor, and new economic problems, the rise of ultra-right individuals and groups in Japan bears careful watching.

The ideology of fascism is not dead—it only lies dormant, waiting for the right social conditions and demagogue to express the discontent. "The soil of modern society, including American society, has been fertilized for fascist seedlings. Fascism is a revenge history takes on an age of mindless moral relativism."[69]

NOTES

1. Ernst Nolte, *Three Faces of Fascism* (New York: Holt, Rinehart & Winston, 1966), pp. 10–14.

2. George H. Sabine, *A History of Political Theory* (New York: Holt, Rinehart & Winston, 1937), p. 905.

3. Fascism in Action (Washington, D.C.: U.S. Government Printing Office, 1947), p. 5.

4. Sabine, *A History of Political Theory,* pp. 884–887.

5. *A Short History of Italy,* edited by H. Hearder and D. P. Waley (London: Cambridge University Press, 1963), pp. 121–140.

6. Ibid., pp. 141–156.

7. Ibid., pp. 157–170.

8. Ibid., pp. 192–196.

9. Alan Cassels, *Fascist Italy* (New York: Crowell, 1968), pp. 15–52.

10. Benito Mussolini, "The Political and Social Doctrine of Fascism, 1932," in *Varieties of Fascism,* edited by Eugene Weber (New York: Van Nostrand, 1964), p. 151.

11. Alfredo Rocco and Mario Palmieri comment on the concept of the state in their essays included in *Communism, Fascism and Democ-*

racy, edited by Carl Cohen (New York: Random House, 1962), pp. 342–343, 377–379.

12. Ibid., p. 377 (Palmieri).

13. "The Fascist Decalogue," in Cohen's *Communism, Fascism and Democracy,* p. 392.

14. Giovanni Gentile, "The Philosophic Basis of Fascism," in *Readings on Fascism and National Socialism,* selected by members of the Department of Philosophy, University of Colorado (Chicago: Swallow Press, 1952), p. 58.

15. Alfredo Rocco, "The Political Doctrine of Fascism," *Readings on Fascism and National Socialism,* p. 27.

16. Benito Mussolini, "The Political and Social Doctrine of Fascism, 1932," *Varieties of Fascism,* pp. 149, 150.

17. Palmieri in Cohen's *Communism, Fascism and Democracy,* p. 375.

18. Ibid., p. 371.

19. Giovanni Gentile, "The Philosophic Basis of Fascism," p. 58.

20. Mussolini, "The Doctrine of Fascism," in Cohen's *Communism, Fascism and Democracy,* pp. 349–357.

21. William A. Smith, Jr., *Twentieth Century Fascism* (New York: Monarch Press, 1965), pp. 65–67.

22. *Facts about Germany,* edited by H. D. Bulka and S. Lücking (Bertelsmann Lexikothek Verlag, 1985), pp. 10, 16, 21, 163. See also "Germany: Country and People" (Bonn, Germany: Press and Information Office of the Federal Government, 1991), p. 5. Translation: Kathleen Müller-Rostin.

23. George Bailey, *Germans* (New York: Avon Books, 1972). See especially Chapters 1–6, 16, 19.

24. *Facts About Germany,* pp. 46–49.

25. C. Briton, J. Christopher, R. Wolff, *Modern Civilization* (Englewood Cliffs, N.J.: Prentice-Hall, 1967), p. 661.

26. Adolf Hitler, *Mein Kampf* (New York: Reynal & Hitchcock, 1941), p. 29.

27. Ibid., see pp. 74–84.

28. Ibid., p. 163.

29. Albert Speer, *Spandau: The Secret Diaries* (New York: Macmillan, 1976), p. 426.

30. Walter C. Langer, *The Mind of Adolf Hitler* (New York: Basic Books, 1972). See Parts II and V.

31. Herman Mau and Helmut Krausnick, *German History, 1933–45* (London: Oswald Wolff Publishers, 1959). See Chapters 2, 3, 5, 6.

32. James P. O'Donnell, *The Bunker* (New York: Bantam Books, 1978). See Chapters 1, 5, 8.

33. Hitler, *Mein Kampf,* p. 406.

34. Ibid., see Chapter 11, pp. 392–405 and 412–456 for Hitler's vicious diatribe against Jews.

35. Alfred Rosenberg in Cohen's *Communism, Fascism and Democracy,* pp. 398–399.

36. *Of Pure Blood,* a film prepared by C. Henry and M. Hillel (PBS-TV).

37. Heinz Höhne, *The Order of the Death's Head* (New York: Ballantine Books, 1971), p. 400. (Pp. 368, 391 also relevant.)

38. Hitler, *Mein Kampf,* p. 595.

39. Ernst R. Huber, in Cohen's *Communism, Fascism and Democracy,* pp. 400, 401.

40. Langer, *The Mind of Adolf Hitler,* Part II.

41. Höhne, *The Order of the Death's Head,* pp. 151–176.

42. Huber, cited in Cohen, pp. 400–401.

43. Hitler, *Mein Kampf,* pp. 30, 301, 615, 626, 704.

44. Ibid.

45. Bailey, *German,* pp. 348–350.

46. Hitler, cited in Cohen's *Communism, Fascism and Democracy,* pp. 405–410.

47. Höhne, *The Order of the Death's Head,* p. 560.

48. Hitler, cited in Cohen's, *Communism, Fascism and Democracy,* p. 411.

49. David Lewis, "The Night of the Long Knives," *International History Magazine* (Switzerland: John Pournaras Publisher, 1973), p. 23.

50. See the following for excellent reviews of "The Night of the Long Knives,": Höhne, *The Order of the Death's Head,* Chapter 6; "The Night of the Long Knives," a PBS documentary aired on January 25, 1983 in Dayton, Ohio; Lewis's article, "The Night of the Long Knives," *International History,* pp. 22–35.

51. Höhne, *The Order of the Death's Head,* p. 407; and Meltzer, *Never to Forget,* p. 81.

52. Richard L. Rubenstein, *The Cunning of History* (New York: Harper & Row, 1975). See Chapter 3.

53. Ibid., p. 72.

54. Flora Lewis, "We Are Five Billion Now and Growing," *Dayton Daily News and Journal Herald,* May 29, 1987, p. 10.

55. R. W. Johnson, "Pig Le Pen," *The New Republic,* May 23, 1988, pp. 18–20 and Elaine Ganley, "French far-right hits boycott," *Dayton Daily News,* June 22, 1995, p. 6-A. See also, *The Guardian* (London), February 15, 2000, p. 20.

56. "Neo-Nazi Violence Rising in Germany," *New York Times,* June 21, 1992, p. A-19. Also—Paul Geitner, "Campaign Focuses on Immigrants," *Dayton Daily News,* July 10, 1998, p. 16-A.

57. John Tagliabue, "On the Dresden Scene," *New York Times,* June 13, 1991, p. A-9; S. Kinzer, "A Wave of Attacks on Foreigners Stirs Shock in Germany," *New York Times,* October 1, 1991, pp. A-I and A-6; "Rowdies Besiege Refugees," *Dayton Daily News,* August 25, 1992, p. 4-A. Louis Salome, "Germans still feel divisions," *Dayton Daily News,* October 2, 1994, p. 14-A. Paul Geitner, "Neo-Nazi Trial May Backfire," *Dayton Daily News,* August 8, 1997, p. 13-A.

58. A. Alexander, "Ethnic Hatred across Europe High," *Dayton Daily News,* September 16, 1991, p. 1. Associated Press, "London Neo-Nazis Spark Disturbance," *Honolulu Star-Bulletin,* January 16, 1994, P. A-24. Richard W. Stevenson, "Racial Tensions in London as Neo-Nazi Wins Election," *New York Times,* September 19, 1993, p. 8. Associated Press, "Italians turn anger on aliens," *Dayton Daily News,* January 6, 1995, p. 8-A. *The Guardian* (London), February 15, 2000, p. 20. Gwynne Dyer, "Europe: Here We go Again?", *Dayton Daily News,* November 9, 1999, p. 7-A.

59. A. E. Scruggs, "Be Aware of Hate Crimes, Police Told," *Dayton Daily News,* August 8, 1991, pp. 12–13. See also, *Dayton Daily News,* April 2, 2000, p. 1-L.

60. *Dayton Daily News,* June 14, 1992, p. 2; "Families Urge Fugitives to End Idaho Standoff," *Dayton Daily News,* August 27, 1992, p. 8-A.

61. Nate Charlow, "Traces of Fascism in the American System," *Daily Nebraskan.* Source: University of Nebraska, Lincoln, NE, Feb. 28, 2005, p. 12.

62. Steven R. Weisman, "Pearl Harbor in the Mind of Japan," *New York Times Magazine,* November 3, 1991, pp. 31–32, 46. See also Robert P. Maddox, *The United States and World War II* (San Francisco: Westview Press, 1992), p. 50.

63. Ibid., p. 47. [For more on this topic see Edwin O. Reischauer, *The Japanese* (Cambridge, Mass.: Harvard University Press, 1981), pp. 204–212 and especially pp. 411–413.] See also, Kwan Weng Kin, "Japan War Shrine," The Strsits, Times (Singapore), April 25, 1997, p. 32. "Japan Cabinet visits Shrine to war dead," *Star Tribune* (Minneapolis MN), August 16, 1998, p. 28-A; Michasl Boxall, "Embracing Defeat," *The Vancouver Sun,* August 14, 1999, p. F-7.

64. James G. Driscoll, "Ugly Practices of Racism, Sexism Stain Japanese Corporate Culture," *Dayton Daily News,* October 21, 1991, p. 11A.

65. Ibid.

66. Willy May Stern, "David and Godzilla," *The New Republic,* February 27, 1989, p. 17.

67. Ibid.

68. Is Japan Moving Towards Militarism? *The Statesman* (India), September 6, 1999, p. 6.

69. George F. Will, "Fascisms Second Spring," *Newsweek,* May 2, 1994, p. 72.

SUGGESTED READINGS

Bailey, George. *Germans.* New York: Avon Books, 1972.
Cassels, Alan. *Fascist Italy.* New York: Crowell, 1968.
Hearder, H., and D. P. Waley. *A Short History of Italy.* London: Cambridge University Press, 1963.
Höhne, Heinz. *The Order of the Death's Head.* New York: Ballantine Books, 1977.

Shirer, William L. *The Rise and Fall of the Third Reich.* New York: Simon & Schuster, 1960.

Speer, Albert. *Inside the Third Reich.* New York: Avon Books, 1971.

Chapter 7

Anarchism

"Property is theft."[1]

Pierre-Joseph Proudhon

"If I can't dance, I don't want to be part of your revolution."[2]

Emma Goldman

"The anarchists are simply unterrified Jeffersonian democrats."[3]

Benjamin R. Tucker

W hen you think of an "anarchist," what comes to mind? For much of the last century, the average American conjured up the image of a fanatical, bearded bomb thrower or deranged assassin. By the turn of this century, the anarchist stereotype had morphed into young, black-clad hooligans smashing up Starbucks and McDonalds, looking for a fight with police, and seeking the violent overthrow of all social order. Yet, despite its bad press, anarchism has also been called the most idealistic of the political philosophies coming out of the Enlightenment. It is certainly a protest doctrine and one of the most complicated and contradictory ideologies we will study. In part, this is because there is no single anarchism but several anarchisms, both left and right-wing, and while most variants clearly share some key goals and assumptions, as a body of political thought anarchism is extremely diverse. Perhaps this is because anarchism itself has undergone several incarnations and has continually reemerged in new guises at different times and in different countries.[4] Some of these variants are directly at odds with each other; they have different emphases and can even be located on opposite ends of the political spectrum—yet they still share the name "anarchism."

That activists situated at so many different points across the political spectrum should claim the name anarchism is itself rather intriguing, because in the United States, the only ideology that carries more negative connotations than anarchism is communism—and the former is arguably even more misunderstood than the latter. Like communism, democratic socialism, and even liberalism, anarchism is a change-oriented ideology. However, while sharing some of the same ultimate goals of the other left-wing worldviews, anarchism offers a distinctly alternative account of historical change—and a dramatically different approach in terms of how to get there. For example, anarchism shares liberalism's insistence on individualism and the protection of natural rights. Yet, anarchism parts company with liberalism over how to get there—so much so that anarchism (of the left or right-wing varieties) has been called "liberalism on steroids."[5]

So, what is anarchism? Rooted in the word "anarchy," which comes from the Greek *anarkhia*, anarchism means "contrary to authority" or "without a ruler." Although many people write off anarchism, believing that the elimination of the state or government will only result in chaos, most anarchists do not call for disorder, chaos, or no administration at all. Rather, they believe that left to their own devices, humans will govern themselves appropriately. They reject conservative arguments that religious and governmental authority is crucial in reigning in negative human impulses. They reject the view that humans need to be led. Rather, according to anarchists, it is the state that creates disorder. From the anarchists' perspective, whether it is "bourgeois democratic" or communist, government (i.e.: the state) tends to be tyrannical and unjust. As far as anarchists are concerned, government is a mechanism by which the minority imposes its will on the majority.[6] Yet, as we will see later in this chapter, proponents of this view do believe that some administration of human relationships is necessary, albeit through a restructured society. The point is, though, that for anarchists, there's a world of difference between government and society. They agree (partly) with Thomas Paine's dictum that society is a blessing, but government, even at its best, is only a necessary evil. At its worst, it is intolerable.[7]

This is one point upon which the left and right-wing variants of the ideology agree. "Question Authority" may be their mantra, but beyond this, anarchists are a diverse lot. They may be religious or atheist, socialist or capitalist, advocates of violent revolution or of civil disobedience. For clarity's sake, much of what we will describe in this section pertains to the majority of anarchist thought, which is marked by a number of divides but is more collectivist and is located on the left side of the political spectrum. As mentioned earlier, anarchy has its right wing, too. However, because it diverges in important ways from the other schools of this ideology, we will restrict our discussion of right-wing anarchism (also known as libertarian anarchism, individualist anarchism, or anarcho-capitalism) to the discussion of conservatism in chapter five.[i]

A SHORT HISTORY OF ANARCHISM

Many of the ideas we today associate with anarchism have been around for a long time. These ideas very likely spurred rebellions as varied as the slave revolts of the Roman Empire and peasant uprisings of Middle Ages, Guy Fawkes' "Gunpowder Plot" to blow up the British parliament in 1605, not to mention the French, Mexican, Russian, and Spanish Revolutions. Still, as a label describing a political movement (or a self-conscious ideology) anarchism usually dates back only to the 1840s. There were certainly people setting out what would become the basic ideas and central tenets of this ideology long before the mid-19th century, although they did not call themselves anarchists. For example, after the French Revolution, a growing number of people had begun to articulate their concerns about the excesses of capitalism associated with the Industrial Revolution. They were particularly alarmed by the growing power of government and the long arm of the law, in the form of restrictions, regulations, and orders.[8]

For setting out his case against government, law and property, the British philosopher William Godwin (1756–1836) is widely considered the father of modern anarchism. Partner of the early liberal feminist Mary Wollstonecraft and father of *Frankenstein* author Mary Shelley, Godwin built on English and Protestant traditions of radical nonconformity to advocate much of what would today be called anarchism. His *Enquiry Concerning Political Justice* (1793) decried the overbearing presence of government and proposed a return to the Puritan ideals of community, decentralization of power, and self-sufficiency. For example, Godwin advocated a form of direct democracy, something he called "face to face democracy," in which individuals took a much more active role in making the decisions which governed their lives. Such views were widely considered laughable at the time, yet Godwin's work later became an underground classic, informing anarchists of the late 19th century and today.[9]

[i]Although they are very similar, some analysts do make distinctions even between these groups on the right.

Another of anarchism's founding fathers (and the first to actually refer to this growing body of thought by the name "anarchism") is Pierre-Joseph Proudhon (1809–1865). Echoing Godwin and adding that property is as oppressive as government, Proudhon famously coined the phrase "Property is theft." Yet, take this statement with a grain of salt—Proudhon did not veer as far left as one might expect, since like Locke and the classical liberals, he also allowed that property is freedom. He would argue that such sentiments are not contradictory. Sure, for Proudhon, property is theft, but he did not oppose all ownership. He wasn't talking about taking what most of us consider our personal possessions. When characterizing property as theft, he was speaking of the landowners and capitalists whose ownership of productive property (like factories and large farms) was unearned, based in conquest and exploitation. For Proudhon, this is very different from property as freedom (in which case he was speaking of peasants and artisans whom he argued had natural right to a home, to land and tools), since these basics are necessary to work and maintain a family. In other words, property is important for personal autonomy as long as it does not involve owning or controlling the livelihoods of others. However, property is theft when a small minority is living off the unpaid wages of the majority.[10]

Before going any further, it should be said that while Proudhon and Godwin are cited as providing the intellectual foundation for left-wing anarchism, the reaction to the unjust misery created by capitalism and the call for a more humane social and economic order has come from other corners as well. Yes, this concern is expressed in liberal and leftish Western ideologies; however, it is also found in non-Western traditions, ranging from Taoism and Buddhism in the East to the indigenous roots of Mexico's Zapatista rebel movement. What these varied traditions share is their rejection of hierarchies and external authority and an emphasis on consensus finding and bottom-up organization that values solidarity without stifling dissent. Western or non-Western, left-wing anarchists agree on another point: capitalism only survives because the majority of us mistakenly believe that there is no alternative to it. The capitalists have done an extraordinary job of convincing us that theirs is the only way. What anarchists must do is show us that there is an alternative and that it is in our capacity to make it happen.[11] As we will see later in this chapter, contemporary anarchists are trying to do just this. These anarchists would probably be the first to admit that their message has not yet gained wide acceptance. But their campaign against corporate globalization and calls an alternative or "authentic globalization"—one which borrows from a variety of traditions, takes a bottom-up approach, and recognizes the importance of both global alliances and local resistance—is a view that is beginning to draw more attention. They predict that people will be looking for another way, particularly as the ugliness of corporate globalization becomes harder and harder to ignore.[12]

ANARCHISM'S FIRST PRINCIPLES

Whether their source is Godwin, Proudhon or Subcommandante Marcos,[ii] what most anarchists share is a belief that 1) freedom is inviolable, and 2) the state seeks to destroy freedom and must therefore (in one way or another) be eliminated. As the paramount value for anarchists, freedom is defined as the ability of individuals and communities to control their destinies as much as possible. In their pursuit of personal liberty, anarchists claim to celebrate the purest expression of individualism. Like liberals, anarchists maintain that humans are born free, with inalienable rights. Yet, all states are constantly infringing on these freedoms—even democracies. Anarchists believe that this practice has been around since well before Godwin warned about it, and has only accelerated in recent years, as the US had led and other countries followed a declared "global war on terror" in which the state reserves the right to impinge on our most fundamental civil rights and liberties. For example, since 9/11 the US government has given itself the right to invade the privacy of its citizens, to "sneak and peek" around their homes, their financial and medical records—even their library records—without a warrant or even notifying the individual that s/he is under surveillance. Similarly, due process is hardly what it used to be in the US, because now any individual (including an American citizen) can be detained and held indefinitely by the government without charge.

But these are only the latest abuses. According to anarchists, under bourgeois democracy, government has long served the interests of the ruling class (it is bourgeois because the government is owned by the rich—the "democracy" part only seeks to cloak that relationship). One glance at voter turnout in the US provides ample evidence of widespread citizen apathy and dissatisfaction. The average American doesn't bother to vote because s/he knows that power is unaccountable—even in democracies. It's a vicious cycle that those in power are happy to perpetuate: people are encouraged to be apathetic because apathy makes them passive. They are apathetic because they don't believe that they can do anything to change things.[13] Money rules. Even the average citizen knows that one has to be a millionaire (or have the backing of millionaires) to run a

---

[ii]Leader of Mexico's Zapatistas.

successful political campaign at the state or national levels, and consequently there is a huge gulf between our "representatives" and the people they "represent." Yet, governments claim "a mandate" to pursue unpopular policies when they are elected with far less than 50% of the eligible vote.

It can't be surprising, then, that anarchists characterize democracy as a sham. However, instead of seeking to destroy it, contemporary anarchists seek to reinvent democracy, to create new forms of organization based in horizontal, non-hierarchical or decentralized networks—rather than top-down structures (like political parties) that they characterize as inevitably coercive and corrupting. Because they believe that authority is by nature corrupt and decadent, anarchists agree that no one is fit to rule anyone else.[14] But what anarchists say they want is a purer democracy, an ordered society without government. Whereas many people doubt that order can exist and our freedoms be protected without states or government, anarchists maintain the opposite and argue that what they stand for is the rights of the individual *against* such coercive institutions. The state (or government), organized religion, and corporations, along with their laws, courts and even educational systems actually destroy freedom.[iii] Whether it is organized religion or the schools, around the world these institutions work at controlling individuality and promoting conformity: they maintain order and defend a variety of unequal property arrangements by socializing citizens to be passive and to obey. Moreover, the state claims rights against us as a sovereign ruler. It makes the seemingly-natural claim on our allegiance by embedding itself in the concept of the nation (and playing on our "patriotism" it manipu-

[iii]Although some anarchists allow that religious faith can provide some refuge from capitalism, they argue that the expression of that faith should be a private matter. Most anarchists view organized religion (particularly religious fundamentalisms) as an anathema to freedom. According to anarchists, not only is most organized religion hierarchical and authoritarian, it tends to serve the interests of the powerful. Like bourgeois democracy it is a prop for the status quo as it encourages passive obedience.

However, Christian anarchists contend that authoritarianism, passive obedience to governmental authority, and intolerance are not traditional to their faith. They instead tend to gravitate to Liberation Theology, which renounces both property and the state. Originally conceived by radical Catholics (but also adopted by some Protestants, notably in South Africa), Liberation Theology embraces a version of Christianity that is based on the (some say anarchist) ethics Jesus taught and is therefore inclusive, egalitarian, and activist (see Louise Tierney, "Thinking about Anarchism: Anarchists and Religion," Workers Solidarity Movement, 1995, *www.flag.blackened.net*; Max Skidmore, *Ideologies: Politics in Action* (Orlando: Harcourt, Brace, Jovanovich, 1993); Leon P. Baradat, *Political Ideologies, Their Origins and Impact* (Englewood Cliffs, NJ: Prentice Hall, 1994).

lates us with fears of foreign enemies). But make no mistake—our sense of nationhood is just another tool of mass oppression. The state registers us, taxes us, assesses, licenses and authorizes us—all the while working to benefit the few at the expense of the many.[15]

But don't jump to conclusions too fast. Yes, this sounds a lot like Marx's description of the state as superstructure. However, although they agree on this point, anarchists oppose state communism. A leading anarchist philosopher, Michael Bakunin (1814–1876) early on disputed Marx's assumption that the state would wither away and predicted that the communist experiments of the 20th century would result in dictatorship. Bakunin forecast that the new class of political elites created by communist revolutions would actually reestablish state power to betray peasants and workers to become the new ruling class. It could be argued that he was right; in every revolution of the last one hundred years, the result has been (in some fundamental ways, at least) largely a change of window-dressing. Under the resulting "despotism of the revolutionaries," the communist party has again and again expected to be trusted to make the rules for everyone else. This has greatly disappointed many on the left, as whether in the Soviet Union, China, or Cuba, once in power the communists' actions have mirrored those of capitalist states. The repression of dissidents and protection of elite (party) privilege are just two examples of this misrule.[16]

Therefore, most anarchists oppose not only government (capitalist or communist), but also present systems of ownership, which deprive the majority of the fruits of their labor and are associated with internalized forms of dominance such as patriarchy, racism, and homophobia.[iv] Instead of government, Godwin called for a "community without rules," predicting that once people are truly free, with the basic right to have control over their own lives, these forms of injustice and inequality will disappear. When humans can be involved in the decisions that affect them, they'll challenge the order-givers and take control over their own struggle—all the while voluntarily conducting themselves with mutual respect and compassion. Thus, the end of government will lead not to disorder; rather, it is only through self-imposed moral rules that authentic freedom will be known. The apathy that is so pervasive under our current system will dissipate; as people become more involved in making their own decisions, their confidence in the possibility of changing things for the better will grow.[17]

[iv] Incidentally, anarchists are just as likely to talk about "order-givers" and "order-takers" as they are the rich and poor, noting that the farther down you are on the socioeconomic ladder, the less control you have over your life.

Anarchists on Human Nature

Like many other leading voices of his time, Godwin adhered to a universal view of human nature and morality. He (and most anarchists) assumed that humans are by nature rational, reasonable beings. We therefore can (and should) eliminate laws and courts because (contrary to the conservative view) these institutions do not represent the wisdom of prevailing generations. Rather, as Godwin put it, laws, courts, and similar institutions represent the interests of a few and the passions of their time. Humans, being fundamentally rational and capable of genuinely disinterested benevolence, should be left instead to follow their impulses. We do not need laws or institutions, and once humans live in a system that allows them to abide by their natural inclinations, we will see that we don't need government as we know it, either.[18]

According to anarchist and naturalist Petr Kropotkin (1842–1921), the law of nature (or human nature) is based in cooperation. Disputing Social Darwinists, he argued that human success is due to cooperative, not competitive instincts. The core impulses commonly identified by Kropotkin and other anarchists as universal to humankind are solidarity, mutual support, sympathy, and concern for others. This view has been taken up by contemporary anarchists who argue that we are capable of being governed by moral rules alone—and without need of government for enforcement. In effect, the good life is one free from government.[19] Anarchists disagree heartily with conservatives who argue that humans need the threat of punishment to compel obedience—without it, humankind will return to a dog-eat-dog, chaotic world. Rather, anarchists contend that when humans perceive the rules as just, working in the interests of all, our instinct is to fulfill our duties and to work cooperatively. If you don't believe it, consider the fact that although we hear a lot everyday about those who break such rules, the vast majority of us obey them and live cooperatively without even thinking about it.[20]

Because human nature is essentially peace-loving and cooperative, moral and rational, humans left to their own devices will not result in harm to society, or the atavistic "law of the jungle" that the right predicts. Anarchists know that people sometimes do bad things. Sure, anti-social behaviors and biased, exploitative societies currently exist, but they do so largely because existing institutions subdue our natural human impulses. Governments divide people; they turn class against class and country against country. No doubt, the world is a mess. Capitalism teaches that those at the top (and the bottom) somehow deserve what they get; yet inequality is not natural and inevitable. Nor is the present corruption of human nature fixed or immutable. It is largely governed by our current way of living and will eventually change once our way of living changes. In other words, anarchists believe that once dehumanizing, corrupting, hierarchical institutions are removed and this natural impulse for cooperation and the mutual good is no longer subdued, a self-imposed harmony—in which all will benefit equally and none will suffer—will be the norm. The revolution they call for will give us the space to create the kind of lives for ourselves that will allow our true humanity to shine through.[21]

This isn't just pie in the sky for anarchists. Fed up with the abuses of both capitalism and state communism, anarchists argue that the time for change has come. From their point of view, it is long overdue, as government has clearly become an impediment to progress, and humans have outgrown whatever need they might ever have had for it. Without government, anarchists are highly optimistic about the potential for progress and predict that society will grow, change, and evolve to meet human needs. Yet, how do we get there from here? It won't be easy; the anarchists' preferred world begins with the removal all limits and restraints on human conduct.[22]

Anarchism and the State

Not surprisingly, competing ideologies deem such a model to be impracticable. Consequently, the anarchists' most insurmountable obstacle is the tendency to discount the anarchist utopia as a real political and social possibility. Yet, anarchists maintain that the stateless societies they speak of are not only possible but were the norm until about 10,000 years ago. Such societies were part of larger federations of self-sufficient and self-governing, highly decentralized communities. Anarchists point to the long span of human history to remind us that the modern nation-state is a relatively recent form of socio-political organization. For millions of years communities did without it. Based in cooperation, small, voluntary, self-regulating communities performed all the functions of states and bureaucracies—and much more humanely. During much of human history, the alienation, lawlessness, and sense of powerlessness (so common in modern state societies) were relatively unknown.[23] It hasn't always been this way, and for these reasons anarchists know that it doesn't have to be this way.

All ancient history, you say? Anarchists answer with contemporary examples of the anarchist model at work. Anarchist experiments in social organization thrived in parts of Spain during the 1930s, and anarchists point to a number of other examples of their ideas in action today. The spirit of voluntary cooperation without government involvement still exists in organizations such as voluntary associations, cooperatives, and even one of the oldest of non-governmental organizations, the Red Cross.[24] Although the potential for spontaneous cooperation based on a common need or interest has been largely stifled and repressed by states and other agents, it exists as a real alternative to the globalized, corporate capitalism of today. Humans have developed multiple patterns of socially beneficial self-help organization without the state. The evidence for this—in the form of sports clubs, babysitting networks, trade unions, professional associations and the like—is all around us. And there's room for more, as the potential for mutual aid lies barely beneath the surface of everyday life.[25]

Anarchists and Economic Organization

Anarchists seek to encourage the development of such human relationships by removing the obstacles to cooperation and by promoting direct democracy. They foresee a world comprised of autonomous and self-governing associations—an alternative form of governance which is based on non-exploitative rules and which values social solidarity above all else. Although they disagree on the fine points of how this would actually work, anarchists do often speak of some of the same guiding general principles, such as federations of voluntary associations of workers (or "producing units"), common ownership of the means of production, and banks which make credit available with no interest.

The most well-known example of an alternative, non-capitalist method of agricultural and industrial production is the cooperative. Based in the West on the medieval craft guilds, cooperatives have existed in different parts of the world throughout history to bring together people with common needs, skills, and interests to pool their resources and work cooperatively within a common framework. Cooperatives (or "co-ops") are a great example of the practice of mutual aid associated with a grassroots-based or bottom-up globalization. They are collectively owned, and the owners share responsibility in running the co-ops to achieve their common aims. Hundreds of thousands of people worldwide choose to organize their enterprises this way, and co-ops are found in virtually any area of human activity.[26]

Many anarchists also advocate the idea of equal exchange, which is a system of skill exchange based on work certificates. Under such a system, individuals and groups would earn certificates or points for their efforts, which reflect the unit of work performed. For example, an item that required one hour of work to produce would be "sold" for a certificate or points reflecting one hour of work time. The certificates could then be exchanged for barter. Equal exchange has been attempted; a few small stores put the idea into practice in the nineteenth century in England and the US.[27]

170

Contemporary anarchists, seeking to expand and reinvent the old ideas of cooperatives and skill exchange systems to solve 21st century problems, argue that today's revolution in communications and information systems would allow this system to operate efficiently and on a larger scale. Like capitalism, this alternative system allows for the exchange of goods and services, but anarchism's emphasis is on bringing people together to access the basic essentials of life and to promote self-sufficiency. It would mean, as Graham Purchase describes it, solving simple problems in more imaginative ways, and also making more sustainable use of derelict and underutilized resources.[28]

Some anarchists offer up examples of "Green Cities" which establish urban nature reserves to ensure the greening of significant sections of the city as an exciting and rational alternative to America's suburban sprawl. Such cities would be based on federations of neighborhoods and would promote self-sufficiency through the efficient recycling of each community's own wastes and the development of locally-based clean energy sources. Such a change would mean rescaling and redesigning our living areas so that we live a more regionally-determined lifestyle, consuming more of what is produced locally.[29] Movements of this sort, aimed at supporting local, small-scale food producers are gaining popularity in several parts of the US—and the world.

In sum, the anarchist theory of organization seeks to create entities that are voluntary, functional, and small. Although the emphasis is on the local level, anarchists argue that this form of organization is appropriate to the scale of the modern, globalized world, as localities can combine and be integrated through a global federation or complex network of ecological regions—all without a central authority.[30] Because they can offer no actual large-scale examples of how it would work, though, anarchists struggle against a great deal of cynicism about the possibilities for progress without centralized government. It is often said that modern society is too complex for the utopian "hippie communes" they're describing. The perennial question posed is "who will clean the toilets?" Given the resistance they face, anarchists know that the obstacles to change can seem insurmountable. Yet, many of these idealists are refreshingly straightforward in admitting that they aren't sure what a complex society based on their principles will look like. They do know that continuing the way we are going (perhaps most obviously as concerns the environment) is impractical and impossible. And they reject the idea that the only alternative to the state is lawless barbarism. Given the environmental devastation, structural unemployment, corporate monopoly, and gross inequality characteristic of the status quo, anarchists are adamant that there must be another option. For anarchists, another world is possible.[31]

Anarchists and the Use of Violence

Our way of living must change, and anarchists are confident that humans have the ability to create that new reality. Just as capitalism was once a new world replacing the way of living that was feudalism, anarchists know that capitalism as a way of living will eventually be replaced with a new and different reality. In this sense, they echo much of the dialectical materialism of the Marxists. Although they don't necessarily agree with Marxists that progress (in the way Marxists define it) is inevitable, these leftists agree that history is dynamic, ever-changing, and new realities are always being forged.[32]

Perhaps the most obvious difference between Marxists and anarchists is that anarchists absolutely believe that individuals can have a part in making that new reality, while Marxists doubt this, and pin their hopes on class war. Another difference is that Marxists hold out hope for the Dictatorship of the Proletariat, while for anarchists, all authority is illegitimate. Therefore, according to anarchists, it is one's duty to resist when government is wrong (which it almost always is) and it is our duty to seize power. However, beyond this, anarchists disagree about how to reduce government or eliminate it. Although they agree that government is the single greatest perpetrator of violence, the vast majority of anarchist thought does not advocate the use of violence to overthrow government. Godwin (who, you may recall, is credited with setting out anarchism's central tenets) was a Calvinist minister and pacifist who discouraged the use of violence because he believed that it was unnecessary. Rather, according to Godwin, the state can be destroyed simply by contracting different human relationships and by behaving differently with one another.[33]

Similarly, another major influence on anarchism, Henry David Thoreau (1817–1862) argued that government would be unnecessary if humans followed their own consciences. In the meantime, he counseled that the individual must not surrender to authority but be true to his/her own conscience. Although Thoreau maintained that it is one's duty to resist when government dictates conflict with what one knows is right, he advocated the use of nonviolent cooperation or civil disobedience, which could include any variety of actions, including ignoring traditional authority or denying it support.[34]

Like Thoreau, Proudhon and other anarchists advocated various forms of civil disobedience to induce state collapse. Proudhon urged citizens to refuse to participate in the activities of government, to boycotts elections or hold office, or to admit to the state's legitimacy in any way. Viewing the state as an evil institution, a principal source of violence in the world, these anarchists sought to destroy the state by ignoring it. An advocate of non-violent non-cooperation or passive resistance, he was joined by many others who argue that if enough citizens refuse to carry out immoral orders, if they drop their hands and walk away, no government can enforce its dictates. For instance, Thoreau, in opposition to the Mexican-American War, practiced what he called "the duty of civil disobedience."[35] In an act of insubordination he refused to pay his taxes (arguing that they would go to support this war), and went to jail for it. Over 100 years later, the young Americans who refused to register for the Vietnam draft or report for induction were refusing to cooperate with unacceptable order—and using the same tactics that have appealed to activists across the world and the political spectrum, including Gandhi and Martin Luther King, Jr., both of whom are known to have read Thoreau.[v] All three of these men refused to bow to illegitimate authority, and for all three the only meaningful way to create an ideal society was through nonviolent change.[36]

Yet, as opposed to the pacifists who argue that there is never any legitimate use of force, who believe that the means and ends cannot be separated, there are early anarchists (such as Proudhon) who did cautiously accept the need for revolution, arguing famously that it is the purposes of violence that determine its good or evil character.[37] Building on this idea, some anarchists allow that there is no legitimate initiation of force, but that reactive force may be justified.[38] For them, the line between violence and non-violence is decided by the state. Yet, this anarchist belief in reactive violence (and, consequently, the belief that anarchists are dangerously violent, even terrorists) is often traced back to the aftermath of the 1871 Paris Commune uprising, in which a group of anarchists sought to avenge the repression and violence perpetrated against them by the state with a series of attacks. For about thirty years (from 1880–1910), groups of anarchists advocated "propaganda by deed," promoting terrorism and assassination to "waken the masses," incite mass uprisings and insurrection, and "speed up" the collapse of the state. Although these acts of terror were carried out by a few extremists, the label stuck. For example, anarchism was blamed for the violence famously occurring in 1886 at Chicago's

---

[v] Although Dr. King was no anarchist, Gandhi declared himself one more than once. An advocate of *satyagraph* (Gujurati for "truth force"), Gandhi embraced many core anarchist principles, calling for a decentralized economic system and autonomy through localization (see Sean M. Sheehan, *Anarchism* (London: Reaktion Books, Ltd., 2003).

Haymarket Square.[vi] Soon anarchists became known as bomb-throwers and assassins. They were feared as the major terrorist threat a century ago, said to be responsible for the deaths of hundreds in the US and Europe.[39]

Often identified as the founder of violent anarchism, Michael Bakunin could be characterized as the anarchists' Osama bin Laden. Arguing that the ends justify the means, he accepted the use of violence, stealth, deceit, treachery and terror to destroy the state. Some extremist protégés of Bakunin's, the Nihilists, received even more attention for maintaining that society was rotten to the core, rejecting all established values and viewing any sort of conformity as enslaving the human spirit. In its place they advocated the most chaotic use of arbitrary violence and willful destruction, arguing that only the few things that managed to survive such an onslaught would turn out to have been worth saving.[40] It is Alexander Berkman, however, who came to personify the stereotypical anarchist. Through propaganda by deed he sought to hasten the revolution with his (unsuccessful) assassination attempt against the industrial magnate Henry Clay Frick. Unfortunately for Berkman and his followers, such an approach only succeeded in impeding any serious consideration of anarchist ideas. In fact, although 1880–1910 is generally recognized as the heyday of anarchist terrorism, anarchism has been conflated with terrorism ever since, to punish anarchists and effectively discredit the movement.[41]

So even though it was nearly 100 years ago that Teddy Roosevelt denounced anarchism as the enemy of humanity, for decades anarchists were cast in the role of terrorists, accused by the state of "fighting a war to the death against society."[vii] Yet, for anarchists, it is the state that has crossed this line again and again, against protesters in venues as diverse as Selma, Soweto, Tiananmen, and Genoa.[viii] It is the state that is using terrorist tactics, not the protestors. Most of today's anti-globalization anarchists define violence as attacks against persons and abhor it. However, for some of these anarchists, making mayhem such as smashing the windows of Starbucks and Nike stores is fair game—it is a state-

---

[vi]Eleven workers were martyred when authorities sought to break up a union action calling for workplace reforms such as an eight-hour workday. In retaliation against what labor activists characterized as police brutality, riots broke out and unknown assailants set off a bomb, killing seven policemen. Despite little evidence of their guilt, four anarchists were hanged for the crime.

[vii]Theodore Roosevelt, "Message to the Senate Committee of the Judiciary Regarding the Transmission through the Mails of Anarchistic Publications," April 9, 1908.

[viii]During anti-globalization protests of a Group of Eight meeting in Genoa in July 2001, hundreds were beaten and a 23-year-old man was shot dead by police.

ment against the free market fundamentalism colonizing the world—it is not violence.[ix] Participants rationalize their attacks on property, which is symbolic of corporate globalization and elite privilege, by asking us to remember the various forms of structural violence committed on a daily basis by corporate elites in the name of private property rights.[42] Calling themselves non-violent but not pacifists, some anarchists are committed to confront police violence with violence, if necessary. Such sentiment is commonly found in black blocs, the most radical wing of the anti-globalization movement. Black blocs are neither groups nor a movement, but individuals who dress in black and come together in what are called "breakaway marches" or mass rallies to perform hit-and-run acts of civil disobedience, to escalate the costs of state repression by making a situation ungovernable.[43] According to those participating in black blocs, their violence is a drop in the ocean compared to the violence perpetrated every day by the state. Yet, they would argue that the terrorist label has been pinned to them (and stuck, especially since September 11th) by those who feel most threatened by the attack on capitalism.[44]

To paint all anarchists with such a broad brush is unfair, since despite anarchists' longstanding sinister reputation as evildoers and bomb-throwers, most of what today's anarchists are actually practicing is direct action. Based on Godwin's idea of face to face democracy, direct action (as opposed to representative democracy) seeks to reinvent democracy to involve everyone affected. Through direct action they attack a target in a variety of ways: symbolically, artistically, criminally, legally, violently, and peacefully. Instead of the traditional marches and petitions, some non-violent groups choose to fight class war through direct action by "bashing the rich." This involves a variety of tactics, such as activists harassing the rich at their regattas and hunt clubs, and pressing their faces against posh restaurant windows "where the rich feed."[45] As we will discuss at the end of this chapter, anarchists also participate in massive, enormously creative, non-violent anti-globalization protests whose soldiers take the form of clowns, enormous puppets, drummers, and fairies armed with feather dusters. Obviously, while there are some very real, clear divisions concerning the most appropriate tactics for promoting change, there are certain core principles that all anarchists share. With this introduction to anarchism behind us, let us now turn to a discussion of some of the varieties of this ideology.

[ix]As in earlier eras, anarchists today are divided on the use of any such actions, as they so often inadvertently serve counterrevolutionary agendas.

ECO-ANARCHISM

Unlike the most ardent advocates of capitalism (or communism, for that matter), anarchists have often displayed an intense interest in ecological management and called for a reorganization of social, political, and economic life to avert environmental disaster. Perhaps two of the most influential early thinkers associated with eco-anarchism are Charles Fourier (1772–1837) and Petr Kropotkin (1842–1921). Fourier was an early anti-statist philosopher who coined the term "harmonium" to describe the ideal society, one that is small and self-sufficient, integrated with the surrounding environment. Influenced by Fourier, it was the Russian aristocrat and geographer, Kropotkin, who took this ideal further, challenging the misinterpretations of Darwinism that were used to justify competitive capitalism. Taking the anarchist position on human nature, Kropotkin argued that as a precondition for survival, competition within the species was a far less significant instinct than cooperation.[46] Like so many other anarchists, Kropotkin called for the creation of more systems for mutual aid, the humanization of work and the establishment of more green and harmonious living spaces. He was joined by others over the years who sought to harness our instinct for cooperation by finding ever more sustainable, efficient and technologically advanced (but appropriately scaled) forms of agro-industrial production. In effect, these eco-anarchists advocate a holistic approach to development that reduces humans' impact on the environment.

Another aspect of the eco-anarchist plan is to encourage people to shift their identification from the nation-state to the eco-regions in which they live. Hardly your isolated 1960s commune, eco-anarchists foresee a world in which these small-scale, self-sufficient farming and industrial communities working together through direct democracy to form a global federation of eco-regions. In effect eco-anarchists have laid out a blueprint for how to live in a way isn't satisfied with just minimizing the damage done to the earth—it actually seeks to improve its ecological health.[47]

Eco-anarchism's faith in innovation and (appropriate) technology's ability to overcome a variety of problems has resurfaced periodically over the last one hundred years. More modern eco-anarchist movements such as EarthFirst! draw from Murray Bookchin (1921–), who pioneered the idea of social ecology in the 1950s and 1960s. Bookchin criticized eco-reformists, contending that a more action-oriented radical green political theory was needed to produce environmentally-friendly "green outcomes." Like other anarchists, he was concerned about the political inequality that exists even in the most celebrated democracies. The social ecologists who followed him seek the elimination of all hierarchies, including anthropocentrism (human-centeredness), sexism, classism, racism, etc. According to this school, we must understand that all forms of domination, control, and exploitation—including humans' domination of nature—are interconnected.[48]

Because capitalism is the root of so many social and environmental problems, Bookchin and contemporary eco-anarchists contend that green outcomes are only possible with its overthrow.[49] Capitalism, with its concern for profit above all else, promotes (among other ills) industrial irresponsibility and ceaseless consumption. Such corporate-driven economies are unsustainable—not only ill-suited, but actually incompatible with the creation of an ecologically viable society. Yet, as much as they would like it, many eco-anarchists don't see revolution around the corner. In the meantime, they advocate the development of new technologies associated with clean, renewable energy and a sustainable consumption which emphasizes a green consciousness. Such a consciousness, based on a redefinition of wants and needs, would reorder our priorities to ensure that sufficient goods are produced to meet the physical needs of society. Green consciousness aims at not only stopping the harm we're doing to the earth, but actually improving our environment. Associated with what is sometimes called a "survival economy," eco-anarchists accept a simpler standard of living and demand a dramatic change in mainstream orientation. This would include radical changes aimed at altering the way we live on earth, which starts with reducing consumption and developing a keener understanding of sufficiency or "enoughness."[50] Gone too far, have they? Perhaps it will help to learn, then, that several eco-anarchist ideas (such as the animal liberationist contribution that non-human animals are sentient beings) are now widely accepted. In addition, cooperative efforts such as recycling, once a practice relegated to the fringe, but is now pretty mainstream.

ANARCHOSYNDICALISM

Another flavor of anarchism shifts its emphasis from the environment to worker's rights. Verging on broad acceptance in parts of Spain, the US, and France in the early 20th century, anarchosyndicalists such as George Sorel (1847–1941) advocated worker control of industry through the radical trade union movement, or a federation of industrial associations. Originally distancing themselves from political parties, the trade union movements in these countries saw themselves as agents of revolutionary change. They envisioned their task as encouraging workers to throw off the shackles of their oppression and

177

challenge the conditions of their work. Because in their view the state represented only the interests of the economic elite, anarchosyndicalists sought to foment state collapse. Through the use of direct action (mostly in the form of general strikes) they predicted that one day the unions would eventually take charge and become managers bound in a loose federation of unions representing the various trades.[51]

For example, the US anarchosyndicalist movement, the Industrial Workers of the World (IWW), founded in 1908, sought to create "one big union" representing all industrial workers. The IWW pushed for equality for every worker, "the unskilled and uncounted," not just skilled workers. As opposed to established unions which the anarchists deemed too conservative for being entwined with management and the state, the IWW "Wobblies" advocated use of the general strike (as opposed to short-run strikes with their goal of limited economic gains) which sought to "expropriate the expropriators." Their aim was to run the factories themselves, to pool resources to create a fairer, communal system of production and distribution based on needs and availability, not supply and demand. This experiment in self-management promised to create what they called a "just economy." Such an economy was to be participatory, local, and based on non-hierarchical forms of community, as opposed to Soviet-style central planning (which was notorious for a variety of problems, including its inefficiency). Remarkably, in this effort, anarchosyndicalists succeeded (most notably from 1936–1939 in Spain, as nearly three million people organized 2,000 collectives to manage their own affairs). Although this historic achievement was eventually forced to a halt by the Franco regime and its heyday is long past, many things that most Western workers have come to expect (such as an eight-hour workday and compensation for overtime) were first championed by anarchosyndicalists.[52]

To be sure, the movement never achieved all of its aims in part because of various assaults from the left, including some communists and socialists, as well as internecine rifts between anarchist reformers and revolutionaries. True to anarchist form, the anarchosyndicalists were unique in their attempt to avoid the centralized hierarchies associated with contemporary unions (which were set up to defend the worker, but have too often become just another large, unaccountable and dysfunctional bureaucracy).[53] However, some would argue that it was the very lack of bureaucratic organization that left the movement plagued by the inefficiencies that would ultimately lead to its demise. Not all agree on the cause of death. According to most anarchists, the IWW and other large-scale, authentically independent unions, such as the Spanish National Confederation of Workers (CNT), were eventually co-opted or destroyed by the capitalist state, which recognized the threat they posed. Yet, perhaps even the reports of anarchosyndicalism's death are greatly exaggerated. As long as we speak of goals such as "liberating work" and recognize that worker satisfaction (and productivity) is related to autonomy, anarchosyndicalism's tenets live on.[54]

ANARCHAFEMINISM

Anarchafeminism, sometimes referred to as "lifestyle anarchism," applies anarchist principles to aspects of living not considered by the other schools presented here. For anarchafeminists, issues of sexuality are intimately bound up with the exercise of political power. For example, the anarchist rejection of authority expressed through anarchafeminism is a call for the abandonment of all sexual taboos. Such taboos are enforced by patriarchal institutions such as the family, religion, and the state, which aim to promote obedience, conformity and sexual repression to reinforce the status quo. Like their anarchist cousins, anarchafeminists demand liberation from these constraints and a revolutionary shift in values and attitudes to allow for equality between the sexes and the dismantling of all hierarchies, particularly those associated with sexism and heterosexism.[55]

Although they might be called sexual libertarians, anarchafeminists disagree with the classic libertarian take on sex work (which argues that individuals should be free to choose this line of work if they so please). It is true that anarchafeminsts also criticize taboos which stifle sexual freedom. However, they view sex work as something more than just the exploitation of labor. While patriarchy has long been blamed for its treatment of women as property, anarchafeminists blame capitalism for commodifying sex—offering the bodies of women and children up (and with globalization, on an ever larger scale) for male consumption.[56]

Like Marxist feminists, anarchafeminists borrow heavily from Frederick Engels' (1820–1895) description of "the world historical defeat of the female sex." Both ideologies criticize the institution of marriage as promoting asymmetric power relations (namely, the male ownership of females), since in capitalist society female sexuality is considered the property first of her father and then her husband. As opposed to patriarchal views promoting chastity and monogamy, anarchafeminists contend that (like property) sex is a communal gift of nature and that there should be no laws or moral constraints binding it. Women (and men) should be free to select and move among sexual partners as they wish—without double standards or fearing other sanctions.[57]

179

While these views have their modern advocates, they are most associated with perhaps America's most famous anarchist, Emma Goldman (1896–1940).[x] Years before anyone else, Goldman began talking about how the personal is political, in ways that would later be taken up by the women's movement of the 1960s and 1970s. One hundred years ago, Goldman called upon women to refuse the right to anyone over their bodies, to refuse to bear children unless she wanted them, and to refuse to be a servant to God, the state, society, her husband, or her family. "Red Emma," as she was known, encouraged women to free themselves from the fear of public opinion and public condemnation. She argued that they should be free to practice free love, to reject marriage as a farce that is degrading to men and women, and to instead form "free unions" (as opposed to those licensed by the church or state).[58]

For these reasons, it probably comes as no surprise that both Goldman and anarchafeminism has had its share of critics from the right (Goldman was imprisoned in the US and deported to Russia for her activism. At her deportation hearing, FBI chief J. Edgar Hoover is said to have described her as "one of the most dangerous women in America").[59] Interestingly, anarchafeminism has also drawn fire from the left, as some anarchists see such concerns as a bourgeois distraction from other, more primary concerns.[60] However, because it deals with so many real life issues such as reproductive rights (the right to safe motherhood as well as contraception and abortion on demand) and the need for quality, affordable child care—and because its sexual politics are all based in anarchism's core values (i.e.: personal freedom)—anarchafeminism must be included in any discussion of anarchism as an ideology.

ANARCHISM AND THE ANTI-GLOBALIZATION MOVEMENT

We wind up this chapter with a discussion of anarchism's influence on the anti-globalization movement, because this movement is so diverse, and because it serves as a prism, bringing together all the different facets of anarchism that have been discussed thus far. Although not all anti-globalization activists call themselves anarchists, anarchism does appeal to a variety of young radicals concerned with the multitude of justice issues associated with globalization. From environmentalists and animal rights activists, to those advocating labor rights, the elimination of poor countries' debts, and the rights of indigenous peoples,

[x]Goldman spent her life working for a variety of progressive causes, particularly as a war resister and for freedom of speech and workers' rights.

180

traditional leftist anarchist principles such as opposition to capitalism, hierarchies and suspicion of the state (and all authority, for that matter) holds sway—so much so that anarchism is often called the heart of the anti-globalization (or more appropriately, the *alternative* globalization) movement.[61][xi]

Attracted by anarchism's egalitarianism and its association with decentralized organizational structures and decisions made by consensus, anti-globalization activists came to the world's attention in the late 1990s, seeking to transform globalization, if not stop it. Concerned about the greed and violence associated with corporate capitalism, individual activists from around the world networked to develop new modes of contestation (mostly peaceful means of disruption) that are part street theatre, carnival, and circus.[62] Their "affinity groups" are not organized as groups in the way that most of us think. They have no leaders and they often do not exist as a group outside of the event itself. Rather, affinity groups are based on the belief that at the grassroots people can lead themselves. They take part in what have been described as modern pilgrimages to come together spontaneously to collaborate in direct action and just as quickly disperse. Described as purposefully fragile, transient, and "decidedly in the moment," some analysts argue that these groups are more likely to gravitate to anarchism as a source of organizational strategy than to commit to it as an ideology, or blueprint for the future.[63] Although its members are so militant in their advocacy for individual rights that the movement has been called "liberalism on steroids," they sound even more leftist than liberal as they take stands against class exploitation, neo-liberalism, state coercion, and US imperialism.[64] No doubt, the individuals and groups comprising the anti-globalization movement have their ideological and tactical differences (i.e.: whether the enemy is corporate power or capitalism itself, as well as whether the two should be reformed or abolished).

Despite these divisions, those drawn to this movement agree that there is a tension between the way things are and the way they should be. Striking for its creativity, even the most militant part of the anti-globalization movement doesn't bank on an old-style revolution or forceful overthrow of the existing

[xi]Some analysts suggest that the anti-globalization movement was set off in Mexico in 1994 with the Zapatistas' sudden appearance on the political scene to defend indigenous and peasant populations against the North American Free Trade Agreement (NAFTA) (see Karen Goaman, "The Anarchist Traveling Circus: Reflections on Contemporary Anarchism, Anti-Capitalism, and the International Scene," pp.163–180 in *Changing Anarchism: A Theory and Practice in a Global Age*, Johnathan Purkis and James Bowen (ed.s) (Manchester: Manchester University Press, 2004); Jen Couch, "Imagining Zapatismo: the Anti-globalisation Movement and the Zapatistas," *Communal/Plural*, 9:2 (2001), pp. 243–260.

order. Unlike other radicals, they haven't adopted the insurgent model of political change. Rather, they argue that times have changed, and different tools are needed to contest power. Namely, anti-globalization activists seek a profound change in our way of thinking about power and government. They don't desire to seize power as much as to expose, delegitimize, and dismantle it.[65] As opposed even to democratic socialists, these groups are explicitly anti-political in the sense that they refuse to enter the arena of traditional electoral politics or to be co-opted—as they argue all political parties inevitably are.[66]

What then are the radical, signature techniques of the movement? The answer is mass nonviolent civil disobedience, played out in any variety of ways. As David Graeber describes it,

Where once it seemed that the only alternatives to marching along with signs were either Gandhian non-violent civil disobedience or outright insurrection, groups like the Direct Action Network, Reclaim the Streets, Black Blocs or Tute Bianche have all, in their own ways, been trying to map out a completely new territory in between. They're attempting to invent what many call a 'new language' of civil disobedience, combining elements of street theatre, festival and what can only be called non-violent warfare—non-violent in the sense adopted by, say, Black Bloc anarchists, in that it eschews any direct physical harm to human beings.[67]

What these contemporary anarchists seek is a "teachable moment." They want to expose what they see as the hollowness of capitalist existence by taking over or appropriating spaces of power, whether it is a World Trade Organization or International Monetary Fund conference site, a Group of Eight summit, or symbol such as a seat of government. The protest is described as play and becomes spectacle, as men and women don elaborate suits of padding, fairy costumes and chemical-proof white jumpsuits to chant, drum, and dance. They push through police barricades and attack police with balloons and water pistols, or tickle them with feather dusters.[68] These activists are also known for using puppets and symbols and erecting ingenious barricades, such as enormous yarn spider webs strung out across major city intersections which make them impossible to cross, giant puppets whose arms outstretched can block a four lane highway, and snake dances as mobile blockades. Huge catapults have been created in the middle of cities to lob soft toys at meetings promoting global capitalism. At other venues, such as the US Republican Convention in 2004, "Billionaires for Bush" dressed in campy tuxedos and evening gowns to present cops with fake cash, thanking them for repressing dissent. The Revolutionary Anarchist Clown Bloc does a keystone cop routine, confusing the police by attacking each other, and favors chants such as "Democracy? Ha Ha Ha!" and "The Pizza United Can Never Be Defeated."[69]

While casual onlookers might be perplexed by all of this, what these anti-globalization activists have been putting on has been called "a post-modern rebellion," aimed at challenging authority and finding alternatives to all of the so-called universal assumptions coming out of the Enlightenment. Yet, ultimately, the anarchist sensibility behind so much of the anti-globalization movement appeals precisely because it is audacious, fresh and new while the demands of this uprising against elite, unaccountable institutions—for the ideals of freedom, justice and democracy—are timeless.[70] Anarchism has always been about these ideas, despite the fact that even in its latest incarnation it is still reviled by the mainstream as terrorist. For all of these reasons, it is important not simply to write off anarchism, but to consider seriously just why this very old ideology has enjoyed a revival and why it continues to inspire and appeal, especially to the young—in ways that other ideologies of the left have not.

CONCLUSION

Although they adhere to the slogan "another world is possible," it is clear that anarchists have not yet changed society in the ways they have hoped—but, for that matter, the same can be said of every one of the ideologies described in this volume. Although anarchism is arguably the most maligned and repressed of all ideologies, as a core idea it is resilient and has endured. Today anarchism may be more a style of life, a posture, or a state of mind than a movement. Yet, this "philosophy of non-submission," based in the idea that people should have more control over their lives, has made a contribution. It is thanks to anarchism and civil disobedience that a series of smaller liberations identified in this chapter have lifted a huge load of human misery. If people didn't break the law, anarchists point out, America would still be a British colony, slavery would still exist, women wouldn't be able to vote, and the Vietnam War might still be going on.[71]

And there is much more work still to be done, since (from an anarchist perspective) the current state of the world—war, famine, environmental devastation, poverty, and injustice—is patently unacceptable. Similarly, anarchists are alarmed by the way governments have manipulated public fears and used the terrorist threat since 9/11 to justify the expansion of government powers without limits—or with any end in sight. According to anarchists, in their war on terror, these governments are becoming the terrorists; not only are they trampling civil rights at home, they are condoning the use of torture, practicing terror abroad.

This is an extremely dangerous time for human freedom, they argue, but anarchists maintain that all is not hopeless. They believe that the ideal world they advocate (in effect, radical participatory democracy) *is* attainable, lying just beneath the surface of everyday life. Sure, it is easy to call anarchists utopians, to criticize them for not explaining exactly how it is that we'll get from here to there. In response, they leave us with two simple questions: if such an ideal is truly unattainable, then why is it so? And, given the fact that so few of us can possibly be satisfied with the existing state of affairs, why do so many of us simply accept the world as it is?[72]

NOTES

1. "Anarchist Quotations," *blackcrayon.com*, nd.

2. George Crowder, *Classical Anarchism: The Political Thought of Godwin, Proudhon, Bakunin, and Kropotkin* (Oxford: Oxford University Press, 1991).

3. "A Brief Introduction to Philosophical Anarchism," *blackcrayon.com*, nd.

4. Colin Ward, *Anarchism: A Very Short Introduction* (Oxford: Oxford University Press, 2004); James Bowen and Jonathan Purkis, "Introduction: Why Anarchism Still Matters," pp. 1–19 in *Changing Anarchism: Theory and Practice in a Global Age*, Jonathan Purkis and James Bowen (eds.) (Manchester: Manchester University Press, 2004).

5. Barbara Epstein, "Anarchism and the Anti-Globalization Movement," *Monthly Review*, 53:4 (September 2001).

6. Andrew Flood, "Thinking about Anarchism: Smash the State," Workers Solidarity Movement, *www.flag.blackened.net*, 1994.

7. Thomas Paine, "Common Sense," in *100 Key Documents in American Democracy*, ed. Peter B. Levy (Westport, CT: Greenwood Press, 1994).

8. Ward, *Anarchism: A Very Short Introduction.*

9. Ibid.

10. Ibid; Max Skidmore, *Ideologies: Politics in Action* (Orlando: Harcourt, Brace, Jovanovich, 1993); Alan MacSimoin, "Thinking about Anarchism: Private Property," Workers Solidarity Movement, *www.flag.blackened.net*, nd.

11. Alan MacSimoin, "Thinking about Anarchism: Are Anarchists Violent?" Workers Solidarity Movement, *www.flag.blackened.net*, 2001.

12. David Graeber, "The New Anarchists," *New Left Review*, 13, January–February 2002.

13. Sean M. Sheehan, *Anarchism* (London: Reaktion Books, Ltd., 2003); Alan MacSimoin, "Thinking about Anarchism: Direct Action," Workers Solidarity Movement, *www.flag.blackened.net*, nd.

14. Leon P. Baradat, *Political Ideologies, Their Origins and Impact* (Englewood Cliffs, NJ: Prentice Hall, 1994).

15. Ibid.; Sheehan, *Anarchism.*

16. Skidmore, *Ideologies: Politics in Action*; Ward, *Anarchism: A Very Short Introduction*; MacSimoin, "Thinking about Anarchism: Private Property."

17. MacSimoin, "Thinking about Anarchism: Private Property."

18. Ward, *Anarchism: A Very Short Introduction*; Irving Louis Horowitz, "Introduction to the Transaction Edition," pp. xi–xx in *The Anarchists*, ed. Irving Louis Horowitz. (London: Transaction Publishers, 2005).

19. Skidmore, *Ideologies: Politics in Action.*

20. Tom Lane, "On Anarchism: Noam Chomsky Interviewed by Tom Lane," *ZNet*, December 23, 1996.

21. George Crowder, *Classical Anarchism: The Political Thought of Godwin, Proudhon, Bakunin, and Kropotkin* (Oxford: Oxford University Press, 1991); Sheehan, *Anarchism*; Skidmore, *Ideologies: Politics in Action*.

22. Skidmore, *Ideologies: Politics in Action*.

23. Graham Purchase, *Anarchism and Ecology* (Montreal: Black Rose Books, 1997).

24. Jonathan Purkis and James Bowen, "Conclusion: How Anarchism Still Matters," pp. 213–229 in *Changing Anarchism: Theory and Practice in a Global Age*, Jonathan Purkis and James Bowen (ed.s) (Manchester: Manchester University Press, 2004).

25. Purchase, *Anarchism and Ecology*; Jonathan Purkis and James Bowen, "Conclusion: How Anarchism Still Matters," pp. 213–229 in *Changing Anarchism: Theory and Practice in a Global Age*, Jonathan Purkis and James Bowen (eds.) (Manchester: Manchester University Press, 2004).

26. Purchase, Anarchism and Ecology.

27. Ibid.

28. Ibid.

29. Ibid.

30. Ibid.; Ward, *Anarchism: A Very Short Introduction*.

31. Sheehan, *Anarchism*; Graeber, "The New Anarchists."

32. Sheehan, *Anarchism*.

33. Ward, *Anarchism: A Very Short Introduction*.

34. Skidmore, *Ideologies: Politics in Action*.

35. Ward, *Anarchism: A Very Short Introduction*.

36. Ibid; Skidmore, *Ideologies: Politics in Action*; Sheehan, *Anarchism*.

37. Skidmore, *Ideologies: Politics in Action*; Horowitz, "Introduction to the Transaction Edition."

38. No author, "A Brief Introduction to Philosophical Anarchism," *www.BlackCrayon.com*, nd.

39. Horowitz, "Introduction to the Transaction Edition."

40. Baradat, *Political Ideologies, Their Origins and Impact*.

41. MacSimoin, "Thinking about Anarchism: Are Anarchists Violent?"

42. Epstein, "Anarchism and the Anti-Globalization Movement."

43. Jeffrey Paris, "The Black Bloc's Ungovernable Protest," *Peace Review*, 15:3 (2003) 317–322.

44. Sheehan, *Anarchism*; Skidmore, *Ideologies: Politics in Action*; Jacob H. Fries, "Anarchy Has an Image Problem," *The New York Times*, January 28, 2002.

45. Sheehan, *Anarchism*; MacSimoin, "Thinking about Anarchism: Direct Action."

46. Ward, *Anarchism: A Very Short Introduction*.

47. Purchase, *Anarchism and Ecology*; Crowder, *Classical Anarchism*.

48. Murray Bookchin, "What Is Social Ecology?" pp. 93–107 in *Radical Environmentalism: Philosophy and Tactics*, ed. Peter C. List (Belmont, CA: Wadsworth Publishing Co, 1993).

49. Alan Atkisson, "Introduction to Deep Ecology: An Interview with Michael E. Zimmerman," *In Context*, Summer 1989.

50. Ward, *Anarchism: A Very Short Introduction*; Purchase, *Anarchism and Ecology*; Neala Schleuning, *Idle Hands and Empty Hearts: Work and Freedom in the United States* (New York: Bergin and Garvey, 1990).

51. Ward, *Anarchism: A Very Short Introduction*; Sheehan, *Anarchism*.

52. Ibid.

53. MacSimoin, "Thinking about Anarchism: Direct Action."

54. Skidmore, *Ideologies: Politics in Action*; Ward, *Anarchism: A Very Short Introduction*; Purchase, *Anarchism and Ecology*.

55. Sheehan, *Anarchism*.

56. Ibid; Patricia McCarthy, "Anarchism's Greatest Hits No. 3: Emma Goldman," Worker's Solidarity Movement, *www.flag.blackened.net*, nd.

57. Ibid.

58. O'Carroll, 1992; Neala Schleuning, *To Have and To Hold: The Meaning of Ownership in the United States* (Westport, CT: Praeger, 1997).

59. McCarthy, "Anarchism's Greatest Hits No. 3: Emma Goldman."

60. Sheehan, *Anarchism*.

61. Epstein, "Anarchism and the Anti-Globalization Movement;" Karen Goaman, "The Anarchist Traveling Circus: Reflections on Contemporary Anarchism, Anti-Capitalism, and the International Scene," pp.163–180 in *Changing Anarchism: Theory and Practice in a Global Age*, Johnathan Purkis and James Bowen (eds.) (Manchester: Manchester University Press, 2004).

62. Epstein, "Anarchism and the Anti-Globalization Movement."

63. Goaman, "The Anarchist Traveling Circus;" Fries, "Anarchy Has an Image Problem."

64. Epstein, "Anarchism and the Anti-Globalization Movement."

65. Sheehan, *Anarchism*; Graeber, "The New Anarchists."

66. Purkis and Bowen, "Conclusion: How Anarchism Still Matters."

67. David Graeber, "The New Anarchists," *New Left Review*, 13, January–February 2002, np.

68. Goaman, "The Anarchist Traveling Circus."

69. Goaman, "The Anarchist Traveling Circus;" Graeber, "The New Anarchists."

70. Ibid.

71. Ward, *Anarchism: A Very Short Introduction*; Sheehan, *Anarchism*; Horowitz, "Introduction to the Transaction Edition;" Fries, "Anarchy Has an Image Problem."

72. Crowder, *Classical Anarchism*.

Chapter 8

Islamism

"Islam is the solution"[1]
Islamist slogan

I t is often said that Islam is a faith and Islamism an ideology; but it is easy to conflate the two, since the religion offers a worldview and program of action, and the ideology is based in faith. Yet, with a global war on terror aimed against mostly Muslim adversaries, it has become more and more urgent that some distinctions be made. For several years prior to the attacks of September 2001, Western academics had predicted a "clash of civilizations," portraying "fundamentalist Islam" (more recently, "political Islam" or "Islamism") as a threat to West. This characterization has only been amplified since 2001, and in a battle reminiscent of the Cold War, President Bush and British Prime Minister Tony Blair have on multiple occasions described Islamism as the latest manifestation of barbarism, a fanatic, hateful, evil ideology, ruthless in its ambitions, seeking global conquest and the establishment of a caliphate (or Islamic empire) that reigns over not just the Middle East, but from Indonesia to Spain.[2]

Moreover, these days it is not uncommon to hear Islamism compared to fascism. According to this view, Islamism is built on a cult of death and promises an Islamic-flavored totalitarianism defined by its hatred of Jews, Christians, and any Muslims who dare disagree.[3] While Bush and Blair have taken pains to argue that they are not denouncing the entire community of Muslims (that the terrorists are not "good Muslims") their administrations could be accused of contributing to a growing Islamophobia that is expressed in a variety of ways. For example, political Islam is commonly accepted in the West as a monolithic,

191

antagonistic political force, the enemy of democracy and freedom.[4] But it is not just Islamism that is portrayed this way. Stereotypes of Muslims run rampant and (given restrictive government policies that target Muslims—particularly Arabs—including profiling and mass arrests without due process) it is hard not to come away with the idea that the West is at war with not just Islamism, but Islam itself.

There are many in the West who argue that such an approach is perfectly appropriate. For them, Islam is Islamism—the religion has not merely been "hijacked" by extremists. Rather, there is no moderate Islam. In his best-selling book, Sam Harris contends that most Muslims are fundamentalists—even "moderates" believe the *Qur'an* is the literal word of *Allah*, or God. Moreover, according to this view, Islam is undeniably a religion of conquest, which teaches that all infidels are to be converted to Islam, subjugated or killed. Therefore, Islam and Western liberalism are irreconcilable. The *Qur'an* instructs the faithful to despise non-believers. Until this changes, he argues, we should ready ourselves for a permanent state of war.[5]

But is such a stance based in dangerously broad generalizations? And even if we separate Islam from Islamism, is it really accurate to speak of a monolithic Islamism? First of all, the religion is largely split into two major sects, Sunni and Shiia Islam. While one might legitimately expect that the 1.4 billion people who consider themselves Muslim share some common values, beliefs, and codes of ethics, we know that any group of individuals' socioeconomic, political and cultural realities vary greatly. Although many people commonly use the terms "Muslim," "Arab," and "Middle Eastern" synonymously, less than a quarter of the world's Muslims are Arab, living in the Middle East. Rather, the world's most populous Muslim countries are Asian: Indonesia, Pakistan, Bangladesh, and India (where Muslims comprise a large minority).[6]

In addition, like any other part of the world, countries with predominantly Muslim populations have changed over time. The Muslim world is known for its diversity, so much so that analysts speak of the development of different "Islams" (different religious interpretations and practices)—both between countries and within them.[i] Scholars concur on the importance of context in understanding Islam: religion provides the guidelines but societies interpret and apply these guidelines according to their own conditions, cultures, and histories). In other words, the interpenetration of religion and local culture shapes different manifestations of Islam.[7]

---

[i]"Muslim world" commonly refers to the collection of countries whose population is predominantly Muslim.

For example, in predominantly Muslim Turkey, the law decrees secularism and there *is* a clear separation of church and state. In theocratic Iran (where the church *is* the state), Islam is applied in strict, conservative fashion. While Iran and Turkey amount to two ends of the spectrum, most predominantly Muslim countries fall somewhere in between the two.[8]

If the practice of Islam varies according to different interpretations of the requirements of Islam and the prevailing conditions and political culture of the societies in which they are applied, surely it is important that we recognize that different Islamisms exist in this way as well. Why? The war against terror is an emotional issue for many in the West. Whether or not one agrees with how it is currently being fought, to achieve the most effective policy, Americans in particular might benefit from putting aside their preconceived notions and engage in a more serious discussion of what is political Islam, and what is driving it. We also need to understand that although it gets the lion's share of media attention, militant Islamism is only one variant of this ideology.[9] The majority of Islamists aren't *jihadists* (those who support a *jihad*, or holy war) and the majority of Muslims aren't even Islamists. Estimates vary, but Daniel Pipes, a known critic of political Islam, contends that Islamists comprise only 10% of the Muslim population worldwide (and *jihadists* a fraction of that)—amounting to a small but active minority.[10]

Although it is more than a minority of Muslims who generally share umbrage at what they see as continuing Western imperialism, political Islam itself is not monolithic, nor is it intrinsically anti-Western or anti-modern. Not every Islamist is a retrograde fanatic rabidly resisting all change or innovation. In fact, political Islam's mainstream is dominated by moderate, even progressive strands that are growing in influence across the Islamic world. These Islamists don't necessarily find all that the West has to offer abhorrent; still, they don't consider all that the West has to offer worthy of emulation.[11]

Just as Islamisms line up across the political spectrum from left to right (or at least from conservative extremist to moderate liberal), there are also considerable differences in the methods and tactics preferred by different Islamist groups.[12] Some Islamists emphasize concrete changes in this world; others prioritize inner reforms based in mysticism and the renewal of faith and spirituality.[13] In fomenting change, some Islamists advocate a top-down, statist approach, while others prefer a bottom-up, grassroots effort that begins with the individual. As we will discuss later in this chapter, some Islamists advocate the use of violence to bring about change, but others seek to change the world using a variety of forms of peaceful protest, centering on democratization. Some Islamists are fiercely ideological, unwilling to compromise in their vision, while others are

193

much more pragmatic in their approach, integrated into the "normal" politics of their countries. In fact, there are so many significant divisions within this single ideology that it is often said that they are locked in a "battle for the soul of Islam."[14]

WHAT IS ISLAMISM?

Before going into some of its varieties, what is the core of Islamism and the common denominator of all Islamist movements? More than anything else, this ideology calls for a return to Islam. To be more specific, Islamism promotes political change to regulate, in whole or in part, governance and public conduct in accordance with Islamic principles.[15] Islamists believe that Islam as a body of faith is a message sent by God to civilize humanity and give human existence a divine purpose. "Islam," which means "submission to God," is also a call to action. Providing direction concerning all aspects of life, this 1,400-year-old religion has something important to say about how politics, economies, and society should be ordered in the contemporary Muslim world. Islamists are simply those who use Islam as the basis for their political ideology.[16]

This ideology galvanizes its adherents more as a reaction to Westernization than modernization (since Islamists do generally embrace modernization in the forms of science, technology, and development). Islamists seek to replace what they see as the foreign imports of secularization and the "shallow freedoms" associated with cultural modernity with their own faith-based value system.[17] As we will see, political Islam has tremendous appeal as a form of imperial resistance; Islamists often promise to purge Muslim societies of the Western "impurities" that they have suffered with over the last fourteen hundred years, which they see as the cause of Muslim decline.[18] In offering an alternative to the existing order, Islamists draw on religious scripture as well as the beliefs, symbols, language of Islamic traditions to inspire, shape, and animate political activity.[19] No other ideology in the Muslim world has as much appeal, with the possible exception in some countries of ethnic and sectoral nationalisms. As opposed to the capitalist and socialist models that failed their people, these political activists offer Islamism as a third way to development. Although they often disagree on how to go about it, Islamists share an interest in shaping their societies in accord with their own beliefs and values and defining their own place in the global community.[20]

In effect, Islamists are practicing revivalism. However, in calling for a return to Islam, they are not necessarily calling for the restoration of the caliphate or for a return to the world as it existed during the Prophet Mohammed's time. Despite its 7th century basis, Islamism is a modern ideology as much as any other described in this textbook. Since its beginnings as a movement in the late 19th century and through its most recent resurgence (usually traced to the 1950s–1960s) Islamism has been descriptive, speaking of a world in crisis. It is also prescriptive, offering a specific political program to right the world's wrongs: a strictly Islamic policy.[21] To deal with today's challenges, Islamists (whether moderate or radical) seek to return to the major sources of Islamic authority and to reinvent concepts from Islamic tradition to promote a moral and cultural transformation, to help Muslims regain their true identity and reestablish the greatness of the *umma*—the community of believers (or followers of the Prophet Mohammed).[22] This revival would most certainly include the application of all of the sacred texts of Islam: the *shari'a* (or the body of Islamic law developed after Mohammed's death by religious scholars), as well as the *sunna* (the customs or "traditions" of the Prophet), the *hadiths* (the sayings of Mohammed, a guide to the practice of Islam), and of course the *Qur'an* (the book of revelations), believed to be the literal word of God (providing general ethical principles and guidelines for the faithful).[ii]

All Islamist movements call for the application of *shari'a* as a source of law. However, that in itself has led to some debate, as some Islamists, particularly moderates, also include a place in this Islamic renaissance for *ijtihad* ("rational interpretation") or human reasoning, to elaborate on *shari'a* law or to provide answers to questions for which the *Qur'an* and *sunna* are silent. According to moderate Islamist scholars, *shari'a* (which in Arabic means "the path to be followed") is not a single, well-defined legal code, but a complex body of rules that serves as an ethical and spiritual guide. It (like Islam itself) has a timeless message that is not static, but dynamic, spanning centuries and developing over time. It is the rethinking associated with *ijtihad* that renews legal codes and enables them to respond to the needs of contemporary society. Therefore, these centrists contend that some *shari'a* prescriptions such as the *hudud* laws (which advocate punishments such as amputation, caning, stoning, etc.) are products of their time hundreds of years ago and should be reinterpreted to reflect contemporary mores.[23]

Not all Islamists agree with this view; conservatives and traditionalists consider *shari'a* to be a set of laws that is wholly divine in origin. If this is the case,

---

[ii]Muslims believe that God's revelations to Mohammed occurred over a 22 year period, beginning in 610 and continuing until just before the Prophet's death in 632.

then it is easy to understand the absolutist argument that there is no room for independent human reasoning or reform when it comes to *shari'a*, no need for evolution.[24]

So, while they disagree about whether to take a literal or reformist approach to understanding some of the sources of Islam, Islamists across the spectrum insist that this body of faith is a superior alternative to all other ideologies for resolving the social, political and economic problems of modernity. For true believers, Islam's message is one of justice, mercy, compassion, and enlightenment. Islam is the solution; it alone offers pragmatic solutions with immediate applicability.

MAUDUDI AND QUTB: THE FOUNDING FATHERS OF ISLAMISM

While Islamists agree that the primary sources of their ideology are the *Qur'an*, the *hadiths*, and the other sacred texts of Islam, there are several important religious scholars (such as Yusuf al-Qaradawi, Hasan al-Turabi, Muhammad Husayn Fadlallah) who have influenced Islamism and drive it today. However, two particular philosophers and activists, Sayyid Abul Ala Maududi and Sayyid Qutb (pronounced "*kutt-tahb*") provide so much of the philosophical basis for this ideology for radical Sunni Muslims that they are widely recognized as the founding fathers of Islamism.[iii]

Sayyid Abul Ala Maududi (1903–1979) is known throughout the Islamic world as one of most influential intellectuals and activists of the 20th century. Born in Aurangabad, India, Maududi was descended from a long line of spiritual leaders who traced their ancestry to the Prophet Mohammed. At a young age Maududi joined the anti-imperial struggle, working as a journalist and opposing the British colonial occupation of India while promoting the rights of Muslims. After India's independence and partition in 1947, Maududi moved to Pakistan to build a purely Islamic state and society. Strongly opposing the Western concept of democracy, suspicious that Indian nationalists would seek to de-Islamize Muslims, and (later) critical of Pakistan's secular governments, he founded the Islamist party Jamaat-e-Islami (JEI) in 1941. The JEI, which has been linked to terrorist groups but seeks to attain political power through elections, has won representation in Pakistan's parliament. It continues to organize today as a leading voice of the opposition. A revivalist, Maududi taught the

[iii]For most Shiites, the Ayatollah Ruhollah Khomeini is the leading architect of Islamism. However, because 80–90% of the world's Muslims are Sunnis, this chapter will focus on Sunni Islamism.

uniquely Indian variant of Deobandi Islam, a strict school of Islamic law that urges pious individuals to purify and transform society from within Islam. He argued that change should begin with individual transformation, which leads to the development of communities of faith. This in turn leads to the growth of movements to bring peaceful societal change and the gradual establishment of an Islamic state. Although he has been accused of advocating violent change (for restating a core teaching of Islam, that *jihad* is a duty for all Muslims), Maududi focused on the individual transformation that begins with *dawa* (long-term education and preparation) in the religious schools (*madrassas*).[25][iv]

One of the most prominent Muslim authors of the 20th century, Maududi was a prolific writer, but his most influential book is *Towards Understanding Islam*. In it Maududi taught the core tenets of Islamism: that religion provides the frame of reference for all human activity and therefore state and society must be subordinated to Islamic law. He advocated strictly Islamic solutions for reform and upliftment, maintaining that the answer to every problem could be found in the *Qur'an* and *hadiths*. He argued that Muslims should look inward to find strength in Islam and struggle for a more just society based on Islamic principles. In addition, Maududi set out a blueprint for the workings of an Islamic state, discussing the functions of the executive, legislative, and judicial branches, as well as specifics on the rights and duties of citizens and the role of parties.[26]

Whereas Maududi's emphasis was on change from within, Sayyid Qutb (1906–1966) is often interpreted as agitating for a much broader change. Although he is regularly cited as political Islam's chief ideologue, Qutb spent much of his career in the Egyptian civil service, eventually rising to senior rank

[iv]There are many different interpretations of *jihad* (or "religious struggle"), which is one of the five pillars of Islam (along with prayer, fasting, alms giving, and pilgrimage). Although most non-Muslims know only of outer *jihad* (or holy war), there is an equally important inner *jihad*. Outer *jihad* is generally understood as a war of defense against non-believers; it is the duty of all Muslims to fight infidels and apostates for the sake of Islam. However, most Muslims believe that indiscriminate violence (such as terrorism) is forbidden by Islam and is not part of outer (or military) *jihad*. Military *jihad* is essentially defensive and subject to strict rules of engagement. For example, according to these rules, any violence undertaken as *jihad* should be proportionate, and suicide is strictly forbidden. Most scholars of Islam argue that military *jihad* is in fact the lesser *jihad*. The greater duty is actually the inner *jihad*—the internal struggle against one's own failings. In other words, the most important struggle for people of faith is to wage war against one's own sinfulness, to improve oneself morally and spiritually, and to live as God wants us to live (see Bruce Maddy-Weitzman, "Islamism, Moroccan-Style: The Ideas of Sheikh Yassine," *Middle East Quarterly*, X, no. 1 (Winter 2003); M.A. Muqtedar Khan, "Radical Islam, Liberal Islam," *Current History*, 102. no. 688 (December 2003), pp. 417–421).

in the Ministry of Education before a dramatic change of path in the 1960s. After two years of graduate study in the US, he came away a changed man, resigned his position, and broke ways with the Nasser government. Disgusted by America's racism, materialism, and sexual promiscuity (and by his own government, which sought to follow in the US' path), Qutb rejected Western values and set out to put his country on what he saw as the right course. Arguing these points, he published a number of important works, including *Signposts* (sometimes translated as *Milestones*), which is widely recognized as the manifesto for radical Islamism.[27]

Like Maududi, Qutb was also an activist; he played an instrumental role in the development of the Muslim Brotherhood. The oldest Islamist party, the Muslim Brotherhood was founded in Egypt in 1928 by Hasan al-Banna. After al-Banna's assassination in 1949, Qutb became the party's leading voice. Yet, Qutb's influence goes well beyond this particular Islamist party. His philosophy combined with others to provide the basis for al-Qaeda and Islamic Jihad, as well as other, less extremist groups. Each group's vision and approach is unique and reflective of its differences of experience, the context and the constraints under which it operates. Yet, strip away much of this and virtually all Islamist movements admit that they owe some debt to Qutb, who was known to be very much influenced by Maududi's teachings—so much so that if Qutb is the Islamist Lenin, agitating for revolution, then Maududi may well be its Marx.[28]

Like Marx, Maududi (and Qutb) predicted that the end of history is inevitable. However, instead of the Marxists' class-based revolution, for Islamists the true transformation will come only when Islam triumphs over ignorance. All three theorists described history as unfolding through continuous struggle, but for Maududi and Qutb the only authentic struggle is between Islam and ignorance. In writing his classic works, Qutb drew from Maududi to elaborate on a key concept for Islamists: *jahiliyya*, or the state of ignorance that existed among tribes in Arabia before God's revelations to Mohammed. Qutb divided the world into black and white, between pure believers and those living in ignorance. He argued that most modern day societies suffer from *jahiliyya*— even those ruled by political leaders who claim to be Muslims. Their populations suffer under this pre-Islamic barbarism, because too many of these leaders are illegitimate, actually imposing infidel, European and American values.[29] Thus, with these works the enemies were identified, the goals set; while there would continue to be some dispute over how to get there, this was the world as the leading architects of Islamism saw it.

WHAT IS ISLAMISM'S APPEAL?

Just as Maududi and Qutb were reacting to the world around them, political Islam is often said to be rooted in the experiences of Muslims, their interaction with the West, and the sociopolitical conditions of the Muslim world in the 19th and 20th centuries.[30] In this sense, both local and international dynamics have contributed to the ascendancy of Islamism.[31] Just as there are different schools of Islamism, Islamisms appeal to different people for different reasons—and to different extents. We need to be very careful in making generalizations about Islamists, just as with any group of people. Islamists certainly agree that *jahiliyya* prevails, but they disagree about whether internal factors (i.e.: Muslims' lack of faith or unity) or external factors (i.e.: infidel aggression) are more important in explaining the crisis Muslims face. In addition, Islamists are divided about how best to resolve the problem. For example, Islamists disagree about how to read Maududi and Qutb. Extremists interpret their message as an angry call for *jihad*, while moderates advocate a very different path and take a significantly softer line on many of the arguments that follow. Still, whether moderate or extremist, Islamism appeals to many Muslims because it offers a path to personal empowerment for the disenfranchised and disenchanted—a way to reclaim their dignity.[32] Experts on political Islam agree on this fundamental point: like other ideologies, it beckons to those who feel that their backs are pressed against a wall.

Like other ideologies, Islamism also appeals because it offers hope. It hearkens back to the golden age of Islam, when the Islamic world was an equal or dominant power in the world. Islamism explains how the Muslim world, renowned for its accomplishments in the arts and sciences for hundreds of years, could have been subjugated during colonialism and since. They agree the 19th and 20th centuries were near-catastrophic decades for the Middle East, Asia, and Africa, years of humiliation and subjugation by the West. Across much of the Middle East in particular, this was a period of transition and crisis, beginning with the demise of the caliphate, continuing through a period of Western colonial domination, and the failures of independence under nationalist, secular governments. Proponents of this intensely anti-imperialist ideology contend that this crisis continues today in the form of corruption, decadence, and underdevelopment—all directly attributable to colonialism and continued Western domination.[33]

In order to overcome these problems and reassert the proper, respected place of Islam among the world's civilizations, Islamists call for a return to cultural authenticity. Conservative Islamists maintain that, just as the faithful must

199

reject the Marxist emphasis on class conflict, they must also avoid foreign ideologies such as nationalism and feminism, which are Western ruses to divide Muslims.[34] Instead of mimicking the West, believers must unite and work to regain their true cultural identity. They can do this only by embracing the message of Islam, following the superior path of Islamic civilization and by pursuing the creation of a pristine Islamic state, modeled after that which existed during the Prophet's life, because it was the most perfect human society.[35]

As a result, it can't be surprising that political Islam's hallmark combination of anti-imperialism and hostility to the infidel has (to varying degrees) such broad appeal in the Islamic world. Many Muslims are sickened by what they perceive as Western attacks on Muslim values. The publication of Danish cartoons depicting the Prophet Mohammed as a terrorist not only insulted Muslims, it violated Islamic injunctions against picturing the prophet. As the image was reproduced around the world in early 2006, moderate Islamists criticized the cartoons but appealed for calm. However, they were mostly overshadowed by radicals, who had a field day in many countries where the cartoons incited an outcry and violent protests. While many Western non-Muslims characterize this clash simply as a freedom of speech issue, many Muslims see it as hate speech, disrespect for other cultures, and yet another example of the Western assault on Islam. President Bush may proclaim that Islamists hate America for its freedoms, but there is plenty of evidence to suggest that what Islamists (and many non-Islamist Muslims) take offense to is flagrant Western disrespect and being treated like second-class citizens.[36]

This catalogue of wrongs is too long to list here, but it is crucial for Americans understand that the Israeli occupation of Palestine has tremendous resonance in the Muslim world—so much so, that it amounts to a "vicarious humiliation" of Muslims everywhere.[37] Although this indignation is most keenly felt in Arab countries, many Muslims identify with the Palestinian cause, as they consider all Muslims to be potential Palestinians, dispossessed and dishonored with impunity. The US-led occupation of Iraq has further angered many Muslims worldwide, who see the war as a ruse to control oil, weaken Muslims, and consolidate Israeli hegemony in region.[38] Although such views are often dismissed in the West as irrational fanaticism, many people throughout the Islamic world are angry and upset by what they perceive as an unjust, anti-Islamic American foreign policy. They are incensed by US double standards (on human rights, nuclear proliferation, etc.), but particularly by its unfailing loyalty to Israel. Islamists of all stripes have been able to capitalize on this resentment, and to varying degrees are united in their cultural and political antagonism toward the West, particularly the US and Israel.[39]

If Israel and the West are depicted as the Islamic world's "far enemies," its "near enemies" only somewhat less despised.[40] It is often hard to separate the two, as the most virulent anti-Americanism in the Muslim world exists in the countries whose regimes are the closest allies of the US: Saudi Arabia, Egypt, and Pakistan. For many people (again, not just Islamists) living in these countries, these "near enemies" have lost all legitimacy.[41] Citizens are frustrated by the corruption and impotence of their governments, by the sense that their governments have sold out to the West and have not fought against Western domination. In the case of extremist Islamists such as al-Qaeda in particular, it is the fact that these "infidel Muslim" governments allow the West's presence in the Middle East, particularly in Saudi Arabia, that is most unacceptable. Saudi Arabia is home to Mecca and Medina, the two most holy places for Muslims, and the presence of US troops in Saudi territory amounts to a desecration.[42]

In other words, Islamists are responding to what they see as a crisis. From many people's perspective, governments like those of Saudi Arabia and Egypt have lost all legitimacy and must rely on repression to remain in power. Since these countries' independence in the mid-20th century, many nationalist governments in predominantly Muslim countries have attempted to remain in power by crushing the opposition. Although these authoritarian rulers were largely successful in overwhelming their secular opponents, the religious opposition has often occupied a unique, relatively safe political space.[43] Because Islamism uses the vocabulary of religion, it has been more able to circumvent the obstacles authoritarian governments put in its way, sending out political messages as sermons. Secular governments have tried various means of controlling Islamists (including attempts at co-optation), but they have been more careful about closing down mosques and imprisoning religious leaders. However, when these techniques have failed, governments have turned to repression. In Egypt, Syria, Tunisia and elsewhere, Islamists were (and still are) harassed, imprisoned, or exiled. In fact, Qutb (who was eventually hanged by the Egyptian government) was repeatedly tortured and spent so much time writing from prison that he has been called the Islamic world's Solzhenitsyn. Maududi also spent a good deal of his life as a political prisoner, the guest of Pakistani dictators.[44]

This continues today, as Islamists are more likely to be victims of political violence than perpetrators of it. Although sometimes such treatment has opened a Pandora's Box, radicalizing the movement, the reaction of most Islamist groups to government repression shows that their commitment to nonviolence is real.[45] To counter Islamists, governments have often tried to strengthen their own Islamic credentials by broadcasting prayers, appointing religious leaders to prominent posts, and "talking the talk," but to Islamists they are not even Muslim anymore. They are un-Islamic, irreligious "apostate regimes," unresponsive to needs of their people and deserving to be overthrown (or at least cast out of power). According to moderate and radical Islamists, these secular governments have been disasters in all senses for Muslims; not only have they allowed Western decadence to permeate their societies, they have enriched themselves and flaunted their material excess while not providing the majority.[46]

Moreover, where secular governments (and the international community) have failed to deliver even the most basic services to the majority, it has been Islamist, grassroots-based organizations that have taken over many of the functions of the state. Through their charitable work, Islamists have demonstrated that Islam is a religion of development and social justice. Islamist organizations have won over untold numbers because they are clearly efficient at delivering services and social programs to the rural and urban poor, providing what the government is not: education, health care, and various other social welfare services.[47] Such services have significantly improved the quality of life for many Muslim families and have won political Islam a great deal of goodwill.

In summary, Islamists have demonstrated that Islam offers more than a remedy for failed political leadership—it provides pragmatic solutions to every political, social, and economic problem.[48] Islam answers questions and provides remedies in ways that are vastly superior to ideas and institutions offered by modernity.[49] Political Islam, comprised of a number of well-organized mass movements, has proven that it can mobilize its constituency to put this plan into action. And it is uniquely placed to do so, since unlike its secular counterparts, it is only the religious opposition that has (within limits) been allowed the political space to channel and express popular discontent. As we will see in the sections that follow, this discontent can be channeled in any number of ways.

MILITANT ISLAMISM

Although Western media coverage would lead one to believe that Islamism is synonymous with militant *jihadism*, only a small minority of Islamists are militant extremists or *jihadists*, on the radical right-wing of the Islamist spectrum. In fact, members of groups such as the multinational al-Qaeda, Indonesia's Jema'ah Islamiah or Iraq's Ansar al-Islam would most accurately be characterized as "rogue" Islamists because the overwhelming majority of Islamists carry out their activities peacefully. This majority often accuses *jihadists* of worsening the situation for Muslims and corrupting the essence of Islam by promoting it as an ideology of hate.[50]

Yet, those Islamists who seek to destroy the US, who embrace the use of violence and confrontational tactics, have made an undeniable impact on the world. How did these groups come about and how do they rationalize their tactics? Although the first suicide bombing associated with radical Islam dates back to the 1983 attack on the US Marine barracks in Lebanon, it wasn't until the early 1990s that the number of extremist attacks began to take off. A variety of reasons exist for this choice of tactics, including the end of the Cold War, the political exclusion of Islamist parties in Algeria and Egypt, as well as government repression against Islamist groups.[51] Such efforts have proven counterproductive, as government crackdowns have bred more right-wing militants. For example, many of today's extremists are veterans of the Afghan war. Fleeing government crackdowns in Egypt and Saudi Arabia in the late 1970s and 1980s, thousands of Islamists (including Osama bin Laden) went to Afghanistan to fight as *mujahedeen* (holy warriors) against the Soviet Union and its puppet regime. After the Soviet withdrawal, these veteran soldiers (who had been armed by the US to fight the Soviets) were convinced that because they had defeated one superpower, they could go on to lead a global *jihadist* movement to defeat another.[52]

How do Islamist extremists rationalize the use of violence? One common argument is that Islamists have not chosen violence, rather it was thrust upon them.[53] Consequently, they are fighting a defensive war for a just cause, a *jihad*. Borrowing from Qutb's teachings about *jahiliyya*, they argue that most governments in the Muslim world are heretical regimes, deserving of violence, and therefore legitimate targets for attack. The West keeps these governments in power, and because the US is the leader of the West, the US is also a target. Much of the anti-Americanism associated with militant Islam is based in the belief in a Western conspiracy aimed at destroying Islam; this is a threat that emerged with the Crusades and continues today. Even before 9/11, *jihadists* considered themselves to be living under a state of siege. Although the most obvious example is the US support of Israel, militant Islamists could point to any number of US wrongdoings to justify their need to strike out in self-defense. In his "Letter to America" written in 2002, Osama bin Laden justified his "aggression against civilians for crimes they did not commit" arguing that because Americans elected their government and have not required a change in policy, they are targets, too.[54]

Islamist extremists such as the Egyptian-born British imam Abu Hamza are known for speeches urging their followers to kill *kaffirs* (non-believers) for any reason—or for no reason at all.[55] These speeches are often viciously anti-Semitic and spewing hatred and (what to outsiders appear to be) bizarre Zionist conspiracies. They justify armed struggle and deliberate attacks on non-combatants (or the use of terror) as one of the only instruments available to them to challenge the West's continued global dominance. From their point of view, they are fighting the world's largest, most powerful militaries, and given the imbalance of power, they argue that there is no way that Islamists can fight a conventional war against the West. Militant Islamists contend that the West and Israel have committed countless acts of state terror against Muslims and their governments have done little in response. Under such constraints, what the West views as terrorism is for them a defensive war, a suitable means of fighting for subnational groups.[v] For them, "terrorism" is only another form of guerilla warfare; the use of transnational attacks and unorthodox fighting methods is deemed the only way to overcome the asymmetry in power between Muslims and the West.[56]

More importantly, besides demoralizing the enemy, militant Islamists argue that highly publicized, spectacular acts of terrorism help to prepare and instigate the *umma* to unite against their oppressors across ethnic, racial, geographical, political boundaries.[57] By destroying the aura of US power, Muslims everywhere are encouraged and spurred to action. Such attacks show that something can be done and change is conceivable.[58]

MODERATE ISLAMISM

From Morocco to Palestine, from Bangladesh to Indonesia, religious opposition groups are showing that nonviolent routes to change are also conceivable. Who leads the biggest pro-democracy movements and who has the strongest voice calling for transparent elections and political participation in the Muslim

[v] Interestingly, Danner contends that al-Qaeda struck on September 11, 2001 with the aim of drawing the US "out of its hole." In other words, al-Qaeda wanted the US to attack a Muslim country (it expected that Afghanistan would be the target but celebrated when the US went on to Iraq). This would not only show the world that the US was on a crusade against Islam everywhere; it also predicted that the US would fall into an endless quagmire that would be costly and politically fatal (see Mark Danner, "Taking Stock of the Forever War," *The New York Times Magazine*, September 11, 2005).

world? More often than not it is Islamists, most of them moderate (or liberal).[vi] They comprise the mainstream of Islamism, representing the vast majority of Islamists. Although there is considerable diversity within this group, mainstream groups share two key characteristics: 1) they reject the use of violence (with the notable exception that almost all support the right of Palestinian resistance against Israel); and 2) they seek political power through elections.[59]

Hardly imitators of Western philosophy, liberal Islamists argue that their liberalism predates that of the West and is based in life as it was lived by Mohammed and the original community of believers. For them, there is no contradiction between Islam and democratic principles such as consent, accountability, and an alternation (or rotation) in power.[60] These moderates argue that in calling for democracy they are also calling for a return to Islam because if the goal is to create a society based on the *umma*, or the first community of the faithful, then its basis is *shura*, or consultation of the believers. Utilizing the principle of *shura* as well as *ijma* (consensus), the Prophet consulted with his companions but made decisions on his own. After his death, the community deliberated on public matters collectively.[61] While this may sound like the perfect recipe for New England-style democracy, don't get carried away. Most scholars of Islam warn that even if an Islamic democracy is possible, it is not going to look much like a Western model (nor should it, they warn). The *umma* was held together by the moral authority of Mohammed, who served as a conduit between individual Muslims and God.

Keeping in mind the Muslim belief that absolute sovereignty belongs to God, what does "consultation of the believers" mean, exactly? Is it binding on leaders, or is it discretionary? That continues to be a critical matter of debate, although many analysts contend that *shura* describes a true democracy and an accommodation between religion and politics. It requires leaders to be in frequent contact with the entire society, to ask about its needs and to be open to its ideas about how problems might be resolved. In effect, under a system of *shura* political leaders are obliged to respect what they're told.[62]

How far does this go, and how are the leaders selected? There is not much agreement among Islamists on this particular issue, either. Maududi can be interpreted as allowing for democracy, in that he wrote that the leaders of an Islamic state could be determined in a variety of ways, including elections.[63]

[vi]The term "liberal" is not favored in much of the Islamic world because of its association with the West. Also, it is important to recognize the distinction between from liberal democratic parties that are secular versus those that are Islamist.

However, more conservative Islamists disagree with such interpretations, arguing that human rule is illegitimate and blasphemous. For them, democracy is a heretical religion, promoting a rejection of Allah and Islam because it places the people's wishes above the word of God.[64] According to this view, Muslims must answer to God alone. All forms of governance over Muslims are illegitimate except Islamic states, in which political power is highly centralized and decision-making power is reserved for the most revered religious elites or scholars. They contend that government should be modeled after Iran's theocracy, where elections are held, but religious elites have the right to select and appoint political leaders and to decide whether legislative decisions would be allowed to stand or not, based on whether they are consonant with the *shari'a*.[65]

On the other hand, more liberal Islamists counter that all Muslims agree with the *Qur'anic* injunction "there is no God but God." It only follows that God intended for humans to have the right to control their rulers (even the most revered religious elites). This Islamist view clearly echoes the Western liberal belief in God-given natural rights. It holds that God gave humans the right to advise and to criticize their rulers through a system of governance that we would recognize today as based in popular sovereignty and a decentralization of power.[66] If we look to *shura* and the precedent that was set during the Prophet's lifetime we can see how it is theoretically possible to have an Islamic democracy. Such a democracy would uphold Muslim values and be defined by limited government and a separation of powers while allowing for public debate, the free expression of opinion, and a free press.[67]

Therefore, for moderate Islamists, the basis of their Islamic democracy is Islam's sacred texts. However, they recognize that various human interpretations of these texts have proven to be conflicting and fallible. Admittedly, there are some "gray zones" in which Islamic sources are unclear and seemingly inconsistent on the crucial matters of political and civil rights (i.e.: the rights of women, non-Muslims, and atheists). For example, there is much disagreement among Muslims concerning personal status issues for women (i.e.: polygamy, inequitable rights to divorce, child custody, and inheritance, etc.). While conservatives argue that such rules are ordained by Allah, the most progressive Islamists argue that these are not messages of Islam. Rather, they are based in pre-Islamic social customs of 7th century Arabia that could not be eradicated by the time of Mohammed's death.[68]

Moderate Islamists attempt address other ambiguities in this gray zone by promising to uphold freedoms—"within the framework of Islam." However, as you might imagine, this only leads to more questions. According to Brown, Hamzawy, and Ottaway, such ambiguity could be characterized as duplicity on the part of Islamists, but it is more likely due to the ongoing debate about these issues between traditionalists and reformers—one that is unlikely to be resolved soon.[69]

Although there is no guarantee as to how they will wind up on crucial questions of human rights, moderate Islamists hold out hope for reform. They point out that relatively speaking, Islam has traditionally been tolerant of minority communities, and its values are compatible with democracy and pluralism.[vii] With a few notable exceptions, moderate Islamists have supported political rights for women. Moreover, Indonesia, Pakistan, Bangladesh may not be liberal democracies, but they all have had some experience with democracy, and these predominantly Muslim countries managed to elect female prime ministers long before most Western countries.[70]

Mainstream Islamists seek to join the democratic process, to reap political rewards through "normal politics," or participation in legal, mainstream political channels. Contending such an approach is appropriate under Islam, they argue that humans are created free, and restrictions on freedom contradict divine will.[71] Just as the *Qur'an* teaches that "there can be no compulsion in religion" (that people should be free to choose their faith), people should also be free to choose their political leaders. Building on Maududi's lessons, mainstream Islamists contend that individuals will choose Islamists if they are educated, enlightened, and peacefully persuaded.[72]

Are they right about this? There is substantial variation among countries in terms of the success rate of moderate Islamist movements. In Iran, a declared Islamist state, a reformist movement seeking more democratization (led by liberal Islamists such as President Mohammed Khatami) had a promising start in the late 1990s but lost elections in 2005 and appears (for the time being at least) to have been shut down by the conservative Islamist government.

However, elsewhere (whether such movements are legal or not) support for Islamist parties seeking power through the ballot box has grown, partly because

---

[vii]Islamists generally believe that where they are religious minorities, non-Muslims (especially those who practice monotheism) should be free to organize their own affairs on issues of worship and personal status. In more heterogeneous settings, moderate Islamists have often advocated equal rights for the different religious communities (see Nathan Brown, Amr Hamzawy, and Marina Ottaway, "'Islamist' Movements and the Democratic Process in the Arab World," Carnegie Endowment for International Peace, Paper No. 67 (March 16, 2006), *www.carnegieendowment.org*).

of people's frustration and dissatisfaction with ineffective, kleptocratic governments and weak economies. It is often predicted that if predominantly Muslim countries in Asia, Africa, and the Middle East were to have free and fair democratic elections today, Islamists would be the likely winners.[73] The Iraqi case, where an alliance dominated by Shiia Islamists in 2005 won more seats in parliament than any other party, is testament to this. There, and in recent elections in Egypt, Jordan, Morocco, and Turkey, mainstream Islamist parties have played by the rules of the game—although under varying levels of government constraint. Even when they have had to put forward candidates as independents because their own parties are banned, Islamists have won office at the local and national level.

For example, although Egypt's Muslim Brotherhood has been outlawed since 1954, when members were arrested for the attempted assassination of then Prime Minister Gamal Abdel Nasser, the organization has not only proven resilient, it has branches in nearly 70 countries, making it the largest Sunni Islamist movement in the Arab world. In the 1970s it rejected the use of violence and today describes itself as a moderate Islamic association that seeks to create an Islamic state and institute religious law through peaceful means.[74] In 2005, in Egypt's freest elections in 50 years, the still-banned Brotherhood managed to put forward candidates and gained five times the number of parliamentary seats it won in 2000.[75] Although it controls only about one-fifth of the parliament, there is no doubt that the Muslim Brotherhood is the strongest opposition force in the country; some experts even characterize it as a parallel power to the government.[76]

In Turkey, because overtly Islamist parties are not permitted to participate in that country's relatively secular politics, many of these groups have moderated and reframed their message as less threatening—as "Islamically oriented" instead of Islamist.[77] There is little evidence that groups such as the Justice and Development Party (which won parliamentary elections and formed the government in 2002) have any link to militants or have substantially changed Turkey's pro-Western foreign policy. In fact, these Islamists have helped to modernize the country's human rights laws and pushed forward the effort for Turkey to join the European Union. Although it is accused by its opponents of having a radical Islamist agenda, the Justice and Development Party likens itself to Europe's conservative Christian Democrats, who balance religious values with a democratic political system. Instead of saying Turkey is not religious enough, the governing Justice and Development Party criticizes it as not being democratic enough. It has effectively positioned itself as a progressive, sophisticated protest party that emphasizes the civilizational and cultural aspects of

Islam. Calling for social justice, religious freedom, ethnic tolerance, and a market economy, this Islamically-oriented party, which has excellent relations with Israel, disproves the view that all Islamists who win elections will work to create an Iranian-style theocracy.[78]

Such parties have been so successful that illiberal regimes in predominantly Muslim countries now recognize moderate Islamist parties as their leading opponents. The overwhelming majority of people living in the Islamic world today may not consider themselves to be Islamists, but they look to these parties as an alternative. Most analysts believe that these parties win some votes from people who reject the governing party's monopoly on power and the slow pace of political and economic change in their countries. Interestingly, given President Bush's hopes for democracy in the Middle East, the more democratic the region becomes, the more Islamists will come to power.[79] Once in power, if these democratic governments are truly representing the opinions of their citizenry, they are likely to adopt policies that appear to be anti-Western.[80] This will be true even of moderate Islamist governments. The US may not like this situation, but if it seeks to reverse course—if its commitment to democracy is perceived as hinging on the outcome of elections—the greatest beneficiary of such a policy will undoubtedly be hardliners and radicals.

THE TWO PRONGED APPROACH

"With One Hand We Will Build, With the Other We Will Fight." This slogan, employed by the Palestinian Islamist group Hamas, is indicative of how still yet a third group of Islamists (those living in territories occupied by Israel, including Lebanon's Hezbollah) favor the use of bullets and ballots simultaneously.[81] Hamas, the Palestinian offshoot of the moderate Islamist Muslim Brotherhood, was formed after the first *intifada* (or "uprising") against Israel in 1987. With its political wing seeking power through the democratic process and its military wing sworn to defeat Israel, Hamas promises a better life for Palestinians and has successfully presented itself as a "clean" (or uncorrupt) alternative to Fatah, the political wing of the secular Palestine Liberation Organization (PLO).

The PLO (which was once also considered a terrorist organization) has been portrayed by Hamas as a corrupt sell-out to Israel for recognizing the state of Israel and participating in the 1993 Oslo peace process. Since the breakdown of that process just a few years later, Palestinian militancy has grown and Hamas has gained political support, perhaps more for its community services and social work than its war against Israel.[82] This support has continued to grow as

209

younger generations increasingly have come to view the Fatah party (which ruled the Palestinian Authority without interruption from 1994 until 2006) as corrupt and incompetent.

To almost everyone's surprise, the strategy worked—and Hamas became the first Arab Islamist party to attain power through democratic means. In nearly a two to one vote, Hamas won a surprise landslide victory in the January 2006 election.[83] Most analysts consider this win more of a protest vote against Fatah than a vote for Hamas (and a vote for internal reforms rather than permanent war against Israel). However, given its push for democracy in the Middle East, this turn of events certainly presented a problem for the Bush administration. The new Palestinian government would now be dominated by members of a terrorist organization who had long insisted that Hamas would never give up its weapons or its avowed goal of destroying the state of Israel (because of its occupation of lands that Hamas believes were given by God to the Palestinians).

Soon after these historic elections, however, Hamas' tone appeared to be softening a bit. Analysts began to debate whether Hamas would moderate itself much as the Palestinian Liberation Organization had since in the late 1980s. The PLO's transformation took years, and the reality of governing may well change Hamas; few opposition groups behave the same way once they are elected to government. Especially if Israel leaves the West Bank (admittedly less likely now), Hamas may be compelled have to give up some of its grander goals and accept coexistence with Israel. In what might be read as a sign of moderation, Hamas' 2006 election platform did not directly call for the destruction of Israel. Some Islamists have talked about the possibility of a long truce. As the new Hamas government was forming, leaders such as Mahmoud Zahar were talking about the possibility some sort of dialogue, perhaps by negotiating with Israel through a third party (although Israeli Prime Minister Ehud Olmert rejected this idea).[84]

So, will this hard-core movement become more pragmatic and change some of its most fundamental demands? Analysts are divided on this question and there is likely some division even within Hamas on which way to go. We have seen such transformations elsewhere—in Ireland and in Central America. However, such shifts toward pragmatism (if they ever happen) take time. Hamas may not be afforded that luxury. Thrown off-guard by the Hamas win, the US (joined by the European Union and Russia) immediately declared that it would not deal with Hamas—and threatened to cut off millions of dollars in financial assistance to the aid-dependent Palestinian Authority—unless the new government recognizes Israel and commits itself to nonviolence. While the West may hope that the combination of isolation and sanctions will compel Hamas to bend (or doom the new government to failure) a total cut off of aid is just as likely to further destabilize the region, strengthen hardliners (who will persuasively blame the peoples' problems on the US and Israel) and solidify Hamas' relationship with new donors (such as Iran and Syria).[85]

Studies of political transitions tell us that the way internal divisions between reformers and hardliners play out is often influenced by how external powers choose to deal with these groups. When external powers adopt heavy-handed policies, the reformers lose out. Therefore, if the West believes that more democratization is in everyone's interests, it should avoid a "one size fits all" policy and tailor its approach to Islamist groups on a case by case basis.[86] Although many Americans agree that the US should refuse to recognize a Hamas government or provide it with aid because it a terrorist organization, analysts point out that Hamas does belong to a different category of political Islam than al-Qaeda.[87] They argue that it is significant that Hamas' violent activity has been restricted territorially and is directed against specific targets. Hamas has not attacked American targets in two decades nor has it been driven by a hatred of the West (in the same way that al-Qaeda is). Compared to al-Qaeda's visions of an international *jihad* and restoration of the caliphate, perhaps Hamas has more fixable grievances (depending on how one defines "Palestine"). No doubt, there are plenty of analysts who discount such ideas, arguing that Hamas will never comprise its principles. However, it may be that Hamas is more akin to old-style terrorist groups like the Irish Republican Army, which has renounced violence and joined the political process. Perhaps the lesson is this: give people a legitimate way to get what they care about most and they may drop their more extreme aims, including the use of terror.

Some point to the Islamist theocracy in Iran and call this naïve. For them, liberal Islamists' claims and assurances about the possibilities of an "Islamic democracy" ring hollow. For example, Harris argues that the term "religious moderate" is an oxymoron, because to be moderate and truly tolerant, one would have to assume the equal validity of all faiths. This is impossible for Muslims (or Christians or Jews, for that matter). There is no moderation if one is a true believer, because ultimately you think that you're right.[88]

Other Western analysts agree, arguing that Islamists (whether liberal or radical) are hardly tolerant, freedom-loving democrats. Sure, Islamists seek to come to power through elections, but they embrace the democratic process for instrumental reasons, as an expedient way to establish themselves in power. Once in power they will revert to radicalism, allowing nothing they deem counter to Islamic law and putting a halt to the democratic process that might remove them. In other words, Islamist support for democracy is a facade; the Islamist agenda is "one man, one vote, one time."[89]

Therefore, according to this view, Islamists are opportunists, biding their time. Consequently, the West must be very careful about pushing for elections (or even for authoritarian governments to relax restrictions on them) because if Islamists come to power, they will create enormous problems, not only for the people who live under them, but for the entire international community. "Islamic democracies" will be rogue, dangerous states committing a vast array of human rights abuses and contributing to arms proliferation, terrorism, and anti-Americanism.[90]

Other analysts disagree with such dire assessments, arguing that they are used by authoritarian regimes (and the West) to maintain the status quo. Sure, it is likely that governments of predominantly Muslim states truly representing the will of the people would likely object to much of US policy. But it also is possible to take an "anti-American" stance while accepting the rules of democracy and condemning violence.[91] Although even moderate Islamists advocate home-grown alternatives to Western-style liberal democracy, in countries where they have been permitted to participate in the political process, they have been playing by the constitutional rules of the game. Many Islamist parties appear to accept the values of democracy and pluralism, promising protections for minorities, and a willingness to cooperate with non-Islamist parties. There are examples, from Morocco, to Turkey, to Indonesia, of how progressive change can come from within Islam.[92]

CONCLUSION

Can we expect that the majority of Islamists would continue to moderate if allowed to participate in normal politics? Are they genuinely committed to democracy? The answer is hard to predict, because (so far, at least) there have been so few democratically-elected Islamist governments. It is also likely that different Islamist groups will behave differently, given their various circumstances. However, to be fair, as of yet there is no evidence that Islamists are more likely than other groups to suspend the democratic process if elected. As mentioned earlier, if history serves as any guide, the reality of governing tends to encourage compromise and mute radicalism.[93] Would this make a policy of engagement of moderate Islamism the most constructive solution in the war against terror? Your answer to this question largely depends on your own ideology.

NOTES

1. Nathan Brown, Amr Hamzawy, and Marina Ottaway, "'Islamist' Movements and the Democratic Process in the Arab World," Carnegie Endowment for International Peace, Paper no. 67 (March 16, 2006), *www.carnegieendowment.org*.

2. Daniel Pipes, "Bush Draws the Distinction between Islam as a Faith and the Political Ideology of Islamism," *The Jerusalem Post*, August 18, 2004; "Blair Lashes Out at 'Evil Ideology' of Islamist Extremism," *Agence France Presse*, July 16, 2005.

3. Amir Taheri, "Fascism in Muslim Countries," *American Foreign Policy Interests*, 26 (2004), pp. 21–30; Pipes, "Bush Draws the Distinction between Islam as a Faith and the Political Ideology of Islamism."

4. Haleh Afshar, "Feminisms, Islamophobia, and Identities," *Political Studies*, 53 (2005), pp. 262–283.

5. Sam Harris, *The End of Faith: Religion, Terror, and the Future of Reason* (New York: W.W. Norton and Co., 2004).

6. Fareed Zakaria, "Islam, Democracy, and Constitutional Liberalism," *Political Science Quarterly* (Spring 2004), pp. 1–20.

7. Amina Mashhour, "Islamic Law and Gender Equality—Could There be a Common Ground?: A Study of Divorce and Polygamy in Sharia Law and Contemporary Legislation in Tunisia and Egypt," *Human Rights Quarterly*, 27 (2005), pp. 562–596; Mohammed Ayoob, "Political Islam: Image and Reality," *World Policy Journal*, 21, no. 3 (Fall 2004), pp. 1–14; "Living Islam: Three Themes of Inquiry," Inder Broadcasting Associations (2002), *www.ibaradio.org*.

8. David Rohde, "A World of Ways to Say 'Islamic Law,'" *The New York Times*, March 13, 2005.

9. Martin Kramer, "Coming to Terms: Fundamentalists or Islamists?" *Middle East Quarterly* (Spring 2003), pp. 65–77.

10. Pipes, "Bush Draws the Distinction between Islam as a Faith and the Political Ideology of Islamism."

11. Brown, Hamzawy, and Ottaway, "'Islamist' Movements and the Democratic Process in the Arab World;" Malin Wimelius, "On Islamism and Modernity: Analysing Islamist Ideas on and Visions of the Islamic State," Ph.D. Dissertation (Umea, Sweden: Umea University 2003).

12. F. Zakaria, *The Future of Freedom: Illiberal Democracy at Home and Abroad* (New York: W.W. Norton, 2003).

13. Graham Fuller, *The Future of Political Islam* (New York: Palgrave, 2003); Henri Lauzière, "Post-Islamism and the Religious Discourse of 'Abd-Salam Yasin," *International Journal of Middle East Studies*, 37 (2005), pp. 241–261.

14. Wimelius, "On Islamism and Modernity;" M.A. Muqtedar Khan, "Radical Islam, Liberal Islam," *Current History*, 102. no. 688 (December 2003), pp. 417–421.

15. Gareth Jenkins, "Muslim Democrats in Turkey?" *Survival*, 45, no. 1 (Spring 2003), pp.45–66.

16. Khan, "Radical Islam, Liberal Islam;" Fuller, *The Future of Political Islam*; Zakaria, "Islam, Democracy, and Constitutional Liberalism."

17. Wimelius, "On Islamism and Modernity."

18. Ayoob, "Political Islam: Image and Reality."

19. Robert H. Pelletreau, Jr., "Symposium: Resurgent Islam in the Middle East," *Middle East Policy* (Fall 1994), p. 2; Alejandro Colás, "The Re-Invention of Populism: Islamist Responses to Capitalist Development in the Contemporary Maghreb," *Historical Materialism*, 12, no. 4 (2004), pp. 231–260.

20. Fuller, *The Future of Political Islam*.

21. Kramer, "Coming to Terms: Fundamentalists or Islamists?"

22. Henry Munson, "Islam, Nationalism and Resentment of Foreign Domination," *Middle East Policy*, X, no. 2 (Summer 2003), pp. 40–53; Ayoob, "Political Islam: Image and Reality."

23. Mashhour, "Islamic Law and Gender Equality;" Colás, "The Re-Invention of Populism: Islamist Responses to Capitalist Development in the Contemporary Maghreb."

24. Mashhour, "Islamic Law and Gender Equality;" Fuller, *The Future of Political Islam*; Khan, "Radical Islam, Liberal Islam."

25. Wimelius, "On Islamism and Modernity."

26. Ibid.

27. Sayyid Qutb, *Milestones* (Cedar Rapids, IA: Unity Publishing Company, 1980); Ayoob, "Political Islam: Image and Reality;" John Kifner, "A Tide of Islamic Fury, and How It Rose," *The New York Times*, January 30, 2005.

28. Reuven Paz, "Islamists and Anti-Americanism," *Middle East Review of International Affairs*, 7, no. 4 (December 2003).

29. Kifner, "A Tide of Islamic Fury, and How It Rose;" Ayoob, "Political Islam: Image and Reality."

30. Ayoob, "Political Islam: Image and Reality."

31. Colás, "The Re-Invention of Populism: Islamist Responses to Capitalist Development in the Contemporary Maghreb."

32. Ayoob, "Political Islam: Image and Reality;" Salma Ismail, *Rethinking Islamist Politics: Culture, the State, and Islamism* (London: I.B. Tauris, 2003).

33. Ayoob, "Political Islam: Image and Reality."

34. Munson, "Islam, Nationalism and Resentment of Foreign Domination."

35. Bruce Maddy-Weitzman, "Islamism, Moroccan-Style: The Ideas of Sheikh Yassine," *Middle East Quarterly*, X, no. 1 (Winter 2003); Colás, "The Re-Invention of Populism: Islamist Responses to Capitalist Development in the Contemporary Maghreb."

36. Munson, "Islam, Nationalism and Resentment of Foreign Domination."

37. Jessica Stern, *Terror in the Name of God: Why Religious Militants Kill* (New York: Ecco, 2003).

38. Ayoob, "Political Islam: Image and Reality;" F. Gregory Gause III, "Can Democracy Stop Terrorism?" *Foreign Affairs*, 84, no. 5 (September/October 2005), pp. 62–76.

39. Ayoob, "Political Islam: Image and Reality;" Munson, "Islam, Nationalism and Resentment of Foreign Domination."

40. Mark Danner, "Taking Stock of the Forever War," *The New York Times Magazine*, September 11, 2005.

41. Ayoob, "Political Islam: Image and Reality."

42. Munson, "Islam, Nationalism and Resentment of Foreign Domination."

43. Ayoob, "Political Islam: Image and Reality."

44. Ibid.

45. Brown, Hamzawy, and Ottaway, "'Islamist' Movements and the Democratic Process in the Arab World."

46. F. Zakaria, *The Future of Freedom: Illiberal Democracy at Home and Abroad* (New York: W.W. Norton, 2003); Fuller, *The Future of Political Islam*; Wimelius, "On Islamism and Modernity."

47. Colás, "The Re-Invention of Populism: Islamist Responses to Capital-
    ist Development in the Contemporary Maghreb;" Roksana Bahrami-
    tash, "Myths and Realities of the Impact of Political Islam on Women:
    Female Employment in Indonesia and Iran," *Development in Prac-
    tice*, 14, no. 4 (June 2004), pp. 508–520.

48. Ismail, *Rethinking Islamist Politics: Culture, the State, and Islamism.*

49. Ayoob, "Political Islam: Image and Reality;" Colás, "The Re-Inven-
    tion of Populism: Islamist Responses to Capitalist Development in
    the Contemporary Maghreb."

50. Khan, "Radical Islam, Liberal Islam;" Ayoob, "Political Islam: Image
    and Reality."

51. Mohammed Hafez, *Why Muslims Rebel: Repression and Resistance in
    the Muslim World* (Boulder, CO: Lynne Rienner Publishers, 2003).

52. Danner, "Taking Stock of the Forever War." *The New York Times
    Magazine*, September 11, 2005.

53. Kramer, "Coming to Terms: Fundamentalists or Islamists?"

54. Ayoob, "Political Islam: Image and Reality."

55. "Imams and Nazis," *The Economist*, February 11, 2006.

56. Danner, "Taking Stock of the Forever War;" Ayoob, "Political Islam:
    Image and Reality."

57. Kramer, "Coming to Terms: Fundamentalists or Islamists?"

58. Danner, "Taking Stock of the Forever War."

59. Brown, Hamzawy, and Ottaway, "'Islamist' Movements and the
    Democratic Process in the Arab World."

60. Charles Kurzman, *Liberal Islam* (New York: Oxford University Press,
    1998).

61. Sadek Jawad Sulaiman, "The Shura Principle in Islam," al-Hewar Center, 1999, *www.alhewar.com.*

62. "Living Islam: Three Themes of Inquiry;" MacFarquhar, "Will Politics Tame Egypt's Muslim Brotherhood?"

63. Wimelius, "On Islamism and Modernity."

64. Nir Rosen, "Iraq's Jordanian Jihadis," *The New York Times Magazine,* February 19, 2006.

65. Kifner, "A Tide of Islamic Fury, and How It Rose;" Wimelius, "On Islamism and Modernity."

66. Kurzman, *Liberal Islam.*

67. Maddy-Weitzman, "Islamism, Moroccan-Style;" Wimelius, "On Islamism and Modernity;" Kurzman, *Liberal Islam.*

68. Brown, Hamzawy, and Ottaway, "'Islamist' Movements and the Democratic Process in the Arab World;" Kurzman, *Liberal Islam.*

69. Brown, Hamzawy, and Ottaway, "'Islamist' Movements and the Democratic Process in the Arab World."

70. Wimelius, "On Islamism and Modernity;" Zakaria, "Islam, Democracy, and Constitutional Liberalism;" Kurzman, *Liberal Islam.*

71. Khan, "Radical Islam, Liberal Islam;" Radwan Masmoudi, "The Silenced Majority," *Journal of Democracy,* 14, no. 2 (April 2003).

72. Masmoudi, "The Silenced Majority;" Wimelius, "On Islamism and Modernity."

73. Gause, "Can Democracy Stop Terrorism?"

74. "The Muslim Brothers: Getting Stronger?" *The Economist,* June 4, 2005.

75. Neil MacFarquhar, "Will Politics Tame Egypt's Muslim Brother-hood?" *The New York Times*, December 8, 2005.

76. Michael Slackman, "With No Status as a Party, Egyptian Group Wields Power," *The New York Times*, August 16, 2005; Michael Slackman, "Under Duress, Egypt's Islamist Party Still Surges at the Polls," *The New York Times*, November 27, 2005.

77. Gareth Jenkins, "Muslim Democrats in Turkey?"

78. Ayoob, "Political Islam: Image and Reality;" R. Quinn Mecham, "From the Ashes of Virtue, A Promise of Light: The Transformation of Political Islam in Turkey," *Third World Quarterly*, 25, no. 2 (2004), pp. 339–358; "Erdogan: Turkey Could Mediate Between Hamas and Israel," *Deutsche-Press Agentur*, January 28, 2006.

79. Gause, "Can Democracy Stop Terrorism?"

80. Fuller, *The Future of Political Islam.*

81. "Hamas: Talks with Israel "Not a Taboo," *Associated Press*, January 23, 2006; Kramer, "Coming to Terms: Fundamentalists or Islamists?"

82. Colás, "The Re-Invention of Populism: Islamist Responses to Capital-ist Development in the Contemporary Maghreb."

83. Matthew Kalman, "Landslide for Hamas—Limbo in Middle East," *Associated Press*, January 27, 2006.

84. Stephen Erlanger, "Hamas Leader Sees No Change Toward Israelis," *The New York Times*, January 29, 2006; Kalman, "Landslide for Hamas—Limbo in Middle East;" Stephen Erlanger and Greg Myre, "Palestinian Leader to Ask Hamas to Form New Government," *The New York Times*, January 27, 2006.

85. Kalman, "Landslide for Hamas—Limbo in Middle East."

86. Brown, Hamzawy, and Ottaway, "'Islamist' Movements and the Democratic Process in the Arab World."

87. Ayoob, "Political Islam: Image and Reality."

88. Harris, *The End of Faith*.

89. Pipes, "Bush Draws the Distinction between Islam as a Faith and the Political Ideology of Islamism;" Maddy-Weitzman, "Islamism, Moroccan-Style."

90. Pipes, "Bush Draws the Distinction between Islam as a Faith and the Political Ideology of Islamism;" Harris, *The End of Faith*.

91. Gause, "Can Democracy Stop Terrorism?"

92. Bahramitash, "Myths and Realities of the Impact of Political Islam on Women;" "Democracy in the Middle East: Mainstreaming Terrorists," *The Economist*, June 25, 2005; Ayoob, "Political Islam: Image and Reality."

93. Fuller, *The Future of Political Islam*.

Chapter 9

African-American Political Thought in the 20th and 21st Centuries:

SOME OF THE MAJOR IDEOLOGUES—LEFT, CENTER, RIGHT

Left   "Capitalism cannot reform itself, it is doomed to self-destruction. No universal selfishness can bring social good to all. Communism ... this is the only way of human life."[1]

> W.E.B. DuBois
> (Application for Membership in the Communist Party of the U.S.A.)

Center   "So I say to you, my friends, that even though we must force the difficulties of today and tomorrow, I still have a dream. It is a dream deeply rooted in the American dream that one day this nation will rise up and live out the true meaning of its creed—we hold these truths to be self-evident, that all men are created equal."[2]

> Martin Luther King Jr.
> ("I Have a Dream" Speech)

"We've sent out a wrong message through our welfare system, and new people aren't trying. ... We have two generations that haven't tried, and ... their abilities are lagging so far behind that one more generation of this and we will have a permanent underclass of people who cannot mobilize themselves."[3]

> Starr Parker
> ("Black Conservatives Seek Abolition of Welfare System")

Right   (The President should have) the *absolute authority* to appoint all his lieu-
        tenants from cabinet ministers, governors of states and territories, adminis-
        trators and judges to minor officers . . .[4] "We are looking toward political
        freedom on the continent of Africa, the land of our fathers."[5]

Marcus Garvey
(Philosophy and Opinions)

CLASSICAL THOUGHT

Left   The philosophers have only interpreted the world, in various ways; the
       point, however, is to change it."[6]

Karl Marx, *Theses on Feuerbach* (xl)

Center   "The sole end of which mankind are warranted, individually or collectively,
         in interfering with the liberty of action of any of their number, is self-
         protection. That the only purpose for which power can be rightfully exer-
         cised over any member of a civilized community, against his will, is to
         prevent harm to others."[7]

John Stuart Mill, *On Liberty*

"It is with infinite caution that any man ought to venture upon pulling
down an edifice, which has answered in any tolerable degree for ages the
common purposes of society, or on building it up again, without having
models and patterns of approved utility before his eyes."[8]

Edmund Burke, *Reflections on the Revolution in France*

Right   "Unless either philosophers become kings in their countries or those who
        are now called kings and rulers come to be sufficiently inspired with a gen-
        uine desire for wisdom; *unless, that is to say, political power and philosophy
        meet together* . . . There can be no rest from troubles . . . for all mankind."[9]

Plato, *The Republic*

T he four quotations by African-American or black political thinkers and
      the four classical theorists clearly demonstrate the many parallels
      between classical literature and black political thought. More impor-
tantly they alert us to the diversity of opinion, the range of ideological commitment and the nature of political thought.

Diversity of opinion is the common denominator in African-American political thought. As the text will show, blacks disagree and argue about virtually

everything—the role of violence, the nature and role of religion, the role of women and the rewards and penalties of interracial coalition. Though the vast majority may *agree* that life in American society is racist, they *disagree* on what to do about the psychological and social domination, economic problems, discrimination, and segregation they experience. Agreement and disagreement characterizes black thought.

African-American political thought covers the spectrum from left to right. Consider the following personalities and their ideological predispositions:

LEFT
- Communism/Marxism: W.E.B. DuBois, Huey Newton, Angela Davis
- Socialism/Radicalism: A. Philip Randolph, Malcolm X (1964–65), Cornel West, Ronald Dellums

CENTER
- Liberalism: Martin Luther King Jr., Jesse Jackson, Shirley Chisholm, Barbara Jordan, Ron Brown, Roy Wilkins, Julian Bond
- Conservatism: Thomas Sowell, Shelby Steele, Starr Parker, Clarence Thomas, Walter Williams, Alan Keyes

RIGHT
- Nationalist Authoritarianism: Marcus Garvey, Mittie Gordon, Cyril Briggs
- Black Power Authoritarianism: Elijah Mohammed, Louis Farrakhan, Malcolm X (1952–64)

Two fundamental issues pervade the nature of black political thought. One overriding theme concerns integration or segregation. Can blacks and whites ever live in an authentic human community together? Is the history of blacks and whites in America so hostile, so contentious, that a life together is impossible? Is a colorblind society possible, probable, or impossible? Some argue that this is *the* underlying issue in all African-American political thought. Another underlying theme that generates tremendous disagreement is how does one most effectively achieve the liberation enterprise. Is the basic problem social or individual? That is, does the key to success involve a fundamental change of the social order, or is it necessary to radically transform individual human beings?

223

Or—is the remedy to be found in some combination of the two? What is to be done?[10]

INTRODUCTION

The African-American or black struggle for freedom and justice involves politics—the arena of constant disagreement on issues that must be continually faced and resolved in various ways. To even begin to resolve controversy implies discussion and understanding of the various viewpoints (ideologies) and an exchange of information. What we attempt here is to identify and explain the complex nature of black politics by an inquiry into some of the fundamental issues which divide this large constituency of about thirty-four million Americans (12.8%) into six broad ideological categories of the Left, Center, and Right.

Virtually all of the great issues of politics are involved in the answers given to the perennial questions such as:

- What is the proper role of government—"Nanny" or Constable?
- Is the American creedal identity as defined in the Declaration of Independence and Constitution a "dream" or a "nightmare?"
- Should the political tactics of blacks be always, everywhere, all-times violent or non-violent?
- Are the problems of blacks best solved by personal or social initiatives?
- What is the origin of our human rights and are these rights and needs the province of individuals or the community?
- Should African-Americans enter into, or avoid, coalition politics with whites? Is black-white brotherhood/sisterhood an oxymoron?
- What form of government would be best to secure freedom and justice for blacks—concentration or dispersion of political power?
- What role, if any, should religion play in the struggle to realize the goals of blacks? What limits, if any, should there be on government? Simply—should blacks subscribe to constitutional or authoritarian government?
- How should we understand human beings—that is, what constitutes human nature and psychology? Are we mere beasts as Machiavelli states or can we transcend ourselves and become new, different, and yes, better human beings?

224

All these and many more are answered in the ideological kaleidoscope of African-Americans. The literature is vast. The individual personalities, male and female, are fascinating. The answers to the questions are as varied as the spectrum. The singular goals of blacks for freedom and justice stand in stark contrast to the many methods suggested. Let us begin then with our inquiry into these varied ideologies.

One last question deserves attention, that is, *why* were the particular individuals discussed herein chosen as opposed to others that are omitted or merely mentioned? We applied a number of criteria to the host of possibilities and made the decision on the basis of the following: range of thought, dedication to the task, organizational skills, reputation as an outstanding spokesman, audacity and activism in politics, style of politics, leadership and personality, and nature of their ideas. Others certainly might have been selected, but space and subjectivity are limiting factors for every author.

LEFT

Huey P. Newton (Communism)

Huey P. Newton was born in New Orleans, Louisiana on February 17, 1942. As the youngest of seven children, Newton was the favorite in a close-knit family. His father, a sharecropper and a Baptist minister, and mother, Armelia Newton, moved to Oakland, California when Huey was one year old. They lived in the leaden, drab ghetto of the central city. To survive, Newton's father worked at two or sometimes three jobs at a time.[11]

Newton attended public school, but was pegged as a slow learner by his teachers. Demoralized, he frequently missed classes and was suspended from various schools a number of times. Though he was virtually illiterate, he graduated from Oakland Technical High School. Recognizing that he had to overcome the illiteracy barrier, he forced himself to read Plato's *Republic* five times. Once he understood this text he "gobbled up" everything he could get at the library. He went on to earn an associate arts degree at Merritt College—a two-year institution in Oakland. While at Merritt, he met Bobby Seale, became interested in politics and there co-founded the Black Panther Party in October 1966. This party became a national paramilitary organization dedicated to black "self-defense." Eldridge Cleaver joined the new group and Newton, Seale, and Cleaver recruited new members from the Oakland ghetto. Newton was minister

AFRICAN-AMERICAN OR BLACK POLITICAL THOUGHT

	ANTHROPOLOGY		SOCIOLOGY		
	Human Nature	Alienation	Society	Economics	Politics
LEFT					
A. Communism					
B. Socialism/Radicalism					
CENTER					
A. Liberalism					
B. Conservatism					
RIGHT					
A. Nationalist Authoritarianism					
B. Black Power Authoritarianism					

Before reading this chapter on African-American or Black political thought in the 20th century, students might find it helpful to review the detailed description of the concepts LEFT, CENTER, RIGHT, as outlined in Chapter One.

Having said this, we suggest the following single standard for easy recall: "Call moving toward socialism and state control - LEFT and moving toward individualism and free markets - RIGHT.

The LEFT thus includes the ideologies of Communism/Marxism and Socialism/Radicalism; the CENTER contains Liberalism and Conservatism; and the RIGHT is membered by Nationalist Authoritarianism and Black Power Authoritarianism political thought.

Two principle categories of analysis provide the framework for this analysis of Black political thought -- ANTHROPOLOGY and SOCIOLOGY. Under anthropology, topics such as human nature/psychology and alienation will be discussed. When making our analysis of sociology we inquire into the social, economic, and political thought of the selected theorists.

Figure 9.1   Political Spectrum and Categories of Analysis of African-American Political Thought

of Defense, and with their clenched-fist salutes, leather jackets, berets, and armed patrols they had frequent problems with the police. Newton was jailed for assault in 1964, imprisoned for murder in 1968 (acquitted), and jailed again in 1978 and 1988 because of possession of weapons.[12]

Newton immersed himself in the literature of DuBois, Malcolm X, Franz Fanon, Karl Marx, and Lenin, but seemed to benefit the most from the writing of Mao Tsetung and Che Guevara. In 1980 he earned a Ph.D. from the University of California at Santa Cruz. *To Die for the People* and *Revolutionary Suicide* constitute his major contributions to knowledge.

Seriously addicted to drugs, he was killed in a drug dispute on August 23, 1989 in Oakland.[13]

Anthropology   Newton embraces Marx's materialism (theory of what constitutes ultimate reality) and dialectics (theory of how one can come to know that reality). For Newton, like Marx, *change* is the rule of life and this change occurs continually in ideas, institutions, and individuals.

Newton sees human beings as a part of nature and the material world, but distinguished from nature by two special characteristics—the existence of the human spirit and the unending quest for knowledge. These attributes combine to make human beings more than mere matter. As he says, "The dignity and beauty of man rests in the human spirit which makes him more than simply a physical being. This spirit must never be suppressed for exploitation by others . . ."[14] Newton's second unique attribute of human beings is Faustian in nature, i.e., human beings possess an insatiable striving for knowledge and mastery. Human beings are constantly troubled and tormented by the quest to know the unknowable—"when the extraordinary is not explained, when the unknown is not known, then there is room for God because the unexplained and the unknown is God."[15]

Next, human beings must have freedom. "Without freedom life means nothing. We have nothing to lose but our shackles and freedom to gain."[16] To Newton, to be free is what it means to be an authentic human being. The slave is therefore the very antithesis of what it means to be human and if the quest for freedom involves death, then so be it—"we escape to freedom" through death. Newton goes on to distinguish between two kinds of suicide—reactionary suicide and revolutionary suicide. Reactionary suicide is the act of accepting reactionary conditions, "accepting the situation and allowing ourselves to die . . . (this is) the death of the Jews in Germany."[17] Revolutionary suicide is "the death of the Jews in Warsaw . . . then, at least, I can claim the dignity of a man and die the death of a man rather than the death of a dog."[18]

To Newton, the problem of the black male is to overcome his constant state of rage, shame, doubt, and a life built on mistrust, role confusion, isolation, and despair. The black male is often unskilled, marginally employed, ineffectual in providing for his family—an invisible nonentity. Worst of all "he is dependent upon the White man ('THE MAN') . . . and (so) he hates 'THE MAN' and he hates himself."[19] In order to escape these destructive psychological problems, blacks must take control of every aspect of their lives—social, economic, and political. Only then can they transcend exploitation and change from a worthless to a worthwhile existence. Blacks must become "producers rather than consumers" in society or the transition is impossible.

Sociology   Politically, "The Black Panther Party is a Marxist-Leninist party because we follow the dialectical method and we integrate theory with practice."[20] But Newton is careful to distinguish Black Panther ideology from mechanistic Marxism, that is, the dogmatic application of Marx's ideas to social realities. Rather he characterizes the group's ideological orientation as "creative Marxism"—one open to constant change and analysis and a Marxism wherein human individuals can and do make a difference.

In his speech delivered at Boston College on November 18, 1970, Newton discusses five stages of political evolution and development of the state: Nationalist, Revolutionary Nationalist, Internationalist, Inter-Communalist, and ultimately the withering away of the state.[21] In 1966, the Party was called the Black *Nationalist* Party. It was assumed that the establishment of the nation was primary. This was found to be inadequate and the Party decided that *Revolutionary Nationalism* was the answer, that is, "nationalism plus socialism." The next level of development of the state for the Party was the *Internationalist* mode. Here solidarity with nations of the world was sought. But this too was shown to be inadequate because of the rapid development of technology and the Party moved dialectically onward and upward to the *Intercommunalist* state. This is the epoch where the people take control of all productive forces and factors and by so doing create the conditions for the *stateless society*. Newton, like Marx, arrives at the new day, the new society, the new human being by a series of progressive steps.[22]

All this political development is, of course, made possible by the full-time professional revolutionaries in the Black Panther Party—the *Vanguard* of the revolutionary forces in society. Finally, insofar as politics is concerned, Newton sees the Party working "with White radicals" to achieve their goals, willing and anxious to employ careful analysis of circumstances rather than rote violence at all times to realize the program (the reason for the split with Eldridge Cleaver), and the crucial role of the Party in raising the consciousness of the people to the exciting possibilities available through political action.

Newton's economic thought conceives of "a real intercommunal economy that transcends culture. Perhaps his most interesting ideas on economics concern the evolution of capitalism from *Democratic Capitalism* to *Bureaucratic Capitalism*. Under Democratic Capitalism he characterizes the American economy with attributes such as small population, fertile land, agricultural emphasis, social mobility, and the rapid development of the entire economy. Two hundred years later, argues Newton, we have an overdeveloped economy so infused with profit and greed that we have replaced the old relations of capitalism with bureaucratic capitalism. Free opportunity is negated by constraints placed on human beings by large corporations. These new economic giants seek particularly to increase profit at the expense of racial and ethnic minorities.[23]

Newton contends that blacks cannot afford the luxury of individualism which he sees as "sheer madness, impotence personified." Newton wants blacks to reject capitalism and instead encourages blacks to support and patronize businesses that return some of their profits to the people on a regular basis.[24]

Socially, the Black Panther Party's task is to "serve the needs" of the people by setting up programs for free clothing, food, shoes, breakfast, health, and research on health problems of particular concern to blacks such as Sickle Cell Anemia.

Finally, Newton sees the Black Panther Party as the field blacks rather than the house blacks. By this he means that the Party is the Party of the working blacks, the proletariat, not the Party of the house blacks—the bourgeoisie. Newton does not want to be controlled by the white radicals or the black bourgeoisie.

Angela Y. Davis (Communism)

Angela Davis is probably the most prominent black woman of the left today. She was born on January 26, 1944 in Birmingham, Alabama. She grew up in a segregated black neighborhood, was a straight "A" student in school, helped form interracial study groups for youths, and at fifteen moved to New York City. After graduation from high school, she entered Brandeis University as a French major, spent her junior year at the Sorbonne in Paris, returned to Brandeis and came under the direction of the eclectic Marxist, Herbert Marcuse. He considered her "the best student" he had taught in thirty years. She earned her bachelor's degree from Brandeis in 1964, and from 1965 to 1967 she studied philosophy at the Goethe University in Frankfurt, Germany under Theodore

Adorno. She earned her M.A. degree from the University of California at San Diego in 1968, but has never finished her dissertation on Immanuel Kant in the doctoral program in philosophy at Berlin's Humboldt University. In 1968 she joined the Communist Party U.S.A. and later, in 1980 and 1984, ran as this group's vice presidential candidate.[25] At the present time she is a tenured professor at the University of California at Santa Cruz, where she teaches courses on feminism and African American studies.

In 1970, in a highly publicized trial, Davis was charged with conspiracy in a murder, went into hiding, appeared on the F.B.I.'s ten-most-wanted list, was captured in New York, and extradited to California. There she was released on bail and subsequently acquitted. The trial, called the case of the Soledad Brothers, brought Davis worldwide attention. She is an internationally known speaker and crusader against racial, sexual, and economic oppression. To realize her goals, Davis favors a United Front, a black-white coalition, as opposed to black separatism. Her economic strategy seeks to take over the productive forces of society and to operate them for the general welfare. She contends that social, not individual, transformation is the key ingredient needed to realize black liberation.

Her books include, *If They Come in the Morning, Angela Davis: An Autobiography,* and *Women, Culture and Politics.* In the latter work she makes powerful comments on women, international issues, and culture. Regarding women, Davis argues "it is incumbent upon women in the United States to study the lessons . . . that emerge from the experiences of women in the Soviet Union. (There) dramatic strides have been made toward the social, economic, and political equality of Soviet women.[26] On international issues, Davis is a passionate supporter of the United Nations Decade for Women. She contends that "the global movement for women's emancipation is finally becoming cognizant of the links between our struggles as women and the worldwide opposition to capitalist exploitation, racist oppression, and nuclear militarization."[27] Finally, on culture, Davis argues that the fight to build and expand ethnic studies programs in America has much to learn from the experiences of the socialist countries. The world is being transformed and the socio-economic structures of the capitalist system are defunct.[28] Her latest publication is entitled, *Are Prisons Obsolete?*

A. Philip Randolph (Socialism)

A. Philip Randolph (1889–1979) was born in Crescent City, Florida on April 15, 1889. After study at Cookman Institute in Jacksonville, Randolph went to New York where he worked as a porter and an elevator operator. He took some courses at City College of New York and started the *Messenger* in 1917 with Chandler Owens.[29] Later, Randolph organized the Brotherhood of Labor and was one of the best "soapbox" orators. At one of his rallies, the Department of Justice arrested him "on sedition charges for urging blacks not to fight in World War I."[30] These charges were eventually dropped and after the war, Randolph moved more and more away from journalism and toward labor organization. In 1925, Randolph began organizing work for the Brotherhood of Sleeping Car Porters. He was opposed, naturally, by the Pullman Company. But by 1928, Randolph controlled over half of the porters in the United States and in 1931 this union, the first black union, was finally recognized by the Pullman Company.[31]

In 1941 Randolph organized a March on Washington Movement designed to pressure the government to allocate a fair share of the defense industry jobs to blacks. Roosevelt sent his wife, Eleanor, to talk to Randolph and persuade him to call off the march. The talks failed and Roosevelt then met with Randolph on June 18, gave in to Randolph's demand, and issued Executive Order 8802 prohibiting discrimination in defense industries.[32]

Twenty-two years later, Randolph helped organize a second March on Washington to end discrimination. This march took place and was the scene of Martin Luther King Jr.'s famous "I Have a Dream" speech. President Johnson awarded Randolph the President's Medal of Freedom. By this time, Randolph was the civil rights movement's leading statesman. Randolph brought magnificent oratory to his obvious intellectual prowess. He died in his New York apartment at age ninety on May 16, 1979.[33]

Anthropology   In almost all times and places, human beings have been divided by inequality of wealth, power, physical well-being, skill, and respect. The problem is that the lives of human beings are dramatically affected by these inequalities. Some theorists contend these inequalities have natural causes. Others argue the inequalities have social causes.

At the very center of A. Philip Randolph's thinking was his belief in the essential *equality* of all human beings. Randolph rejected the notion of hierarchy where some people exist only to serve others. For him, the distinguishing attributes of human nature were the "power of reason and his belief in people's common destiny." This faith in reason and common destiny separates him from

231

contemporary socialists such as Cornel West who cogently argues in his book, *Race Matters,* that the injuries of racism create barriers that reason alone cannot transcend. For Randolph, human nature and psychology is characterized by a reasoned balance between one's self-interest and by a concern for the common good.

On *alienation,* Randolph saw the solution to the problems of blacks in an alliance, a coalition, with the white working class. In his speech of September 27, 1942 in Detroit, Michigan, he says, "Our policy is that it be all-Negro and pro-Negro, but not anti-white or anti-Semitic or anti-labor or anti-Catholic."[35] Randolph condemned the ideology of Marcus Garvey for its racially-separatist doctrines and he criticized also the slogans of the Black Power Movement saying that "slogans don't solve anything."[36] If Randolph was anything, he was a superb organizer and his abilities were directed toward closing the gap of racial alienation, separation, and estrangement by building coalitions of working men and women—both white and black. He fought for "the common man" regardless of race. He wanted to realize equality, freedom, and justice for blacks, and all working people regardless of race, and he believed that human beings were brave enough and honest enough to achieve these goals. The American creed is Randolph's creed—but one that demands practice in conjunction with theory.

Sociology   Randolph was a socialist and ran, as a socialist, for New York Secretary of State. But Randolph always rejected communism and when the Socialists in the United States split into Left and Right wing groups after World War I, he sided with the Right. He worked, organized and was later invited to be the Socialist candidate for Vice-President of the United States.[37] He never trusted the communists saying, "We cannot sup with the communists, for they rule or ruin any movement. This is their policy. Our policy must be to shun them."[38] Randolph was a democratic socialist. He believed that for blacks "our fate is tied up with the fate of the democratic way of life."[39] His political goals were to make American democracy an operative ideal for all Americans and to end the empire system in the underdeveloped countries that he argued was brought about by monopoly capitalism. It was the duty of blacks to fight, and if need be die, to realize their civil rights. He knew it would take a protracted struggle to gain these rights as they "will not be given." His tactic in politics was to use non-violence and this technique is probably best seen in the 1963 March on Washington where over 200,000 people participated. Some have characterized this March as his political high-point.

In economics, Randolph's message is straightforward. He sought to improve the capitalist system with the "medicine" of socialism so that it worked for all rather than just some people. He wanted to improve the economic system in America—not destroy it which was the goal of the Communists.

Randolph attacked discrimination in white-dominated trade unions, he organized blacks and whites into political coalitions, he attacked the "economic royalists" of big business, and in particular, fought to end Jim Crow laws throughout America that denied jobs to blacks. When the AFL and CIO merged in 1955, Randolph was named one of two vice-presidents of that organization. Randolph understood, perhaps better than most, the economic roots of racism and fought all his life to tear down these barriers.

Randolph's social vision was broad. He went "toe to toe" with both Franklin D. Roosevelt and Harry Truman to end the Jim Crow practices in the armed forces and all the other aspects of life in America. He was rewarded for these efforts when on July 21, 1948 Truman issued Executive Order 9981 which states that "there shall be equality of treatment and opportunity for all persons in the armed services."[40]

At his death in 1979 at the age of ninety, Randolph's reputation as the most important labor leader to come out of the black community in America was accepted by all as a truism.

Cornel West (Socialism)

Cornel West is a faculty member in the Department of Religion at Princeton University (2002). Prior to that West was at the Harvard Divinity School and Harvard College's department of Afro-American studies. He was one of only fourteen of the university's 2,000 faculty to hold the title of university professor. In his 1993 book, *Race Matters,* West writes about the crisis in black America and calls on black leaders to forsake the failed approaches of both liberals and conservatives in favor of solutions based on ethical not political principles.

West was born in Tulsa, Oklahoma in 1953. His mother was a teacher and principal and his father was a civilian administrator for the air force. The family moved frequently but settled in Sacramento, California where West had problems in school, was suspended, and subsequently transferred to a more progressive school across town. Besides his family, West was inspired during these formative years by the Baptist church he attended, the Black Panthers who introduced him to activism and the writing of Karl Marx, and by Theodore Roosevelt, an asthmatic sufferer like West.[41]

In 1970, West entered Harvard College and so became part of the first generation of young blacks to attend prestigious institutions of higher learning in significant numbers. There West majored in philosophy and near eastern languages

233

and literature. At Harvard his Christian vision of democratic socialist values was influenced by the writing of Franz Fanon, Leon Trotsky, Reinhold Niebuhr, Leszek Kolakowski, and Marxist humanists like Milo Markovic and Stojanovic. West graduated magna cum laude from Harvard and then went to Princeton for two more years of study in philosophy. Here he became committed to the values of individuality (the sanctity and dignity of the individual) and to democracy as a way of life. He then returned to Harvard as a Du Bois fellow to write his dissertation. In 1980 he received his Ph.D. from Princeton university.[42]

In the fall of 1977 West began teaching at Union Theological Seminary in New York City as an Assistant Professor of philosophy and religion. There he immersed himself in the literature of liberation theology and joined Michael Harrington's Democratic Socialists of America (DSA). In 1984 West moved from Union to the Yale Divinity School where he studied Antonio Gramsci's thought. He spent the spring of 1987 at the University of Paris and when he returned to the United States he again began teaching at Union Theological Seminary for one year. Princeton then persuaded West to join its Department of Afro-American studies in the fall of 1987. He remained there until he went back to Harvard in 1994 as a faculty member of the Harvard Divinity School and that college's department of Afro-American studies.

West is a tall (6'1"), easygoing man with a drawl and a habit of wearing three-piece suits. He is slender, has a goatee and is a superb orator. His wife, Elleni, is Ethiopian-born, and he has a son from his first marriage who lives with him.[43]

Anthropology

West's conception of human nature and psychology begins with a frank acknowledgement of the basic humanness of each discrete human individual. As he says in *The Ethical Dimensions of Marxist Thought,* "I became convinced that the values of individuality—the sanctity and dignity of all individuals shaped in and by communities—and of democracy—as a way of life and mode of being-in-the-world, not just a form of governance—were most precious to me" . . . (To West this is the demand) "to view each and every individual as having equal status, as warranting dignity, respect, and love . . ."[44] Because of this posture, West sees black nationalism as a "gallant yet misguided" effort to understand African identity in a hostile white society and in so doing limits the discussion on race. Interracial interdependence, to West, is a reality in America—there is no escape.

Black alienation, isolation and the "numbing detachment from others" leads to nihilism in America's Black communities—a lived experience of coping with a life of horrifying meaninglessness, hopelessness, and (most important;) love-lessness.[45] For West, this loss of hope, absence of meaning, love, and alienation is the major enemy of black survival in America. This nihilism pervades black society and contributes to forms of escape (sports and sex) and criminal behavior. West writes approvingly of Toni Morrison who decries blacks' self-image in America—and the lack of self love and love of others. For West and Morrison, these are the most potent weapons of all.

Sociology

Cornel West characterizes himself as a "non-Marxist socialist" which he sees as a viable alternative to the "world-encompassing capitalist order" that rules the globe today. West is a member and also honorary co-chair of the Democratic Socialists of America (DSA). But his fundamental ideological posture, his mentality, is founded in his embrace of Christianity mediated by the traditions of the Black Church "that produced and sustains" him.

To understand West's politics and economics one must understand Antonio Gramsci, for he calls himself a Gramscian Democratic Socialist in the essay, *The Ethical Dimensions of Marxist Thought*. To Gramsci, the role of the intellectual is crucial, but Gramsci's organic intellectuals differ from the traditional intellectuals (priests and teachers that reinforce the status quo) in that they bond to the working class and the new revolutionary class. These intellectuals are to educate the masses and train them to be the ruling group. This in order to establish hegemony. This fabric of hegemony is woven by the organic intellectuals through reform, education and compromise, and a fully developed hegemony must rest on active consent. Hegemony cannot be reduced to manipulation. For Gramsci, and thus for West, this is the historic task of the intellectual, i.e., to create a continuous expansion of consent and a strategy of transition to socialism. Hegemony is the key concept in Gramsci's *Prison Notebooks* that comprise 2,350 printed pages in thirty notebooks.

West laments America's "chocolate cities and vanilla suburbs" that erode the tax base of major cities. He sees social breakdown, cultural decay and a consumer culture that promotes spiritual impoverishment. He is, as noted, a prophetic Christian freedom fighter because Christian existential wisdom, i.e., of what it means to be human and how we should act toward each other transcends Marxist social theory. Marxism is silent about "the existential meaning of death, suffering, love and friendship owing to its preoccupation with improving the social circumstances under which people love, revel in friendship, and confront death."[46] West works out of the Christian tradition—the prophetic Christian tradition.

In his book of essays, *Race Matters*, West discusses the failed Black leadership in America today, decries the nihilism in the Black *community*, and demystifies black sexuality, black nationalism and black conservatives. West's current project is a book entitled, *The Tragic, the Comic and the Political*. His is an authentic new voice in America that addresses the crucial issue of race in our society.

CENTER

Liberalism and Conservatism   The ideological center of black political thought contains a great reservoir of men and women. Those who embrace liberalism include people like Martin Luther King, Jr., Jesse Jackson, Shirley Chisholm, Barbara Jordan, Roy Wilkins, Julian Bond, Thurgood Marshall, Medgar Evars, Andrew Young, and a host of others. If there is a center of gravity in black political thought it is based in liberalism.

Today however, more blacks are adopting the ideology of conservatism, including Clarence Thomas, Walter Williams, Thomas Sowell, Starr Parker, Shelby Steele, Stanley Crouch, Glenn Loury, Julius Lester, Stephen Carter, Langston Hughes, Alan Keyes, Errol Smith, Larry Elder, and Armstrong Williams. Liberalism is still dominant, but black conservatives are making their voices heard on talk radio, syndicated newspaper columns, and television. The ideological balance in the black community appears to be making a small move to the right. How far right or how many blacks will make the psychic move remains to be seen. The point is black conservatives are suggesting that it is time for blacks to embrace a new ideological direction—and some who hear and read their ideas now heed the call.

Martin Luther King, Jr. (Liberalism)

Martin Luther King, Jr. is the best known black in American history even though his life ended when he was only thirty-nine years old. His public career began in December of 1955 when he assumed the leadership of the Montgomery, Alabama bus boycott. It ended with an assassin's bullet in Memphis, Tennessee, in February of 1968.

King was born in Atlanta, Georgia on January 15, 1929. His mother was a college graduate and his father a minister. Both parents sensitized their son to questions of morality and justice as opposed to mere law and order. He was educated at Morehouse College (sociology major) and then attended Crozier Theological Seminary in Chester, Pennsylvania. In 1955 he earned a Ph.D. at Boston University.

Besides his parents, the intellectual influences that shaped the mind of King involved the great philosophers (Plato, Aristotle, St. Thomas Aquinas, Hobbes, Locke, and Rousseau), Mahatma Gandhi's non-violent tactics, the social gospel of Walter Rauschenbusch, and the writing of Karl Marx. King agreed with Marx's analysis of the weaknesses of capitalism and his challenge to the Christian Church, but disagreed with Marx's materialist view of history. Contrary to Marx, King believed that history is primarily guided by spirit and not matter.[47] One more very influential factor on King cannot be overemphasized, i.e., the famous essay of Henry David Thoreau entitled, "Civil Disobedience." Law and order are one thing. Justice is something else. Justice to Thoreau and King transcended mere order and was something worth living and dying for.

King was married to Coretta Scott in 1953. The family moved to Montgomery, Alabama in 1955 and King helped form the Montgomery Improvement Association (MIA) in 1955. This group sought to strike down the Jim Crow laws in the south. King was president of the association and became nationally famous because of his involvement in the bus boycott in Montgomery. The boycott of the busses by blacks was prompted by Rosa Parks, a black woman, who refused to give up her seat to a white rider. King's great contribution to the 382 day boycott that followed was his oratory.[48]

The next twelve years in King's life were a period of social activism matched by very few human beings. In 1957, King and others formed the Southern Christian Leadership Conference (SCLC) to spread the word about King's philosophy of non-violent civil rights protest. He was active in this group the rest of his life. In 1960, King resigned his position as pastor of Dexter Church and went to Atlanta to concentrate all of his energy on the program of the SCLC. There he came into contact with the newly formed Student Non-violent Coordinating Committee (SNCC) and served on their Adult Advisory Commission. As the 1960s civil rights movement gathered momentum, King became involved with the Congress on Racial Equality (CORE) and their freedom riders. Then in 1962–63, he joined in the Birmingham, Alabama struggle to desegregate lunch counters and hire more blacks. Eugene "Bull" Connors, the local police commissioner, got a court order to bar demonstrations, but King defied the order and was sent to jail. There he wrote, "Letter from a Birmingham Jail."[49]

As the recognized leader of the Civil Rights Movements in America, King and others organized the August 1963 March on Washington. Here he delivered his inspirational, "I Have a Dream" speech to over 250,000 people. In 1964, he was Man of the Year on *Time* magazine's cover and he was awarded the Nobel Peace Prize. In 1965, King led a voter registration drive in Selma, Alabama and participated in the Selma-Montgomery March in the spring of 1965. In 1966, King moved to Chicago to address the problems associated with the urban ghetto. Finally, in 1968, King went to Memphis, Tennessee to head a protest march of black sanitation workers—a forerunner of a planned Poor People's March in Washington. It was in Memphis that King was killed by a sniper's bullet at the motel in which he was staying.[50] "Martin Luther King, Jr. was more than the principal leader, catalyst, architect, and prophet of the Black Revolution; he was a chief theorist and interpreter of it as well . . . He was to the Black Revolution what Washington was to the birth of the nation.[51]

Anthropology   "King believed strongly in the idea that all people are related to one another, because God is the parent of all."[52] Human beings are both spiritual and physical and they possess *free will*—the capacity to choose between doing good or evil. King sees human nature as both good and evil. He argues that all human beings are created equal, and each human individual has certain natural rights, rights given to them by God, which include liberty, equality, and justice. King believed every human being possessed a divine spark and a limitless potential for growth.[53]

For King, God is the creative force in the life of human beings and love was to him the most powerful factor in the world. As long as human beings recognize God's central role in their lives, human freedom can operate within history. God and human beings, working together, can change human history. *Reason* and *emotion* both operate in dialectical tension within human beings. This basic dualism is characteristic of King's conception of human nature—all human beings, all times, everywhere. Human nature is not perfect, but it is perfectible.[54]

Alienation, in King's thought, has three facets: self, neighbor, and God.[55] A human being is self-alienated when the individual is not *becoming* ever more human. This self-alienation occurs when one's actual condition and essential nature do not correspond. Reality has given way to virtual reality. The authentic human individual is constantly striving to close the gap between image and reality, condition and nature. Humans should not live abstract lives but concrete ones. When human beings bow down and worship the abstract (blackness or whiteness) then they alienate themselves.

Alienation of neighbor, in King's thought, refers to any form of isolation or estrangement that separates one human individual or group from another. Therefore, every kind of alienation should be avoided—be it founded on race, gender, religion, or ethnicity. All these so-called "important attributes" are, to King, alienating forces and factors in the world today. Tribalism, nationalism, racism, etc., all must be avoided.

The ultimate alienation to King is that between human beings and God. King rejects philosophical and cultural relativism and instructs his followers that values are not relative. To King, every system of belief is not equally valid and it is not necessary to tolerate diversity. Virtue is better than vice and the human tragedy is the separation between humans and God. Human beings are sinners and need God's forgiving grace. King believed that through struggle and suffering, human beings will become ever more noble, gentle and heroic. For King, "means are as important as ends."[56]

Sociology   In politics, King constantly referred to the Declaration of Independence and, in the Constitution, the Bill of Rights as the basis of the rights of black people. He believed in the principles expressed in these documents, considered them the moral foundation of the country, and sought all his mature life to make practice in America correspond with the magnificent theory expressed in the document. These rights of *all* Americans were, to him, God given and he sought to drive out the white racism that distorted the American dream. "Whenever King had an occasion to speak about the virtues of America, he usually began by enthusiastically praising the Declaration of Independence and the Constitution."[57]

What is particularly unique in King's politics is not its ends, its goals, but the *means* he demanded his followers employ. King used non-violent protest. He knew his method involved suffering and that many would call it impractical but "the way of non-violence means a willingness to suffer and sacrifice. It may mean going to jail ... It may mean physical death,"[58] but in King's philosophy, *how* one achieves one's ends is as important as the ends themselves. King's method of civil disobedience, non-violent resistance, and direct action required spiritual as well as physical strength, and there were many who were unable to cope with his methods. As he said, "non-violence is a powerful and just weapon ... It is a sword that heals ... non-violent direct action proved it could win victories without losing wars."[59] King derived his non-violent method from

Mahatma Gandhi and he was quite willing to seek the support of northern white liberals to realize his goals. King resisted laws that he considered unjust, but his pacifism and direct action are what make his practices so unique.

In economics, King was acutely aware of the internal relationship between politics and economics. He advocated radical economic changes, but he "was a strong advocate of the Protestant work ethic and urged blacks to exercise thrift as they began to earn greater wealth."[60] In 1963, King put forward a "Bill of Rights for the Disadvantaged." He advocated the need to establish black credit unions, savings and loan associations, and cooperative economic enterprises. He preferred a mixed economy or a democratic-socialist system as opposed to one that is exclusively capitalist.[61]

Socially, King wanted the central government to assert strong leadership. He criticized blacks for high crime rates, the waste of money on non-essentials and demanded that they join him to achieve social progress. Perseverance and struggle, not sloth, were the keys to an evolutionary-developmental black community. Government can and should help, but the role of the individual is of equal import. Finally King believed formal education to be a potent instrument for African-American liberation. Education can create the condition for blacks to transcend their existing mentality and go beyond this to a new and liberated future. Only education can enable human beings to overcome prejudice, ignorance, and stereotype.

King was a remarkable man and thinker. But his intellectual skills were complimented by his activism. This is why King is perhaps the most important black American of the twentieth century.

Shirley Anita Chisholm (Liberalism)

Shirley Chisholm was a politician and author. She was born in 1924 in Brooklyn, New York of West Indian parents (Barbados). During the Depression, the economy was so bad that Shirley and her sister were sent back to Barbados to be cared for. Chisholm returned to the United States in 1924, attended high school in New York and later attended and graduated from Brooklyn College cum laude. She joined the NAACP and worked with the Urban League and later took an M.A. at Columbia University. All her life she was deeply influenced by Garveyism and the racial pride this ideology taught. She became involved in Democratic politics in New York, was elected to the New York legislature in 1965 and to the United States Congress in 1969—the first black woman ever elected to Congress. In Congress, she opposed the Vietnam War, did pioneering work on women's rights, and refused to knuckle under to the seniority system. In 1972 she attempted to gain the Democratic Party nomination for the Presidency, but lost to George McGovern. She retired from politics in 1982 for two reasons: a desire to return to private life, and frustration in affecting change in an ever increasing conservative atmosphere in Congress. She lived in Williamsville, New York. Chisholm was an activist and a pragmatist.[62] She was the champion of the rights of the disadvantaged who derived her power from people rather than through the regular party organization. She died on January 1, 2005.

Shirley Chisholm was a political maverick while in Congress. She was a political pluralist and argued against the leftists and the separatists who claimed that black liberation could never be realized within the framework of the American political system. She believed that blacks could achieve their goals in America and she was quite willing to cross race or party lines to gain success (she even endorsed John V. Lindsay for reelection to the office of Mayor of New York City on the Liberal ticket). Pluralists, like Chisholm, view violence as counterproductive and instead employ economics as their principle weapon in politics—boycott, rent strikes, and work stoppage.[63] Shirley Chisholm used the strategy of coalition politics. Consider her own explanation: "Coalition politics is issue oriented instead of party oriented. It draws together disparate groups, who combine—temporarily, in all probability—around some issue of overriding importance to them at that time and place. By its nature, it confronts the traditional politics of expediency and compromise."[64]

Chisholm believed strongly in the American creed and individualism. Respect for the human individual was her top priority—ahead of race and class. And to her, one of the primary barriers to realizing the American dream is Congress itself. She claims congressmen "act like aristocrats," and that Congress is "ruled by a small group of old men"[65] who gain power by seniority. Seniority alone determines who rules and who obeys—not "competence, character, past performance, background, or orientation."[66]

Chisholm embraced the ideology of democratic liberalism. Human beings had the capacity for social consciousness and altruism, all was not greed and avarice. Her supreme value was the human individual in society, and this meant all human beings, not just some. But more than anything, Chisholm was an advocate of change. Change was possible, probable, if one persevered, and could be progressive. The American creed and the American dream can be realized. The basic organization of the country is sound.

Walter E. Williams (Conservatism)

Walter E. Williams was born on March 31, 1936 in Philadelphia, Pennsylvania. He was raised by his mother alone after his father abandoned the family. His home was in the slums of Philadelphia during the Depression. He was educated at Benjamin Franklin High School (1950–1954), took his A.B. at California State University, and a Ph.D. in economics at the University of California at Los Angeles. He was an instructor in economics at Los Angeles City College during the 1967–68 academic year and accepted a post as assistant professor at California State University at Los Angeles and was there from 1967–1971.

Williams left academic life briefly to work at the Urban Institute as a member of their research staff from 1971–1973. He then went back to academic life when he accepted a post at Temple University as an associate professor of economics from 1973–1980. He transferred in 1980 to George Mason University in Fairfax, Virginia as John W. Olin professor of economics where he remains to this day.

He is the author of two major monographs, *All it Takes Is Guts* and *The State Against Blacks*, and he writes a syndicated newspaper column that appears frequently in over 100 major newspapers across the United States. Williams has been a substitute on the Rush Limbaugh radio show many times and is "a pioneering black conservative" who speaks out against what he considers "an outworn liberal orthodoxy."[67]

Williams sees the liberal programs associated with welfare as a failure and that what is needed is a correction of black behavior and a new consciousness that embraces the work ethic. The present black leadership, to Williams, suffers from denial. Hard work and the free market are the solutions for blacks in the United States.[68] Williams, along with Thomas Sowell, Stanley Crouch, and Shelby Steele, form the phalanx of black men who have attacked affirmative action, minority scholarships, and social programs. Williams and his colleagues contend that such programs create the condition for an inner stigma and negativity and they want these programs dismantled to reduce the stigma.

Anthropology   In his essay, "Greed Makes the World Go 'Round," Walter Williams outlines his theory of human nature and psychology. Self-interest and greed are the essential attributes of human beings. Given this conception, everything else in his political, economic, and social thought follows. Consider the implications of the following quotation:

"What is the noblest of human motivation? Some would say love. Others would say courage. What about greed? The desire in each of us to have the things we enjoy is the motivation that creates the greatest good in the world."[69]

Like his mentor, Adam Smith in *The Wealth of Nations*, Williams assumes the prime psychological drive in human beings is as an economic being. There is something inherent in all human beings, the "propensity to barter and exchange," and this attribute is common to all human beings, all times, everywhere. Why do human beings struggle and work so hard? "Can love for our fellow man explain all this effort? No, it's the desire to have more—greed."[70]

The generation of human freedom and liberty to act is also central to Williams' thought. Human beings possess natural rights that flow from a body of law higher than human law, and "the most important right in the preservation of freedom is one's right to his property."[71] He goes on to argue that if blacks are not as successful as they should be in the economy, it is because the economy is no longer free and open to all.

Williams presupposes antagonistic groups struggling for advantage over each other. To him, "discriminated-against people generally do better under a system where there is a market allocation of goods and services than when there is political allocation of goods and services."[72] The problem in America for blacks, contends Williams, is in government efforts to resolve these problems through such legislation as minimum wage, occupational and business licensing, and regulation of transportation.[73] The invisible victims of such actions are blacks and the poor. The remedy to much of the isolation, estrangement, and hostility of the races in America is to get the state out of the economy. Williams argues that for years the federal government has attempted, by the legislative process, to reduce racial discrimination against African-Americans. He contends that these efforts have been ineffective and that equal opportunity can never be legislated.

Sociology   "Anarchy plus the constable" comes close to synthesizing Williams' conception of the proper role of the state. The "one legitimate role of government is to provide national defense (to prevent our foreign fellow man from confiscating our property) and a domestic defense (to prevent the same by our fellow countryman)."[74] To accomplish the latter goal, government must set up a judicial system to settle disputes and claims. Finally, to provide for the general welfare, government may be involved in water, health, and highway projects.

At this point, Williams draws the line and argues that in America today federal, state, and local governments far exceed their scope of legitimacy.[75] Williams sees virtually all taxes as "confiscating the property of one American and giving it to another."[76] He holds that this practice violates governments very reason for being. Williams' definition of social justice is, "I keep what I earn and

243

you keep what you earn. Do you disagree? Well then tell me how much of what I earn belongs to you—and why."[77]

Williams claims that economic planning and regulation is inherently impossible. No government agency can possibly coordinate the millions and billions of decision makers involved in their daily struggle to get ahead financially. Williams has very little faith in government's ability to solve economic problems. "Government has no resource of its own . . . (thus) we are forced to acknowledge that the only way government can give one American a dollar is to take it from another American."[78] For Williams, the free market is not a utopia, but it serves the masses of people and all their varied needs and wants better than government can ever hope to do. He cautions us that there is no such thing as a free lunch—somebody is paying for it and it isn't government which produces nothing. Of particular concern to Williams are programs like "farm handouts," where the government pays the farmer *not* to produce. Payment in kind (PIK) is legalized theft and typical of the insane legislation that results when government gets involved in the economy.[79] Adam Smith's "invisible hand" is still the best guide to rational policy in the area of economics. Government's job in the economy is simple—protect the populace from force and fraud. That's it.

In his social thought, Williams differs dramatically from all black liberals and some conservatives. Williams argues that *welfare* has had a devastating effect on the black family, that welfare bails people out year after year, generation after generation, and that we need a "withdrawal program." Blacks are victimized by the welfare policies of liberals. "I have always said welfare has done to black families what slavery, reconstruction, and the rawest racism could not have done."[80] Political swaps are just bad deals for blacks. For example, blacks received $4 billion worth of food stamps, but they have their food prices raised by $15 billion due to farm subsidies.[81]

On the education of blacks, Williams argues that if you want to get black children educated you need to expel the troublemakers, establish discipline, structure and high expectations, get rid of the sex clinics in high school which, he claims, is the equivalent of calling in an arsonist to put out a fire, and drop the free lunch programs because the majority of this goes to middle class children who don't need it.[82] In the process of civilizing children, a well-justified spanking[83] may be the wisest course.

Williams approvingly quotes Princeton professor John J. DiIulio who says, "America does not have a crime problem, inner-city America does."[84] Poor, law-abiding blacks and Hispanics are the principal victims of crime in America. And *why* is this so, according to Williams? Because of "liberal hair-brained schemes

244

on how to treat criminals.[85] The liberals believe that those predators on poor blacks would go to college if they had the chance." Williams thinks this is not sense, but nonsense.

Walter E. Williams certainly deviates from standard treatments suggested to resolve the issues associated with racial inequity. His is a libertarian vision, a liberating vision in his view, of how the world really works in America.

RIGHT

Marcus M. Garvey (Nationalist Authoritarianism)

Marcus M. Garvey was born on August 17, 1887 in St. Ann's Bay, a rural town on the north coast of Jamaica, the eleventh child of Marcus and Sarah Garvey. His parents were both of pure black ancestry and descended from the Maroon—a group of African slaves that had defied the Jamaican slave system and established "independent black communities in the mountains from 1664 to 1795."[86] Garvey was fiercely proud of his black skin and Maroon background and distrusted light-skinned blacks such as W.E.B. DuBois, a mulatto, who he claimed "hated the black blood in his veins . . . black, to him, is ugly, is hideous, is monstrous."[87]

Garvey left school at age sixteen and became a printer in Kingston, Jamaica. By the age of twenty, he was a foreman and in this job he became aware of the prevailing relationship between class and race—upper class white, middle class brown, lower class black. As he became increasingly conscious of the internal relations between race and the political economy, Garvey published, in 1910, his first newspaper, *Garvey's Watchman*. When this failed, he went on a Latin American odyssey that included Costa Rica, Panama, Ecuador, Nicaragua, Honduras, Columbia, and Venezuela. In these countries, he established more newspapers and worked to organize the black labor force. He then spent time in Europe and North Africa and in 1914 returned to Jamaica where he established The Universal Negro Improvement Association (UNIA). In March of 1916, Garvey arrived in the United States and with his arrival the Garvey Movement began in America.[88]

In the United States, he toured the country, met many black leaders in the thirty-eight states he visited, and was unimpressed with the vast majority who he saw as mere "opportunists." He set up his base of operations in Harlem and in 1919 began publication of a weekly newspaper *The Negro World,* the official voice of the UNIA. In 1920 Garvey founded The Black Star Steamship Line as a commercial operation.[89] Garvey's movement flourished after World War I and he was seen as a leader with worldwide ambition. The centerpiece of Garveyism was its clarion call for a return to Africa, the expulsion of the colonial powers from Africa, the need for self-determination for the entire African continent, and racial separation.

Garvey was an aggressive leader, had a charismatic personality, and a fierce racial pride. Because of his style of leadership and the ideology of Garveyism, he had numerous critics including the NAACP, Communists, and Socialists. He also alienated the black middle class and those blacks who had no interest in returning to Africa. Finally, America's allies in Europe criticized Garvey for his ideas and actions designed to free Africa from colonialism and imperialism and bring about self-determination for the continent.[90]

In 1925 Garvey was convicted of mail fraud and given a five year term in the penitentiary at Atlanta. President Coolidge pardoned him and he was deported to Jamaica where he died in 1940. With his death, the movement suffered a gradual eclipse and it lay dormant until the 1960s when some of his ideas were resurrected in the Black Power Movement.[91]

Anthropology   The equality of all human beings lies at the heart of Garvey's conception of human nature and psychology. All human beings are equal, regardless of race, because "that God we worship and adore has created man in His own image, equal in every respect, wheresoever he may be; let him be white; let him be yellow; let him be red; let him be black."[92] God wants, nay demands, that blacks recognize their equality with all other human beings, their possession of certain natural rights common to all human beings, and the need for blacks to lift themselves from the "lethargy of the past" and realize the new "resurrected life" that is possible.[93] For Garvey, all human beings stand on an equal plane, all must be respected for being human individuals, and all individuals in society must be given the opportunity to defend his or her own interests. All races, except blacks, have accepted this equalitarian ethos and it is time for blacks to awake to and operationalize this reality in their personal lives. Again and again Garvey's rhetoric is focused on his effort to instill racial pride and equality in the black psyche.

Next, human beings are responsible for their fate on earth. God has made human beings free moral agents, and if you want to care for or destroy your body, commit suicide, or live, that is the "same privilege and prerogative" given to all human beings. Each of us has a free will, we can choose the kind of life we will lead. It is pointless to blame one's misfortunes related to our physical life on

"Christ and God the Father." God is concerned about the spiritual aspects of humankind, but, "if you want to break your physical life up, that is all your business."[94] Garvey ends his speech at Liberty Hall, December 24, 1922, with the following ringing charge. "Blame not God, blame not the white man for physical conditions for which we ourselves are to be blamed."[95] To Garvey, blacks are masters of their own destiny and fate.

Blacks, like people everywhere, pursue their own individual self-interest and often are selfish and corrupt. But to Garvey, these are common attributes of all human beings in all races. Of particular concern to Garvey are "selfish Negro preachers and politicians" who have exploited blacks for years. Their ravings and machinations of blacks must cease. To Garvey, the task at hand for all blacks is take control of their lives, and work to go beyond, to transcend, the selfish proclivities of humankind. It can be done, says Garvey, if we act as the free, moral agents we truly are.

Finally, Garvey is concerned that human freedom and liberty become a reality for all blacks. "Liberty or Death" is Garvey's battle cry for blacks in America. "In our corner of the world, we are raising the cry for liberty, freedom, and democracy . . . we give out a spirit that knows no compromise, a spirit that refuses to turn back."[96] Garvey goes on to lucidly expound his ideas on liberty.

"If liberty is good for certain sets of humanity it is good for all. Black men, colored men, Negroes have as much right to be free as any other race that God Almighty ever created, and we desire freedom that is unfettered, freedom that is unlimited, freedom . . . to rise to the fullest of our ambition."[97]

Sociology   Garvey is a revolutionary nationalist. Blacks need a nation of their own. Nations are natural political entities, separate and distinct, and as such the only means whereby human beings can realize their freedom. They achieve this freedom by immersing themselves in the cultural milieu of the nation. Hundreds of times, Garvey stresses the need, the necessity, for racial nationalism. He contends that only the UNIA fights for an independent self-determining black nation. Garvey supports separation *not* integration of the races as does the NAACP. For Garvey, black equality implies black independence and self-determination for black states.

To Garvey, the politics and governing of the ideal state is an effort to "apply the corporate majesty of the people to their own good."[98] The problem is that the selfish and greedy nature of the individual ends up corrupting the system and the goal is not attained. Garvey points out the failure of communist, socialist, and noncommunist states as examples. Africa must develop an "aristocracy of its own"—an aristocracy based on service and loyalty to the people. Garvey argues persuasively that "government should be absolute" and that all ministers and governors of territories are completely responsible. Government leaders who violate their oath of office should be disgraced and then "stoned to death."[99] In reading Garvey on the selection and operation of political officials, one is quickly conscious of the many parallels between his vision of the state and Plato's conceptions as outlined in the *Republic* with its philosopher kings. Africa must be free and the "entire Negro race must be emancipated."[100] Such is the task of the ruling elite—and it is a ruling elite, not a class system, as Garvey conceives it.

Garvey writes with passion about economics. He argues that socialism is "the dreamer's vision," that is, the myth that rich people of the world will voluntarily give up their wealth. Communism fares even worse in Garvey's thought. He sees communism as "more dangerous to the Negro's welfare than any other group at present."[101] Paradoxically, Garvey argues that "the only convenient friend the Negro worker or laborer has in America at the present time is the white capitalist."[102] This is so because the selfish capitalist seeks only the greatest profit and is quite willing to use black labor, white labor, or any other labor if the cost is to his advantage.

"Capitalism is necessary to the progress of the world, and those who unreasonably and wantonly oppose or fight against it are enemies to human advancement."[103] Garvey supports capitalism in much the same manner as Adam Smith does—it is the system that most nearly corresponds to his theory of human nature and psychology. Self-interested and greedy human beings should have a system that flows logically from human attributes. For Garvey that is capitalism. He talks about some limitations on possession, but he casts his economic die for capitalism.

Finally, in his social thought, Garvey contends that blacks should avoid race mixing and integration. "Miscegenation will lead to the moral destruction of both races."[104] Garvey teaches the "unity of race," but racial unity that denies "color superiority or prejudice." In his essay, "An Exposé of the Caste System Among Negroes," he says on pages 57–60 that the NAACP and individuals such as W.E.B. DuBois are doing great damage to the black community with their constant commentary on the need for more and more integration. These are false prophets to Garvey.

Garvey encourages blacks to get all the education they possibly can, formal and informal, inside or outside the classroom. He reminds his followers that education is not only for the mind, it is also for the "soul, vision, and feeling"[105] of the human individual.

Marcus Garvey won an audience, kept and enlarged that audience, because "he preached the doctrine of revitalization at precisely the right time (and) he preached it in the right syllables."[106] His words were instantly recognized by all who embraced traditional American ideology. Most of his ideas corresponded to the American value-belief system. He showed his followers that his ideas could lead them to liberation.[107]

Malcolm X (Black Power Authoritarianism)

Malcolm Little (Malcolm X) was born in Omaha, Nebraska on May 19, 1925, the son of a West Indian mother and a fiery black preacher who embraced the traditions of both the Baptist Church and the secular teaching of Marcus Garvey. White vigilantes harassed the family in Omaha and they moved to Lansing, Michigan where members of a white supremacist group burned the Little home and later severely beat his father and threw him to his death under a streetcar.[108]

Malcolm X was an intelligent student in high school, but also a "stormy and rebellious" one. He hoped to be a lawyer but was discouraged by his teacher from pursuing that goal. He dropped out of school after the eighth grade, went to Boston and later Harlem, and lived the life of a street hustler—a "zoot-suited, bop-gaited" life. He became known as Detroit Red (later Big Red) and dealt in drugs, the numbers racket, burglary, and prostitution. This lifestyle eventually earned him a seven-year sentence in the Charleston State Prison in 1946. In prison he underwent a psychic transformation and became a devoted Muslim. There he read and studied the theological and ethical teaching of Elijah Muhammad, leader of the Nation of Islam,[109] and embraced the new creed with genuine enthusiasm. This conversion occurred in 1948, and Malcolm said, "The truth of Muhammad's teachings was like a 'blinding light.'"[110]

Upon his release from prison in 1952, Malcolm, went to Detroit to meet Elijah Muhammad. There he changed his name to Malcolm X, advanced rapidly in the organization, and in 1954 became minister of the Black Muslim Mosque in Harlem. He was the trusted disciple and spokesman for Elijah Muhammad for years and without doubt the Nation of Islam's most effective and inspired minister. "His blistering condemnation of white racism, advocacy of retaliatory violence, and critiques of the civil rights movements"[111] attracted support from ghetto blacks. Eventually his charisma and style were too successful for his own good because his verbal militancy created enemies in both the white and black community. He was "silenced" by Elijah Muhammad for three months in November of 1963, learned of Muhammad's siring of children with young Muslim women, and left the Nation of Islam.

In 1964 he made a pilgrimage (The Hajj) to Mecca and adopted orthodox Islam's multiracialism. Upon his return Malcolm X preferred the name El Hajj Malik el Shabazz. In June of 1964, Malcolm formed the Organization of Afro-American Unity (OAAU) which put him into direct competition with Elijah Muhammad and the Nation of Islam. On February 25, 1965, Malcolm X was assassinated "by three members of the Nation of Islam, in New York City."[112]

Malcolm X was not a scholar in the sense of W.E.B. DuBois or Angela Davis. He was primarily a speaker of exceptional ability. Yet Malcolm X is seen as "the most heroic symbol of the Black Power Movement of the 1960s . . . he developed into a fearless propagandist . . . (saying) that Afro-Americans had a right to use any means necessary—violent or non-violent—to attain these human rights."[113] He was the conscience of the Black Power movement, a follower for twelve years and a leader for one year. Malcolm X transformed Muhammad's tiny Muslim sect into a large respected militant wing in the black struggle.

Anthropology   To understand the thought of Malcolm X, one must give careful attention to the ideology and theology espoused by Elijah Muhammad. This is so because Malcolm X is the disciple of Elijah and "until his defection, Malcolm had accepted without question the Black Muslim theology . . . he became a famous organizer in a system developed not by himself but by Elijah Muhammad."[114] America's creedal identity is founded on human equality. Black Islamism stands in direct opposition to this and is based on human inequality. Black Muslims insist that human beings are born unequal and the degree of inequality is based on one's race. The black Muslim hierarchy of spiritual grace, that is, one's relation to Allah, is as follows: blacks and non-whites who practice Islam; blacks and non-whites who do not practice Islam; blacks and non-whites who have rejected Islam; all whites are seen as children of the devil.[115] To Muhammad and Malcolm X, human beings possess a "weak human nature," one motivated by self-interest, greed, and the desire for property. But with God's help the really defiant black and non-white person can overcome these attributes and emerge as a conqueror and a civilized person.

Malcolm and Muhammad's self-transforming message demanded that blacks strengthen their self-discipline, self-confidence, and self-love and by doing so blacks could realize a "triumph of the stronger, superior African over the shrewd, devilish Caucasian."[116] Blacks can thus transcend the present epoch and construct a new human being and a new society. Again and again, Muhammad and Malcolm, call for personal discipline as the prerequisite to authentic freedom.

Black separatism is a doctrine "to which Malcolm X was beholden for most of his life after his first psychic conversion to the Nation of Islam."[117] To Malcolm X, black separatism with its black supremacist explanation of the origins of white people, was important because Malcolm believed "the other major constructive channels of black rage in America—the black church and black music"[118]—were not as effective in producing a new mentality in blacks as the ideology of the Nation of Islam. Black supremacy plays a major role in Malcolm's view of the psychic conversion necessary for blacks in America. This goal, psychic conversion, was the precondition for everything insofar as a positive change in black human nature is concerned. Black people must not view themselves through the prism of white lenses. This implies self-destruction and self-loathing to Malcolm and he would have none of it. He commented often on the days in his youth when he tried to change his hair to look like whites. Malcolm X's rhetoric always affirmed black attributes, and he was very pessimistic throughout his life about white America's capacity to shed racism.

Sociology   In politics, the issue of authoritarian organization loomed large in Malcolm X's thought. He was pessimistic about American democracy and shunned the American political system. From 1952 until his second conversion in 1964, his political message to blacks reinforced the Nation of Islam's doctrine of authoritarian distribution of power. Malcolm X and the Black Muslim Nation of Islam movement was a distinctive form of authoritarian arrangements which imposed a top-down disciplined corps of devoted followers and a good deal of paternalism regarding women.[119]

Malcolm X was critical of Martin Luther King, Jr.'s non-violent resistance and compared King's and his perspective on use of violence to that of the house Negro versus the field Negro. Malcolm X argues the need, the necessity, for blacks to use retaliatory violence—direct action. He was definitely not one to "turn the other cheek" as King suggested. He always was defiant in his demand for the right of self-defense and complete independence for black people.[120]

Malcolm X's black nationalism envisaged a "separate black homeland," but with the emergence of the many new states in Africa in the 1960s, Malcolm advocated a "psychological" rather than a physical return to Africa. This to be realized by ridding blacks of white domination. His brand of black power nationalism always included a special relationship with black Africa—a black nationalism committed to language, culture, pride, hope for the future, land or territory.[121]

"The African-American Zion was predicated on capitalistic economic practices . . . (Malcolm and Muhammad) espoused notions such as the work ethic, profit motive, competition, private property, incentives, and the free market."[122] Malcolm's vision of economic self-reliance presupposed a body of fertile land that could support a growing population. He was certain that the skills of black farmers and scientists could overcome any challenge. The Muslims desperately wanted land, a racially separate territory, voluntarily separated, where blacks could endure their own culturally distinctive forms of self-government and particularly economic self-reliance and cooperation.[123]

Socially, Malcolm X feared any kind of cultural hybrid. He fought against interracial marriage and integrated schools. This fear was rooted in his own personal hybrid (his grandfather was white).[124] For Malcolm, education was seen as critical to blacks and he demanded educational facilities equal to those of whites. He often times used himself as an example of a person who could overcome his past through education.

Black Muslims were to be governed by a strict code of private and social morality. Malcolm X argued that fulfillment for blacks was only possible if one lived out the Muslim ethic, that is, restraint in the consumption of food, sexual morality, a life characterized by sober living (no drugs or alcohol), hard work and complete devotion to the family.[125] To achieve these social goals in America, Malcolm X called for school boycotts, rent strikes, housing rehabilitation, and programs for unwed mothers and drug addicts. Malcolm's vision gave priority to race over class as the fundamental reality of American politics.

Malcolm X's second conversion occurred in 1964 after his trip to Mecca. On this Hajj, he visited the pyramids, completed the seven circuits required of those who make the Hajj, ate, drank, and slept with Muslims of all races, and embraced the brotherhood of all mankind. When he returned to America he had changed. In the last year of his life, he formed the Organization of Afro-American Unity (OAAU) and switched from a racially separatist capitalist to a universalist, Pan-African, quasi-socialist. In politics he encouraged voter registration drives, black candidates, and independent voter status for all blacks. His vision of capitalism gave way to favorable comments on socialism. He even made appeals to non-racist whites for their support. The second conversion, the new psychic conversion for Malcolm, was to end in a matter of months. He was assassinated in February of 1965.

When one talks of Malcolm X, one must be clear which one is being discussed—Malcolm Little the hustler, Malcolm X the disciple of Elijah Muhammad, or El Hajj Malik el Shabazz. One thing is clear, his significance for Black Power Authoritarianism flows from his role as the disciple of Elijah Muhammad—he was the Nation of Islam's most outstanding orator and organizer for twelve years.

252

Louis Farrakhan (Black Power Authoritarianism)

Louis Eugene Wolcott was born in New York City on May 11, 1933 and grew up in the Roxbury section of Boston, Massachusetts. Both of his parents were from the Caribbean area—his mother from the Bahamas and his father from Jamaica. He attended St. Cyprian Episcopal Church in Roxbury and Boston English High School. There Wolcott was an honor student, a track star and an outstanding performer in music and the theater. After graduation he enrolled at predominately black Winston-Salem State Teacher's College in North Carolina and studied there for the period 1950–52. When his wife, Betsy, became pregnant he dropped out of college at the end of the year and began his career as an entertainer in Boston. There he was known as Calypso Gene and the Charmer. In 1952 he met Malcolm X and three years later, while working in Chicago,[126] he joined the Nation of Islam at their Savior Day service after hearing an address by Elijah Muhammad. "I went looking not for a new religion, but for a new leadership that would address the concerns of black people. And I found Malcolm X and Elijah Muhammad."

As a Black Muslim, Farrakhan discarded his "slave" name and adopted the name Louis Abdul Farrakhan. Back in Boston, Farrakhan advanced quickly and became a minister of the Boston mosque in 1956. He held this post until 1965. In 1963, the Nation of Islam was torn apart by rumors of Elijah Muhammad's sexual activities with six of his female secretaries. Malcolm X relayed this to other Muslim leaders and was subsequently silenced and replaced as minister of the Harlem mosque by Louis Farrakhan. Later Farrakhan wrote, "The die is set and Malcolm shall not escape. . . . Such a man is worthy of death."[127] When Elijah Muhammad died in 1975, his son W. Deen Muhammad became chief imam (teacher) of the Nation of Islam. He swiftly moved away from his father's doctrines, changed the name of the Nation to World Community of Al-Islam and aligned himself with the worldwide Islamic movement as a non-racial Islamic organization.

Then in 1977, Farrakhan resurrected the Nation of Islam and traveled extensively to rally new support. Under Farrakhan's leadership, the message of black supremacy was continued and in addition a heavy dose of anti-Semitism was introduced. Though his ideas instilled pride and discipline in the lives of the members, it stressed that women were to be subservient to men and that obedience was more important than democracy. The *Economist* of October 12, 1985 reports that, "The targets of Mr. Farrakhan's blistering attacks are established black leaders, white folks in general, and Jews in particular." Farrakhan is a charismatic leader and in 1995, after his Million Man March of Washington D.C. he must be considered a major player in America's political scene.

Farrakan's social thought preaches racial separation in contradiction to traditional Islam's advocacy of racial harmony. Orthodox Muslims believe Allah created all mankind; but Farrakhan for years has taught that the white race is the consequence of a failed experiment. Like Marcus Garvey, Farrakhan's most provocative and protracted theme is that blacks must separate themselves from the rest of society. The first mass movement of urban blacks organized around this thesis was led by Marcus Garvey in the 1920s. Farrakhan's vision for the Black Muslim movement dismisses integration as a viable option and argues for separation. America's creedal identity is based on equality. Black Muslims in the Nation insist that human beings are born unequal and the degree of inequality is based on one's race. Whites are seen as children of the devil. To Elijah Muhammad, the young Malcolm X and Farrakhan, human beings have, implicitly, a weak human nature—one motivated by greed and self-interest. On politics and economics Farrakhan contends that, "Black people can take care of themselves if they establish their own businesses and produce their own products in their own communities."[128]

Then in March of 2000, Farrakhan reconciled with his arch-rival Imam W. Deen Muhammed and "proclaimed the Nation of Islam's entry into the Muslim mainstream. . . . Rarely has an American religious group changed its doctrines so radically and so swiftly."[129] Orthodox Islam embraces the brotherhood of all races; but the Nation of Islam characterized whites as devils, advocated racial separation, and even wanted their own territory in the United states. In addition, the Nation taught that Allah appeared in the person of Fard Muhamad and his successor Elijah Muhammad. All this was forgotten as W. Deen Muhhamad embraced Louis Farrakhan. In a two hour speech, Farrakhan demoted Fard and Elijah from Gods to "pioneers" and said that Mohammad of Arabia was a white man and spoke for a faith of all races."[130] This is a stunning new orthodoxy for Farrakhan. W. Deen Muhhamad appears to have won the struggle for the minds of America's Black Muslim community. In July of 2003, Farrakhan agreed to host a series of conferences on the principles of reparations. This is his latest major project.

Summary

Aristotle says in *The Politics* that man is a political animal—a social being that is autonomous and one moved by reason and ideas. The rhetoric of black Americans as revealed in this chapter demonstrates that they participate with gusto in the clash of ideas all along the political spectrum from left to right. The words of the leading black men and women are employed by them to move the black masses to action—to achieve the goals of the particular ideology of the spokesperson. The essence of each spokesperson reviewed in this chapter is revealed in what he or she *thinks* because the history of blacks is the history of minds, of blacks as free, moral agents.

Every black leader discussed herein attempts to resolve the crucial questions of anthropology (human nature and alienation) and sociology (social, economic, and political institutions). Some suggest that blacks can realize full liberation by separation. Others fight for integration. But all recognize that civic engagement of blacks in America is crucial to liberation. Some argue that blacks can make democracy work by getting people involved in organizations that cut across race and class. Others reject this "horizontal" approach and argue for a "vertical" solution. Whatever one thinks after reading the answers supplied here, one can only conclude that taken together their work must stand alongside such great social science as that done by Frederick Douglass, W.E.B. DuBois, and Nat Turner.

NOTES

1. W.E.B. DuBois, "Application for Membership in the Communist Party," in *W.E.B. DuBois,* edited by William M. Tuttle, Jr. (New Jersey: Prentice-Hall, 1973), p. 112.

2. Martin Luther King, Jr., "I Have a Dream" in *The Voice of Black Rhetoric,* edited by Arthur L. Smith and Stephen Robb, (Boston: Allyn and Bacon, 1971), p. 196.

3. Julia Malone, "Black Conservatives Seek Abolition of Welfare System," *Dayton Daily News,* December 9, 1994, p. 4A. (Malone quotes Starr Parker, a black conservative female who founded the 10,000-member conservative Coalition on Urban Affairs.)

4. Amy Jacques Garvey, editor, *Philosophy and Opinions of Marcus Garvey,* Volume 2 (New York: Atheneum, 1969), p. 74.

5. Marcus Garvey, "The Principles of the Universal Negro Improvement Association," in *The Voice of Black Rhetoric,* edited by Arthur L. Smith and Stephen Robb, (Boston: Allyn and Bacon, 1971), p. 104.

6. Karl Marx, "Theses on Feuerbach," in Robert C. Tucker (ed.), *The Marx-Engles Reader,* 2nd edition, (New York: WW Norton, 1978), p. 145.

7. John Stuart Mill, On Liberty, in Andrew Hacker, *Political Theory: Philosophy, Ideology, Science* (New York: The Macmillan Company, 1961), p. 591.

8. Edmund Burke, *Reflections on the Revolution in France* (London: Dent, 1910), p. 58. Also Hacker, *Political Theory,* p. 352.

9. Plato, "The Republic," in Hacker, *Political Theory,* p. 56.

10. Charles Krauthanuner, "Conservatism Took a Left Turn Somewhere," *Dayton Daily News,* March 20, 1990, p. 4.

11. *Current Biography: 1973,* (New York: H.W. Wilson Company) p. 308.

12. Ibid., pp. 308–309.

13. John T. McCartney, *Black Power Ideologies* (Philadelphia: Temple University Press, 1992), pp. 135–140.

14. Huey P. Newton, *To Die For the People* (New York, Random House, 1972), p. 220.

15. Ibid., p. 64.

16. Ibid., p. 221.

17. Ibid., p. 22.

18. Ibid., p. 22.

19. Ibid., p. 81.

20. Ibid., p. 25.

21. Ibid., p. 31.

22. Ibid., pp. 30–32.

23. Ibid., pp. 156–157.

24. Ibid., pp. 107–110.

25. Angela Y. Davis, *Current Biography, 1972*, pp. 97–100. Also "Angela Y. Davis" by Joan Curl Elliott in *Notable Black American Women*, p. 253.

26. Angela Y. Davis, *Women, Culture and Politics* (New York: Random House, 1989), p. 93.

27. Ibid., p. 110.

28. Ibid., p. 195.

29. Arthur L. Smith and Stephen Robb, eds., *The Voice of Black Rhetoric* (Boston: Allyn and Bacon, 1971), p. 110.

30. Kenneth O'Reilly, editor, *Black Americans* (New York: Carroll and Graf Publishers, 1994), p. 307.

31. Ibid., also Smith and Robb, *The Voice of Black Rhetoric*, p. 110.

32. O'Reilly, *Black Americans*, p. 308.

33. Ibid., p. 309.

34. John Hope Franklin and August Meier, editors, *Black Leaders of the Twentieth Century* (Urbana: University of Illinois Press, 1982), p. 165.

35. Smith and Robb, *The Voice of Black Rhetoric*, p. 113.

36. Franklin and Meier, *Black Leaders in the Twentieth Century,* pp. 162–165.

37. Ibid., pp. 139, 145, 146, 152, 153.

38. Smith and Robb, *The Voice of Black Rhetoric,* p. 113.

39. Ibid., p. 112.

40. Franklin and Meier, *Black Leaders in the Twentieth Century,* p. 159.

41. *Current Biography Yearbook,* p. 594–594.

42. West, *The Ethical Dimensions of Marxist Thought,* Monthly Review Press, New York, pp. xvii and xx,xxi.

43. *Current Biography Yearbook,* p. 596.

44. West, *The Ethical Dimensions of Marxist Thought,* pp. xx and xxviii.

45. Cornel West, *Race Matters,* Beacon Press, Boston, 1993, p. 14.

46. West, *The Ethical Dimensions of Marxist Thought,* p. xxvii.

47. John T. McCartney, *Black Power Ideologies* (Philadelphia: Temple University Press, 1992), pp. 97–99.

48. John White, *Black Leadership in America 1895–1968* (New York: Longman, 1990), pp. 128–131.

49. Ibid., pp. 131–137.

50. Ibid., pp. 138–142.

51. Hanes Walton Jr., *The Political Philosophy of Martin Luther King, Jr.* (Westport: Greenwood Publishing, 1991), p. xxxiii.

52. Peter J. Paris. *Black Religious Leaders* (Louisville: Westminster/John Knox Press, 1991), p. 112.

53. McCartney, *Black Power Ideologies,* pp. 103–110.

54. Walton, *The Political Philosophy of Martin Luther King, Jr.,* pp. 49–58.

55. McCartney, *Black Power Ideologies,* p. 105.

56. Walton, *The Political Philosophy of Martin Luther King, Jr.,* p. 58.

57. Paris, *Black Religious Leaders,* p. 133.

58. Walton, *The Political Philosophy of Martin Luther King, Jr.,* p. 57.

59. Ibid., p. 65.

60. Robert M. Franklin, *Liberating Visions* (Minneapolis: Fortress Press, 1990), p. 117.

61. McCartney, *Black Power Ideologies,* pp. 99–109.

62. John T. McCartney, *Black Power Ideologies* (Philadelphia: Temple University Press, 1992), pp. 152–153.

63. Ibid., p. 153.

64. Shirley Chisholm, *Unbought and Unbossed* (Boston: Houghton Mifflin, 1970), p. 128.

65. Ibid., p. 110.

66. Ibid., p. 111.

67. Larry Platt, "The Black Rush" in *Philadelphia,* July, 1994, pp. 19, 20.

68. Ibid., pp. 21, 23, 25.

69. Walter E. Williams, "Greed Makes the World Go 'Round," in *All It Takes Is Guts* (Washington, D.C.: Regnery Books, 1987), p. 53.

70. Ibid., p. 53.

71. Ibld., p. 83.

72. Walter E. Williams, *The State Against Blacks* (New York: McGraw-Hill, 1982), p. 142.

73. Ibid., pp. 33–53, 67–74.

74. Williams, "Freedom and Coercion," in *All It Takes Is Guts,* p. 51.

75. Ibid., p. 52.

76. Ibid., p. 52.

77. Williams, "Defining Social Justice," in *All It Takes Is Guts,* p. 62.

78. Williams, "Spending, Taxing, and Regulating," in *All It Takes Is Guts,* p. 91.

79. Williams, "Farm Handouts Expose Congressional Hypocrites," in *All It Takes Is Guts,* p. 103.

80. Walter Williams, "White Illegitimacy: Bad News That's Kind of Good," *Dayton Daily News,* January 7, 1994, p. 9A.

81. Williams, "Political Swaps and Other Bad Deals," in *All It Takes Is Guts,* pp. 14 and 15.

82. Williams, "Producing Poor Children," in *All It Takes Is Guts,* pp. 107–110.

83. Walter Williams, "'Sound Good' Public Policy Hurting U.S.," *Dayton Daily News,* December 2, 1994, p. 15A.

84. Walter Williams, "We've Had Enough of Crime," *Dayton Daily News,* December 17, 1994, p. 19A.

85. Ibid.

86. John White, *Black Leadership in America: 1895–1968* (New York: Longman Group, 1985), p. 72.

87. Marcus Garvey, *Philosophy and Opinions of Marcus Garvey,* Vol. 2 (New York: Arno Press and the New York Times, 1969), p. 311.

88. White, *Black Leadership in America,* p. 73.

89. Ibid., p. 75–77.

90. John T. McCartney, *Black Power Ideologies* (Philadelphia: Temple University Press, 1992), pp. 79–80.

91. Ibid.

92. Marcus Garvey, *Philosophy and Opinions of Marcus Garvey,* Vol. 1 (New York: Arno Press and the New York Times, 1968), p. 89.

93. Ibid., p. 90.

94. Ibid., p. 33.

95. Ibid., pp. 33, 91.

96. Ibid., p. 94.

97. Ibid., p. 96.

98. Garvey, *Philosophy and Opinions,* Vol. 2, p. 74.

99. Ibid., pp. 74, 75.

100. Garvey, *Philosophy and Opinions,* Vol. 1, p. 74.

101. Garvey, *Philosophy and Opinions,* Vol. 2, p. 70.

102. Ibid., p. 69.

103. Ibid., p. 72.

104. Ibid., p. 62.

105. Garvey, *Philosophy and Opinions,* Vol. 1, p. 17.

106. Lawrence W. Levine, "Marcus Garvey and the Politics of Revitalization," in *Black Leaders of the Twentieth Century,* edited by John H.
Franklin and August Meier (Chicago: University of Illinois Press,
1982), p. 118.

107. Ibid., p. 118.

108. John White, *Black Leadership in America: 1895–1968* (New York:
Longman Group, 1990 printing), p. 103.

109. Robert Michael Franklin, *Liberating Visions* (Minneapolis: Fortress
Press, 1990), p. 77.

110. James H. Cone, *Martin and Malcolm and America* (New York: Orbis
Books, 1993), p. 50.

111. White, *Black Leadership in America,* pp. 107–108.

112. Ibid., p. 114.

113. John T. McCartney, *Black Power Ideologies* (Philadelphia: Temple
University Press, 1992), p. 186.

114. Ibid., pp. 184 and 185.

115. McCartney, *Black Power Ideologies,* pp. 172–173.

116. Ibid., p. 83.

117. Cornel West, *Race Matters* (Boston: Berea Press, 1993), p. 99.

118. Ibid., p. 100.

119. West, *Race Matters,* pp. 99–104.

120. White, *Black Leadership in America,* pp. 108–112.

121. Franklin, *Liberating Visions,* pp. 79–80.

122. Ibid., p. 97.

123. Ibid., p. 87.

124. West, *Race Matters,* p. 101; Franklin, *Liberating Visions,* p. 87.

125. Franklin, *Liberating Visions,* pp. 82–84.

126. Arthur J. Magida, *Prophet of Rage,* Harper-Collins, New York, 1996, p. 32.

127. Current Biography Yearbook: 1982, p. 192.

128. Ibid.

129. Richard N. Osting, "Muslim Unity Could Remake America's Religious Landscape," *West Hawaii Today,* March, 10, 2000, p. 18-B, from an AP report.

130. Ibid.

Chapter 10

Gender Ideologies
in America:
Left, Center, Right

> "Madonna is the true feminist. She exposes the puritanism and suffocating ideology of American feminism, which is stuck in an adolescent whining mode. Madonna has taught young women to be fully female and sexual while still exercising control over their lives."[1]
>
> Camille Paglia

> "Our bodies have been taken from us, mined for their natural resources (sex and children), and deliberately mystified."[2]
>
> Robin Morgan

> "A central problem within feminist discourse has been our inability to arrive at a consensus of opinion about what feminism is . . ."[3]
>
> bell hooks

These quotes by prominent writers illustrate the diversity of opinion among women on the subject of gender politics. Camille Paglia expresses the libertarian view that contemporary feminism has evolved into a stifling ideology embodied by the feminist establishment. Robin Morgan is a radical feminist who believes that women are a colonized people, and that the problems of women and of contemporary society are directly attributable to men. The view expressed in 1984 by African-American writer bell hooks reflects the diversity within feminist thought.

Gender ideologies will be discussed within the left-center-right continuum, as indicated in Figure 10.1 below. On the left are Marxist, socialist and radical feminists. The liberal feminists constitute the center of the spectrum. These perspectives are critiqued by libertarians, conservatives and the New Right.[4]

RADICAL FEMINISTS

As described by Rosemarie Tong, feminist thought is not one but many theories or perspectives, and "each feminist theory attempts to describe women's oppression, to explain its causes and consequences, and to prescribe strategies for women's liberation."[5] Specifically, feminism argues that women are oppressed and dominated by men and that social, economic, cultural and political arrangements constitute the *patriarchy* maintaining this oppression. Regarding this domination as morally wrong, feminism became a social movement to correct it.[6] Feminist theory combines description, explanation, and prescription by incorporating analysis, social criticism and political action. In other words, feminist theory is ideology.

GENDER IDEOLOGIES IN AMERICA: LEFT CENTER RIGHT

Left	Center	Right
Marxist Feminists	Liberal Feminists	New Right
Radical Feminists	Libertarians Conservatives	
Socialist Feminists		

Figure 10.1 The Political Spectrum of Gender Ideologies

The Radical Critique

The literature of radical feminism abounds with descriptions of society as oppressive, patriarchal, and male dominated. The analysis of society and the economy by Marxist and socialist feminists is rooted in the concepts of materialism and economic conflict. They regard social class as being as important as gender and sex roles in explaining the position of women in society. Radical feminists, the most influential of the leftist feminist groups in the United States, rely on the ideas of Marxist and socialist thinkers, although the radicals emphasize gender as being more important than social class or race for understanding society, economics and politics. In the radical feminist critique of society, *gender* (meaning sex roles) and conflicts based on gender replace class as the key unit of analysis. These varieties of leftist feminist critiques are similar to one another and will be discussed here as variations of a radical critique of society and capitalism.

Radical feminists believe that women are an oppressed group, that women's oppression is the most fundamental form of oppression, and that their oppression is worldwide and deep-seated. Oppression is defined broadly to include art, culture, religion, reproduction, mothering, sexuality, employment and politics. The radical feminist analysis of society is a systematic critique encompassing property, the economy, sexuality, marriage and the family, as well as politics and various reform proposals.[7]

Property   Leftist feminists believe that the system of private property produces a male dominated class system which manifests itself as corporate capitalism and imperialism. For Marxist feminists, women's subjugation is the product of political, social, and economic structures of capitalism. The system of private property gives power to male property owners to exploit working-class men and nearly all women. Therefore, leftist feminists believe that women's liberation will require that the property system be replaced by socialism in order to end the economic dependency of women and their exploitation by men.

Politics and Patriarchy   In 1949, *The Second Sex,* an influential book about the condition of women, was published in France, and translated into English four years later.[8] The author, Simone de Beauvoir (1909–1986), was a prominent philosopher and left-wing political activist. Her analysis contended that women are a product of society as well as nature, and that the subordination of females to males is a result of various social, economic and political forces. In her lifestyle de Beauvoir embodied the ideal of the educated liberated woman, choosing never to marry nor have children. In France, she was active in the campaign for women's liberation and abortion rights, stating that "we must fight for the situation of women, here and now, before our dreams of socialism can come true."[9]

"The personal is political" became a maxim of the women's movement after the publication of *Sexual Politics* in 1970, by Kate Millett. Contending that male-female relationships are political because they are based primarily on power, Millett concluded that women's oppression is rooted in a patriarchal system of sex and gender. Millett's analysis illustrates the major theme of radical feminist thought: that the patriarchal system oppresses women. Feminists believe that male control, and the patriarchy that enforces female submissiveness, must be eliminated. Patriarchy maintains male dominance by means of socialization and coercion, and by supporting a culture that exaggerates biological differences between men and women.[10] Describing why the personal is political, Susanne Kappeler contends that "What *is* a historical fact is women's exploitation in the slave labour of 'love' and care, coerced out of them through a patriarchal social order which allowed no alternatives."[11] In the radical feminist analysis patriarchy is characterized by power, dominance, hierarchy and competition. Patriarchy cannot be reformed and must be transformed totally, including legal and political structures, and social and cultural institutions.

The Economy   Radical feminists assert that the family is related to capitalism, that women's domestic work is trivialized, and women are generally given menial and low-paying jobs. This came about, they argue, because prior to capitalism, the division of labor within the extended family was such that women made an important and valued contribution. Industrialization transferred production from the private household to the public workplace. Many women did not enter the workplace and their labor in the home came to be regarded as nonproductive. According to the radical analysis, capitalism needs to keep women working for free in the household, and/or for low wages in the workplace. If women enter the work force without relief from socially necessary domestic chores, they are doubly exploited. Radical feminists advocate socialization of domestic work (child-rearing and housework), communal or subsidized child care, or monetary compensation for women for their work at home.[12] As part of their economic agenda, feminists advocate equalization of pay to overcome pay inequities resulting from the sexual division of labor in the workplace. Jobs traditionally held by women (teaching, nursing, clerking) are compensated with lower pay than jobs usually held by men. As with the household, labor in female-dominated occupations is undervalued. One means of addressing this problem is the concept of *comparable worth*, which proposes that jobs be evaluated on the basis of skills, knowledge, working conditions, and responsibility, and that similar jobs should be compensated at the same rate.[13]

Marriage and the Family   In *The Origin of the Family, Private Property and the State*, published in 1845, Friedrich Engels analyzed bourgeois marriage as an institution to promote the control and transmission of private property from the husband to his male heirs.[14] The critique of marriage by anarchist Emma Goldman is even more blunt: "Marriage and love have nothing in common; they are as far apart as the poles; are, in fact antagonistic to each other."[15] Goldman was a radical anti-war activist and feminist who was deported from the United States. She was imprisoned three times, including once in 1915 for giving out birth control information. Her anarchist doctrine regarded marriage as one of the oppressive institutions of the capitalist state.

The Marxist analysis assumes that the abolition of property will liberate women and render the family obsolete. Employment outside the home, supported by communal living and childcare arrangements will free women to pursue intellectual and creative interests, and enable them to become economically independent. "Since there is to be under socialism no private property for the family to own and pass on to subsequent generations, there will be no need to rear children privately and consequently no need for women to be tied to the home."[16]

In the radical view, society perpetuates the "myth of motherhood" to bind women to their reproductive role so that men may pass along their genes, names and property to their heirs. Goldman stated that woman's development and independence can come only through herself: "First, by asserting herself as a personality, not as a sex commodity. Second, by refusing the right to anyone over her body; by refusing to bear children, unless she wants them; by refusing to be a servant to God, the State, society, the husband, the family . . . Only that, and not the ballot, will set women free . . ."[17]

In order to be liberated, radical feminists argue that women must seize control of the means of *reproduction* by taking control of their bodies, their sexuality and the reproductive process away from men. Liberation from reproduction may take the form of contraception, abortion, communal child rearing, celibacy, lesbianism and/or sexual separatism.

Gender and Sexuality   Of particular interest to radical feminists are issues of sexual dominance, especially the ways in which men attempt to control women's bodies and sexuality. Radical feminists assert that through sexual oppression, meaning male sexual domination and female submission, men have controlled women's sexuality for male pleasure by using social, economic and legal control to define women's sexuality in ways that serve the interests and needs of men. Examples range from beauty pageants, pornography, prostitution, and sexual harassment to spousal abuse, rape, sexual mutilation, and witchburning.[18] The radicals believe that women must redefine female sexuality in ways that liberate them from male dominance and meet their own needs. Consider, for instance, the protests against the Miss America Pageant first organized in 1968 by the New York Radical Women. To these radical feminists the pageant symbolized the objectification and exploitation of women by the patriarchal system. They expressed their dissatisfaction by dealing only with newswomen and refusing to speak with male reporters, by organizing a demonstration against the pageant, and by crowning a sheep on the boardwalk in Atlantic City.[19]

Summary   Clearly rooted in leftist ideas, radical feminism, by emphasizing the primacy of gender, has developed an original and imaginative critique of society. A new approach is necessary, the radicals contend, because existing ideologies are male defined and traditional politics is male dominated. This statement by Robin Morgan (from an essay entitled "The Wretched of the Hearth") captures some of the flavor of radical feminist rhetoric: ". . . the Left, the Right, and certainly the Center as we know them are male defined—and have all exploited women for their own purposes and then betrayed women in their own fashions."[20] Radical feminists emphasize gender, sex roles and male control of female sexuality as the major causes of women's oppression. The radicals contend that this oppression will continue until sex roles and sexuality are redefined by women in a manner that emphasizes the needs and interests of women rather than men.

LIBERAL FEMINISTS

Victoria Woodhull was a successful 19th century businesswoman who ran a brokerage house in New York. In testimony before Congress in 1871, she argued that women must have the right to vote, and that denial of this right constituted taxation without representation. Her statement to the Congress contains the essence of liberal feminist beliefs: "I come before you, to declare that my sex are entitled to the inalienable right to life, liberty and the pursuit of happiness . . . I ask the right to pursue happiness by having a voice in that government to which I am accountable."[21]

Liberal Feminism

Rooted in classical thought, *Liberal Feminism* reflects the traditional liberal values of individuality, rationality, freedom and political equality. Liberals believe that female subordination is rooted in custom and law. A set of legal, political and economic controls block women's entrance into, and success in, the world outside the home. "Because society has the false belief that women are, by nature, less intellectually and/or physically capable than men, it excludes women from the academy, the forum, and the marketplace. As a result of this exclusion, the true potential of many women goes unfulfilled."[22]

Mary Wollstonecraft, an early advocate of women's equality, wrote *A Vindication of the Rights of Woman* in 1790, in which she advocated the same civil rights and economic opportunities for women and men. She argued that women are not less intelligent, rational or capable than men, nor are they more emotional and weaker. Wollstonecraft believed that most significant gender differences in temperament and intellectual skills were products of custom, socialization and environment.[23] John Stuart Mill, in his essay "The Subjection of Women," made similar arguments in 1869."[24]

Modern Liberal Feminists

Liberal feminist thought reflects the traditional liberal view of Wollstonecraft and Mill that the route to equality for women requires society to grant political and legal equality to women. Many contemporary liberal feminists are more sympathetic to the radical critique of society, contending that mere political equality is not sufficient to eliminate discrimination against women. These more activist and reform-minded liberals believe that the government must take more positive and forceful measures to promote women's equality.

The Feminine Mystique   One of the more important modern liberal feminists is Betty Friedan, who wrote *The Feminine Mystique* in 1963. This widely read and influential book contributed to the growth of the women's movement of the 1970s. Friedan identified as the source of women's discontent and oppression the widespread social acceptance of the myth of femininity. The myth, or mystique, of femininity is the idea that women can and should find satisfaction exclusively in the traditional role of wife and mother. The mystique, by encouraging women to choose marriage and motherhood over career has left housebound women feeling empty and unhappy. Friedan's remedy is for women to become educated and seek satisfying and creative work outside the home.[25] According to Friedan: ". . . these problems cannot be solved by medicine, or even by psychotherapy. We need a drastic reshaping of the cultural image of femininity that will permit women to reach maturity, identity, completeness of self, without conflict with sexual fulfillment."[26]

Legal Equality   The National Organization of Women (NOW) was founded to promote the principles of liberal feminism, in particular legal equality and the repeal of discriminatory laws and policies. The Organizing Statement of NOW (written by Betty Friedan in 1966) states: "We . . . believe that the time has come for a new movement toward true equality for women in America, and toward a fully equal partnership of the sexes . . . The purpose of NOW is to take action to bring women into full participation in the mainstream of American society now . . ."[27]

Sexuality and Women's Liberation   *The Female Eunuch,* by Germaine Greer, was published in 1970 and became a bestseller. The title is a reference to the "desexualization" of women by the Victorians and in Freudian theory. Greer's book was a call for women to liberate themselves by reclaiming their sexuality: ". . . we can, indeed we must, reject femininity as meaning *without libido,* and therefore incomplete, . . . and rely upon the indefinite term female, which retains the possibility of female libido."[28] Sexual awakening and emancipation are regarded as an important aspect of the liberation of women from tradition and convention. Reproductive rights, meaning free access to birth control and abortion, are an important part of the liberal feminist agenda.

Government Policy   Nearly twenty years after the publication of *The Feminine Mystique,* Friedan wrote *The Second Stage* in which she shifted from the traditional liberal view that gender-neutral laws and equal opportunity were sufficient to liberate women, and assumed a more reformist position favoring government programs to assist single mothers with job training, childcare and direct subsidy.[29] Because of gender stereotyping, women are often assumed to be unqualified for many jobs, especially "masculine" jobs. Once women decide to enter the job market they may encounter overt discrimination or the "glass ceiling" blocking their access to jobs and promotions. In 1991, The Glass Ceiling Commission was established within the United States Department of Labor. The Glass Ceiling Commission released a report on March 15, 1995, showing that more than 90 percent of senior managers of *Fortune* 500 companies were white males, and that in *Fortune* top 2000 companies, only 5 percent of senior managers were women. In response to this report, Labor Secretary Robert Reich stated: "This is a wake-up call to corporate America. Talented women and minorities are being ignored."[30]

Summary   The goal of modern liberal feminism is the liberation of women from gender roles that justify giving women a lesser place in economy and society. Liberal feminists favor reforms in employment opportunities, salaries and compensation, abortion rights, child care access, and an end to discriminatory practices in economic, social and political life. Specifically, liberal feminists seek two sets of remedies. The first is the traditional liberal objective of legal equality, meaning the repeal of laws and policies that are discriminatory against women. Modern liberal feminism has moved beyond this gender-neutral approach and now advocates government policies to overcome past discrimination and protect women's status in the workplace, including subsidized affordable child care facilities, maternity leave from work, protection against sexual harassment on the job, and affirmative action to assure that women have access to jobs for which they are qualified. Liberal feminism is now concerned with persistent women's issues such as the feminization of poverty, cutbacks in social services, reproductive freedom, domestic violence, sexual harassment, equal opportunity in employment and education, and working women's need for childcare. For example, NOW organized a rally near the Capitol in Washington, D.C. on April 9, 1995 to protest "violence against women"—a term they applied to political assaults on welfare, spending on social programs, abortion and affirmative action, as well as to rape and battery.[31]

The Liberal Critique of Radical Feminism

Since the 1980s the debate between radical and liberal feminists has intensified. The decreasing notoriety and influence of liberal feminists has been matched by the growing influence and notoriety of radical feminists. In addition to questions of strategy and tactics, this debate concerns the politically acceptable definition of what constitutes a "feminist." Some liberal feminists contend that radicals have gained control of the movement's leadership and agenda, resulting in the growth of anti-male attitudes and values within feminism and the alienation of a majority of young American women from the ideology of feminism.

Numerous public opinion polls show that a majority of women in the U.S. support the liberal feminist ideals of political and economic equality for women. These polls also show that a majority of American women do not describe themselves as feminists. For example, a 1989 *Time*/CNN survey reported that a majority of American women believed that feminism had advanced women's rights but only one-third of the sample considered themselves to be feminists, and three-fourths paid little or no attention to the women's movement. Another poll (in 1992) showed that only 39 percent believed that contemporary feminism reflected the views of a majority of women, and that only 29 percent considered themselves to be feminists.[32] This raises the question: Why do many

273

women who believe in equal rights not identify with the women's movement or call themselves feminists? Susan Faludi, author of *Backlash: The Undeclared War Against American Women,* contends that the failure of many American women to embrace feminism is the result of a widespread media conspiracy against feminism orchestrated by men in media, business and politics.[33] Other feminist authors have been less willing to blame men for the current state of feminism, choosing instead to look critically at the leadership and ideology of contemporary feminism.

Who Stole Feminism? How Women Have Betrayed Women was published in 1994.[34] The author, Christina Hoff Summers, describes herself as a feminist who does not like what feminism has become. This book reports the results of her investigation of the sources used by feminist writers to support their findings and conclusions. Summers' critique of feminist scholarship describes a pattern of misleading and inaccurate statistics used by feminists to support a radical agenda. For example, a number of publications by feminist writers make the assertion that 150,000 American women die each year of anorexia nervosa, an eating disorder. Some authors attribute these alleged deaths to men, sexism or the male dominated culture. Naomi Wolf, for example, has compared male-induced anorexia to the genocide of the Nazi Holocaust: "When confronted with a vast number of emaciated bodies starved not by nature but by men, one must notice a certain resemblance."[35] However, Ms. Summers reports that correct statistics, according to the American Anorexia and Bulimia Association, show that approximately 150,000 Americans *suffer* from anorexia, and that there were 54 deaths from this disorder in 1991.[36] Summers' investigation questions the reliability of a variety of statistics and studies on eating disorders, sexual harassment, battery and rape used by radical feminists writers "to drive home the message that maleness and violence against women are synonymous."[37]

The New Victorians   Rene Denfeld is a journalist and author of *The New Victorians: A Young Woman's Challenge to the Old Feminist Order.* In her analysis of feminism, published in 1995, she concludes that the leaders of contemporary feminism are out of touch with the values of the younger generation of American women. The leadership of the women's movement, and the curriculum of women's studies programs at many colleges have, according to Denfeld, adopted the values of radical feminism. This more than any factor, Denfeld believes, explains the alienation of many young women from feminism. "The fact is that feminism has changed—dramatically . . . It has become bogged down in an extremist moral and spiritual crusade that has little to do with women's lives . . . For women of my generation, feminism has become as confining as what it pretends to combat."[38]

The focus of Denfeld's investigation is the organized women's movement, which she defines as women's groups such as NOW, women's studies programs at colleges and universities, and feminist leaders. These are the people and institutions which determine the meaning of feminism. Denfeld's analysis describes a shift in leadership and ideology within the feminist establishment. The founders of the women's movement of the 1970s have, for the most part, faded from the scene or moved on to other interests. Germaine Greer and Betty Friedan have begun writing about issues of aging, and Gloria Steinem's most recent book addresses questions of self-esteem and spirituality.[39] Friedan, one of the founders of NOW, has been excluded from the feminist establishment because of her moderate views and her willingness to criticize some of the trends in feminism.[40] Denfeld contends that, by the early 1990s, a new generation of radical feminists had taken control of the organized women's movement and established themselves as the voices of feminism. Especially influential among the radical feminists are: Robin Morgan, the 1960s activist, who was editor of *Ms.* magazine from 1990 until 1993; Catherine MacKinnon, an attorney who is leader of the radical feminist anti-pornography and date rape crusades; and Andrea Dworkin, an anti-pornography activist who regards heterosexual intercourse as rape and all men as potential rapists.[41]

The important point for Denfeld is that, until the late 1980s, these women were considered part of the feminist fringe. In the 1990s they dominated the organized women's movement and defined feminist ideology. Their writings and those of other radical feminists constitute the core of the curriculum in women's studies programs at many colleges and are taught as mainstream feminist theory. By means of their writings, activism and appearances on the television talk show circuit and, in the case of MacKinnon, legal scholarship and litigation, they have become the feminist establishment.

Sexuality   According to Denfeld's critique, there are a number of beliefs that constitute the core of radical feminism, but the central theme is that women are the victims of men. The feminine mystique has been replaced by the victim mystique. Denfeld identifies a number of different ways in which this theme manifests itself, beginning with male bashing and an attack on male sexuality (which she calls "the antiphallic campaign"). The radical view of male sexuality, articulated in the 1960s and 1970s by Kate Millett and Susan Brownmiller, became mainstream feminist doctrine during the 1980s.[42] In the radical view all men benefit from women's oppression. Men maintain social, economic and political control by means of legal and sexual coercion, including rape, which is seen as political terrorism. According to Brownmiller, rape is "a conscious process of intimidation by which all men keep all women in a state of fear."[43]

A branch of radical feminism is sometimes described as lesbian-feminism. The prevailing view of this faction is that women are innately lesbians who have been repressed by the institution of "compulsory heterosexuality."[44] Given their view that heterosexual women are sleeping with the enemy, a lesbian life style is regarded not simply as a matter of personal choice but as a mandatory political statement.

Pornography   Denfeld contends that the position of feminists regarding pornography illustrates both the degree to which the women's movement has been radicalized and the extent to which it has embraced neo-victorian values. A movement that at one time advocated the sexual liberation of women has become part of a crusade to eradicate sexually explicit material. Radical feminists now find themselves allied with religious conservatives demanding censorship of books, magazines, motion pictures, record covers and even billboards. Regarding the distinction between erotica and pornography, Andrea Dworkin stated that "erotica is simply high-class pornography."[45] Radical feminists object to pornography on two grounds, believing that pornography degrades and subordinates women and, that by depicting explicit and graphic acts of violence, pornography causes violence against women. Researchers who study rapists and pornography are not in agreement about a link between pornography and sexual violence.[46]

Liberal feminists responded by organizing to oppose censorship. Betty Friedan, author Erica Jong and numerous authors and liberal activists joined organizations such as Feminists for Free Expression, The National Coalition Against Censorship, and the Feminist Against Censorship Taskforce (FACT). Wendy McElroy, the former president of the Canadian branch of Feminists for Free Expression, has written a defense of the anti-censorship position entitled *XXX: A Woman's Right to Pornography.*[47] McElroy argues that pornography benefits women by encouraging women's sexual imagination, feelings and fantasies. She critiques the radical feminist anti-pornography crusade as hostile to sexual freedom and in league with conservatives in an attempt to control female sexuality. The liberal feminists' resistance to censorship has been denounced by the radicals as a betrayal of women.

AFRICAN-AMERICAN WOMEN AND FEMINISM

Black women writers who analyze feminist thought are of course interested in racism. In common with white women, black women have experienced exploitation of their labor and denial of political rights. In addition, black women bear the burden of racial discrimination. The analysis of feminist thought by black women writers is also distinguished by the degree to which black feminists describe racism and classism *within* the feminist movement. Their critique is directed at radical and liberal feminists. For example, Patricia Hill Collins states that: "Even today, African-American, Hispanic, Native American, and Asian-American women criticize the feminist movement and its scholarship for being racist and overly concerned with white, middle-class women's issues."[48] Black feminist bell hooks is more blunt: "Racism abounds in the writings of white feminists, reinforcing white supremacy . . ." and "white women who dominate feminist discourse today rarely consider whether or not their perspective on women's reality is true to the lived experiences of women as a collective group."[49]

Mainstream feminism in the United States is frequently described by black feminists as one-dimensional, reflecting primarily the concerns of middle-class white women. Despite occasional radical pretensions, the white feminist movement is seen as not addressing the pressing concerns of the masses of women. In particular, liberal white feminists, perhaps unintentionally, embrace racist and classist assumptions by generalizing from their own rather narrow range of experiences. Consider the critique by bell hooks of Betty Friedan's *The Feminist Mystique*. Friedan's analysis, according to hooks, did not describe the condition of women in society, but "actually referred to the plight of a select group of college-educated, middle and upper class married white women—housewives bored with leisure, with the home, with children, with buying products, who wanted more out of life."[50] Moreover, working women often cannot share the liberal feminists' assumption that work outside the home will empower women and enable them to gain personal satisfaction. As hooks points out, many women already work outside the home, frequently in an exploitive situation, most often out of economic necessity. Mainstream feminism in the United States is perceived as primarily a bourgeois ideology serving the interests of white liberal feminists.

Describing radical feminism as not only racist but sexist, hooks states: "Militant white women were particularly eager to make the feminist movement privilege women over men. Their anger, hostility, and rage was so intense that they were unable to resist turning the movement into a public forum for their

277

attacks ... Fundamentally, they argued *that all men are the enemies of all women* ..."[51] According to hooks, this has undesirable effects, including dividing black women from black men and decreasing unity within feminism. The criticism of the traditional family structure by some radical feminists, especially the suggestion that feminism should seek the abolition of the traditional family, is threatening to many women, particularly women of color.

The familiar argument that black women have endured not only racial but class and gender discrimination does not minimize the importance of sexism; rather, it is intended to place sexism into a larger context. Black women writers emphasize that sexism is part of a larger inter-connected network of discrimination and dominance. Therefore, the goal of feminism ought to be elimination of the system of domination, not simply assuring that educated women have better access to jobs within the power structure. This goal requires that feminism focus on the need to eradicate the underlying cultural basis of sexism, racism, poverty and other forms of group oppression.[52]

LIBERTARIAN WOMEN

The goal of libertarians is to promote individual liberty in all areas of human endeavor. Libertarians desire minimal control by society over individual thought and behavior. They seek to liberate human thought and action from limits imposed by custom, tradition, government and religion, to increase human freedom and privacy, and to reduce unnecessary social controls. Ayn Rand was a prominent libertarian writer whose books have sold more than 20 million copies. Her novels, including *The Fountainhead* (1943) and *Atlas Shrugged* (1957), are well known statements of the libertarian position. Rand was frequently critical of social conservatism. She stated in a letter to *The New York Times* in 1976, "I am profoundly opposed to Ronald Reagan. Since he denies the right to abortion, he cannot be a defender of any rights."[53] The irony is that, because of her defense of laissez-faire economics, Rand's novels are popular with conservatives.

Camille Paglia is an author and lecturer on popular culture whose controversial libertarian views and energetic speaking style have earned her considerable notoriety. She is a critic of radical feminism, describing herself as "a feminist who wants to radically reform current feminism, to bring it back to common sense about life ... My kind of feminism stresses independence and personal responsibility for women."[54] She adds, "I want to save feminism from the feminists."[55]

Like novelist Ayn Rand, Paglia is neither a liberal nor a conservative. "My thinking tends to be libertarian. That is, I oppose intrusions of the state into the private realm—as in abortion, sodomy, prostitution, pornography, drug use, or suicide, all of which I would strongly defend as matters of free choice in a repre-sentative democracy."[56] As a libertarian, she believes in maximizing human liberty in social, economic, political and cultural affairs. Paglia states that her position "should not be mistaken for conservatism: I am radically pro-pornography, pro-prostitution, pro-abortion, and pro-legalization of drugs."[57]

Sexuality   Paglia believes that sex is one of the ways that women exercise power over men. In *Sex, Art, and American Culture,* she states: "Feminists are currently adither over woman's status as a sex object . . . For me, sexual objecti-fication is a supreme human talent that is indistinguishable from the art impulse."[58] In rejecting mainstream feminism and the New Victorianism, Paglia states that the age of consent should be lowered to fourteen, that artists have no responsibility to society other than to produce art (meaning government should not censor art, even if it is pornographic), and that women must take responsi-bility for their actions by not placing the blame for their personal situations on men, or on society. She uses the radical feminist charge that "nothing that demeans women can be art" as an illustration of the "fascism of the contempo-rary women's movement."[59]

Paglia is an out-spoken advocate of the libertarian position regarding women's rights. As a libertarian, she favors government policies that encourage maximizing human liberty and expression in social, economic, political and cul-tural affairs. Contending that contemporary feminists have abandoned the goals of equality and liberty for women, Paglia asserts that women are entitled to political and legal equality, but not preferences. Rather than promoting strong and independent women, Paglia believes that radical feminist policies will return women to the status of those who need special protections, and who are not capable of handling equality.

THE CONSERVATIVE CRITIQUE OF FEMINISM

Katherine Kersten is the author of an essay entitled "How the Feminist Estab-lishment Hurts Women," published in 1994 in *Christianity Today.* She describes herself as a lawyer and M.B.A. who decided to become a full-time mother.[60] Kersten begins her critique by acknowledging that historically, feminism has played an important role in attaining equal rights for women. Kersten's basic

279

premise is that while equal treatment of the sexes is a worthwhile goal, feminism, especially radical feminism, fails to address the most important issue in America, namely, the moral, cultural and social environment in which children are growing up. Conservative women, according to Kersten, believe that a mother's most important duty is to their children. "Clearly, society's most pressing need at the moment is not more lawyers and accountants. What we need . . . is more decent people, of the kind only strong families and dedicated parents can produce. We need people of character—self-controlled people who know right from wrong and are committed to the common good."[61]

Kersten joins Paglia and Denfeld in arguing that contemporary feminism, especially its radical variants, perpetuates a victim status for women by providing women with an excuse to blame others for personal problems. Kersten states that feminism's image of women has changed drastically in the last hundred years. Early feminists (in the 19th and early 20th century) portrayed women as capable and intelligent, needing only equal rights in order to make a contribution to society outside the home. Beginning in the 1950s and 1960s, the image of women as strong and capable was superseded by a new and very different image that Kersten calls "the empty vessel." Kersten describes this image as portraying women as timid, weak, and bewildered creatures who are defined by their suffering and victimhood. "She lacks the internal resources to cope with suffering, to put it into perspective, and to distinguish between garden-variety irritation and real injustice."[62]

Women of the New Right

Phyllis Schlafly is a journalist, attorney and author. She rejects the gender-neutral approach to public policy because, she believes, there are sex-based differences that need to be acknowledged by society, public policy and law. She rejects with equal vehemence the libertarian view that women ought to seek sexual liberation and economic and political equality. Schlafly favors laws that recognize the *right* of a woman to be a full-time wife and mother by requiring husbands to provide the primary financial support and a home for their wives and children. She supports equal opportunity which, for her, does not include preferential treatment or "reverse discrimination" for women. However, Schlafly *does* support the right of employers to give preference to wage earners supporting dependents, and to protect women from strenuous job requirements (as in the armed forces, the police, or in factories). In line with the New Right conservative agenda, Schlafly favors government regulations to outlaw pornography, and requirements that school textbooks endorse the "family values" of "monogamous marriage, woman's role as wife and mother, and man's role as provider and protector."[63]

In summary, some conservative women favor social recognition of women's role as mother and wife, advocating that women be permitted to choose a traditional path. Others favor stronger government policies to assure that women (particularly married women) are provided with financial security and protections from strenuous job requirements, pornography and prostitution.

CONCLUSION

Conservative critics of feminism argue that biology is destiny, meaning that females are destined to have a more burdensome reproductive role than are males. Conservatives insist that males and females are innately different. Males tend to exhibit "masculine" psychological traits such as assertiveness, aggressiveness, rationality, logic and control of emotions, while females display traits of gentleness, empathy, sensitivity and intuition. Conservatives believe that these differences are natural and that society should preserve this natural order by permitting men to be manly and women to be feminine.[64]

Ironically, some feminists are now advancing arguments similar to those of conservatives. An ideological debate around feminism is the issue of equality versus the need for special protections for women. The debate between egalitarian and protectionist feminism poses a dilemma for women. As described by Wendy Kaminer, author of *A Fearful Freedom: Women's Flight from Equality,* the danger of protectionist feminism is that it has always aligned feminists with the enemies of emancipation. "Any feminist who finds herself allied with Jerry Falwell (and) Phyllis Schlafly . . . on matters of sexual justice has good reason to question her judgment."[65] Whether the feminist agenda will be served by alliance with conservatives seems dubious at best. Social conservatives and radical feminists have relatively little in common other than their shared loathing for pornography.

Conservatives are not likely to embrace proposals for social reform on women's issues such as the feminization of poverty, cutbacks in social services, reproductive freedom, domestic violence, sexual harassment, equal opportunity in employment and education, and working women's need for childcare. Liberals, both male and female, are likely to resist attempts to impose censorship and controls over sexuality. The outcome of the debate within feminism will determine the capacity of the ideology to attract a range of supporters and sympathizers from the political center.

NOTES

1. Camille Paglia, *Sex, Art, and American Culture* (New York: Vintage, 1992), p. 4.

2. Robin Morgan, "On Women as a Colonized People," in Robin Morgan, *The Word of a Woman: Feminist Dispatches 1968–1992* (New York: Norton, 1992), p. 76.

3. bell hooks, *Feminist Theory: from margin to center,* Boston: South End Press, 1984, p. 17.

4. A number of authors use the same or similar classifications. See: John Charvet, *Feminism* (London: J. M. Dent, 1982); Janet A. Kourany, James P. Sterba and Rosemarie Tong (eds.), *Feminist Philosophies* (Englewood Cliffs New Jersey: Prentice Hall. 1992); and Rosemarie Tong, *Feminist Thought: A Comprehensive Introduction* (Boulder: Westview Press, 1989).

5. Rosemarie Tong, *Feminist Thought: A Comprehensive Introduction* (Boulder: Westview Press, 1989), p. 1.

6. Sondra Fargains, *Situating Feminism: From Thought to Action* (Thousand Oaks, Ca.: Sage, 1994), p. 15.

7. In addition to Tong, *Feminist Thought,* see: Alison M. Jaggar and Paula S. Rothenberg, eds., *Feminist Frameworks* (New York: McGraw-Hill, 1984.); Catherine A. MacKinnon, *Toward a Feminist Theory of the State* (Cambridge, Mass.: Harvard University Press, 1989); and Alison M. Jaggar, *Feminist Politics and Human Nature* (Totowa, New Jersey: Rowman & Allanheld, 1983).

8. Simone de Beauvoir, *The Second Sex* (New York: Alfred A. Knopf, 1953).

9. Alice Schwarzer, *After the Second Sex: Conversations with Simone de Beauvoir,* trans. Marianne Howarth (New York: Pantheon, 1984),

p. 32, cited in Miriam Schneir (ed.), *Feminism in Our Time: The Essential Writings, World War II to the Present* (New York: Vantage, 1994), p. 5.

10. Kate Millett, *Sexual Politics* (Garden City, NY: Doubleday, 1970).

11. Susanne Kappeler, *The Will to Violence: The Politics of Personal Behaviour* (New York: Teachers College Press, 1995), p. 27. Emphasis is Kappeler's.

12. Tong, *Feminist Thought: A Comprehensive Introduction,* pp. 51–54. See also Alison M. Jaggar, *Feminist Politics and Human Nature* (Totowa, New Jersey: Rowman & Allanheld, 1983).

13. Tong, *Feminist Thought: A Comprehensive Introduction,* p. 59.

14. Friedrich Engels, *The Origin of the Family, Private Property and the State* (New York: International Publishers, 1972), pp. 137–139.

15. Emma Goldman, "Marriage and Love," in *Emma Goldman, The Traffic in Women and Other Essays on Feminism* (Washington, N.J., 1970), p. 37.

16. John Charvet, *Feminism* (London: J. M. Dent, 1982), p. 48.

17. Emma Goldman, "Woman Suffrage," in *Emma Goldman, The Traffic in Women and Other Essays on Feminism,* p. 63.

18. Tong, *Feminist Thought: A Comprehensive Introduction,* p. 5.

19. Robin Morgan, "Women vs. the Miss America Pageant," in Robin Morgan, *The Word of a Woman: Feminist Dispatches 1968–1992* (New York: Norton, 1992), pp. 22–23.

20. Robin Morgan, "The Wretched of the Hearth," in Robin Morgan, *The Word of a Woman,* p. 31.

21. Victoria Woodhull, "Testimony before Congress," in Pat Andrews (ed.), *Voices of Diversity: Perspectives on American Political Ideals and Institutions* (Guilford, Connecticut: Dushkin, 1995), p. 71.

22. Tong, *Feminist Thought: A Comprehensive Introduction*, p. 2.

23. Mary Wollstonecraft, *A Vindication of the Rights of Woman*. Carol H. Poston, ed. (New York: W.W. Norton, 1975).

24. John Stuart Mill, "The Subjection of Women," in John Stuart Mill, *Three Essays*, Richard Wollheim, ed. (New York: Oxford University Press, 1975), pp. 427–549.

25. Betty Friedan, *The Feminine Mystique* (New York: Norton, 1974), pp. 1–70.

26. Friedan, *The Feminine Mystique*, p. 364. For a literary treatment of these issues see Marilyn French, *The Women's Room* (New York: Jove, 1978).

27. NOW, Organizing Statement, 1966, in Pat Andrews (ed.), *Voices of Diversity*, p. 142.

28. Germaine Greer, *The Female Eunuch* (New York: McGraw-Hill, 1970), p. 61.

29. Betty Friedan, *The Second Stage* (NY: Summit, 1981).

30. Darlene Superville, "Diversity stops at top, glass-ceiling study says," Associated Press, reported in the *Dayton Daily News*, March 16, 1995, p. 5A.

31. "Rally calls political assaults violent crime against women," *Dayton Daily News*, April 10, 1995, p. 5A.

32. The surveys are cited in Rene Denfeld, *The New Victorians: A Young Woman's Challenge to the Old Feminist Order* (New York: Warner, 1995), p. 2.

33. Susan Faludi, *Backlash: The Undeclared War Against American Women* (New York: Crown, 1991).

34. Christina Hoff Summers, *Who Stole Feminism: How Women Have Betrayed Women* (New York: Simon & Schuster, 1994).

35. Naomi Wolf, *The Beauty Myth* (New York: Doubleday, 1992), p. 207, cited in Christina Hoff Summers, *Who Stole Feminism*, p. 11. See also, Gloria Steinem, Revolution from Within: A Book of Self-Esteem (Boston: Little, Brown, 1992), p. 222.

36. Summers, *Who Stole Feminism*, p. 12.

37. Summers, *Who Stole Feminism*, p. 13.

38. Rene Denfeld, *The New Victorians*, p. 4.

39. See Germaine Greer, *The Change: Women, Aging and Menopause,* Betty Friedan, *The Fountain of Age,* and Gloria Steinem, *Revolution from Within: A Book of Self-Esteem* (Boston: Little, Brown, 1992).

40. Rene Denfeld, *The New Victorians*, p. 6, 7.

41. Rene Denfeld, *The New Victorians,* p. 8. See, for example: Catherine MacKinnon, *Toward a Feminist Theory of the State,* Catherine Mac-Kinnon, *Only Words* (1993), Andrea Dworkin, *Pornography: Men Possessing Women,* and Andrea Dworkin, *Fire and Ice: A Novel* (New York: Weidenfeld & Nicolson, 1986).

42. In addition to Millet, *Sexual Politics,* see Susan Brownmiller, *Against Our Will: Men, Women and Rape* (New York: Simon and Schuster, 1975).

43. Brownmiller, *Against Our Will: Men, Women and Rape*, p. 15.

44. In particular see Adrienne Rich, "Compulsory Heterosexuality and Lesbian Existence," *Signs: Journal of Women in Culture and Society,* 5, no. 4: (1980), p 637.

45. Rene Denfeld, *The New Victorians*, p. 101. See also Andrea Dworkin, *Pornography: Men Possessing Women* (New York: Putnam, 1981).

46. See Denfeld's discussion in *The New Victorians*, pp. 91–123.

47. Wendy McElroy, *XXX: A Woman's Right to Pornography* (New York: St. Martin's, 1995.)

48. Patricia Hill Collins, *Black Feminist Thought* (New York, Routledge, Chapman and Hall, 1990), p. 7.

49. bell hooks, *Feminist Theory: from margin to center* (Boston: South End Press, 1984), p. 3.

50. Ibid., p. 1.

51. Ibid., p. 33, emphasis is hooks'.

52. See, among others, Cellestine Ware, *Woman Power: The Movement for Women's Liberation*, New York: Tower Publications, 1970.

53. Rand's letter is cited by Maureen Down, "Where *Atlas Shrugged* Is Still Read—Forthrightly," *The New York Times*, September 13, 1987, p. 5.

54. Paglia, *Sex, Art and American Culture*, p. 56.

55. Ibid., p. 262.

56. Ibid., Introduction, p. viii.

57. Ibid., p. 244.

58. Ibid., p. 17.

59. Ibid., p. 262.

60. Katherine Kersten, "How the Feminist Establishment Hurts Women," *Christianity Today*, June 20, 1994, p. 20.

61. Ibid., p. 20.

62. Ibid., p. 22.

63. Phyllis Schlafly, "The Power of the Positive Woman," in Andrews, *Voices of Diversity*, pp. 207–211.

64. See George Gilder, *Sexual Suicide* (New York: Quadrangle Books, 1973).

65. Wendy Kaminer, *A Fearful Freedom: Women's Flight from Equality* (Reading, Mass.: Addison-Wesley, 1990), p. 215.

Chapter 11

Gay and Lesbian Rights: Left, Center, Right

"Gay is Good."[1]

Frank Kameny

"No American, no human being, should have to give up her or his difference in order to be treated equally under the law."[2]

Evan Wolfson

"AIDS is nature's retribution for violating the laws of nature in many ways. I think the promiscuous homosexual lifestyle is not only wrong, it is medically ruinous. And I think it is socially destructive."[3]

Patrick Buchanan

Should the right to equal treatment under the law be accorded to all humans? Is it as simple as that? Or, for people whose primary difference may be based in a choice (one which a large and vocal part of the public disapproves), would the recognition of such rights amount not only to "special rights" for some—but possibly even the downfall of Western civilization? Such questions are hardly arcane. For many analysts, the biggest surprise of the 2004 US presidential election was that the reelection of George W. Bush was presumably more about "moral values" than it was about Iraq, the economy, or even the threat of terrorism. For many American voters, "moral values" was shorthand for protecting the family, which translated for most into opposition to gay mar riage. For a while, it looked as if same-sex marriage had replaced abortion as the hot button issue of the times. While that may no longer be the case today, it is likely that Americans remain as divided as ever over what rights (if any) gay and lesbians should be able to demand as citizens.[i]

A SHORT HISTORY OF HOMOSEXUALITY IN THE US

Most historians agree that homosexuality has likely existed in the US since the first days of human settlement. Yet it was only in the late 19th century that the terms "homosexual" or "lesbian" became widely defined as a new class of people whose primary erotic interest is in the same sex. Prior to this time in the US as well as in Western Europe, some men and women engaged in what we would now describe as homosexual behavior, but neither they nor society defined persons as essentially different in kind from the majority because of it. In effect, "homosexual" was an adjective—it described certain behaviors, not certain people.[4]

According to John Emilio, this absence of rigid categories of homosexual and heterosexual should not be taken to suggest some wide social approval of same-sex eroticism. Social tolerance or acceptance, if not approval, varied by time and place. For example, colonial legal codes prescribed death for sodomy (and although it was relatively rarely enforced, some accused "sodomites" were executed under these laws). Certainly, anti-homosexual interpretations of ancient religious codes contributed to a hostile climate for gays. Yet, D'Emilio argues that although it was not unusual in the US for various communities to severely punish individuals for such behavior, such acts (though stigmatized) were generally considered a discrete transgression, a misdeed comparable to other sins.[5]

---

[i]In this chapter we will occasionally employ the term "sexual minority" as short-hand for gays and lesbians. Although there is no agreement on what percentage of the US population belongs to this minority group, common estimates range from 3–10 percent or higher, depending on whether bisexual and trans-gendered persons are included. The inclusion of these groups is increasingly common, as it is not unusual for discussions of gay and lesbian rights to be represented as "GLBT" (or gay, lesbian, bisexual and trans-gendered) rights. However, because of the significant differences in self-definition between these groups, this chapter will focus only on the struggle over homosexual rights. For brevity's sake, the term "gay" should be taken to refer to homosexual men and women.

However, by the late 19th century, a conceptual shift had occurred and from that time people who participated in same-sex eroticism were labeled as homosexuals, whose very nature was believed to be sharply distinguishable from "normal" heterosexuals. Although many gays and lesbians likely suffered from what D'Emilio calls a profound sense of difference, no movement to advocate for their rights could come about until these individuals came to perceive themselves as sharing an identity as an oppressed minority. This constituency had to be created before it could be mobilized. Yet, as people became labeled as homosexuals and were viewed as inferior, less moral, respectable, or even healthy, most people's first inclination was to retreat, rather than to organize.[6]

For example, homosexuals were routinely diagnosed by physicians as diseased, although the debate as to whether homosexuality was based in an acquired form of insanity or a congenital defect continued for nearly 100 years.[ii] During those years various medical mistreatments in the name of a "cure" were widely accepted. Large numbers of gay men and lesbians were committed to asylums and subjected to medical experimentation. Their medical care included everything from hypnosis and psychotherapy to electroshock and treatment with untested drugs, castration and hysterectomy.[7]

Similarly, homosexuality was classified as a felony (lesser only than the crimes of murder, kidnapping, and rape) in most US states until 1950. As late as 1986, in *Bowers v. Hardwick*, the US Supreme Court upheld that the criminalization of sodomy was constitutional.[iii] Although various "crimes against nature statutes" were relatively rarely enforced, they posed a constant threat in the lives of many people. The existence of sodomy laws continued to cast a legal stigma on same-sex relationships as it equated homosexuality with criminality. Sodomy laws threatened to destroy the lives of gay men and lesbians in a variety of other ways as well. For example, a sodomy conviction could mean the loss of a job, the right to child custody, or even visitation rights. Moreover, on a daily basis nationwide a range of other penal code provisions were routinely used by police and courts around the country to shame, harass and in some cases terrorize gay men and women.[8]

[ii]The American Psychiatric Association only removed homosexuality from its list of mental disorders in 1974. It took the World Health Organization nearly ten years more to do the same in 1981.

[iii]Although over the years more than half of all states eventually repealed sodomy laws, sexual activity between consenting adults of the same sex was only decriminalized with the 2003 Supreme Court ruling in *Lawrence v. Texas*.

Given the threat of social reprobation, during much of the early through mid-20th century, most homosexuals took great pains to conceal their sexual preferences and lived isolated, invisible lives, fearing exposure and the trouble that would inevitably follow. This was not always the case; for some gay men and lesbians living in larger American cities starting in the 1870s, life was relatively easier and more open. By the 1930s a class of people had emerged who recognized their erotic interest in members of their own sex, people found ways of meeting each other in saloons, clubs, literary societies, and parks, so that participation in a gay subculture was possible. Especially after World War II and through the 1950s, gay subcultures developed as the shift to industrial capitalism was complete. As more people left their small towns and farms for the cities, larger numbers of people seeking autonomous personal lives came into contact with each other for the first time. But it was also during this period that a number of forces, most notably McCarthyism, converged to produce a political climate hostile to difference or movements for social change.[9]

Despite the 1950s-era persecution, a number of Supreme Court split decisions during that time suggested the existence of a changing social climate. Growing numbers of gay men and lesbians, joined by straight supporters, quietly formed what would be known as the homophile movement.[iv] This movement took an incrementalist approach, seeking to first develop among homosexuals a sense of group consciousness as an oppressed minority. It also encouraged gays to overcome their shame and to take pride in their homosexuality as a unique culture with a positive contribution to make. The homophile movement included a variety of groups (many of which felt compelled to operate in secrecy) such as the mostly male Mattachine Society and the predominately lesbian Daughters of Bilitis (DOB).[10]

Although they were both part of this early movement, the Mattachine Society and Daughters of Bilitis did not necessarily share the same priorities. Founded in 1955, the Daughters emphasized lesbians' dual identity as homosexuals and as women, and their unique economic and social challenges as females. There were other differences within the movement as well. Some homophile organizations of the 1950s and 1960s preached defiant, collective action to promote equality. The Mattachine Society, for example, started out in 1951 in southern California as a relatively radical group. However, along with the DOB it

---

[iv]As a sign of the times, the term "homophile" was preferred in the 1950s because it suggested same-sex friendship and love, but without the negative connotations associated with "homosexual" (Henry L. Minton, *Departing from Deviance: A History of Homosexual Rights and Emancipatory Science in America* (Chicago: University of Chicago Press, 2002).

settled on a more accommodationist approach which minimized the differences between homosexuals and heterosexuals. It eventually became known as the "NAACP of the movement" for its cautious moderation.[11]

Despite the lack of cohesion within the 50 or so relatively small groups comprising this movement, it is important to recognize that resistance to discrimination and other forms of marginalization did exist prior to the gay liberation movement of the 1960s. The homophile movement did not substantially change laws or policy, but it did pave the way for later successes, by helping to establish a sense of group identity and by broaching homosexual rights as a topic for discussion.[12]

What was it about the 1960s that would lead to the dramatic rise of this movement, and the adoption of such a radically different strategy and approach? The birth of the gay civil rights movement is often identified with the Stonewall riots of June 1969. In a country where homosexual relationships were illegal, bars provided a refuge of sorts, a place for sexual minorities to socialize in relative safety. Yet, throughout the country, such bars and their patrons were under constant attack by city administrators and police. It was this rising sense of resentment that led to a profound shift in the consciousness of many gay men and lesbians. Stonewall (which refers to the Stonewall Inn, a bar in Greenwich Village) became a symbol of the movement and a catalytic event because it was there that a small group of bar patrons led by drag queens spontaneously fought back against incessant police harassment. The resulting riots, which lasted for days, drew the world's attention because they were so audacious; it is estimated that 400 people joined in and forced the police to barricade themselves in the bar before the crowd set it on fire. Stonewall no doubt marked a turning point in US history, but it was the community coming out of this shared experience that became a mass movement within a few years. Stonewall inspired a new generation of activists who set out to transform an entire society.[13]

THE POLITICAL SPECTRUM

Stonewall was just the first major battle on one front in the US' ongoing culture wars— the struggle over gay and lesbian rights. As we have done throughout the rest of this book, the full range of opinion on this topic will be represented, which includes ideological divides over values such as equality, self-determination and privacy, as well as definitions of morality. We will describe gay rights movements (and counter-movements) and place them along the political spectrum from left, to center, to right. As you will soon see, those who support the

293

rights of sexual minorities in this country are hardly monolithic in their ideology, primary concerns, or approach to change. Neither are those who seek to restrict or oppose them. In this chapter, revolutionary, reformist, and status quo ideologies all will take their places on one of today's major ideological battlefields—the right to marry.

Like the civil rights movements that demand racial and gender equality, the struggle for gay and lesbian rights includes a broad range of topics. Similarly, there is consensus within this movement only on a core set of goals. As you will see in the sections to follow, gays, lesbians, and their allies are as divided ideologically as the race and gender-based movements have been—over strategy and tactics, and over working within the system versus taking it on. Some organizations within this movement are broad in their approach, while others have focused on a single issue, such as AIDS. Some seek reformist change through litigation, others offer practical assistance, while still others focus on the media to educate for larger, transformative social change.[14] Like the other civil rights movements, it has not been unusual for gay and lesbian organizations to attempt to unify but to break apart over ideological, class, and other differences. For many years, the gay rights movement in the US was largely dominated by middle and upper-class white gay men and their interests and priorities (and some say it still is). Finding patriarchy alive and well in these boys' clubs, some lesbians split off to form separatist organizations, which have also had problems with racial inclusion.[15] In other words, just as other civil rights movements had their Martin Luther King/Malcolm X divides, or the Liberal Feminist/Radical Feminist splits, such schisms also existed (and exist) within the gay and lesbian rights movement.

Until now, we've been using the terms "gay rights" and "gay liberation" interchangeably, but it is important to recognize that to many people they do mean very different things and are most appropriately located at different points along the political spectrum. Those who call for gay liberation are likely to identify with the political left. Often derided by mainstream America as militants, gay liberationists embrace this identity and with it their outsider status (as opposed to what they would characterize as the accommodationist, insider status embraced by gays and lesbians inhabiting the political center). Some analysts contend that by turn of the 21st century, its overwhelming focus on the right to marry indicates a conservative shift within the gay and lesbian movement (which one observer likened to the movement passing into middle age).[16] Others point out that because there is such a significant overlap in interests between the left and center that the two groups are not so separate and distinct as some may care to think. What is clear is that the left and center are confronted by a right wing that is formidable in its unity. Yet, it is just as clear that America's larger heterosexual population is divided over the question of gay rights. So, where does this leave us? Before attempting to resolve this question, let's turn to a discussion of what distinguishes and distances the various groups along the political spectrum.

THE LEFT

Inspired by the "Black Is Beautiful" motto, the gay left proclaimed its radicalism in the late 1960s with the simple slogan "Gay Is Good." How is this so radical? Well, for mainstream Americans grappling with the sexual revolution—extending this revolution to include homosexuality came as something of a shock. Yet, for leftists such as Frank Kameny, being gay wasn't something to be closeted or simply tolerated—it was to be accepted as a positive identity.[v] Gay liberationists agreed (and agree) that homosexuals and heterosexuals could not be more different, but that homosexuality is the moral equivalent of heterosexuality. According to Kameny, it is important to be clear and unequivocal that homosexuality is moral, right, good, and desirable—for the individual participants and for society as a whole. For nearly forty years the left has sought to force America to reexamine its prejudices by seeking visibility. With their pride celebrations and defiance of external authority, those on the left have demanded the right to the public sexual expression that heterosexuals take for granted. Maintaining that they owe apologies to no one, these activists have been characterized as militants for staging kiss-ins and chalking and chanting slogans such as "We're Here. We're Queer. Get Used to It."[17]

Ideologically speaking, the gay left is not necessarily Marxist (any more than the religious right is fascist). However, each end of the spectrum is associated with certain characteristic core principles and values, and both are on the fringes of the political spectrum and fairly militant on the issues. As usual, the left has a transformative agenda; it is viewed as aggressively calling for something that is

[v]For many people, the question of identity is central to any discussion of gay rights. Is homosexuality merely a sexual preference? Or is it a sexual orientation—akin to a worldview, about much more than the gender of one's sexual partner? Moreover, is homosexuality an active choice? Or, is it involuntary and an immutable characteristic, as fixed and unchanging as gender or race—something that one is born with? Some gays (and lesbians, in particular) are social constructivists who agree that sexuality is all about choice. Others maintain that sexuality is an essential part of one's nature over which s/he has little control. These debates remain unresolved.

truly revolutionary—the complete sexual liberation of all. Known as libera-tionists (as opposed to reformists), groups such as the Gay Liberation Front (GLF) and the Gay Activists Alliance (GAA) are associated with an explicitly radical view. Calling for the abolition of all existing social institutions that sup-port only one narrow view of human sexuality, they demand the end of racism, sexism, and economic injustice.[18]

Coming of age in the late 1960s, the liberationists were often contemptuous of the older, homophile generation whose moderate approach, they argued, was obsolete. This newer generation of leftist activists accused their elders of being naïve or complacent, to be disdained for continuing to live closeted lives in fear of discrimination.[19] Instead, the liberationists advocated the use of confronta-tional tactics, including sit-ins to denounce the publication of demeaning images of homosexuals, disruptions of medical conventions whose membership contin-ued to regard homosexuality as a mental illness, and public outings of their own (which proved and continue to prove controversial within the gay community).[vi]

Whereas in the gay community, "coming out" had traditionally been respected as the private decision of the individual, liberationists recast it as a political act, the first step toward freedom, and the symbolic shedding of inter-nalized homophobia. Similar in principle to Black Power, liberationists argued for Gay Power, rejecting all efforts at inclusion as assimilation. In many ways, this too was a separatist movement, calling for liberation instead of equality, self-determination over integration, preserving autonomy and celebrating dif-ferences instead of minimizing them. Therefore, much of this liberation was about sexual liberation, undoing the damage of the past, and building pride in an identity as a sexual minority. By the late 1970s, the movement had effectively gotten its message out; there were thousands of activist gay organizations in the US.[20]

Yet, the movement would change markedly in the 1980s with the coming of AIDS. AIDS represented a dramatic turn in the direction of the movement, much as the 1969 Stonewall riots had a generation before. However, AIDS had a contradictory impact on the struggle for gay and lesbian rights. On the one hand, AIDS was originally thought to be a "gay plague" because it primarily tar-geted homosexual men. This provided the liberationists' enemies with a power-ful weapon in the counterassault against gay rights. At the same time, though, AIDS stimulated an unprecedented level of gay and lesbian activism. Because it had the potential to decimate a population, the disease reshaped the priorities

---

[vi]To "out" someone is to pull him or her "out of the closet," or to publicize someone else's homosexuality.

of the movement. For years, AIDS drew attention away from other concerns. In many ways, AIDS changed everything. It may even have contributed to a political shift in the movement, associated with the (centrist) push for the right to marry.[21]

For those firmly on the left, though, AIDS also proved critical to the emergence of a new wave of radical gay activism. By the 1990s, new, liberationist organizations such as ACT UP (the AIDS Coalition to Unleash Power) were thoroughly frustrated with the slow pace of government efforts to deal with the disease. It was clear to them that the more moderate approach of going through official channels was not working. So the liberationists pushed the system, turning again to extrajudicial, confrontational tactics such as direct action and civil disobedience. They aimed to shock; activists marched on Washington, unfurled safe sex banners at baseball games, and resuscitated 1970s techniques to disrupt meetings, including those of the Food and Drug Administration (FDA) to demand more research and access to AIDS medicines.[22] In effect, the 1990s radicals returned to their roots, demanding media visibility—and they got it, for better or worse.

More militant and sophisticated than ever before, a variety of liberationist movements besides ACT UP formed on the left since the 1980s. One example is Queer Nation, which provocatively appropriated the once-derogatory term "queer," and transformed it into a statement of pride, power, and militancy. In its rejection of all attempts at assimilation, queer nationalists are separatists. Echoing Kameny's 1960s radicalism, these activists celebrate being on the margins and embrace all individuals considered sexually marginalized. They do so both to unify the movement and to play up their difference, to make the point to straight America in fact that gays are as different from straights as they could possibly be. The playwright Tony Kushner, for example, argues for the existence of a unique gay culture or "queer outlook." For him, sexual orientation is more than simply a "preference"...it is as central to one's worldview as is race or religion.[23]

Therefore, on the issue of marriage, many on the gay left resist pressures to fit into relationships and family patterns designed by and for heterosexuals. Not all gays and lesbians want to marry, nor should they. Instead of fighting for the right to enter into what they regard as a dysfunctional, corrupt, and oppressive institution—"a tool of the capitalist establishment"—the left seeks to broaden our understanding of what constitutes a family. Radicals don't want their relationships to be just like straight ones; they want to gain respect for a variety of sexual identities and fear that if gay marriage is sanctioned, those who choose less conventional arrangements will wind up even more marginalized. Why should the state recognize only one kind of emotional arrangement between people and reward it with legal, financial, and social benefits, they ask. Consequently, the gay left generally either rejects marriage or ranks it as a low priority. Although it isn't an opinion one hears much of these days in the mainstream press, for sexual minorities on the left, the freedom to marry isn't nearly as crucial as simply the freedom to be themselves without fear.[24]

The right to be free to live one's life without fear is a tall order for homosexuals in this country even today; ultimately it involves a transformative agenda. The leftists who advocate such an approach are not satisfied with changing a specific law or meeting a particular need, they are focused on a whole system of oppression. Yet, not all of them agree on what is the most appropriately "leftist" position on marriage. For example, instead of being dismissive of the institution, given the reaction gay weddings have provoked from straight society, marrying up with someone of the same sex might just be the most transgressive and revolutionary gesture one can make. Recognition of marriage equality for same-sex couples could be viewed as amounting to a profoundly revolutionary step because it would require a transformation of the nature of marriage—and society. There are plenty of gay radicals who contend, therefore, that this is actually the most orthodox leftist position—and they have served notice that they will continue to marry whether mainstream America likes it or not.[25]

Therefore, allowing for differences within this camp, the left is in agreement on its insistence upon a fundamental rethinking, not only of sex and gender, but of constitutional guarantees to life, liberty, and the pursuit of happiness.[26] In their efforts to combat institutionalized homophobia while demanding no less than full equality, it is the without a doubt the liberationists who have done the most to increase the visibility of gays and lesbians in America. The question remains, however, as to whether the left has attracted the kind of attention the gay rights movement wants—or needs.

THE CENTER

As opposed to the direct action, in-your-face liberationists, many other people who identify as part of the post-Stonewall generation just want to be left alone to live their lives in peace. For the most part they see themselves as living in a world in which ignorant rhetoric is still far too common. But they take some respite in the fact that the most rabid anti-gay expressions are becoming more unacceptable in polite society. They know far too well that discrimination and worse still exists in America, but sexual minorities of this generation consider themselves to be freer than any before to get on with their lives and to live as they wish, like anyone else.[27]

Such views are characteristic of a "creeping cycle" described by social change theorists, in which social justice movements started by radicals are eventually repudiated and supplanted by moderates.[28] Like their pre-Stonewall counterparts of the 1950s, today's gay center (as shared by liberals and conservatives) is relatively conventional, mainstream and reformist, seeking to win equal rights for sexual minorities within the existing system. In terms of approach, the center is shared between gays and straights who advocate tolerance (if not acceptance) of homosexuals. For them, transformative cultural change is not necessary because whether liberal or conservative, centrists believe that American institutions are valuable and the system is essentially fair. As centrists, both liberals and conservatives are distinguished from the far left and right by their preference for reformist, gradualist tactics and accommodationist agendas based in legislative change.[29]

Therefore, gay and lesbian centrists pin their hopes on the core ideas of integration, or inclusion: the idea that if the heterosexual mainstream realizes that homosexuals are just like everyone else (or that the only differences between us are unimportant), there will be no reason to object to equal treatment. Clearly, this is a major point upon which the left and center diverge. Centrists contend that the left's separatist approach will only heighten hostility against gays and lesbians. They want to win allies and gain support from heterosexuals, whom they hope will see that their lives too are changed for the good by a policy of inclusiveness. Making an emotional appeal, centrists hope to build on empathy. They believe that if heterosexuals realize that they know people who are gay, they are likely to view homosexuals as morally worthy and comparable to heterosexuals. They are also more likely to be supportive of changing laws and policies to promote equal rights.[30]

In this effort, centrists have been criticized for encouraging what liberationists dismiss as middle-class assimilation (urging homosexuals to become more like heterosexuals). Most gay centrists resist such characterizations. Yet, at the risk of being labeled conformists, centrists are more likely to admit to wanting what some consider the American dream: to be free to form committed relationships, raise their kids, and pursue their careers.[31]

It is this desire that has led to the push for universalizing marriage, a battle that goes back to the early 1970s. For centrists, the right to marry is in many ways the biggest hurdle of all because full recognition of gay marriage demands more than tolerance—it demands acceptance.[32] In a more practical sense, the right to marry is important because it carries with it over 1000 rights, such as access to health benefits, inheritance, and the right to make crucial medical and financial decisions for one's mate. While some states, municipalities, and employers now recognize domestic partnerships, many people regard this as a half measure that discriminates against homosexuals, establishing them as second-class citizens.[vii] They argue that domestic partnerships (or even civil unions, which go a step further, granting gays and lesbians most of the legal and financial benefits of marriage, but without allowing marriage) are in no way a satisfactory compromise most crucially because the right to marry is important symbolically. As Chambers puts it, marriage is an enchanted term reserved for the most highly valued, committed sexual relationships. It is about the emotional satisfaction that comes from being recognized by society as partners.[33] Although they are accused by some of attempting to destroy the institution by joining it, gay centrists argue that the effort to universalize marriage underscores the institution's value and social function. Not only would universalization (or marriage equality) encourage as many people as possible to live more stable and productive lives; it would reaffirm the message that individuals and society flourishes when love, sex, and marriage go together.[34]

As you may recall, classical liberals generally believe that all people are born free and equal. They are bestowed with certain natural, God-given, and inalienable rights, including the right to life, liberty, and the pursuit of happiness. While Jefferson and the other liberal architects of the US Constitution may not have been thinking of the rights of sexual minorities at the time that they coined the phrase, centrists interpret this message as an endorsement for expanding individual rights. It was cited by the civil rights movements for blacks and women, as it is now being used by gay advocacy groups such as the Lambda Legal Defense and Education Fund, as well as the Human Rights Campaign. Although some people reject the use of such parallels, gay centrists disagree.[viii] They point to important similarities between the struggle for racial equality and their own,

[vii]Domestic partnerships grant unmarried (gay and straight) couples in committed relationships many of the legal benefits and burdens of marriage.

[viii]Some centrists contend that if one's sexuality is biologically determined, as innate as one's race, then it is as wrong to discriminate because of sexual orientation as it is to discriminate based on race. Taking this view, African-American civil rights leaders such as Coretta Scott King endorsed a number of gay-friendly reforms. However, other centrists reject attempts to equate the struggle for gay rights with the struggle for racial equality, arguing that the experiences of African-Americans and gay Americans are deeply different. For them, gays do not comprise a "bona fide" minority for a variety of reasons. For example, they question whether sexual orientation is involuntary and whether homosexuals truly comprise an oppressed group (Andrew Sullivan, "Integration Day," *The New York Times*, May 17, 2004; Lee Badgett, "Income Inflation: The Myth of Affluence among Gays, Lesbians, and Bisexual Americans" (New York: NGLTF Policy Institute, 1998).

and predict that gay marriage may well follow the same trajectory as inter-racial marriage, which only became legal in all states about 40 years ago. Supporters of marriage equality for same-sex couples argue that such unions don't diminish the validity or dignity of opposite-sex marriage, any more than marrying someone of a different race devalues marriage between those of the same race. They argue that the right to marry is a fundamental civil right, it is a private, personal choice, and the government has no business deciding who anyone can marry.[35]

Proponents of this view believe that the Constitution backs them on this claim. As centrists, both liberal and conservatives pursue insider strategies and are more inclined to work within more traditional political structures than is the left.[ix] As reformists, they share a legal rights strategy, trusting that the Constitution protects their rights as it forbids the creation of second-class citizens. They recognize that social change (i.e.: ending segregation, legalizing abortion and interracial marriage, etc.) has tended to be driven by the courts; they have tried to capitalize on this tradition, but they don't count on the courts to resolve these questions in their favor. Gay or straight, centrists also seek access to politically powerful elected officials through lobbying and interest groups to promote legislative change.[36] In all this the two wings comprising the center are alike. Otherwise, as always, liberals and conservatives have their differences.

Liberals

As mentioned earlier, gay liberals make the point that their only difference from heterosexual America is relatively unimportant. Rather than being separatists, they seek to join the mainstream, desiring full and equal rights to political participation and representation. By 1980 gay liberals had largely won inclusion within the Democratic Party, as a gay rights plank became part of its platform. Yet, their incrementalist approach did not appear ready to pay off until ten years later with the election of Bill Clinton. Clinton, more than any Democratic nominee in US history, had campaigned promising to promote gay rights and had lobbied hard for their votes.[x] President Clinton sought to reward

[ix]Many of those seeking to universalize marriage consider themselves moderate centrists. Yet, these same-sex couples' weddings may signal a return to unconventional politics, as nothing so eloquently forces heterosexual America to confront its prejudices publicly. Out-of-state couples who lined up to wed outside Massachusetts' courthouses and the 4,000 committed couples married by the San Francisco mayor's office may symbolize a growing resistance, a form of civil disobedience sometimes used by the center, which also works to attracts media coverage and highlight the injustice of discrimination (Craig A. Rimmerman, *From Identity to Politics: The Lesbian and Gay Movements in the US* (Philadelphia: Temple University Press, 2002).

this support when in 1993, as one of his very first domestic initiatives, he launched an effort to overturn the military's ban on gay and lesbians, permitting homosexuals the right to serve their country without fear of harassment or discrimination. However, as is described fully elsewhere, Clinton was surprised by the furor set off by the policy, retreated, and ended up disappointing many people on all sides with the problematic compromise of "Don't Ask/Don't Tell/Don't Pursue."[37] [xi]

Moreover, many gays and lesbians seeking equal rights to marriage were dealt a blow by Clinton's 1996 signature of the Defense of Marriage Act (DOMA), which for federal purposes defined marriage as only existing between a man and a woman, and therefore granted the federal benefits of marriage exclusively to those unions which fit this description. DOMA also gave states the right to refuse to recognize same-sex marriages performed in other states, so that a couple legally married in one state may not be recognized as married in another. Although some legal scholars characterize DOMA as unconstitutional, it has not yet been effectively challenged in the courts.

[x]It is estimated that Clinton won approximately 75% of the gay and lesbian vote in 1992 and that sexual minorities contributed more than $3 million toward his campaign (see John D'Emilio, "Cycles of Change, Questions of Strategy: The Gay and Lesbian Movement after Fifty Years," 31–53 in *The Politics of Gay Rights*, ed.s Craig A. Rimmerman, Kenneth D. Wald, and Clyde Wilcox (Chicago: University of Chicago Press, 2000).

[xi]The policy overturns a ban on all homosexuals in the military, barring only openly gay men and lesbians from serving. In effect, the military is not allowed to ask enlistees if they are gay, but to pursue a career in the military, gay servicemen and women are required to hide their sexual orientation and abstain from homosexual sex. Widely criticized as repackaging discrimination and undermining the military's core values, advocates for equality continue to seek its repeal in the courts. The policy, which President Bush refuses to overturn, is perceived by many to be vulnerable to constitutional challenge, particularly since sodomy was decriminalized in 2003.

Furthermore, multiple studies have found that Don't Ask/Don't Tell has failed in its mission of creating a less hostile climate for gays in the military. Since the policy was enacted in 1993, the number of service members discharged for being gay has actually risen, to over 10,000. At a time when the military is already stretched to fight concurrent wars in Afghanistan and Iraq, this loss of personnel has led some policymakers to call for a reconsideration of the ban. For more on this topic, see Tim McFeeley, "Getting It Straight: A Review of the 'Gays in the Military' Debate," 236–250 in *Creating Change*, ed.s John D'Emilio, et al (New York: St. Martins, 2000) and John Files, "Gay Ex-Officers Say 'Don't Ask' Doesn't Work," *The New York Times*, December 10, 2003.

There would be other setbacks for centrists at the state level, with repeals of legislative remedies against other forms of discrimination based on sexual orientation. Yet, on the other hand, some liberals would count it as progress that over Clinton's two terms during the 1990s, several other important initiatives promoting the rights of gays and lesbians were placed on the legislative agenda. One example of such reform, the Local Law Enforcement Enhancement Act (LLEA), seeks to strengthen and update hate crimes legislation by allowing the federal government to assist state and local authorities in investigating and prosecuting hate crimes. As currently defined by law, hate crimes are acts motivated by prejudice and directed against particular persons or groups because of their real or perceived race, ethnicity, national origin, or religion. If passed, the LLEA would amend existing hate crime laws to also include persons not randomly selected but intentionally victimized because of their sexual orientation, gender, gender identity, and disability. The LLEA's proponents consider it a crucial tool for law enforcement, since currently it is estimated that only 20 percent of all hate crimes result in arrest.[38]

Another piece of proposed legislation aimed at promoting equality is ENDA (the Employment Non-Discrimination Act), which would make it illegal to fire someone simply because of his or her sexual orientation.[xii] Currently there is no federal law protecting homosexuals from workplace discrimination and in most states it is legal to discriminate against workers based on their real or perceived homosexuality. However, for years corporations have taken the lead; half of all Fortune 500 companies include homosexuals in their nondiscrimination policies, as do some state and local governments.[39] To the dismay of liberals, while both ENDA and the LLEA have some bipartisan support, even if they get through Congress, neither is likely to be signed into law by President Bush.

Looking back, most gay liberals would probably agree that although Clinton proved unwilling to take risks to promote equality in this area, by putting these issues on the agenda and by making some important appointments of openly gay officials, he did more to promote their cause than any US president had thus far. In this, Clinton is probably representative of most (straight) liberals who don't want to appear gay-unfriendly, but have generally remained agnostic on whether gay is actually good. Instead, liberals generally portray homosexuality as being as morally neutral as heterosexuality. For example, both Democratic presidential contenders since Clinton, Al Gore and John Kerry, continued Clin-

---

[xii]As a compromise measure, ENDA exempts a variety of employers, including religious organizations and the military, which would remain free to discriminate based on sexual orientation.

ton's tradition of inclusion but compromise. Hardly a champion of gay rights, Kerry did join with those who supported the expansion of hate crimes laws and ENDA. In this, he is like many moderates (Democrats and Republicans) who oppose equal marriage rights—but while also opposing a constitutional amendment seeking to bar same-sex marriage.[xiii] This position appeals to many centrists and seems safer politically; it allows liberals to support initiatives important to gay reformists without going so far as promote full equality. However, such nuance has been lost on many Americans, and the most conservative Republicans have effectively portrayed any support of gay rights as offensively liberal.[40]

They did this so well in fact that countless analysts have argued that same-sex marriage may well have been the issue that cost the Democrats the 2004 election. There is evidence that a counterassault against gay rights had been building for some time. For liberals, the turn of the 21st century was a time in which advances were made in terms of homosexuals' visibility and (perhaps) acceptance in popular culture.[41] [xiv] However, this increased visibility has apparently been followed by a lack of social consensus on gay rights, if not a powerful backlash against it, one which threatens to undermine all that its supporters have worked for. In response, it appears that the center is retrenching, making the shift to a new, defensive strategy and more measured approach. For example, although some have characterized it as weak-willed surrender to the right, the Human Rights Campaign, the largest centrist organization promoting the rights of sexual minorities, has reportedly decided to deemphasize the right to marriage—for now. Recognizing that perhaps they had underestimated their opponents, some centrists are backing up and spending more time on educating the public and gaining social acceptance for gays before pursuing more ambitious change.[42]

Conservatives and Libertarians

As you read in Chapter 5, there are many different schools of conservatism, and while some talk more about it than others, each has its own unique stance on gay

[xiii]Put before Congress in May 2003, the proposed Federal Marriage Amendment sought to effectively ban same-sex marriage. Although by 2004 it had failed to win the two-thirds majority needed to amend the Constitution, another vote on the proposal (now known as the Marriage Protection Amendment) is planned for 2006.

[xiv]Examples include the 2003 repeal of sodomy laws and Vermont's recognition of civil unions in 2000. This step was followed by the Massachusetts' Supreme Court's landmark decision legalizing gay marriage as of May 17, 2004.

rights. However, one group of conservatives with much to say on this issue is the Log Cabin Republicans. The most well-known national organization of gay conservatives, the Log Cabin Republicans consider themselves to be part of a much larger group of an estimated one million gay men and women who are fiscal conservatives, are pro-military and support the war in Iraq.[43][xv] These conservatives (approximately 10,000 mostly white, middle and upper-class men) argue that they cannot walk away from their ideology any more than they can any other part of their identity. Yet, as opposed to queer nationalists, being gay is just one part of their identity. For the Log Cabin Republicans, homosexuality is simply a personal quality, not a cultural category or something by which they define themselves. Although it seems far-fetched these days, rather than the anathema it is to some, these conservatives would like nothing more than to make homosexuality a non-issue for the Republican Party.[44]

However, currently that is hardly the case; as a result, the Log Cabin Republicans admit to feeling beset by both sides of the political spectrum. Since 1992, the year that gay liberals celebrated Bill Clinton's candidacy for president, Republican platforms and conventions have been explicitly (and increasingly) antigay, reflecting the views of the majority of Republican delegates at the 2004 convention, of whom only 3% supported same-sex marriage.[45] Yet, Log Cabin Republicans argue that gay rights and the party's philosophy are not inimical. They are joined in this argument by many (straight and gay) libertarians, who see gay rights as an issue of individual rights. In addition, because many conservative (straight and gay) businesspeople value their gay employees and customers, major corporations were some of the first entities in the US to offer partner benefits.[46]

Whatever the issue, as with any other ideology, conservatives share certain values and assumptions. One of these certainly is a philosophical opposition to the expansion of government powers. Therefore, it can't be surprising that gay and lesbian conservatives depart from their more liberal brothers and sisters over the issue of whether the government should be involved in the job of eliminating discrimination. In what perhaps most differentiates them from the other side of the center, gay conservatives are not interested in using the law to impose tolerance. They strongly oppose any reforms that smack of special treatment.[47]

Still, as conservatives they also value individual freedoms, and many are concerned by the right wing of the Republican Party's aggressive efforts to push

---

[xv]Sokolove (2004) estimates that there are a total of four million gay voters in the US.

through a marriage protection amendment. As mentioned earlier, the proposed constitutional amendments (supported by President Bush) would override any state court ruling or legislation—effectively banning same-sex marriage. Gay conservatives reject the idea of such a ban, but for them the greater issue is amending the Constitution, which (gay and straight) conservatives by nature are generally reluctant to do. Log Cabin Republicans are joined by moderate conservatives such as Arizona's Senator John McCain and California's Governor Arnold Schwarzenegger, who prefer that the decision to regulate marriage instead be left to the states. These conservatives often wind up in the same camp as the right in their rejection of gay marriage, yet they disagree on how to get there.[48]

Gay Republicans and their allies know that they have a lot of work to do to get the party to acknowledge their concerns, which are admittedly narrower than liberals when it comes to gay rights. In the meantime, they will work within the party against religious conservatives to move it back toward what they see as its libertarian roots. They want the right to marry and all the benefits associated with it, but they will not leave the GOP. For now they recognize the power of the Religious Right and pursue instead a status quo policy, aimed at keeping the Constitution as is, which they see as enshrining their individual rights and the libertarian preference of being left alone.[49]

THE RIGHT

The right wing of the political spectrum on this issue is comprised of a variety of groups joined together by their interest in restoring the traditional social order. No status quo ideology, the right is dominated by the Religious Right, which believes that transformative changes are needed to return America to its moral foundations. Although it must be recognized that not all religious people would fall on the right of the political spectrum when it comes to this (or any other) issue, the Religious Right does gets its name for a reason. Also known as the Christian Right, its members are socially conservative (predominantly Evangelical Protestant but also Catholic and Mormon) Christians. However, just as Christians can be found among the adherents of each ideology (for example, theological liberals are often strong advocates of gay rights) adherents to the views presented in this section could perhaps be more accurately described as religious traditionalists belonging to a variety of faiths.[50]

Although over the years the kind of religious activism associated with the Religious Right has periodically appeared and subsided, the powerful movement we know today has been building in strength since the late 1970s. Currently estimated to attract approximately 20 per cent of American voters, the right is comprised of well-developed local and national networks of social conservatives with tremendous resources at their disposal. It is an increasingly sophisticated, well-funded, and well-organized ideological movement, widely recognized to have galvanized its constituency—the "values voter" so crucial to the election (and reelection) of George W. Bush in 2000 and 2004.[51]

Yet, depending on where they sit on the political spectrum, these analysts are likely to disagree about whether the worldviews described in this section are more appropriately termed conservative or fascist. Although these two rightward ideologies share certain core assumptions and beliefs, there are important differences between them—most notably concerning the use of violence. Because it does not directly espouse the use of violence, most analysts would not characterize the Religious Right as fascist. However, because of the vitriol with which it describes its enemies and because of its calls for a holy war, the right has been blamed for the murders of sexual minorities. Southern Baptist leader Richard Land provides an example of such language, arguing that Christians must fight until the end against gays, who are dangerous predators, spreading AIDS and molesting children.[52] Religious leaders are joined by right-wing Republican politicians in their characterization of sexual minorities. Senators Trent Lott and Rick Santorum, for example, are well-known for comparing homosexuals to alcoholics, sex addicts, and kleptomaniacs.[53] Militants on this end of the spectrum go on to argue that gays are sinners, serving the forces of evil. Land has warned we must stop the sexual paganization of the US and he threatens that if Americans allow same-sex marriage, God will not bless this nation.[54] It can't be surprising that some (young men in particular) have taken such exhortations as an incitement to violence. According to the Federal Bureau of Investigations, more than 8,000 hate crimes were reported in the US in 2000. Of those, far more attacks were motivated by racial hatred than any other category, although 16% of all hate crimes were committed against people because of their real or perceived sexual orientation.[55] [xvi]

It should also be pointed out, however, that the Religious Right is not monolithic. There are those on the right who allow for the possibility of redemption. James Dobson, of the ministry Focus on the Family, believes that sexual orienta-

---

[xvi]The Southern Poverty Law Center also tracks hate crimes and contends that because so many attacks go unreported or uncounted, the actual number of hate crimes perpetrated each year may be five to six times higher (see "Discounting Hate," The Southern Poverty Law Center, 2005, *www.splcenter.org*).

tion is a choice, and Christians' role is to rescue gays from their lifestyles by embracing them, "converting" them, and bringing them back to the church. He argues that Christians need to repent of their hostility to gays, and gays need to know that God loves them but hates their acts.[56] While such language is considered by some to be just as offensive as that associated with Rev. Land, there are significant differences within the Religious Right in terms of the kind of hostility encouraged against homosexuals. We'll leave it to you to decide the significance of these differences. However, allowing for this disagreement on tactics, there is enough agreement on goals that we consider them both in this section.[57]

The goal of the Religious Right is clear: it is dedicated to restoring "traditional values" in public policy. Much of this power is based in the belief that the liberal elite has launched a cultural war in the US, conspiring to replace Christianity with a Godless, state-sponsored secularism that is seeking to destroy the traditional family, morality and order. In this worldview God-fearing people are called upon to fight a crusade in defense of traditional Christian values, a religious war against a variety of enemies—Hollywood, feminists, and of course, homosexuals.[58]

From the perspective of the right, this is a defensive war because these enemies (in this case gays and lesbians) have gone too far. The Religious Right argues that there is a gay agenda, and its aim is promoting a homosexual lifestyle. Hollywood's glamorization of this way of life is aimed at gaining young recruits. Interestingly, while worlds apart on so many issues, the supporters and opponents of gay rights are in some ways mirror images of each other: each side feels that it is fighting for its way of life and the other represents the ruin of America.[59] Each calls the other side unfair, bigoted and mean-spirited, prone to demonize all who disagree.

Yet, this is a war that goes back many years. Much of the legal and medical persecution of gays and lesbians described earlier in this chapter has been based in religious teachings. Most people on the right view homosexuality as a sin, and believe that Judeo-Christian traditions teach that homosexuality is condemned as a heinous abomination, against nature. For them, homosexuality is not an alternative lifestyle, but a moral failure that is irresponsible and tragic. Therefore, it can't be surprising that the right objects strongly to the extension of civil rights to gays and lesbians.[60]

Analysts characterize the right as having adopted a revolutionary ideology that works most effectively when it focuses on clearly defined issues and specifically attainable goals.[61] Legislation that gay centrists support as protecting equal rights (i.e.: laws that recognize attacks targeting victims for their sexual orientation as hate crimes) are viewed by the right as promoting illegitimate "special rights" for gays—even after the Matthew Shepard murder.[xvii] According to this view, all crimes are hate crimes. Shepard was a robbery victim who may have provoked his attackers by making a pass at them.[62] The federal government should not rush in to give people special privileges or protections because of how (or with whom) they choose to engage in sexual relations.

The right also opposes the military's Don't Ask/Don't Tell policy because it encourages deception and because the existence of homosexuals in the military undermines unit cohesion and poses a threat to national security. Similarly, the right has vigorously put forward the view that ENDA would amount to Affirmative Action for homosexuals (a charge its supporters deny). While the right generally rejects such policies as government-sponsored discrimination, this argument has appealed to many voters outside the movement, who see gays as a well-educated, well-paid, and politically vocal elite that do not deserve consideration as a traditionally-oppressed group.[63] As the Reverend Dwight McKissic, an advocate of race-based civil rights (who is also a leader of the Religious Right) argued, "civil rights are rooted in moral authority/gay rights are rooted in a lack of moral restraint."[64]

In its claims to be on the defensive in this cultural war, the Religious Right has proven itself remarkably successful at adapting its message to the changing social and political landscape.[65] It has won over countless moderates with the argument that it is not the right that is not antigay—it is homosexuals who are anti-religious. The homosexuals have an agenda, the institution under siege is the family, and the battleground for this war is the definition of marriage.[66]

It is for these reasons, the right argues, that a constitutional amendment to ban same-sex marriage is absolutely necessary to defend and protect the institutions of marriage and the family. In countries where homosexual unions are recognized (such as the Netherlands, Norway, and Sweden), the effect on the family has been devastating, confusing sexual identity and undermining commitment. They point out that in Norway, 80% of first-born children are conceived out of wedlock.[67] Worse, if somehow marriage rights were extended to same-sex couples, we would wind up on a slippery slope with an "anything goes" definition of marriage, legitimating and requiring us to honor polygamous and incestuous

---

[xvii]Shepard was a 21-year-old University of Wyoming student who in 1998 was beaten and left to die in freezing weather, strapped to a wire fence in an isolated area. In court, his murderers admitted to targeting Shepard because he was gay. However, his attackers later changed their story, arguing that their primary motive was to rob him to buy drugs. The right embraced this version to "de-gay" the highly publicized murder, supporting the view that homosexuals are not deserving of inclusion in hate crimes legislation.

couples as well.[xviii] Moreover, the right contends, homosexuals are not being honest with us. With every victory, they will push further. Because of the natural link between marriage and procreation, if homosexuals are given the right to marry, the right to parent would follow immediately—with, they argue, overwhelmingly negative consequences.[68]

According to the right, this is a very real threat to the majority of Americans who have been forced into a corner by those who seek to circumvent the democratic process. Gays and their liberal sympathizers have adopted a stealth strategy. With the help of what the right sees as unelected, unaccountable activist judges, the left is forcing gay marriage on a country that rejects it.[69] In a society already plagued by problems brought about by an assault on the traditional family, the courts have no business engineering such dramatic social changes. In a democracy, permission for such change should rest with the voters and their elected representatives. Although a federal amendment barring same-sex marriage will take time, the right can already claim vindication: in every one of the eleven states that proposed a constitutional amendment in 2004 defining marriage as only including the union of a man and woman, voters turned out in droves to back it. By February 2006, a total of twenty states were moving toward constitutional amendments limiting marriage and other forms of relationship recognition.[70]

The failure of the Federal Marriage Amendment to win enough votes in Congress in 2004 was only a temporary defeat for the right; a similar proposal, the Marriage Protection Amendment (which also bars civil unions) is supported by President Bush and comes up for a vote in June 2006. Social conservatives have warned their representatives that they must do better this time.[71] The message is clear: any who resist altering the Constitution on this matter should take cover—even conservatives. According to this view, a uniform national definition of this most fundamental institution is necessary. The Bible is more sacred than the Constitution in our country's history, they argue, and we have amended the Constitution for less important things than this.[72] Unequal treatment based on sexual orientation is acceptable, since to allow equal rights for all would destroy

---

[xviii]The right's critics contend that the slippery slope argument is spurious. Incest, bestiality, pedophilia, and the other practices described as following on gay marriage's coattails are illegal and will remain so because they cause irreversible harm. There are tangible victims and sound health reasons for prohibiting such things, but none of these arguments can be made about the consensual union of two unrelated adults of the same sex (for more on this argument see Dahlia Lithwick, "Slippery Slop: The Maddening 'Slippery Slope' Argument Against Gay Marriage," *Slate*, May 19, 2004).

the meaning of the institution of marriage. For the majority of Americans, marriage is a religious matter. It is also the bedrock of civilization and of our democracy—which, in a holy war of sorts, the right plans to fight tenaciously to defend.

CONCLUSION

Although all sides can claim wins and losses, Americans appear divided in this particular ideological battle. How the public reacts to the campaign for gay rights all depends on the way the question is framed—as an issue of traditional moral values or as an issue of fairness. A variety of surveys suggest that in recent years the public has become more tolerant of homosexuality and accepting (at least in the abstract) of the idea of equal rights regardless of sexual orientation. Over the last decade or so there have been some extraordinary changes, particularly in the younger generation's views of homosexuality. This shift in views may be as significant as those associated with improved race and gender relations.[73] Yet, as the leaders of these other struggles would point out, America still has some work to do towards race and gender-based equality. For a variety of reasons presented in this chapter, the task of promoting gay rights may well prove to be even more formidable.

Perhaps we are at a crossroads: gays and lesbians may have won the majority's toleration, or even acceptance, but not its approval. Most Americans, including many who consider themselves supportive of gay rights (i.e.: allowing homosexuals to serve in the military) say that they oppose gay marriage. Polls conducted by the Pew Research Center and CNN/USA Today/Gallup in 2005 showed that 53–56% of Americans opposed same-sex marriage.[74]

In effect, it appears that many Americans have come around to the view that adults should be able to do what they like in private, but society will not say what they're doing is right. In other words, most straight Americans are not going to condone homosexuality, but they don't believe that people should be punished for it either. Americans may consider themselves willing to offer something more than tolerance of homosexuality. But as long as universalizing marriage is deemed unacceptable because it amounts to outright approval (rather than mere acceptance) of homosexuality, then it is clear that Americans haven't really changed as much as we thought we had.[75]

If this is the case, it does not necessarily mean that change on this front will be forestalled indefinitely. As John D'Emilio and others point out, if one looks to the history of this and other struggles for individual rights, progress has come in fits and starts and has nearly always been followed by backlash.[76] Perhaps even more interestingly, almost all changes in the extension of civil rights so far have come during eras of deepening political conservatism. Historians tell us that we should not expect social change to be linear or sustained; rather, as with other struggles, moments of change have been episodic and sporadic. If we look far enough back we can identify a pattern of long stretches of "creeping change" followed by short periods of "leaping change."[77]

It might be argued that that America was in the throes of such a historic moment in the period just prior to the elections of November 2004. However, while it hasn't gone away, much of the drama and excitement associated with the clash of ideologies surrounding gay and lesbian rights has since waned somewhat. All that is clear is that change is not coming as quickly as many had hoped—or feared. Whatever happens in the near-term, is unlikely that this particular struggle for civil rights, which has come from the fringe to occupy the center of American consciousness in just a generation or two, will be on the periphery for long.

NOTES

1. Jose Antonio Vargas, "Signs of Progress," *The Washington Post*, July 23, 2005.

2. Evan Wolfson, *Why Marriage Matters: America, Equality, and Gay People's Right to Marry* (New York: Simon and Schuster, 2004).

3. Susan Yoachum, "Buchanan Calls AIDS 'Retribution:' Gays Angered by his Bid to Win Bible Belt Votes," *The San Francisco Chronicle*, February 28, 1992.

4. "The Man Behind 'Kinsey': Filmmaker Bill Condon interviewed on "Fresh Air," *National Public Radio*, November 20, 2004, *www.npr.org*.

5. John D'Emilio, *Sexual Politics, Sexual Communities: The Making of a Homosexual Minority in the United States, 1940–1970* (Chicago: University of Chicago Press, 1998).

6. D'Emilio, *Sexual Politics, Sexual Communities*; Margaret Cruikshanks, *The Gay and Lesbian Liberation Movement* (New York, Routledge, 1992).

7. Ibid.

8. D'Emilio, *Sexual Politics, Sexual Communities*; Kenneth D. Wald, "The Context of Gay Politics," pp. 1–30 in *The Politics of Gay Rights*, eds. Craig A. Rimmerman, Kenneth D. Wald, and Clyde Wilcox (Chicago: University of Chicago Press, 2000); Rachel Kranz and Tim Cusick, *Gay Rights* (New York: Facts on File, 2000).

9. D'Emilio, *Sexual Politics, Sexual Communities*.

10. Ibid; Henry L. Minton, *Departing from Deviance: A History of Homosexual Rights and Emancipatory Science in America* (Chicago: University of Chicago Press, 2002).

11. Minton, *Departing from Deviance: A History of Homosexual Rights and Emancipatory Science in America*.

12. John D'Emilio, "Cycles of Change, Questions of Strategy: The Gay and Lesbian Movement after Fifty Years," pp. 31–53 in *The Politics of Gay Rights*, eds. Craig A. Rimmerman, Kenneth D. Wald, and Clyde Wilcox (Chicago: University of Chicago Press, 2000); Henry L. Minton, *Departing from Deviance: A History of Homosexual Rights and Emancipatory Science in America* (Chicago: University of Chicago Press, 2002).

13. D'Emilio, *Sexual Politics, Sexual Communities*.

14. D'Emilio, *Sexual Politics, Sexual Communities*; Wald, "The Context of Gay Politics."

15. Jean Reith Schroedel and Pamela Fiber, "Lesbian and Gay Policy Priorities: Commonality and Difference," pp. 97–120 in *The Politics of Gay Rights*, eds. Craig A. Rimmerman, Kenneth D. Wald, and Clyde Wilcox (Chicago: University of Chicago Press, 2000); Kranz and Cusick, *Gay Rights*.

313

16. Tamar Lewin, "The Gay Rights Movement, Settled Down," *The New York Times*, February 29, 2004.

17. Kameny quoted in Cruikshanks, *The Gay and Lesbian Liberation Movement*; D'Emilio, Sexual Politics, Sexual Communities.

18. D'Emilio, *Sexual Politics, Sexual Communities; Cruikshanks, The Gay and Lesbian Liberation Movement*; Chai R. Feldblum, "The Federal Gay Rights Bill: From Bella to ENDA," pp. 149–187 in *Creating Change: Sexuality, Public Policy, and Civil Rights*, eds. John D'Emilio, William B. Turner, and Urvashi Vaid (New York: St. Martins, 2000); Kranz and Cusick, *Gay Rights*.

19. Maureen N. McLane, "To Be Young, Gifted, and Gay," *The New York Times Book Review*, December 14, 2003.

20. D'Emilio, *Sexual Politics, Sexual Communities*.

21. Mark Carl Rom, "Gays and AIDS: Democratizing Disease?" pp. 217–248 in *The Politics of Gay Rights*, eds. Craig A. Rimmerman, Kenneth D. Wald, and Clyde Wilcox (Chicago: University of Chicago Press, 2000).

22. Ibid.

23. Stephen M. Engle, *The Unfinished Revolution: Social Movement Theory and the Gay and Lesbian Movement* (New York: Cambridge University Press, 2001); Cruikshanks, *The Gay and Lesbian Liberation Movement*.

24. Cruikshanks, *The Gay and Lesbian Liberation Movement; D'Emilio, Sexual Politics, Sexual Communities*; David Chambers, "Couples, Marriage, Civil Union, and Domestic Partnership," pp. 281–304 in *Creating Change: Sexuality, Public Policy, and Civil Rights*, eds. John D'Emilio, William B. Turner, and Urvashi Vaid (New York: St. Martins, 2000); Kranz and Cusick, *Gay Rights*.

25. Lewin, "The Gay Rights Movement, Settled Down;" Kranz and Cusick, *Gay Rights*.

26. D'Emilio, *Sexual Politics, Sexual Communities*; Cruikshanks, *The Gay and Lesbian Liberation Movement*.

27. Jonathan Rauch, "Imperfect Unions," *The New York Times*, August 15, 2003.

28. D'Emilio, "Cycles of Change, Questions of Strategy;" Kranz and Cusick, *Gay Rights*.

29. Engle, *The Unfinished Revolution*; Cruikshanks, *The Gay and Lesbian Liberation Movement*; Feldblum, "The Federal Gay Rights Bill: From Bella to ENDA."

30. Engle, *The Unfinished Revolution*; Cruikshanks, *The Gay and Lesbian Liberation Movement*.

31. Chambers, "Couples, Marriage, Civil Union, and Domestic Partnership;" D'Emilio, *Sexual Politics, Sexual Communities*; Kranz and Cusick, *Gay Rights*.

32. Chambers, "Couples, Marriage, Civil Union, and Domestic Partnership."

33. Chambers, "Couples, Marriage, Civil Union, and Domestic Partnership."

34. Rauch, "Imperfect Unions;" Kranz and Cusick, *Gay Rights*; Nathaniel Frank, "Joining the Debate But Missing the Point," *The New York Times*, February 29, 2004.

35. Andrew Sullivan, "Integration Day," *The New York Times*, May 17, 2004; David E. Rosenbaum, "Legal License: Race, Sex, and Forbidden Unions," *The New York Times*, December 14, 2003; Joseph J. Ellis, "A New Topic for an Old Argument," *The New York Times*, February 29, 2004.

36. Chambers, "Couples, Marriage, Civil Union, and Domestic Partnership;" Michael Sokolove, "Can this Marriage be Saved?" *The New*

York Times, April 11, 2004; D'Emilio, *Sexual Politics, Sexual Communities.*

37. D'Emilio, *Sexual Politics, Sexual Communities.*

38. "Frequently Asked Questions: The Local Law Enforcement Act," The Human Rights Campaign, *www.hrc.org.*

39. "Endorsing the Employment Non-Discrimination Act," The Human Rights Campaign, *www. hrc.org.*

40. John Broder, "Groups Debate Slower Strategy on Gay Rights," *The New York Times*, December 9, 2004.

41. D'Emilio, *Sexual Politics, Sexual Communities*; Engle, *The Unfinished Revolution.*

42. Broder, "Groups Debate Slower Strategy on Gay Rights."

43. Sokolove, "Can this Marriage be Saved?"

44. Richard Tafel, "Caught Between Two Worlds: Gay Republicans Step Out, and Into the Political Fray," pp.115–130 in *Creating Change: Sexuality, Public Policy, and Civil Rights*, eds. John D'Emilio, William B. Turner, and Urvashi Vaid (New York: St. Martins, 2000); Sullivan in Kranz and Cusick, *Gay Rights*; Sokolove, "Can this Marriage be Saved?"

45. "A Kinder, Gentler Republican Party," *The Denver Post*, August 31, 2004.

46. John C. Green, "'Antigay' Varieties of Opposition to Gay Rights," pp. 121–138 in *The Politics of Gay Rights*, eds. Craig A. Rimmerman, Kenneth D. Wald, and Clyde Wilcox (Chicago: University of Chicago Press, 2000).

47. Sullivan, "Integration Day;" Kranz and Cusick, *Gay Rights.*

48. Tafel, "Caught Between Two Worlds;" Sokolove, "Can this Marriage be Saved?"

49. Ibid; Kranz and Cusick, *Gay Rights.*

50. Thomas C. Caramagno, *Irreconcilable Differences? Intellectual Stalemate in the Gay Rights Debate* (Westport, CT: Praeger, 2002); Green, "'Antigay' Varieties of Opposition to Gay Rights."

51. Green, "'Antigay' Varieties of Opposition to Gay Rights."

52. Tom Strode, "Thousands Rally in Nation's Capital for Traditional Marriage," *Baptist Press News,* October 18, 2004.

53. Ibid.

54. Ibid.

55. "Frequently Asked Questions," The Human Rights Campaign.

56. Strode, "Thousands Rally in Nation's Capital for Traditional Marriage."

57. Green, "'Antigay' Varieties of Opposition to Gay Rights."

58. Green, "'Antigay' Varieties of Opposition to Gay Rights;" Caramagno, *Irreconcilable Differences?*; Craig A. Rimmerman, *From Identity to Politics: The Lesbian and Gay Movements in the US* (Philadelphia: Temple University Press, 2002); Steven Shaw, "No Longer a Sleeping Giant: The Re-Awakening of Religious Conservatives in American Politics," pp. 7–16 in *Anti-Gay Rights: Assessing Voter Initiatives,* eds. Stephanie L. Witt and Suzanne McCorkle (Westport, CT: Praeger, 1997).

59. Wald, "The Context of Gay Politics;" Caramagno, *Irreconcilable Differences?*

60. Cruikshanks, *The Gay and Lesbian Liberation Movement.*

61. Wald, "The Context of Gay Politics;" Shaw, "No Longer a Sleeping Giant."

62. Dave Cullen, "Gay Panic Lite," *Salon.com*, November 2, 1999.

63. Ibid.

64. Marc Rogers, "McKissic: Homosexual Rights Not the Same as Civil Rights," *Baptist Press News*, October 22, 2004, *www.ivotevalues.com*.

65. Caramagno, *Irreconcilable Differences?*; Rimmerman, *From Identity to Politics*.

66. Rogers, "McKissic: Homosexual Rights Not the Same as Civil Rights."

67. James Dobson, "Eleven Arguments Against Same-Sex Marriage," Citizenlink, May 23, 2004, *www.family.org*.

68. Frank, "Joining the Debate But Missing the Point;" Richard Viguerie, *America's Right Turn: How Conservatives Used New and Alternative Media to Take Power* (Chicago: Bonus Books, 2004).

69. Green, "'Antigay' Varieties of Opposition to Gay Rights;" Caramagno, *Irreconcilable Differences?*

70. "What the Definition of Marriage Act Does," The Human Rights Campaign, *www. hrc.org*.

71. Jamie Coomarasamy, "US Evangelicals Warn Republicans," *BBC News*, March 17, 2006, *www. news.bbc.co.uk*.

72. Dwayne Hastings, "Land: Marriage Debate is Over Society's Basic Building Block," *Baptist Press News*, September 22, 2004, *www.ivote-values.com*.

73. Feldblum, "The Federal Gay Rights Bill: From Bella to ENDA;" Clyde Wilcox and Robin Wolpert, pp. 409–432 in *The Politics of Gay*

Rights. eds Craig A. Rimmerman, Kenneth D. Wald, and Clyde Wilcox (Chicago: University of Chicago Press, 2000).

74. Katherine Q. Seelye and Janet Elder, "Strong Support Is Found for Ban on Gay Marriage," *The New York Times*, December 21, 2003; "Law and Civil Rights," *www.pollingreport.com.*

75. Feldblum, "The Federal Gay Rights Bill: From Bella to ENDA;" William Saffire, "On Same-Sex Marriage," *The New York Times*, December 1, 2003; "Gay Marriage: Another Thirty Years War in the Making?" *The Economist*, May 22, 2004.

76. D'Emilio, "Cycles of Change, Questions of Strategy;" Broder, "Groups Debate Slower Strategy on Gay Rights."

77. D'Emilio, "Cycles of Change, Questions of Strategy."

Glossary

agitation Lenin's notion that party workers must exacerbate and/or create problems to do good political work.

alienation Refers to the separation, isolation, and estrangement of human beings from each other and society.

anarchism Meaning "contrary to authority" or "without a ruler," it rejects religious and governmental authority and is based in the belief that left to their own devices, humans will govern themselves appropriately.

anti-Semitism Hatred and discrimination against Jews as individuals and as a racial and religious group.

aristocracy Political system in which power is vested in a minority, usually based on hereditary nobility.

authentic globalization Also known as alternative (as opposed to corporate) globalization. It takes a bottom-up approach, recognizing the importance of both global alliances and local resistance in countering the ill-effects of global capitalism.

authoritarian political system A system in which power is concentrated in the hands of a few groups, usually economic, clerical, military, and political elites. Political power is not subject to constitutional limitations and is used to control political activity and suppress opposition.

black blocs The most radical wing of the anti-globalization movement; groups of people who dress in black and come together in mass rallies to perform hit-and-run acts of civil disobedience (such as vandalism).

blitzkrieg Lightning-like military offensives by massed mechanized ground and air forces. Such attacks were initiated by the Nazi armed forces in World War II.

Bolsheviks Faction of the Russian Social-Democratic Worker's party headed by Lenin. Advocates of a highly centralized and disciplined Communist party organization.

bourgeoisie In Marxist theory, the class of modern capitalists that owns the means of production and employs wage labor.

capitalism An economic system that advocates private ownership, competition, profit, and a market economy.

Castroism A variety of communism operative in Cuba until the mid-1980s that advocated military combat in gaining power and military involvement abroad. It draws its inspiration and legitimacy from Fidel Castro.

center The political center includes the ideologies of liberalism and conservatism, which have in common a commitment to private property and constitutional government.

charisma The extraordinary magnetic power of a political or military leader to arouse loyalty and widespread popular support.

civil disobedience A form of protest based on citizens' refusal to participate in the activities of government, or to admit to the state's legitimacy in any way.

class In Marx's theory, one's class is determined by one's relationship to the means of production as either an owner or a worker.

class struggle Marx's theory of the basic relationship between the property--owning class and the propertyless class. Also the engine of social change.

cold war A period of tension and confrontation between the Western Alliance and the Soviet Union lasting (approximately) from the end of World War II (1945) until the administration of President Bush (1990–1991).

Comintern (Third Communist International-1919–1943) An international communist organization established and dominated by the Soviet Union and used to further Soviet foreign policy.

communism (Marxism) A classless society where private ownership of productive forces has ended, the state has withered away, and human alienation has ended.

conservatism (1) An attitude of skepticism regarding the desirability of rapid change. (2) An ideology that reflects this attitude, maintaining that ordered liberty, private property, and constitutional government may best be conserved by emphasizing tradition, stability, and gradual social and political change.

containment The doctrine that American interests required the United States to oppose Soviet expansion in Europe and, by implication, communist expansion worldwide.

cooperatives Enterprises that are collectively owned, when people with common needs, skills, and interests pool their resources and work cooperatively within a common framework.

corporatism In Mussolini's Italy, the corporate state was proclaimed as an alternative to capitalism and communism. Twenty-two corporations directed and coordinated the Italian economy.

Defense of Marriage Act (DOMA) A 1996 US law which for federal purposes defines marriage as only existing between a man and a woman; it also gives states the right to refuse to recognize same-sex marriages performed in other states.

democracy Originally meaning government by the people, in the modern context democracy most often refers to a system of representative government based on competitive elections and constitutional protection for civil liberties.

democratic socialism A movement striving to attain the goals of socialism within the context of representative constitutional government. **determinism** The doctrine that human consciousness as well as social phenomena and social change are predetermined by causes over which the individual has no control.

dialectical materialism This concept describes Marx's philosophy; that is, what constitutes ultimate reality ("materialism") and how one can come to know and understand that reality (dialectically).

Dictatorship of the Proletariat Marx's name for the transition period that occurs after the epoch of capitalism ends and before the era of communism begins.

Don't Ask/Don't Tell/Don't Pursue A policy which overturned a ban on homosexual service members, it allows homosexuals to pursue a career in the military, but requires them to hide their sexual orientation.

elitism The belief and advocacy of rule by a group perceived as socially superior because it possesses some unique quality (knowledge, military skills, religious insight, and so on).

ENDA (the Employment Non-Discrimination Act) Proposed legislation which would make it illegal to fire someone simply because of his or her sexual orientation.

equal exchange Advocated by anarchists, a system of skill exchange in which individuals and groups earn certificates for nits of work performed and the certificates are exchanged for other goods or services through barter.

ethics Involves distinctions between right and wrong, moral duty and obligation, and the relation of ends to means.

Eurocommunism A Marxist variant in Western Europe in the 1970s that claimed communism is compatible with constitutional democracy. Advo-cated democratic pluralism and rejected the notion of the Dictatorship of the Proletariat.

Fabians Nineteenth-century British democratic socialists.

fascism A post-World War I phenomenon that had its origin in Italy in 1922 and in Germany in 1933 where it was called national socialism.

feminism A reform movement seeking to establish the legal rights of women, end sex discrimination, and eliminate sexist attitudes and values in society.

feudalism A social system, prevalent in the Middle Ages, characterized by small, self-sufficient agricultural communities with rigid feudal relationships between lord and vassal.

fuhrer The German Nazi name for their leader, Adolf Hitler.

gay liberationists Often derided by mainstream America as militants, these activists advocate transformative, revolutionary changes based in the complete sexual liberation of all.

geopolitics Argument that the growth, development, and power of a state can only be understood in terms of its physical location, geography, and relationship to other states.

ghetto A part of a city in which Jews are forced to live by socioeconomic, political, and legal pressures.

Great Society Liberal programs of the administration of President Lyndon B. Johnson attempting to improve the lot of the disadvantaged segments of American society.

green cities Advocated by anarchists as an alternative to suburban sprawl, they promote self-sufficiency, recycling, the development of locally-based clean energy sources, and the redesign of public living spaces to include urban forestation.

hadiths The sayings of the Prophet Mohammed, a guide to daily behavior for Muslims.

Hamas Formed out of the first *intifada* (or "uprising") against Israel in 1987, this Palestinian group (which vows that it will never give up its weapons or its avowed goal of destroying the state of Israel) in 2006 became the first Arab Islamist party to attain power through democratic means.

historical materialism Marx's theory of social change and development. Marxists consider it his most important contribution to social thought. Holocaust Refers to the 6 million Jewish victims murdered in areas under German control during Nazi rule in Europe (1933–1945).

humanism An ideology in which the human individual is the central measure of value. This philosophy asserts the dignity of human beings and reason as the mechanisms of self-actualization.

human nature Those essential elements of human beings that are changeless and common to all.

ideology A systematic political doctrine that claims to provide a universal theory of the individual and society.

ijtihad Also knows as "rational interpretation" or the use of human reasoning to elaborate on *shari'a* law, it provides answers to questions on which the *Qu'ran* and *sunna* are silent, renews legal codes and enables them to respond to the needs of contemporary society.

imperialism The policy or practice of extending the power of one state by direct · political control over a foreign territory.

Islamic fundamentalism The revival of Islam as a powerful political force in the Middle East. It is characterized by strict adherence to the principles of Islam as the law of the land and all aspects of life.

Islamism Also known as political Islam, it calls for a return to Islam, urging Muslims to shape their own politics and societies in accordance with Islamic principles.

jahiliyya A core concept for Islamists, it describes pre-Islamic barbarism, or the state of ignorance that existed before God's revelations to Mohammed.

Justice and Development Party (JDP) Turkish Islamist party which won parliamentary elections and formed the government in 2002 based on a platform calling for social justice, religious freedom, ethnic tolerance, and a market economy.

jihad One of the five pillars of Islam and a duty of all Muslims, it includes an inner (the internal struggle against one's own failings) and an outer jihad (or holy way, a war of defense against non-believers).

jihadists Muslims who support a *jihad*, or holy war against threats to Islam.

Keynesian economics Policies associated with the theories of British economist John Maynard Keynes, who advocated government tax and spending programs to manage business cycles.

Kuomingtang The ruling political party of China under Chiang Kai-shek. Driven from power in 1949 by the communists headed by Mao Zedong, they retreated to Taiwan.

labor theory of value Marx's theory that the amount of labor power congealed in an object is the ultimate determinant of value.

laissez-faire The doctrine of free market economics, advocating a minimum of government involvement in economics.

left The political left includes the ideologies of communism and socialism, both of which exhibit hostility to large concentrations of privately owned capital, and an emphasis on economic equalitarianism and the social welfare state.

Leninism A Marxist worldview that argues the primacy of politics and the Communist party as the ultimate source of power. Party discipline and centralism are central to Leninism.

liberalism (1) Classical: the ideology of individualism, private property, and limited government. (2) Modern: within the context of private property and constitutional government, modern liberalism strives to use social programs to create conditions conducive to individual development.

liberation theology Originally a radical Catholic response to poverty in less developed countries, it argues that Jesus taught a version of Christianity that is inclusive, egalitarian, and activist.

libertarianism An ideology advocating a minimum role for government in society as the means of maximizing personal liberty.

Local Law Enforcement Enhancement Act Proposes providing federal assistance to state and local authorities in the investigation of hate crimes, and amending existing federal law to include under recognition as hate crimes violent acts targeting victims because of their sexual orientation, gender, gender identity, or disability.

Log Cabin Republicans Pro-military, gay fiscal conservatives who believe that gay rights and the Republican Party's philosophy are not inimical.

lumpenproletariat Marx's name for the lowest class; that part of society composed of thieves, prostitutes, and so on.

Maoism A unique modification of traditional Marxism-Leninism operative in China during Mao Zedong's rule and characterized by guerrilla warfare and the revolutionary role of the peasant.

Marxist-Christian dialogue Discussions and activities carried on by select Christian and Marxist intellectuals and leaders throughout the world in an effort to change their relationship from anathema (intense dislike and denunciation) to dialogue (exchange of ideas and opinions).

Mensheviks A minority faction of the Russian Social-Democratic Worker's party headed by Martov. This opposition group fought for a more democratic and broader-based Communist party.

mode of production (Marxism) Concerns what is produced, how it is produced, and how it is exchanged. Simply, a measure of technological development.

Muslim Brotherhood Founded in 1928 by Hasan al-Banna, this Egyptian Islamist movement has been banned since the 1950s, but remains a major player in Egyptian politics, winning one-fifth of the seats in parliament in late 2005.

nationalism (1) The doctrine that a nationality should be self-governing. (2) The doctrine that advocates the supremacy of the nation-state as the appropriate means of political organization.

natural rights Basic rights derived from natural law or God. In liberalism these include life, liberty, and property.

Nazi The word Nazi emerged out of the German pronunciation of the first two words of the Nazi party's official name (National Socialist German Workers party).

neoconservatism A variation of modern conservatism that combines social conservatism with free market economics.

neoliberalism A variation of modern liberalism that places less emphasis on social programs and greater emphasis on economic development.

New Deal The liberal program of the administration of President Franklin D. Roosevelt (1933–1945). Objectives included stabilizing the banks and stock market, revitalizing industrial activity, and creating employment by means of public works.

New Right A movement in contemporary American conservatism. nonalignment An alternative to incorporation into either the United States or the Soviet bloc.

"one country, two systems" A concept advocated by Deng Xiaoping meaning one unified Chinese nation that pragmatically seeks rapid development through both socialist and capitalist institutions.

organic society The theory that societies possess attributes of living organisms, including interdependence, unity, and continuity.

pan-Arabism An assertion by the Arab people of their fundamental unity in language, religion, and tradition.

politburo In states with Marxist-Leninist regimes, the politburo is the center of decision making, the apex of political power.

power: ruling In politics, the possession and/or control of the coercive force of the state that may be used to compel obedience. In nonpolitical situations, power is the capacity to compel others to do one's bidding.

praxis The interaction between thought and action-each impregnated with the other. Praxis is specific to human beings alone.

progressives A reform movement of middle-class origin in the early twentieth century United States, seeking to increase democracy in politics, to regulate concentrated economic power, and to eliminate corruption in politics and business.

proletarianization Mao Zedong's theory that it is possible to transform the consciousness of a person from bourgeois to proletarian by education.

proletariat In Marxism, the class of propertyless wage-laborers who sell their labor power to capitalists.

propaganda The spreading of ideas and information for the purpose of realizing political advantage or injuring one's enemies.

propaganda by deed Advocated by anarchists who promoted the use of terrorism and assassination to "waken the masses," incite mass uprisings and insurrection, and speed up the collapse of the state.

Qur'an The book of revelations. Believed by Muslims to be the literal word of God as spoken to the Prophet Mohanned, it provides general ethical principles and guidelines for the faithful.

radicalism Advocacy of extensive and rapid social, economic, and political change.

Reformation Initiated by Martin Luther in 1517, this movement rejected and modified Catholic doctrine and eventually gave rise to the Protestant church.

relations of production (Marxist theory) Refers to the property question; that is, who owns and controls the productive forces of society.

Religious Right Also known as the Christian Right, its members are religious traditionalists who believe that transformative changes are needed to return America to its moral foundations. Known for its religious activism, this powerful movement has galvanized its constituency, which is estimated to comprise approximately 20 percent of American voters.

Renaissance The cultural change in Europe that originated in Italy in the fourteenth century and was marked by humanism and the flowering of the arts, architecture, and literature.

revisionists Socialists who challenged the assumptions of orthodox Marxism.

revolution A form of political change characterized by violence, illegality, mass involvement, and deep fundamental social transformation.

right The political right, including fascism, rejects constitutional government, appeals to extremism and violence, and advocates a highly centralized, powerful state with authoritarian leadership.

shari'a "The path to be followed," this body of Islamic law was developed after Mohammed's death by religious scholars.

shura "Consultation," a principle of governance in Islam which refers to the Prophet Mohammed's practice of consulting with his companions before making a decision and the *umma's* collective deliberation on public matters. Although Muslims debate whether *shura* is a binding obligation, liberal Islamists cite it as evidence of the compatibility between democracy and Islam.

social contract In liberal social theory, an agreement among individuals to enter into society, or an agreement by which citizens consent to be governed.

Social Darwinism The view that society progresses only through the competitive struggle among individuals.

socialism An ideology that advocates collective ownership of productive forces along with cooperation, a planned economy, and production for the general welfare rather than individual profit.

Stalinism The version of communism operative in the Soviet Union for 30 years (1924–1953) characterized by dictatorship, use of terror, forced col-lectivization, and central planning of the economy.

state In political science its essential characteristics are sovereignty, territory, population, and government.

statism A state characterized by a centralized and bureaucratic system of authority and organization that runs everything on a day-to-day basis.

Stonewall Refers to a bar which became a symbol of the gay and lesbian rights movement after riots in June 1969 against police harassment drew the world's attention.

sunna The customs or "traditions" of the Prophet Mohammed.

superstructure Institutions such as law, religion, and politics created by the property-owning class to reinforce their privileged position in society (Marxist theory).

surplus value (Marxism) Value produced by the worker that is above and beyond that required for subsistence and appropriated by the capitalist as profit.

Third Reich Established by Adolf Hitler and his Nazis in 1933. Designed to last 1,000 years; it did in fact exist only 12 years and collapsed in 1945 at the end of World War 11.

Titoism A dissident brand of communism that operated in Yugoslavia until the breakup of that state-characterized by worker self-management, nationalism, and nonalignment.

totalitarianism Refers to the scope of power exercised by a political regime. Usually means absolute and unlimited exercise of power with control over all aspects of life.

umma The original community of believers or followers of the Prophet Mohammed.

utopian socialists Nineteenth-century socialist philosophers who advocated planned communities, usually to be organized as producers' cooperatives.

Weimar Republic Name of the German Republic established in January 1919, following World War 1. This republic collapsed in January 1933 when Hitler came to power.

INDEX

Relations of production, 22, 32
Religious Right, 295, 306, 308
Renaissance, 11, 30
Republicans, 84, 150, 304
Revel, Jean Francois, 134
Revolution, 3, 11, 13, 16, 23, 29, 31–32, 34,
    36, 38, 41–43, 59, 63, 84, 87, 130,
    161–162, 167, 169, 171, 174–1766, 181,
    198, 294
Rhineland, 13, 140
Ricardo, David, 16, 24
Right, 1–4, 7–10, 29, 112–116, 123, 129, 137,
    150–152, 161–163, 180, 193, 202–203,
    221–224, 232, 236, 244, 255, 265–266,
    270, 280, 289, 294, 304, 306–311
Risorgimento, 127–128
Robertson, Pat, 112
Robison, Jim, 112
Rocco, Alfredo, 125
Röhm, Ernst, 139, 146
Roman Empire, 125, 136
Romania, 123
Roosevelt, Theodore, 234
Rosenberg, Alfred, 141, 155
Rossiter, Clinton, 99–101, 104, 118, 122
Rothschild strike, 35
Russia, 30–32, 35–36, 40, 110, 128, 137, 180,
    210
Russian Revolution, 110, 163
Russian Social-Democratic Workers party,
    36

Sabine, George H., 127, 153
Schlafly, Phyllis, 280
Schlesinger, Arthur M., Jr., 87–88
Schopenhauer, Arthur, 125
Schutzstaffel (SS or Headquarters
    Guards), 142
Scott, Coretta, 237
Seale, Bobby, 227
Second Reich, 136
Self-determination, 5–6, 45, 4133, 246, 248,
    293, 296
Selma-Montgomery March, 238
Serbia, 137
Shanghai, 39–40
Shari'a, 195–196, 206
Sharia, 156, 158

Shaw, George Bernard, 61
Shepard, Matthew, 309
Shura, 205–206, 218
Sino-Soviet Treaty of Alliance, 41
Slavery, 21, 183, 244
Smith, Adam, 16, 24, 27, 51, 78–79, 242, 244,
    248
Smith, Errol, 236
Sobibor, 136, 148–149
Social Darwinism, 168
Social Security Act, 88
Socialism, 2–4, 14, 16, 20, 23, 27–28, 32, 38,
    40, 57–58, 60, 62–66, 68, 70–71, 83, 123,
    135, 141, 144, 146, 162, 223, 228, 230,
    232, 234–235, 248, 252, 267, 269
Socialism in one country, 6
Soledad Brothers, 230
Sorel, Georges, 125
Southern Christian Leadership
    Conference (SCLC), 237
Soviet Union, 7, 10, 30, 34, 36–38, 45,
    49–50, 90, 108, 110, 118, 140, 148, 167,
    203, 230
Sowell, Thomas, 223, 236, 242
Spain, 4, 66, 123, 129, 134, 140, 169,
    177–178, 191
Speer, Albert, 139, 155, 159
Spencer, Herbert, 105
St. John Lateran, 128
St. Thomas Aquinas, 237
Stalin, Joseph (Iosif V. Dzhugashvili), 7,
    34–36
Stalingrad, 140
Stalinism, 36
Steele, Shelby, 223, 236, 242
Steinem, Gloria, 275, 285
Stonewall, 293, 296
Student Non-Violent Coordinating
    Committee (SNCC), 238
Sturmabteilung (SA. or Brownshirts), 139
Sudetenland (Czechoslovakia), 140
Summers, Christina Hoff, 274, 284
Sumner, William Graham, 105
Sunna, 195
Sunni Muslims, 196
Superstructure, 18–19, 22
Surplus value, 24–25
Sword and the Arm of the Lord, 151

337

About the Authors

Charles Funderburk is a Professor of Political Science at Wright State University. He was chairman of the political science department ar Wright State for seven years and has taught at Florida Atlantic University, Wilmington College, and the University of Basque Country in Bilbao, Spain. He has published numerous articles and books on the American presidency and public policy. He lives in Yellow Springs, Ohio.

Robert G. Thobaben, Professor Emeritus of Political Science at Wright State University, has published numerous books and articles on political ideologies, philosophy, and on biopolitics. He was a Visiting Fellow at Cambridge University (Clare Hall College) in the 1980–81 academic year and a scholar in residence and guest lecturer at The Chinese University of Hong Kong in the winter of 1993. He lives in Centerville,Ohio.

December Green is a Professor of Political Science at Wright State University. She has served as the Director of the International Studies program there for the last five years. Dr. Green has also taught at The Citadel, Pacific Lutheran University, the Governor's School at the College of Charleston, and the University of the Basque Country, in San Sebastian, Spain. The author of several books on Africa and comparative politics, Dr. Green resides in Oakwood, Ohio.